FROM CONFEDERATION
TO NATION

In the era of the Early Republic, Americans determined the meaning of their Revolution and laid the foundation for the United States' later emergence as a world power. This book provides students with an explanation of the major events and developments of one of the most important periods in American History. Focusing on the years between the Revolution and the Civil War, *From Confederation to Nation* presents a narrative of the era's political history along with discussions of the significant social and cultural changes that occurred across the Union's first six decades. Taking a broad approach which examines economic changes, religious influences, political reform, cultural challenges, and racial and gender inequalities in the Early Republic, Atkins' text is useful for a vast array of critical perspectives. *From Confederation to Nation* presents an accessible introduction to the Early American Republic that offers readers a solid foundation for more advanced study.

Jonathan Moore Atkins is Professor of History at Berry College, in Mt. Berry, Georgia.

FROM CONFEDERATION TO NATION

The Early American Republic, 1789–1848

Jonathan M. Atkins

Routledge
Taylor & Francis Group

NEW YORK AND LONDON

First published 2016
by Routledge
711 Third Avenue, New York, NY 10017

And by Routledge
2 Park Square, Milton Park, Abingdon, Oxon OX14 4RN

*Routledge is an imprint of the Taylor & Francis Group, an
informa business*

© 2016 Taylor & Francis

Library of Congress Cataloging-in-Publication Data
Atkins, Jonathan M., 1960– author.
From confederation to nation : the early American republic,
1789–1848 / by Jonathan Atkins.
pages cm
Includes bibliographical references and index.
ISBN 978-1-138-91621-0 (hardback) — ISBN 978-1-138-91622-7 (pbk.) —
ISBN 978-1-315-68978-4 (ebook)   1. United States—History—1783–1815.
2. United States—History—1815–1861.   I. Title.
E337.5.A85 2016
973.4—dc23
2015031294

ISBN: 978-1-138-91621-0 (hbk)
ISBN 978-1-138-91622-7 (pbk)
ISBN: 978-1-315-68978-4 (ebk)

Typeset in Bembo
by Apex CoVantage, LLC

 http://www.routledge.com/cw/atkins

Printed and bound in the United States of America by
Edwards Brothers Malloy on sustainably sourced paper

CONTENTS

FIGURES

PREFACE

The period between the Revolution and the Civil War stands as one of the most important in the nation's history. Though often overshadowed by the "great events" that bookend the era, the Early Republic's importance for American development becomes even clearer the more the passage of time removes us from it. In these years, Americans determined the meaning of their revolution and established the political, social, and cultural institutions that would shape the world of their descendants. The fledgling United States likewise demonstrated that it could defend itself from foreign dominance while laying the foundation for the nation's emergence as a world power. The Constitution proved that it had created a workable government, even as the electorate expanded and adopted democratic practices that would make the United States a model of free government. At the same time, Americans defined the boundaries that would constrain the public roles of women, African Americans, and Native Americans for the next century, constraints whose legacy are still present today.

Fascination with the work of the "Founding Fathers" has kept alive popular interest in the Early Republic. A flood of academic research meanwhile has significantly deepened historians' appreciation of the era. Nevertheless, the absence of a core text has long frustrated instructors of advanced courses on the period. This book seeks to fill that void by providing students and general readers with a relatively short introduction to the Early Republic, broadly defined as the years between the Constitution's ratification in 1789 and the conclusion of the Mexican-American War in 1848. The book does not engage the arguments that usually preoccupy scholars, nor does it necessarily reflect the current state of the profession. Instead, the goal is to present a cohesive narrative for the era, based on the work that recent and past scholars have produced. Through this approach, the work intends to take readers beyond the simplistic, heroic interpretations sometimes presented in popular histories and instead expose them to the reality, complexity, and significance of the era.

Five principal themes guide this account. The first, *federalism*, highlights one of the most underappreciated aspects of the pre–Civil War United States. The Constitution forged a "more perfect union" out of thirteen former colonies that prior to the Revolution had relatively little to do with each other. Revolution sparked a sense of nationalism, but practical politics decreed that the state governments retain responsibility over most domestic issues, including the well-being of a state's people, the role of the courts, and the regulation of its economy. By the 1840s, the states' common Revolutionary heritage, their economic and social development, and the central government's increasing effectiveness strengthened American nationalism. Still, nationalism rested upon a federal political structure that recognized state rights, and Americans continued to see the state and central governments as equals. One of this book's primary goals is to show the development of the federal system that provides the foundation for modern American law and politics. Throughout, it usually refers to the United States as "the Union"—the term most often used in the era—to remind readers of how Americans understood their nation as a unique federal compact.

Republicanism, a second theme, represented an equally important concern for early Americans. After cutting ties with Great Britain, the Revolutionary generation created republican governments for the states and, with the Constitution, the federal Union. Today, Americans assume that government is based on the consent of the governed, and that its purpose is to protect individual rights. It remains difficult for modern generations to appreciate how radical these republican ideals once seemed to a world dominated by monarchy and aristocracy. Before independence, colonial Americans agreed with their European contemporaries that a society based on individual freedom would degenerate into anarchy. Without the stabilizing presence of a king or a titled nobility, republics historically fell prey to military dictatorships more tyrannical than hereditary monarchs. From these presumptions, nineteenth-century Americans continued to wonder whether their "republican experiment" could succeed, especially as they watched the French Revolution succumb to Napoleon Bonaparte's empire and witnessed Europe subsequently fall prey to reactionary conservatism. The Union's accomplishments, and its increasing size and strength, eventually convinced most Americans that their republics had largely succeeded. Still, in a world dominated by tradition and privilege, the survival of governments based on popular consent remained a constant worry.

Economic and social change provides a third theme. Early-nineteenth-century Americans experienced one of the most dramatic economic and population expansions ever seen in world history. At the conclusion of the Revolution, they stood predominantly as a simple agricultural people. Sixty years later, the Union not only stood as one of the world's leading agricultural producers but also had emerged as a potential industrial power. A subtle shift in people's lives underlay the changes. Subsistence-oriented production—giving priority to producing goods for a family's use—gradually gave way to deeper involvement in a market economy, in which people sold goods and services to others in exchange for cash to buy what they needed. Historians refer to this transformation as the "Market Revolution" and recognize that it contributed to an expansion of wealth. They also observe that it profoundly altered the ways in which people related to each other. Americans from small, tradition-bound rural communities increasingly found themselves in a fluid, competitive market economy, with their fates often determined by distant individuals they never met, and with distinct social classes developing and guiding personal relations. Economic transformation thus provoked several important issues that demanded Americans' attention. Their responses to new kinds of problems and conditions shaped the American version of a modern industrial society.

A republic, all agreed, meant a government of "the people." But who were "the people"? That question provides the basis for a fourth theme, the issue of *citizenship*. A citizen stood equal to his peers and enjoyed full membership in American political society, with all the rights and privileges that society recognized. The colonial heritage and republican assumptions instructed Americans at first to limit citizenship to property-owning adult men, who alone enjoyed the economic independence considered necessary for a citizen to make responsible decisions. Economic change and the opportunities apparently available to all white men led to the elimination of property as the basis of citizenship. Voting rights expanded, so that the Union became the world's most democratic nation. At the same time, new presumptions about race and gender more clearly separated citizens from dependents and outsiders. Despite widespread resentment toward foreigners and Roman Catholics, European immigrants' standing as white men allowed them to attain the status of citizens. White women meanwhile found themselves relegated to a "separate sphere," distinct from male-dominated public affairs, while Native Americans, African-American slaves, and free black Americans had to learn how to function in a society to which they clearly would not be admitted.

Foreign relations serves as the book's final theme. Immediately after the Revolution, the Union stood vulnerable to foreign invasion and caught between the western world's two strongest nations in their struggle for dominance. By the middle of the nineteenth century, the nation not only had preserved its independence but had added several new territorial possessions, extending the Union from the Atlantic to the Pacific. Avoiding "entangling alliances" remained a guiding principle, but American leaders proclaimed the United States the defender of the western hemisphere and later waged a war of conquest against a southern neighbor. Americans argued over which would better serve the Union's interests: (a) expansion and free trade or (b) encouraging internal development and limiting territorial acquisition. Still, Americans' belief that the republic offered the world an example of free government, and that "manifest destiny" guided the Union to dominate North America, became cornerstones of the United States' later emergence as an international power.

The structure of this work focuses on presenting a cohesive narrative mainly of the era's political history. An introductory chapter reviews the general conditions of the American states during the 1780s. Three chapters then present the Federalist and Republican conflicts through the conclusion of the War of 1812, followed by three chapters examining important developments that parallel the political history but are better addressed as distinct subjects, including economic and social changes; slavery and sectionalism; religious revivals and reform movements; and the experience of women, African Americans, and Natives. The final three chapters resume the political story following the War of 1812. The attention to political history will strike some as old-fashioned. Nevertheless, I believe that a political narrative remains the best way to organize an introductory work for nonspecialists. The era's politics present a clear, coherent "story" that can provide a foundation for more advanced study. Separate chapters that concentrate on long-term trends avoid overlooking their importance through brief mentions in the political account. Political leaders' actions likewise affected the lives of all Americans, not just those of elite white men like themselves. Finally, if one of the purposes of studying history is to encourage engaged and thoughtful citizenship, studying the political experience of another time and place—especially a politically charged one like the Early American Republic—can only deepen students' appreciation for the types of issues they will face in their own lives.

Like all historians when they produce a book, I owe a debt of gratitude to several individuals for their support. I am blessed to work with great colleagues in the History Department at Berry College. Lawrence Marvin, Christy Snider, Matthew Stanard, and Jennifer Hoyt all read portions of the manuscript or patiently answered my questions while demonstrating that they are outstanding people as well as scholars. Timothy Johnson of Lipscomb University, John Quist at Shippensburg University, and Mark Stegmaier at Cameron University provided helpful critique of my initial proposal for the book. At the project's early stages, Berry's administration provided a sabbatical leave that helped me get the writing off to a strong start. Since then, Tom Kennedy, dean of the Evans School of Humanities, Arts, and Social Sciences, has delivered his support to ensure the project's completion.

Tim Johnson and Larry Marvin both read the entire manuscript and offered crucial feedback. Tim especially provided helpful insights when he used draft chapters in his own Early Republic course, while Larry presented several suggestions to improve the writing as well as the insightful perspective of an accomplished non-American historian. My friend Zack Waters, recently retired from teaching at Rome Middle School, also shared his insights on portions of the manuscript. Several student workers provided vital assistance along the way. At the risk of overlooking someone, I will mention that Justin Henry, Katelyn Boykin, Haley Fortune, and Rachel Renaud each contributed crucial help along the way. At Routledge, Kimberly Guinta and Genevieve Aoki showed tremendous encouragement for this book before they moved on to other positions. Since then, Margo Irvin and Daniel Finaldi have likewise proven a great team to work with as we saw the project to its completion. I also deeply appreciate the perspective of the eight readers whom the press asked to provide comments; though I did not incorporate all of their suggestions, I recognize that each gave the manuscript a careful and thoughtful reading, and their input helped make the final product better. As always, Christie demonstrated her love and support throughout the years of work on the project as we saw Leslie through middle and high school while helping Douglas face the challenges of autism.

Finally, two groups deserve special acknowledgment. Hundreds of historians of the early American republic produced the secondary literature that made this text possible. Their contributions greatly enhanced my knowledge and appreciation of the era. I can only hope that my writing even dimly reflects the brilliance of their work. Likewise, I have had the pleasure of working with a multitude of students in my twenty-four years at Berry College. They have always challenged me with their questions and their desire to learn. My desire is for this work to stimulate the curiosity of future students while satisfying the interest of anyone who wishes to know more about this fascinating period.

I

GEORGE WASHINGTON'S AMERICA

George Washington received official notification of his election as the first president of the United States on April 14, 1789. Two days later, he left Mount Vernon, his beloved Virginia plantation on the banks of the Potomac River, and headed for the Union's capital in New York, accompanied by Charles Thomson, the secretary of Congress; David Humphreys, his former military aide; and William Lee, his personal slave. Triumphant celebrations greeted Washington at several stops on the way, giving his journey the character of a royal procession. But privately, he confessed misgivings about his new responsibility. On the day he left Mount Vernon, he wrote in his journal that he "bade adieu . . . to private life, and to domestic felicity . . . with a mind oppressed with more anxious and painful sensations than I have words to express." He pledged to perform his duties "with the best dispositions to render service to my country in obedience to his will," but, he admitted, "with less hope of answering its expectations."

Washington's reservations stemmed partly from his reluctance to leave retirement. He also recognized the portentous challenges he would face in his new office. As commanding general of the Continental army, he had led thirteen British North American colonies in the successful war to gain independence. War and revolution had created a sense of nationalism, an idea that the citizens of the thirteen states made up one people. Nevertheless, Americans understood the Union—as they usually referred to the United States—as a union of states, joined together in a loose confederation that guarded the states' sovereignty. Different heritages and long-standing tensions among the states made state loyalties stronger than nationalist sentiments, and with the war's end the states' willingness to cooperate waned. Washington himself had recently participated in a convention that tried to create a government that would directly serve all of the Union's people, rather than work for the states like the government it replaced. The states would still play a role in the new government, however, and most Americans remained skeptical about the new constitution's prospects. Washington's actions as president would help determine whether the Union would be preserved. For him and others, the Union's fate would decide the outcome of the Revolution itself.

The States of the Union

Nearly four million people lived in the Union over which Washington would preside. Englishmen had founded the thirteen former colonies more than a century before, as a series of small settlements along the Atlantic coast grew to provide important agricultural products for Great Britain's imperial economy. Most Americans were descended from English settlers, but in the eighteenth century the lure of land and a possibly better life had brought a large number of immigrants from other regions—mainly Scottish inhabitants of Northern Ireland and Germans from central Europe. One-fifth of the inhabitants were African-American slaves, brought to America against their will. English heritage provided the cultural framework for Americans:

English practices provided the basis for the legal, political, social, and religious institutions of each state, and with the dominant English language the states' similarities contributed to the nationalist outlook stimulated by the war.

But England had not founded its colonies as part of a grand, unified strategy. The English government had played only a minor role in the colonies' establishment. Instead, private investors and court favorites oversaw the colonies' settlement, and a wide range of motives, circumstances, and designs guided their plans. Most of their schemes never materialized as they had intended, as the American geography and environment shaped the colonies differently than their founders had intended. Nevertheless, the legacy of the original intentions could still be felt and gave each state a sense of distinction from the others. As colonies, too, each had its own government and developed unique political traditions. While England had expanded its control over colonial trade, the mother country largely allowed the colonial governments to take care of their own internal affairs. Parliament's attempt to subvert local control after 1763, in fact, had driven the colonies to rebel. As independent states, some had more desire to be part of a larger union than others, but all of the state governments jealously guarded their powers and continued to resist outside interference.

Washington's home state, Virginia, was the oldest and largest former colony, both in population and in geography. Founded in the early seventeenth century, Virginia had grown from the tiny coastal village at Jamestown into a series of farms and plantations stretching west. On the map, Virginia extended to the Mississippi and Ohio Rivers, but three-fourths of its nearly 750,000 inhabitants lived east of the Blue Ridge Mountains. Just west of the mountains, German and Scots-Irish farmers raised wheat, corn, and livestock in the Shenandoah Valley, but tobacco remained the dominant crop in the eastern counties. Tobacco's importance deeply influenced Virginia's development, most importantly because the labor required to produce the crop encouraged the importation of slaves, who made up about forty percent of the population. The common interest in tobacco production and the need for white solidarity bolstered the authority of the large planters, who dominated the state government. Widespread voting rights likewise reinforced farmers' support for the planters, as most farmers met the requirement that voters own at least twenty-five acres of land. The planters often bickered among themselves, but their rule in the state for the most part stood unchallenged.

Virginians played a leading role in the Revolution, partly to free themselves from imperial restrictions that kept tobacco prices low and kept many planters in debt to British merchants. War and independence did not improve Virginia's fortunes. The British army invaded the state shortly before the war's end, causing widespread damage and carrying away an estimated thirty thousand slaves. Several planters devoted more of their lands to wheat and searched for another profitable crop, especially after tobacco prices collapsed in 1784 and 1785; Washington himself kept an "experimental garden" at Mount Vernon to test what might grow well on Virginia soil. Most, though, remained deeply committed to tobacco. Overproduction kept prices low until new markets could be found for the crop, and several planters invested in shipbuilding in hopes of creating a state merchant fleet. Despite the difficulties, Virginia's large population and stability put it in a better position than the other states to act independently, and its leaders acted with the expectation that Virginia should be a leader on the continent.

Virginia's size, and the confidence of the planters who led the state, intimidated its northern neighbors. Across the Potomac River lay Maryland, established twenty-seven years after Virginia and intended as a refuge from persecution for English Catholics. Though Protestants outnumbered Catholics from the colony's earliest days, several prominent Catholic families remained, as a legacy of Maryland's original mission. Like Virginia, Maryland developed into a tobacco-producing colony, with large planters as its political and social leaders. But tobacco production proved limited to the southernmost counties along the Potomac, where most of the state's one hundred thousand slaves (about a third of the population) worked. Small farmers on the eastern shore across the Chesapeake Bay, and German and Scots-Irish migrants in the north and west, concentrated on producing food. The need to process and market western farmers' produce had transformed Baltimore, near the mouth of the Patapsco River, into the Union's fifth largest city. On Maryland's eastern border lay Delaware, the least populated state, with only about sixty thousand inhabitants. Slaves made up one-fifth of the population in Delaware, though small farming provided the livelihood for most Delaware inhabitants. Delaware's tiny population, absence of a good port, and location between some of the Union's larger states made it appear vulnerable. During the 1780s, Marylanders turned inward to focus on domestic concerns, but Delaware's leaders attached their hopes to a union in which their state might have some influence.

South of Virginia lay North Carolina, first settled in the late seventeenth century and separated from the southern portion of the Carolina colony in 1719 after the north followed its own pattern of development. Like Virginia, the "Old North State" stretched from the Atlantic to the Mississippi, and with nearly 430,000 inhabitants it stood as the fourth most populous state in the Union. As in Virginia, the vast majority lived east of the mountains, with English descendants dominant in the east and Scots-Irish and German migrants prevalent in the west. Tobacco planting, though, remained restricted to the rich lands in the state's northeastern corner, and as a result slaves made up a smaller proportion—no more than twenty-five percent—of the population. Elsewhere, farmers supplemented their food crops by cutting timber and tapping trees for sap to create products used in shipbuilding like resin, pitch, turpentine, and tar. Poor roads, the absence of navigable rivers or large natural harbors, and the sandy islands of the Outer Banks kept North Carolinians largely isolated: farmers had to wait for heavy fall rains to flood the streams so they could float their produce to Wilmington, New Bern, or one of the other small trading towns along the coast. Tensions between the state's eastern and western halves preoccupied the small planters and farmers who controlled the legislature. Despite the reliance on outsiders for trade, North Carolinians generally displayed little interest in the Union's affairs.

Two states farther south focused on staple-crop production and depended heavily on slavery, but their environment and product gave them a different character from the states around the Chesapeake. The area that became South Carolina was originally intended to provide food and supplies for Britain's sugar colonies in the West Indies. Settlers soon discovered that the tropical climate and coastal lowlands provided an ideal environment for growing rice, a valuable grain in demand not only in the West Indies but also in Britain and southern Europe. Similarly, Georgia had been designed as a colony of small farmers who could work off their debts while serving as soldiers to protect the other colonies from invasion by Spanish Florida, but within a generation the lure of profits from rice production drove out the humanitarian ideals and strategic objectives. Rice plantations thus dominated the coasts of both colonies, with planters splitting their time between their plantation homes and their mansions in Charleston or Savannah. The confluence of two major rivers into its natural harbor had made Charleston the South's largest city, with more than sixteen thousand residents. The intense labor demands for rice production meant that slaves made up the majority in the plantation districts, with the proportion of slaves exceeding eighty percent in several parishes around Charleston.

Rice planters maintained firm control over South Carolina and Georgia during the colonial era. Small farming Scots-Irish and German migrants in the backcountry challenged the planters' authority on the eve of the Revolution, but concessions to the backcountry and the vicious fighting on the frontier between Patriots and Loyalists allowed South Carolina's planters to maintain a firm hold on the state government. In Georgia, the western counties' unity forced planters to share power with the smaller farmers, in one of the Union's more demo-cratic constitutions. In both states, planters relied on slave importations to support their labor force, since hard labor and unhealthy conditions in the rice fields took its toll each year. Lower South planters, too, hoped the Union could help open up new markets for the rice trade, which had not yet recovered from the disruption caused by the war. Georgians likewise looked to the Union for assistance against the Cherokee and Creek Indian nations that occupied most of the state's lands and kept its immigrant population huddled along the coast. But leaders in both South Carolina and Georgia were prepared to reject any outside interference regarding slavery and could join together if the Union failed to meet their needs.

The states farthest north contrasted dramatically with those in the Chesapeake and lower South. New England had been founded by Puritans, the members of an English religious sect heavily influenced by the theology of the Swiss reformer John Calvin. A small group of Sepa-ratists who rejected any connection with the Church of England set up a colony at Plymouth. Most Puritans, however, maintained their connection with the established church with the hope that they could persuade their countrymen to follow their beliefs, and they established Massachusetts as a "city upon a hill," a model society based on Puritan principles that could serve as an example for the corrupt England they had left behind. Disagreements shattered their mission within a generation of their arrival. By the late seventeenth century, Massachu-setts had incorporated Plymouth and still held the lands that would later become Maine, but Connecticut, Rhode Island, and New Hampshire stood apart as separate colonies. The original Puritan zeal faded long before the Revolution, but the Christian faith nevertheless remained central to New England culture. Most inhabitants lived in small towns that were initially designed to foster a sense of fellowship. Thanks to the influence of its founder, Roger Wil-liams, Rhode Island granted religious freedom to its people, but elsewhere the Congregational Church continued to receive state support—in Connecticut, until 1818; in New Hampshire, until 1819; and in Massachusetts, until 1833.

New England also stood as the Union's least prosperous region. Despite the founders' plans, none of the Puritan colonies found the crop or product necessary to make them important contributors in the British Empire. Except along the Connecticut River, the region contained little land that could support commercial farming while providing relatively easy access to markets. New England farmers worked hard to grow what they could from the rocky soil, bartering with their neighbors and selling their limited surpluses to merchants in one of the several seaports. Still, farming supported a rapidly growing population. With about 475,000 residents, Massachusetts ranked second only to Virginia, while Boston, New England's prin-cipal port, emerged as the Union's third largest city, with more than 18,000 inhabitants. The lack of arable land, however, forced numerous young men to look for opportunities outside of their hometowns. Shipping remained the heart of New England's economy, so many went to sea on merchant, fishing, or whaling expeditions, while others went to work on the docks or in shipbuilding. By the mid-1780s, New England commerce had not yet fully recovered from the disruption caused by the war. Merchants generally looked to Congress to negotiate com-mercial treaties that would open new markets. Isolated farmers throughout the region, though, tended to distrust the deliberations of a body that seemed even more distant than their state governments.

Three Middle Atlantic states lay between New England and the Chesapeake, and two had the potential to become continental powers. Small farmers made up the majority in New York, New Jersey, and Pennsylvania. In the colonial era, they had grown the crops that fed the slaves working on the British sugar islands in the Caribbean. Each state's unique heritage had given it a distinct character, and the lure of land had brought thousands of migrants in the eigh-teenth century and given the Middle Atlantic the Union's most ethnically mixed population.

Good harbors at the mouth of the Hudson River and at the confluence of the Delaware and Schuylkill Rivers provided farmers with easy access to Atlantic markets while making New York and Philadelphia the Union's two largest cities, with more than thirty-three thousand and twenty-five thousand inhabitants, respectively. As in New England, merchants had played dominant roles in colonial politics. With independence they remained influential figures and looked to the Union to help expand their trade, but the Revolution brought challenges to the Middle Atlantic's traditional leadership from locally oriented leaders skeptical of any outside authority.

A large Dutch presence in New York reflected its original founding as New Netherland by the Dutch West India Company in 1624. Under the Company's control, the colony remained underdeveloped, making it easy for England to capture the outpost in 1664 and name it for its proprietor, the Duke of York. Under English control, migrants—mainly from England and Northern Ireland, as well as New England—came to work on a series of landed estates along the Hudson River between Albany and New York City. The "Manor Lords" who owned these estates—including the Van Rensselaer, Livingston, Morris, Van Cortlandt, and Philipse families—resembled a European landed aristocracy, since they largely derived their income from rents paid by the tenants working their land. The need to attract labor, though, forced them to grant privileges usually not awarded to tenant farmers, including the right to vote and ownership of improvements on their lands. For most of the colonial period, too, the presence of the Iroquois Confederation west of the Hudson limited New York's expansion. War had broken the Iroquois' hold on the land, and in the decade before independence New York's population doubled as farmers moved for the first time into the western part of the state. With more than 300,000 people in the 1780s, New York ranked as the Union's fifth most populous state, and with its vibrant commercial center and millions of acres of unsettled lands, it stood poised to become one of the Union's wealthiest.

Prosperity and ethnic and religious diversity likewise characterized the other Middle Atlantic states. The Dutch West India Company included in New Netherland the lands that became New Jersey, which as an English colony became a prime location for migrants who hoped to improve their fortunes. New Jersey's politics had been dominated by a division between the descendants of the original English Quaker and Anglican settlers in thriving "West Jersey," as the state's southern portion was known, and the Dutch, German, and Scots-Irish settlers in less-affluent "East Jersey." Sectional arguments continued to divide the state after independence, but leaders of both West and East Jersey agreed that they wanted to free their state from outside influence: since New Jersey lacked a good harbor, Philadelphia and New York merchants controlled New Jersey's trade. The state legislature approved several proposals designed to encourage manufacturing and attract merchants to their own small ports. None of these measures produced results, however, so New Jerseyians united in the hope that the Union might establish a uniform commercial policy that would make the state less dependent on its neighbors.

No such agreement prevailed in Pennsylvania. William Penn had founded his colony partly as a refuge from persecution for his fellow English Quakers, but he had also intended for Pennsylvania to serve as a "Holy Experiment," a society without a government-backed church. The presence of various sects would produce a harmonious society, he believed, since no one in the colony would be forced to violate their conscience. Religious freedom and rich farmland attracted thousands of migrants and made Pennsylvania the third most populous state, with more than 430,000 people. Contrary to Penn's dreams, religion and ethnicity fueled contention in colonial Pennsylvania's politics. English descendants dominated the original counties around Philadelphia. The city's Quaker merchants held firm control of the colonial Assembly, but an English-led "Anglican party" challenged Quaker leadership and shortly before the

Figure 1.1 "The Residence of David Twining, 1785," an idealized view of a prosperous farm in the Confederation era. Oil painting by Edward Hicks (1846). Courtesy American Folk Art Museum, New York; gift of Ralph Esmerian, 2005.8.13; photo by John Bigelow Taylor.

Revolution appealed to the king to take over the colony from the Penn family. Both groups sought support from German settlers, who made up thirty-eight percent of the population and lived in the regions surrounding the English counties, while a "Presbyterian Party" promoted the interests of the Scots-Irish settlers on the frontier between the German counties and the Appalachian Mountains. The Quakers' reluctance to support independence reshaped Pennsylvania politics, but the bitterness from the colonial era remained, contributing to the most caustic politics of any state in the Union.

The Revolution shook the states' internal politics. Not only did independence unleash many of the conflicting interests that tradition and the British presence had somewhat contained, but several states struggled with exactly how to implement a government based on the authority of the people, rather than on the will of the British king. The creation of popular governments that protected liberty while maintaining stability presented a major challenge for each state—more daunting, perhaps, than facing the British army. The war had been necessary, but for George Washington and his countrymen independence was mainly a means to an end. The establishment of effective republican governments gave the Revolution its meaning. Revolutionary leaders intended for their states to stand as models of free government, encouraging the cause of liberty throughout the globe. They were to be, in the words of the Revolutionary pamphleteer Thomas Paine, an "asylum for mankind."

Republican Revolutions

The English and European cultures from which white Americans had come understood a republic to be a representative form of government. Unlike in a pure democracy, where all the citizens actually meet together and rule themselves, in a republic the citizens elect representatives to carry out their will and conduct public affairs. But the eighteenth-century world also considered freedom a limited and potentially dangerous privilege. The vast majority of humans, they believed, were selfish, lacking both the self-restraint and respect for institutions thought necessary for people to live together in society without some check on their behavior. History had shown time and again that a republic, a democracy, or any government based upon individual liberty would degenerate quickly into anarchy, a "war, where every man is enemy to every man," as the philosopher Thomas Hobbes put it in his 1651 work *The Leviathan*, making life "solitary, poor, nasty, brutish, and short."

For a society to function, Europeans assumed that people needed the leadership of a hereditary monarch and a titled nobility, placed in their stations by God. The king and the aristocracy offered wise direction while providing the force necessary to compel individuals to remember their responsibilities. Some liberty could be permitted, in the European view of society. Americans' British ancestors, in fact, considered themselves the world's freest people because their constitutions permitted more freedoms than found in any continental nation. The "rights of Englishmen," including trial by jury, no imprisonment without a formal charge, no unlawful entry of private homes, and taxation only after approval by the people's representatives, protected them from arbitrary authority. In the Revolution, Americans concluded that the king and his ministers had embarked on a plot to eliminate these English rights and subject both Britons and Americans to their absolute will. The need to protect freedom helped propel the colonies into independence and in the process convinced Americans that monarchy and aristocracy were the enemies of popular rights. Britons might accept their enslavement, but in the Revolution the Americans intended to show that the people could rule themselves without the stabilizing but threatening presence of a king or an aristocracy.

As in Britain, in America freedom was not extended to everyone. Voting and participation in public affairs belonged only to those considered independent—that is, those who had the means to support themselves and their families so that they were not under anyone else's direction or influence. Since laws generally dealt with property, and since the vast majority of people made their living in agriculture, most Americans continued to believe that the ownership of landed property provided the best way to determine who had the independence necessary to make wise and informed decisions. Yeomen—small farmers who owned rather than rented the land they worked to provide for themselves—and artisans—master craftsmen with the skills to manufacture the goods that society needed—met the minimum standards for independent status. Presumably they represented the interests of everyone living within their household. Slaves understandably were thought to be completely dependent on their masters, but farm laborers, servants, and the journeymen and apprentices learning an artisan's trade, though protected by the rights of Englishmen, also lacked the vote, because they lived under their employers' legal oversight. To extend the vote beyond property holders, most thought, would not expand freedom but unfairly increase the influence of the household head, who controlled the decisions of those living under his direction.

Women likewise occupied a restricted position in their families. In fact, their gender placed them in the status of perpetual dependents. The law recognized married women as *femmes couvertes*, or "covered women," meaning that they had no legal existence apart from their husbands. Not only were they denied the vote, but they could not own property, hold public office, work outside the home, sit on juries, or even pursue an education without their husband's consent. Single women, or *femmes soles* ("women alone"), could own property and make contracts, but traditional attitudes limited their opportunities. Men and women both assumed that a woman found ultimate fulfillment in her role as a wife and mother, subject to her husband's will. Upon marriage she took her husband's name, and any property she owned immediately became her husband's possession. Notwithstanding the legal restrictions, a woman's actual experience depended heavily on her circumstances and her relationship with her father or husband. The vast majority of women lived under a patriarch's authority, but many assisted their husbands in managing their farms or running a family business. Some Americans recognized women's important economic contributions to farm households as the ones who prepared food, tended gardens, and manufactured necessities like clothes, soap, and candles. Good judgment or service in a position like a midwife even brought many women respect and standing in their communities.

A few women hoped the Revolution might open possibilities for them to play a greater role in public affairs. Abigail Adams asked her husband John to "Remember the Ladies" when making the independent republic's laws; women at least needed protection from men's absolute authority, she insisted, because "all Men would be tyrants if they could." Most Americans, including John Adams, recoiled from these suggestions. As a result, the Revolution produced no significant changes in women's legal status. No state permitted women to vote except New Jersey—thanks to the vague wording in the state constitution until its revision in 1807. Instead, the Revolutionary generation stressed that women should contribute to the Union's success through their roles as mothers of future republicans. As keepers of the domestic side of the household, they should instill in their sons the morality and patriotic values necessary for them to grow up to be virtuous citizens. Advocates for "Republican Motherhood" encouraged women to be informed about public affairs, and many men accepted the idea that women needed a basic education to better pass lessons on to their children. For most women, though, the hard work of supporting a farm remained the dominant experience. Frequent pregnancies and childbearing shortened the lives of many while leaving others in poor health.

Despite these limitations, in the eighteenth-century view freedom flourished in America, and the Revolutionary generation thought their states well-positioned to establish successful republics. Most Americans eagerly embarked on the "republican experiment," because conditions in the states seemed well suited to the creation of successful republican governments. Popularly elected assemblies had governed the colonies' internal affairs with minimal interference from the mother country—Britain's threat to the assemblies' prerogative, in fact, had first provoked the movement that led to independence. The wealthiest colonists controlled the assemblies and also enjoyed economic dominance and social status, but they lacked the prestige and advantages of a landed European aristocracy with entrenched legal privileges, and varying economic fortunes meant that membership in the elite could and sometimes did change. Unlike in England, where property requirements restricted voting to a small number of men, in America most adult males owned enough property for the right to vote. Colonial voters usually endorsed local elites' claims to office, and voter turnout was erratic. Still, the relatively large electorate and the heritage of assembly leadership showed that Americans entered independence with considerable experience in self-government.

The states provided the laboratory for testing the republican form of government—not just because of their heritage as distinct colonies, but mainly because most people assumed a republic could work only in a small geographic region. According to political theorists, in a republic a representative had to know his constituents personally so he could accurately present their interests in a legislature. Representative districts thus had to be small enough for a candidate to meet all the citizens in order to hear their views. A large republic containing too many people would end up with hundreds, and perhaps thousands, of members in its representative branch, making it far too large and unwieldy a body to conduct business effectively. Several states might already prove too large for an effective republic, and in all their governments would be shaped as much by their colonial experience as by republican thought. Nevertheless, most Americans agreed that the United States was too vast and heavily populated for the establishment of a single republican government.

The state governments put republican principles into practice. During the war, American leaders had concentrated on composing their state constitutions. The legacy of the colonial charters—papers that the king had issued to authorize and provide the legal organization of each colony—joined the Revolution's insistence on the people's authority to convince most Americans that the constitutions should be written documents representing the citizens' grant of power to their government. State legislators initially assumed the task of composing constitutions, but as the Revolution progressed more became convinced that the duty of writing a state's fundamental law belonged to a specially elected convention, with delegates specifically charged with the task. Most states' lawmakers declined to submit their work for the voters' approval; unusual circumstances in Pennsylvania led to the calling of the first convention, and protests against New Hampshire's original constitution led to a convention in 1778, followed by another, more successful meeting in 1784. In Massachusetts, meanwhile, an overwhelming majority of town meetings rejected the lawmakers' constitution before a convention wrote a document that received the voters' endorsement in 1780. By the middle of the 1780s, Americans considered constitutional conventions the best way for the people to express their will in the framing or revising of a republic's government, and they expected a popular vote to approve the government before it went into effect.

Beyond approving the constitution, what role the people should play in a republic presented a major point of dispute. All agreed that the Revolution's success depended upon the citizens' virtue: In order to avoid the tragic fate of previous republics, the people needed to follow public affairs and, when necessary, rise above their selfish interests and vote for the public good. For many—especially the planters, merchants, lawyers, and landholders who had controlled colonial politics—responsible voting fulfilled the citizens' duty: Once voters had approved the constitution and selected government officials, they were to defer to the decisions of those with the education and experience necessary to make wise decisions. At the same time, the Revolution's calls for popular action convinced others that the people actually could rule themselves. Colonial leaders inspired by the Enlightenment favored giving the people a greater role, but democracy gained adherents among artisans, small merchants, and professionals in port towns, as well as among small farmers in rural areas or whom the old colonial leadership had in some way alienated. Advocates of democracy strongly condemned anything that resembled aristocratic or monarchical pretensions, and they believed that separation from Britain offered the opportunity to create a truly democratic system, in which the people actually made the decisions and elected officials merely carried out the people's will.

Tensions between those who thought the people should defer to their betters and those who thought citizens had the right to rule affected the shape of most states' new governments. Lawmakers in Connecticut and Rhode Island merely removed their charters' references to royal authority, but in other states conventions made some substantial changes, mainly in reducing property requirements for voting and expanding the size of the legislatures. Most added a senate, a smaller legislative body that would balance the popular will with the wisdom of the "best" members of society, but the powers of state governors were restricted to the point that they stood mainly as figureheads. Planters managed to retain their firm hold on Maryland and South Carolina, while democratic concessions allowed traditional leaders to remain in control of Virginia and Massachusetts, despite the popular rejection of Massachusetts' first constitution. Similar concessions allowed New York's Manor Lords and merchants to give their governor more powers than found elsewhere, though to their shock rural small farmers rejected their candidate in 1777 to elect the popular militia general George Clinton to the first of six consecutive terms. Resentments left over from the colonial era forced the old leadership to share authority with sectional or factional rivals in Delaware and North Carolina. Popular protests from western towns gave the vote to all taxpayers in New Hampshire; Georgia's constitution gave all effective power to a one-chamber legislature, while a coup led by western farmers and Philadelphia artisans implemented almost a direct democracy in Pennsylvania, with a powerful one-chamber assembly with its sessions open to the public, nearly universal white male suffrage, and a requirement that voters approve bills before they became law.

Democratic demands presented a crucial issue to the new republics. The presence of slavery presented a less immediate but equally disturbing challenge. Slavery had been legal in all of the American colonies. The need for workers on the Chesapeake's tobacco plantations and on the rice plantations in the lower South had concentrated the majority of slaves in those regions. Small farmers in New England and the Middle Atlantic had less use for slave labor, but well-off farmers and artisans expanded their production with a slave or two, while wealthy Northerners used slaves as domestic servants like valets, maids, cooks, and coachmen. Before the Revolution, few white Americans questioned the morality or usefulness of slavery. As subjects of the British Empire, most accepted hierarchical distinctions among humans as the divinely ordained natural order and saw slaves as the unfortunates in the lowest rank. The only formal challenge to slavery within the colonies came from the Quakers, a religious sect that had long emphasized the equality of all men before God. Anthony Benezet's and John Woolman's advocacy against the slave trade eventually persuaded several Quaker meetings to condemn both purchasing and owning slaves.

The Revolution's appeals to liberty, however, brought slavery to many more Americans' attention. In the Declaration of Independence, Thomas Jefferson rejected traditional hierarchy, in his dramatic statement that "all men are created equal." Americans disagreed widely about the meaning of equality, but almost all recognized that the existence of slavery directly contradicted one of the Revolution's core ideals. Critics now highlighted the inefficiencies of coerced labor, and many feared that blacks' "uncivilized" behavior and masters' absolute authority over their slaves promoted laziness, arrogance, and selfishness among whites—characteristics contrary to the virtue needed in a successful republic. Many now wanted to eliminate or at least distance the Revolution from slavery. After Congress approved resolutions condemning the slave trade in 1776, several states prohibited further importations, and their small proportion of slaves allowed Northern states to act against the institution. A series of state court decisions in the 1780s brought slavery to an end in New England, where slaves constituted about one percent of the population. Slaves' slightly larger presence—around four percent—allowed the Middle Atlantic states to end the institution through gradual emancipation or "post-nati" laws, which declared that slaves born after a particular date would be freed upon reaching a certain age. Pennsylvania passed the first gradual emancipation law in 1780. Slaveholder resistance delayed the passage of similar laws until 1799 in New York and 1804 in New Jersey, but by the early nineteenth century slavery was well on its way to extinction in the North.

Farther south, slavery proved too deeply entrenched for dramatic action. Abolishing the institution would significantly disrupt Southern states' plantation economies. Moreover, African Americans' supposed ignorance and barbarity, along with the resentments incurred while in slavery, convinced white Americans that the two races could not live together peacefully in freedom. Unless the black population could somehow be removed, immediate emancipation would eventually result in a race war, with consequences far worse than anything currently experienced in slavery. Numerous Southerners—particularly in the Chesapeake—lamented slavery's existence, and many Virginia and Maryland planters freed their slaves or changed their wills to provide for their slaves' emancipation. Until Southerners no longer needed slave labor, and an affordable way could be found to remove blacks from American soil, white Americans throughout the Union accepted slavery's persistence as a "necessary evil"—forced upon Americans, they claimed, by their English ancestors and indispensable now to maintaining stable race relations.

During the 1780s, slavery presented only a minor concern to the Union. Since gaining independence, Congress attempted to present a united front for the states as it dealt with issues that would have intimidated longer-established and more respected governments. The delegates' inability to deal effectively with these problems showed that the states had not given Congress sufficient power. The question remained whether the states would show enough interest in working together to create an effective union.

The Confederation

In contrast to the careful attention devoted to the state constitutions, a government for the Union seemed an afterthought. The Second Continental Congress had convened in 1775 to present a united colonial front against Britain; with the onset of revolution, Congress continued to meet and assumed the responsibilities of a government. Independence brought the need for a more formal basis for the states' cooperation. In June 1776, the delegates to Congress appointed a committee to draft "Articles of Confederation" that would give the Union a legal foundation. The committee's chair, Pennsylvania lawyer John Dickinson, prepared a document that would have given Congress substantial authority over the states, but when he presented it to the delegates they quickly watered down Dickinson's proposals to preserve the states' authority. The war's distractions prevented Congress from approving the Articles of Confederation until November 1777. The document would still not take effect until all the states ratified it, and though ten ratified it within a year, leaders in New Jersey, Delaware, and Maryland feared being overwhelmed by the larger states and refused to give their consent until all had given up any claims to lands north of the Ohio River. Gradually the other legislatures consented, but Maryland's delay prevented the Articles of Confederation from operating legally until March 1781.

Ratification merely legalized the work of Congress, which followed the terms of the Articles of Confederation after the delegates first approved them. In fact, the Articles mainly outlined how the Union had operated since 1775. Rather than creating a government for the American people, the Articles recognized the Union as a compact of the states, a permanent "firm league of friendship," with each state retaining "its sovereignty, freedom, and independence, and every power, jurisdiction, and right" that it had not specifically delegated to "Congress," a term that traditionally referred to an international assembly rather than a legislature. Citizens were guaranteed the right to travel freely throughout the Union, subject only to the restrictions a state placed on its own people, while Congress was given authority over foreign relations, common defense, resolving disputes between the states, and some specific issues across the Union. The states could send to Congress any number from two to seven delegates—compensated, if at all, by the states—and each state would cast only one vote. Any action needed a simple majority, but major issues like declaring war, approving treaties, and borrowing money needed the approval of nine states. All thirteen states had to agree to any changes to the Articles, and since the Articles created neither an executive nor a judicial system, Congress had to rely on the states to carry out its decisions. Likewise, since it lacked the power to tax, Congress could raise money only through requisitions that the state legislatures were expected to pay.

Clearly, the Articles of Confederation did not set up a government representing the people of the Union. As an agent of the states, Congress had to depend upon the states' goodwill and cooperation, while the state governments dealt directly with individual citizens. War and the threat of losing independence had provided a strong motivation for the states to work together; since the conflict remained underway when Maryland ratified the Articles of Confederation in 1781, Congress moved toward assuming long-term guidance of the Union's affairs. To facilitate its business, it established departments of Foreign Affairs, War, and Finance, with New York's Robert Livingston, Massachusetts' Benjamin Lincoln, and Pennsylvania's Robert Morris as secretaries in charge of each respective agency. The official end of the war and achievement of independence came with the ratification of the Treaty of Paris in September 1783; with peace, Congress sent diplomatic missions to represent the United States in London and Paris. A Pennsylvania regiment's mutiny to demand back pay had forced Congress to leave Philadelphia in the summer of 1783 and compelled the delegates to disband the army even before the official peace. After holding sessions in Princeton and Trenton, New Jersey, and in Annapolis, Maryland, in 1785 Congress settled on New York as the Union's capital. In the meantime, the delegates expanded and reformed the postal service set up ten years earlier to improve communication across the Union.

While meeting in various locations, Congress also worked to develop a policy for managing and settling the western lands. The Treaty of Paris recognized the lands south of the Great Lakes, east of the Mississippi River, and north of Spain's Florida Territories as American possessions. Virginia, North Carolina, and Georgia held the lands south of the Ohio; lands north of the river came under Congress' authority as the common property of the states. Various opinions arose among the delegates as to what to do with these lands. Some thought the west should be organized as new colonies under the authority of Congress, with limited rights for the inhabitants and serving the interests of the original thirteen states. Others thought the lands should be opened and either given away or sold for low prices to encourage their rapid settlement and their organization as territories and states under the residents' control. Still others agreed that the lands should eventually become states, but they wanted the lands sold at higher prices. Higher prices would aid speculators, who would buy large tracts and profit from selling smaller parcels to actual settlers, but this process could provide Congress with an important source of revenue. Viewing the lands as an important resource, many also hesitated to leave the west under local control until they had developed stable societies with responsible leaders who would discourage unrestrained democracy.

The states' common interests in the west encouraged the delegates to work out a satisfactory compromise. Through a series of land ordinances, Congress determined that the western territories would eventually enter the Union as states on equal standing with the original thirteen, but their lands would be sold in such a way as to promote orderly settlement. A 1784 ordinance simply declared that the northwest would be organized into territories that would become states "on an equal footing" with the original states. A second ordinance a year later directed that the lands be surveyed and divided into townships of six square miles in size and containing thirty-six sections of one square mile, or 640 acres, each. Once surveyed, the lands were to be sold from land offices located in the eastern states, meaning that speculators or settlers would have to buy and get the title to their lands before moving west. Finally, a third ordinance, known as the Northwest Ordinance of 1787, determined that Congress would govern the territories while outlining the process for them to become states. Three to five territories were to be created north of the Ohio, with Congress appointing a governor, a secretary, and three judges. Once the population reached five thousand, the settlers could elect a territorial legislature, and once sixty thousand lived in the territory they could elect a convention to write a constitution and apply for admission as a state. The ordinance also prohibited slavery from existing in any territory while guaranteeing basic rights for a territory's inhabitants.

Passage of the Northwest Ordinance marked a major accomplishment for the Confederation and established a policy that would long outlive the Articles of Confederation. The ordinance did not, however, guarantee American possession of western lands. Natives—known to Europeans and their descendants as "Indians" ever since Christopher Columbus had misnamed them—remained a formidable obstacle. European expansion to the Americas had brought numerous diseases that devastated Native populations, and growing dependence on European goods severely disrupted their traditional cultures. Nevertheless, Natives fought to maintain their independence and to hold on to their territories. Wars had killed or driven out most Natives from the New England states, but several nations still existed in the northwest and the south. Most had sided with Britain during the Revolution as a way to slow American expansion. The Treaty of Paris made no recognition of the Natives' existence, but the six nations of the Iroquois Confederacy—the Mohawk, Seneca, Oneida, Cayuga, Onondaga, and Tuscarora—still lived in western New York. Several likewise occupied the region north and west of the Ohio, with the Delawares, Shawnees, and Miamis among the most formidable, while the Cherokees, Creeks, Chickasaws, and Choctaws held the lands south of the Ohio claimed by Virginia, North Carolina, and Georgia.

The Articles of Confederation gave Congress the authority to manage Native affairs unless a nation lay within a single state's boundaries, and the majority of delegates wanted to preserve peace while gaining access to more lands for settlement. In September 1783, they issued a proclamation prohibiting settlement or sale of Native lands without congressional approval, and they sent agents to the tribes to work out treaties establishing peace, setting the boundaries between Native and American territories and regulating trade. Most white Americans, though, considered Natives merely an impediment to the Union's rightful possession of the west. Several communities had already been established that either bordered on or lay within Native country, most notably Pittsburgh in western Pennsylvania, Lexington and Louisville in western Virginia, and Nashville and Watauga in western North Carolina. Britain's abandonment of the west, meanwhile, convinced Americans that they had also defeated the Natives, who would now have to accept the Union's sovereignty. Speculators continued to buy tracts from Congress or from Southern state governments, while anxious pioneers pressed into Native lands, showing little regard for Natives' claims.

Natives never considered themselves as having surrendered, however, so the treaties that Congress' agents negotiated did little to stabilize the west. In the Treaty of Fort McIntosh, signed in January 1785, the Delaware, Wyandot, Chippewa, and Ottawa nations agreed to pull back from the Ohio, and hundreds of white settlers flooded into the region and established settlements at Marietta and at Losantiville, which would be renamed Cincinnati in 1790. None of the nations that agreed to the treaty actually occupied the region, however, so settlers faced raids from the Shawnees and Miamis, the tribes who actually lived in the area. General George Rogers Clark organized a local militia for a retaliatory expedition in the fall of 1786, but the excursion only expanded the violence into a full-scale war. Violence also prevailed on the southern frontier. Despite treaties with the Cherokees, Choctaws, and Chickasaws negotiated at Hopewell, South Carolina, in late 1785 and early 1786, speculators and settlers pressed westward, particularly into Cherokee lands. One group of speculators in western North Carolina declared themselves the separate "State of Franklin," demanded admission to the Union as the fourteenth state, and provoked a war to acquire more Cherokee lands. Congress refused to recognize Franklin's existence, and the North Carolina government's suppression of the independence movement in 1788 temporarily restored peace, but Americans' continued movement onto Cherokee lands soon revived the conflict.

Congress' inability to stabilize the west reflected the difficulties it faced when it addressed any of the Union's issues. The Articles of Confederation had given the legislature legal authority, but it lacked the practical powers needed to enforce its decisions. Gaining the majorities among the states necessary for it to take action proved difficult enough. Without an executive, the delegates had to depend on the willingness of the state governments to carry out Congress' decisions; often a state's delegation would vote for a congressional act only to see its state's government resist implementing its provisions. Similarly, because the Articles had not given Congress the power to tax, Congress could raise money only through direct requisitions to the states, with each state's share determined by its population. But the states had their own issues and already imposed higher taxes than Americans had paid during the colonial era; several simply refused to pay or claimed they lacked the funds to contribute their share. An independent source of revenue apart from the states would have allowed Congress to set up an administration to enforce its decisions. Without it, the Union extended no further than the states' willingness to work together.

The lack of money particularly complicated the need to address the debt accumulated during the Revolution. During the war, the Union had borrowed more than $11 million from the French government and Dutch bankers, but it owed considerably more to individual Americans. Congress had purchased war supplies and covered its expenses by issuing paper money and various securities with the promise to redeem them when cash became available. Back pay was still owed to soldiers, and to prevent an uprising the delegates agreed to pay bonuses of five years' pay to officers and four months' pay to enlisted men. Robert Morris, the superintendent of finance, adjusted claims from citizens in 1783 and estimated that the domestic debt stood at about $28 million. All agreed that the foreign debt needed to be paid in full and that at least some provision had to be made for the domestic debt to retain public support and so that Congress could borrow money during a future emergency. The states, however, had their own debts and devoted their resources to those obligations. Without a reliable source of income, Congress stood unable to pay either its expenses or the interest that daily increased the debt. Several states, in fact, began taking on the Union's obligations to their own citizens, which could eventually provide for part of the debt's payment but at the same time reinforced the Union's dependence on the states.

Congress could also do little to address the economic depression that followed the war. Once the fighting stopped, British merchants came back to American ports and offered manufactured goods for sale on generous credit terms. Americans had done without new products for nearly a decade and eagerly bought the British wares, expecting the sale of their produce to provide the funds needed to pay their debts. But the war had seriously disrupted the American economy. Destruction from the armies' movements and the enemy's confiscation of about twenty-five thousand slaves dramatically reduced tobacco and rice production. Independence meanwhile deprived Americans of the advantages of the British Empire. British merchants cut back their purchases and their marketing of American products to international ports, while the royal government stopped paying bounties on American goods and closed their colonies to American ships. Most damaging was the closing of the West Indies trade, where American colonists had profited from selling food and supplies to feed the slave population and support the islands' sugar industry. The loss of the West Indies trade and the overall collapse of the economy forced Americans to pay whatever gold and silver they had toward their debts. Still, large numbers in the population remained heavily indebted, and the loss of wealth further depressed an already troubled economy.

In the long run, the crisis forced Americans to search for new trading partners. Agricultural production recovered; trade with France, Holland, and the French West Indies eventually filled some of the void left by the declining sales to Britain, and in the 1780s merchants made initial contacts for trade with China and India. In the short run, however, the depression produced severe hardships that Congress appeared unable to resolve. Some representatives hoped that

France could replace Britain as the Union's principal trading partner, but the French economy mostly produced expensive luxuries, rather than the practical manufactured goods that came from Britain. Other delegates thought imposing heavy tariffs on British imports might force Britain to relax its restrictions on American exports, and in 1784 Congress proposed an amendment to the Articles of Confederation that would give the legislature the power to pass navigation laws regulating the Union's trade. Merchants, though, feared that the British might retaliate by cutting back their purchases even further, and some Southern planters thought navigation laws might leave the Union under Northern traders' control. Rhode Island likewise refused to support a national policy that might favor its neighbors, and it joined North Carolina to reject and defeat the proposed amendment.

Trade restrictions were only one of America's problems with the former mother country. A more ominous threat appeared in Britain's continued occupation of several northwestern forts. In the Treaty of Paris, Britain agreed to withdraw from all military posts in American territories. Nevertheless, British troops remained in several forts in the Great Lakes region, including Forts Michilimackinac and Detroit on the Michigan peninsula and Forts Niagara and Oswego in western New York. Britain's government justified holding the forts by noting that Americans themselves had not fulfilled their obligations, for no state had restored to the Crown any property confiscated from Loyalists during the Revolution, as the Treaty of Paris "earnestly" recommended. In reality, the forts allowed Britain to continue profiting from the fur trade with Natives and to resist American expansion westward, for settlers suspected that the soldiers encouraged Native attacks on frontier settlements. Yet Congress could do little to challenge the British presence. The states showed limited interest in providing the necessary resources for military action and ignored Congress' recommendations to restore the Loyalists' estates. British officials likewise paid little attention to the entreaties of John Adams, the American representative in London, reminding Adams that they had neither the need nor the desire for another treaty that Congress could not enforce.

In the southwest, Spain likewise obstructed American expansion. Spain had refused to recognize American independence until 1783, fearing that supporting a colonial rebellion might inspire similar uprisings in its own colonial empire. Nevertheless, Spain had joined the war against Britain in 1779 and in the peace gained possession of West Florida, the region between the Mississippi and the Perdido Rivers; East Florida, the peninsula east of the Perdido; and Louisiana, the vast territory between the Mississippi River and the Rocky Mountains. In the Treaty of Paris, Britain recognized the southern boundary of the United States at the 31st parallel, but Spain used Britain's pre-war boundaries for West Florida to claim the territory up to 32° 28', where the Yazoo River flowed into the Mississippi. From their military post at Natchez, Spanish commanders supported Native wars against Americans, at the same time offering protection if settlers would renounce the Union and declare allegiance to Spain. In the meantime, Spain announced in 1784 that Americans could no longer sell their produce in New Orleans.

Closing New Orleans to American trade presented a serious threat, especially to Southern interests. Those who ventured to western Virginia and North Carolina had presumed they could float their crops down one of the several rivers that flowed into the Ohio to the Mississippi for sale to international traders in New Orleans. Without the right of deposit in the city, their only option was to transport their goods on expensive routes over the Appalachian Mountains to one of the ports on the east coast. The cost of overland trade would discourage further settlement and economic development, making the lands all but worthless while offering western residents additional incentive to break from the Union and recognize Spanish authority. Yet again, Congress' efforts to address the problem revealed its weakness. The Spanish government sent Don Diego de Gardoquí to negotiate a commercial treaty if the United

States would renounce any claims to trade on the Mississippi. Congress instructed New York's John Jay, the secretary of foreign affairs, to talk with Gardoquí but to insist on opening New Orleans as a condition for any treaty. Jay quickly realized that Gardoquí offered no hope of opening the Mississippi. Lured by the potential profits that trade in the Spanish Empire would bring to New Yorkers and other Northern merchants, Jay nevertheless asked Congress to change his instructions to allow him to surrender the right of deposit for twenty to thirty years so he could complete a commercial agreement.

Jay's request incited a contentious debate. Northern delegates saw little advantage in the rapid development of the west, and like Jay they eagerly anticipated the profits to be made in colonial Spanish markets. Yet Southerners resented Northern states' willingness to sacrifice Southern lands and strengthen the Spanish presence on their frontiers. Arguments over whether to approve Jay's proposal lasted through the summer of 1786 and produced the bitterest divisions among the states since they had formed the Union. When Congress finally voted on the motion in August, seven states—from Pennsylvania through New Hampshire—favored Jay's request. As a diplomatic issue, however, it needed the approval of nine states, and the five states from Maryland to Georgia joined together to block the change. Jay's negotiations with Gardoquí soon ended, New Orleans remained closed to the west, and American merchants remained excluded from Spanish colonial ports.

The furor sparked by the Jay-Gardoquí negotiations severely strained the states' sense of unity. Some delegates privately wondered whether they might be better off divided into two or three separate confederations. No formal proposal for disunion emerged, and most Americans expected the Union to plod along into the future. But Congress clearly lacked the power to deal effectively with the issues facing the Union, and the states seemed less and less inclined to work with each other. Movements were underway to strengthen Congress under the Articles of Confederation, and an increasing number of Americans expressed a willingness to accept them. Still, it seemed more likely that the Union would die from a lack of interest. The fact that the Union survived, and that the states went beyond merely revising the Articles of Confederation, was the result of luck and of the efforts of a relatively small number of individuals.

The Constitution

From the Revolution's earliest days, a few leaders thought the Union needed a centralized government strong enough to act independently and enforce its will. John Dickinson's original proposal for an effective Congress gained little support, but as the war progressed, more Americans developed a nationalist outlook that saw the Union as something distinct and greater than the states. Several groups supported a stronger union. Army officers like George Washington and his young aide, Alexander Hamilton, dealt directly with Congress and came to see the state governments as obstructions to their plans to defend the Union. Diplomats like Benjamin Franklin likewise represented the Union as one common people. Most members of Congress continued to be primarily loyal to their states, but many grew frustrated with Congress' inability to act. Outside of government, numerous merchants, particularly in the Middle Atlantic states, saw the potential benefits of a national economy managed and regulated by a central authority. Most Southern planters and local leaders jealously continued to guard their power over state affairs, but the need to organize and protect the west persuaded some to overcome their parochialism and at least consider strengthening the Union.

Americans who came from the old colonial elite were among the strongest nationalists. Holding on to the traditional belief that the common people should defer to their betters, many expressed concern at the extent of popular influence in the state governments. Bitter divisions and legislative battles through the 1780s convinced several nationalists that the states were too democratic to function effectively. The growing size of the assemblies and the lower-ing of property requirements left governments dominated by small farmers, smaller planters and merchants, and artisans—"middling sort" property owners whom elites thought lacked the education and experience necessary for enlightened leadership. In their view, the state governments ignored both the Union's and their state's needs, because lawmakers became pre-occupied with local factional battles and passed laws designed only to satisfy their constituents' self-interest, regardless of the greater good. Paper money seemed to symbolize irresponsible government. With money short and trade stagnant, seven states issued unbacked paper money as currency. Georgia, New Jersey, North Carolina, and especially Rhode Island issued so much that the money quickly became worthless, but lawmakers in these states simply declared their notes to be legal tender, forcing merchants and creditors to accept the deflated paper as pay-ment. Beyond paper money, the flood of laws passed in the states—often merely repealing a previous legislature's work to replace it with a new majority's will—indicated to many people that the state governments were headed for collapse.

Nationalist-oriented leaders generally agreed that the people's influence on the state gov-ernments needed to be reined in. Since the legislatures showed little interest in yielding their powers, they worked mainly to increase Congress' authority so it could act without the states' interference. The requirement for unanimous approval for any changes to the Articles of Confederation, however, defeated their efforts. Twice, a single state—first Rhode Island, then New York—rejected a plan to authorize Congress to collect an impost, a five-percent tax on imports that would have given Congress an independent source of income. Southern states, too, refused to approve an amendment authorizing Congress to pass navigation acts, which would allow it to regulate foreign trade. By 1786, most nationalists gave up any hope of secur-ing the unanimous approval necessary to change the Articles. Instead, they concluded that a general convention of the states presented the more likely method of strengthening the central government. Like the meetings that produced the state constitutions, an assembly of delegates from the states selected for one purpose would derive its authority directly from the people and perhaps provide a way to sidestep the states' blocks to reform.

Ironically, a meeting that reflected the states' independence provided an opportunity to call a convention. In 1785, representatives from Maryland and Virginia met at Mount Vernon to establish regulations for trade and shipping on the Potomac, the river that served as their common border. After coming to an agreement, they submitted their work to their respec-tive legislatures for approval. During the subsequent discussions, Virginia legislator John Tyler proposed that all the states should send delegates to Annapolis, Maryland, to discuss similar commercial regulations throughout the Union. Several states expressed interest in a general commercial arrangement, but when the convention opened in September 1786, only New York, New Jersey, Delaware, Pennsylvania, and Virginia were represented. Instead of waiting for more delegates to arrive, the twelve members present approved a statement prepared by New York's Alexander Hamilton that highlighted the Confederation's weaknesses, argued that the problems went beyond anything a commercial agreement could remedy, and called for a general convention in Philadelphia in May 1787 to propose changes "necessary to render the constitution of the Federal Government adequate to the exigencies of the Union."

The call for the Philadelphia Convention came at a time when state leaders were more will-ing than usual to consider strengthening the central government. The acrimonious debate over the Jay-Gardoquí negotiations concluded only a month before the Annapolis meeting. At the same time, the outbreak of rebellion in Massachusetts confirmed for many that the states stood on the verge of anarchy. The Massachusetts legislature had imposed a series of heavy taxes, mainly to service the state debt owed largely to merchants in the eastern part of the state. The taxes particularly burdened small farmers in western counties; with the economy in depression, few could pay, leaving many facing the confiscation and sale of their land. After the legislature rejected a bill for an issuance of paper money, which would have provided small farmers some assistance, western farmers took matters into their own hands. In late August 1786, a mob of about fifteen hundred attacked and shut down the Hampshire County court, where foreclosure proceedings threatened to seize farmers' lands. Similar mobs closed court proceedings in several other counties throughout the fall. Daniel Shays, a former captain in the Continental army, led some of the uprisings and gained recognition as the leader of the rebellion. Word reached Governor James Bowdoin that Shays planned to seize a federal arsenal in Springfield.

The Massachusetts legislature quickly reduced taxes and reformed its courts, while Governor Bowdoin scrambled to restore order. Congress authorized Secretary of War Henry Knox to recruit thirteen hundred men to send to Massachusetts; in the meantime, eastern merchants provided Bowdoin with the funds he needed to raise an army of four thousand that, under General Benjamin Lincoln, dispersed Shays' twelve hundred followers at Springfield. "Shays' Rebellion" proved more a series of riots than an organized revolution, but nationalists portrayed the uprising as a serious threat that demonstrated the need for a central authority that could assist the states against future unrest. Even without this encouragement, fears for the long-term stability of republican government convinced enough state leaders to consider what the Philadelphia Convention might propose. Five states appointed delegates soon after receiving the Annapolis Convention's appeal. Several members of Congress resented the call for a meeting that bypassed their authority, but as the states appointed delegates it appeared it would meet regardless of their objection. Congress finally authorized the meeting in February 1787, stipulating that it should be "for the sole and express purpose of revising the Articles of Confederation." With begrudging congressional support assured, every state but Rhode Island appointed delegates to attend by the time the convention opened on May 25.

By that date, at least one nationalist concluded that the convention should go farther than anyone previously thought. James Madison, the thirty-six-year-old son of a Virginia planter, had served both in Congress and in his state's legislature, and his experience convinced him that Virginia's future would be best served in a strong union, with Virginia playing a leading role. Frustrated with Congress' ineffectiveness while he was a delegate, Madison took on strengthening the central government as a personal mission. After attending the Annapolis Convention, he introduced himself to George Washington and eventually persuaded the hero to lend his prestige by attending the upcoming meeting in Philadelphia. In the meantime, Madison undertook an extensive study of ancient and modern confederations to learn why they had succeeded or failed. His research convinced him that an effective confederation had to have a central government that acted directly on the people, unobstructed by any intermediary power. To Madison, the Union should be no longer a voluntary alliance of the states, but a nation under the authority of a single government. In this case, the Philadelphia Convention would have to do more than recommend amendments to the Articles of Confederation: it would have to scrap them and propose the creation of a national government that derived its authority from the people of all the states collectively, one that could check or even overturn shortsighted or unjust state laws.

Madison rejected the prevailing wisdom that a republic could function only in a small area, where the people actually knew their representatives. He reasoned instead that a government over the whole Union could better serve the people than could the state governments. No common interest united the people, he contended. As he later explained in the essay *The Federalist #10*, a variety of diverse interests, whether economic, religious, or ideological, divided the people in even the smallest state. When the people knew their representatives, they voted for those who best promoted their interests, and once in the legislature the "faction" that gained a majority simply passed laws to benefit its supporters, even if its acts oppressed minority factions. An "extended republic," on the other hand, better promoted stability while protecting the citizens' liberty. In a government over a large geographic area—especially one with poor transportation and communication links like post-Revolutionary America—politicians could not meet every voter to practice the "vicious arts" of campaigning, forcing voters to choose candidates based on their character and reputation rather than on personality or promises; a legislature chosen on these terms, he argued, would more likely know the public good than would the people themselves. But even if selfish representatives ended up in the legislature, a large republic would contain so many diverse local interests that none could hope to control a majority. In this circumstance, lawmakers could pass only acts that they mutually agreed actually served the public welfare.

Gathering enough delegates at Philadelphia to create a national government would be a challenge, but Madison nevertheless drafted a series of resolutions outlining a national system so the convention could consider it as soon as the delegates assembled. Once enough arrived in Philadelphia for a quorum, the delegates elected Washington the presiding officer and agreed to a set of rules to guide their deliberations, including an agreement to meet in secret and not comment publicly on their discussions. With the convention organized, Virginia governor Edmund Randolph introduced Madison's resolutions on May 29. The plan proposed to divide Congress into two chambers, making it more like a legislature than a diplomatic assembly. Representatives would vote as individuals, and in each chamber a state's population would determine the size of its representation—making the states, in the eyes of the national government, nothing more than administrative units. An executive officer and a judicial system both would have extensive powers that would balance the legislature's authority. Voters would select the representatives for the "first branch," who would in turn elect the members of the "second branch"; members of the second chamber would select the executive, who would then appoint justices to the courts. Madison's plan would give the national legislature the power to make laws "in all cases to which the separate states are incompetent." To make it clear that the national government took precedence over the states, he proposed giving the national legislature the power to veto state laws.

The scope of the "Virginia Plan," as it came to be known, caught the majority of delegates by surprise. Nevertheless, they accepted Madison's resolutions as the basis for their discussions. Representation immediately emerged as the crucial issue: Should the national legislature be apportioned according to the states' populations, as the Virginia Plan stipulated—meaning that it would represent the people rather than the states? Or should the states have equal representation, keeping the Union an alliance of states even if the central government had greater authority? Delegates from the four most populous states—Virginia, Massachusetts, Pennsylvania, and North Carolina—stood behind proportional representation, as did those from South Carolina and Georgia, who anticipated that their states would expand in the near future. Delegates from less populated states feared that their larger neighbors would overwhelm them in a national union, and they joined highly independent New York in calling for equal state representation. Delegates from Delaware, New Jersey, Connecticut, and Maryland thus put together a counterproposal. The plan that New Jersey's William Paterson introduced on June 15 would keep Congress a one-chamber assembly, with each state having one vote, but it declared all acts of Congress and treaties with foreign nations "the supreme law of the respective States." Congress would have the authority to tax and to compel the states to pay their requisitions, and a plural executive would be created to enforce congressional decisions. A supreme court would decide cases involving federal acts and international relations.

Paterson's "New Jersey Plan" reflected the type of union that most representatives initially expected the convention to produce. If introduced earlier, it probably would have become the basis of the convention's work. By the time it came before the delegates, however, representatives from the large states controlled the direction of the proceedings, and the convention rejected it by a 7–3 vote. Small states' delegates continued to resist a union under the large states' control, however, and after losing a motion on July 2 to give the states equal representation in the second chamber, small states' delegates seemed ready to abandon the convention. Before taking this step, Connecticut's Roger Sherman suggested appointing a committee, with one member from each state, to try to resolve their differences. Three days later, the committee reported what came to be known as the "Connecticut Compromise": the states should have equal representation in the second chamber, though the members would vote as individuals and not as states; in exchange, all bills involving money would have to originate in the first house, where proportional representation would allow the large states to protect themselves from unfair taxes and irresponsible spending. Delegates from the large states saw no benefit in the proposal, but the committee's work had the desired effect: North Carolina joined the smaller states, changing its vote, and the four delegates from Massachusetts divided, preventing their state from casting a vote. As a result, the convention accepted the compromise on July 16 by a mere 5–4 decision.

Madison and his nationalist allies at first expressed extreme dissatisfaction with the compromise. Giving the states any role in the central government would prevent it from serving as the necessary check on the states, and their equal standing in one chamber threatened to give them the same opportunity to obstruct the central government as they had under the Articles of Confederation. Gradually, though, nationalists reconciled themselves to the compromise and came to a new understanding of what their convention was doing. More and more, they began to identify themselves as "Federalists"—a term that traditionally referred to a loose confederation of states—and explained the Union should be one that was "partly national, partly federal." According to this view, the citizens—the sovereigns in a republic—authorized not one government to serve their needs, but two: the state governments to oversee local affairs and the health, welfare, and morals of the people, and a "general" government to deal with foreign relations, common defense, and issues that addressed the states collectively. Unlike under the Articles of Confederation or the Virginia Plan, each government would be fully empowered to carry out its duties, answerable only to the people. And, since the state and central governments would be charged with distinct, separate responsibilities, they would seldom, if ever, come into conflict with each other.

Once they came to an agreement on representation, the delegates worked out most of the remaining issues with little trouble. They decided that Congress would have the authority to impose taxes on property, trade, and imports, though Southern protests led them to deny it the power to tax exports. In addition to responsibility over foreign affairs and common defense, the central government gained power to regulate interstate and foreign trade and to provide for the "general welfare" of the American people. Moreover, the convention authorized the national legislature to enact any laws "necessary and proper" to carry out its duties while declaring the Constitution, congressional laws, and foreign treaties the "supreme law of the land." The delegates rejected Madison's proposal for a national veto of state laws, but the Constitution prevented the states from entering into alliances, issuing paper money, or taxing imports or exports, and it charged the central government with guaranteeing "a republican form of government in each state." A five-man "Committee of Detail" determined that the executive would be called the "president"; the first chamber would be the "House of Representatives," elected by the states' citizens and with members up for re-election every two years. The second chamber would be called the "Senate," with state legislatures electing senators to serve six-year terms, staggered so that one-third of the Senate would be newly elected every two years.

Several issues involving slavery divided the convention largely along sectional lines, but the general desire to preserve the Union prevented the topic of slavery from becoming as divisive as representation. Southerners expected slaves to be included in the population for determining the size of their representation in the House, but Northerners protested that, since the South considered slaves to be property, only the white population should be counted. Several delegates—from both the North and the South—hoped that the central government would have authority to eliminate the institution eventually, and a majority expected at least to prohibit the importation of more slaves into the Union. South Carolina's and Georgia's delegations refused to consider any moves against slavery, and others' willingness to bargain encouraged compromise. Though the delegates avoided using the terms "slaves" or "slavery," the Convention agreed to add three-fifths of "all other persons" to the white population—the same ratio Congress had used in determining a state's requisition under the Articles of Confederation —when determining the number of seats a state would have in the House of Representatives. Slave importations would be permitted for another twenty years, but Congress would have the authority to prohibit the slave trade after January 1, 1808. The delegates also upheld property rights in slavery by declaring that fugitive slaves caught, even in a state where slavery was illegal, would be returned to their legal owners.

Less controversial but more perplexing was the question of how to select the president. The Virginia Plan proposed that the Senate choose the executive, but several delegates noted that this method would make the president "the mere creation of the legislature." A popular election would avoid corruption, but few potential candidates besides George Washington could be expected to gain the national following necessary for a majority. Voters, too, would probably support a favorite from their state, giving an advantage to the largest states. Another committee finally proposed what seemed a workable solution. Each state would choose, by any method it preferred, electors to serve in an "electoral college." The number of a state's electors would be determined by its total representation in the House and the Senate, but the electoral college would never meet as a body. Instead, electors would meet in their state capital on the same day across the Union, and each would cast two votes for president, with at least one vote given to a person who was not a citizen of the elector's state. The convention presumed that the requirement to vote for someone outside the state would force electors to cast ballots for candidates whose public service had gained them national respect and qualified them for the presidency. The candidate who gained a majority would become the president, with the runner-up the vice president, who would preside over the Senate and assume the presidency if the president became incapacitated. If no candidate received a majority, the House of Representatives would then choose the president from among the five candidates who had received the most votes.

After completing their work on September 17, 1787, the delegates forwarded the proposed Constitution to Congress. Several members of Congress expressed their displeasure because the convention had gone far beyond the charge of merely recommending revisions to the Articles of Confederation, and throughout the Union state leaders expressed shock at the type of government the Constitution proposed. Federalists had anticipated this opposition: several delegates had left the convention early to warn the public of the developments in Philadelphia, despite pledges of silence, and the states could be expected to object to any proposal requiring them to give up their power. The states seldom agreed unanimously even in the best circumstances, so the delegates included in the document a means of improving the chance of securing the Constitution's ratification: Instead of requiring the consent of all thirteen states, the Constitution would become effective once it received the approval of only nine. Also, rather than getting the state government's consent, the Constitution was to be ratified by specially elected conventions called specifically for the purpose of considering the new government. Like the conventions that created the state constitutions, Federalists claimed, ratifying conventions would better reflect the will of the people; privately, they knew that it might be easier to persuade convention delegates to give their approval than it would those entrenched in the legislatures. The nine-state requirement, too, might pressure and bring about ratification in reluctant states that did not want to remain out of a union that might become a rival to their interests.

Concern regarding the range and extent of the powers of the proposed government, however, endangered ratification. Congress formally sent the document to the states without endorsement, and several small states gave their approval quickly, since they considered themselves more in need of the Union and were satisfied that they could protect their interests with equal representation in the Senate. By early January 1788, Delaware, New Jersey, and Connecticut had given their approval, as had Georgia, which hoped for federal protection against Natives in their western lands and against the Spanish in neighboring Florida. Pennsylvania, where a Federalist majority in the legislature managed to rush a convention before their opponents could organize resistance, likewise ratified the document early. The major challenges, Federalists recognized, would come in Massachusetts, New York, and Virginia—states with the resources to stand independently and reluctant to subject themselves to the smaller states' will. Several "Antifederalist" writers in these states and in Pennsylvania published essays and pamphlets urging the Constitution's rejection, criticizing specific features of the proposed government and charging that a powerful central authority would threaten individual liberty as well as state sovereignty. Antifederalists particularly focused on the Constitution's lack of a bill of rights—a list of specific freedoms guaranteed to each citizen—and some proposed another convention, one with its deliberations publicized, to suggest revisions that would protect the rights of the people and the states.

Federalists desperately wanted to avoid a second convention, because a second convention would likely undermine the compromises that had been so difficult to work out in Philadelphia. Several responded to Antifederalist charges with their own writings arguing for ratification, with Madison, Hamilton, and John Jay producing the most extensive case in eighty-five *Federalist* essays. More important than any writings were several advantages that allowed Federalists to retake the initiative. In the aftermath of the failed Jay-Gardoquí negotiations, which highlighted the Articles of Confederation's weakness, the Federalists offered a positive program that could remedy the Union's defects. Antifederalists had little to offer beyond continued discussions. The Constitution likewise enjoyed strong support in cities, towns, and rural areas that lay along rivers and transportation routes—commercially active areas where small farmers and artisans agreed with merchants on the potential benefits of an economy under a national government's oversight. Antifederalist support mainly came from rural areas, where residents

Figure 1.2 "The Looking Glass for 1787." A Connecticut Federalist's drawing, depicting his state mired in debt and weighed down with paper money. Federalists try to pull the state toward the Constitution and prosperity, while Antifederalists seek to lead the state to destruction. Detail from engraving by Amos Doolittle (1787). Courtesy Prints & Photographs Division, Library of Congress, LC-DIG-ppmsca-17522.

were less likely to take an interest in outside affairs. The debate over ratification failed to stir widespread interest, as only about one-third of those eligible bothered to vote for delegates to the ratifying conventions. Federalists thus knew that their push for the Constitution would not likely provoke a popular backlash. Still, they wisely made a major concession when several claimed that, once established, the new government should adopt a bill of rights.

Nevertheless, Federalists had to rely on aggressive politics to get the Constitution rati-fied. Antifederalists held the majority when the Massachusetts convention gathered in Janu-ary 1788, but Federalists eventually persuaded Revolutionary heroes Samuel Adams and John Hancock to give up their initial opposition. Their influence, along with the Federalists' willing-ness to accept recommendations for amendments, persuaded enough delegates to change their position so that the convention ratified the document by a slim margin. Maryland and South Carolina ratified with little opposition, leaving the total one state short of the nine necessary to organize the government. New Hampshire voters returned an Antifederalist majority when its convention opened in December 1787, but Federalists managed to delay a final decision; in the meantime, Antifederalist support weakened as more states accepted the Constitution, and when the convention finally voted in June 1788 it accepted the Constitution by a 57–47 vote. Four days later, Federalist agreement to endorse a list of twenty proposed amendments convinced Virginia's convention to give its consent by a mere ten votes. News that the Consti-tution's government would exist regardless of their decision likewise weakened Antifederalist resistance in New York. Still, Federalists needed a rumor that New York City would secede if the state rejected the Constitution to gain enough votes for ratification in July. Even then, the convention made its decision by only a three-vote margin, 30–27.

With ratification accomplished, Federalists turned to making the new government a reality. Elections held during the fall and winter mostly returned the Constitution's proponents to the first new Congress, and, as expected, the electors unanimously chose George Washing-ton as the first president, with Massachusetts' John Adams as vice president. After appointing Charles Thomson to notify Washington of his election, the lawmakers settled down to business. Despite the Federalists' achievement, several challenges remained. Two states remained out-side of the Union: North Carolina explicitly rejected the Constitution, and Antifederalists so dominated Rhode Island that the legislature refused to even consider calling a convention. The economic and diplomatic problems that had plagued the Confederation Congress still con-fronted the new government's leaders. Skeptical Antifederalists, meanwhile, waited for the new government to fail. These challenges contributed to Washington's misgivings as he prepared to assume the presidency. As he took the oath of office at his inauguration on April 30, 1789, he knew as well as any Federalist that the fate of the Union depended on the effectiveness of the government he and his countrymen were creating.

Suggested Readings

Bernstein, Richard B., and Kym S. Rice. *Are We to Be a Nation? The Making of the Constitution* (Cambridge, MA, 1987).

Boyd, Steven R. *The Politics of Opposition: Antifederalists and the Acceptance of the Constitution* (Millwood, NY, 1979).

Conley, Patrick T., and John P. Kaminski, eds. *The Constitution and the States: The Role of the Original Thirteen in the Framing and Adoption of the Federal Constitution* (Madison, 1988).

Cornell, Saul. *Anti-Federalism and the Dissenting Tradition in America, 1788–1828* (Chapel Hill, 1999).

Finkleman, Paul. *Slavery and the Founders: Race and Liberty in the Age of Jefferson* (New York, 1996).

Holton, Woody. *Unruly Americans and the Origins of the Constitution* (New York, 2007).

Kerber, Linda K. *Women of the Republic: Intellect and Ideology in Revolutionary America* (Chapel Hill, 1980).

Morris, Richard B. *The Forging of the Union, 1781–1789* (New York, 1987).

Newman, Simon P. *Parades and the Politics of the Street: Festive Culture in the Early American Republic* (Philadelphia, 1997).

Norton, Mary Beth. *Liberty's Daughters: The Revolutionary Experience of American Women, 1750–1800* (Ithaca, NY, 1980).

Rakove, Jack N. *The Beginnings of National Politics: An Interpretive History of the Continental Congress* (New York, 1979).

Richter, Daniel K. *Facing East from Indian Country: A Native History of Early America* (Cambridge, MA, 2001).

Travers, Len. *Celebrating the Fourth: Independence Day and the Rites of Nationalism in the Early Republic* (Amherst, MA, 1997).

Waldstreicher, David. *In the Midst of Perpetual Fetes: The Making of American Nationalism, 1776–1820* (Chapel Hill, 1997).

Wood, Gordon S. *The Creation of the American Republic, 1776–1787* (Chapel Hill, 1969).

II

THE FEDERALIST ERA

The convening of the first federal Congress in the spring of 1789 meant that the Federalists' vision had become reality. They had not created the all-powerful national force that some had wanted, but they had gotten the states to approve a central government directly responsible to the people of the Union, a government better designed than that under the Articles of Confederation to deal with the Union's problems. Several challenges remained, but if the new government could act effectively and win over doubters, it could indeed create "a more perfect Union."

The First Congress

The new Congress' first session would be crucial. The Constitution provided the outline; now, the First Congress had to define the details and determine what the Constitution's provisions meant. Conveniently, the session opened at a time when economic conditions had begun to improve, giving legislators the opportunity to remedy one of the old Congress's greatest defects. The government under the Articles of Confederation had lacked the authority to raise revenue independently from the states, but the Constitution authorized Congress "to lay and collect taxes, duties, imposts, and excises." Thus, on April 8, Representative James Madison introduced a bill to impose a five-percent tariff on the value of all imports into the United States. Madison's law included a list of "enumerated articles," like rum, wine, and tea, subject to an additional tax. The bill also proposed a controversial plan to impose additional charges to discriminate against goods imported on foreign ships. American ships importing foreign products would pay an additional six cents per ton of the weight of the ship. Ships from nations that had a commercial treaty with the United States would pay a surcharge of thirty cents per ton, whereas those from nations with which the Union did not have a treaty would pay fifty cents per ton.

Discriminatory duties would clearly give an advantage to American merchants, but Madison mainly wanted to foster increased trade with France, which had supported the Revolution and signed a commercial agreement when it recognized American independence in 1778. Despite the Revolution, British ships brought about eighty-five percent of all American imports and remained the Union's primary trading partner. Britons accepted the loss of their former colonies only grudgingly, though, and now their government refused to negotiate a treaty. Concerned that the economic connection with the former mother country might threaten independence, Madison thought discrimination would reduce dependence on Britain, build up American commerce, and encourage France to fill the void that the cutback in trade with Britain would create. At first his colleagues in the House agreed. After an extensive debate—the first in the new Congress—the representatives passed the tariff bill with the discriminatory rates included. The Senate, though, struck out the discrimination plan. Recognizing that the additional taxes would likely compel Britain to curtail its sales to America, the senators feared that neither American merchants nor French traders could replace the British trade that the higher rates would drive away. The Tariff of 1789 thus left the American economy heavily dependent upon Britain, but Congress had succeeded in establishing a reliable source of income that did not depend upon the will of the states.

After concluding the tariff debate, the House took up the issue of establishing executive departments. The Constitution assumed that the "principal officer" in each department would act as the president's chief advisers, so in creating the Treasury Department, the representatives replaced the three-member board that headed the Confederation's Department of Finance with a single secretary. Because the House had ultimate responsibility for the Union's finances, Congress required the Secretary of the Treasury to prepare for the representatives estimates of public expenditures and revenues and to report "in person or in writing" on any relevant issue requested. An act creating the War Department left it organized largely as it had existed under the Confederation. The same intention guided plans for the proposed Department of Foreign Affairs, but when Delaware congressman John Vining proposed creating a Home Department in charge of the federal government's archives and records, the legislators instead gave that responsibility to the Secretary of Foreign Affairs and renamed his bureau the Department of State. Congress also authorized the appointment of a postmaster general to oversee the Union's mails and an attorney general to serve as the president's legal adviser.

Congress created the attorney general's office as part of the Judiciary Act of 1789, which established a federal court system. The Constitution determined that judicial power would be vested in a supreme court and any "inferior courts" Congress might establish, but it left to the legislators the task of working out the courts' structure and responsibilities. In one of its first actions—before it even completed its discussion of procedural rules—the Senate appointed a special committee, chaired by Connecticut's Oliver Ellsworth, to prepare a bill to set up the federal courts. The resulting Judiciary Act, largely the work of Ellsworth, provided for a supreme court consisting of six justices that would act as the final appeals court on all federal questions; at its discretion, it could also hear appeals of civil cases. Each state would have one federal district court with an appointed judge who would be a resident of the state and with its original jurisdiction limited to subjects specified in the Constitution—that is, cases involving Constitution interpretation, the laws of the United States, and treaties with foreign nations. Three circuit courts, each made up of two Supreme Court justices and one of the district judges, would hear appeals from the district and state courts, and state courts were likewise given the power to address a range of federal issues.

The adoption of a bill of rights perhaps presented the new government's most important task. Most Federalists showed little interest in amending their document once they had secured the Constitution's ratification. Madison, though, recognized that a bill of rights could neutralize the Antifederalists' strongest criticism while actually reinforcing the new government's authority. State ratifying conventions had offered numerous proposals to weaken the national government, but Madison discarded most and instead devised a list of twenty-two amendments that emphasized individual freedoms from government interference—protections that reinforced the notion that the new government dealt directly with all American citizens, rather than the states. The Senate reduced Madison's list to twelve before giving them final congressional approval. The amendments still required the approval of three-fourths of the states, and several states rejected the first two amendments, one of which dealt with the size of congressional districts, the other of which prohibited a sitting Congress from voting itself a pay raise. The remaining ten met with little opposition, and Virginia's ratification in December secured the three-fourths approval necessary to attach the Bill of Rights to the Constitution. Even before this date, the amendments worked to strengthen the Union: North Carolina finally ratified the Constitution and joined the Union in November 1789. North Carolina's decision helped promote the Federal cause in Rhode Island, but the Senate had to pass a bill banning American commerce with Rhode Island before that state became the last of the original thirteen to join the Union in May 1790.

Several blocks away from Federal Hall, in a mansion on Cherry Street, George Washington worked to determine just what the president's role should be. Clearly the president would not be a king, but to ensure respect for the new government, many Federalists believed that the public should give the executive the same homage offered to a monarch; the American president, they contended, should be celebrated as a kingly figure who benevolently ruled over republican subjects. Others thought he should be recognized merely as a respected citizen responsible for carrying out the people's will. The questions surrounding the president's

Figure 2.1 "View of the Federal Edifice in New York." Federal Hall, the first home of Congress under the Constitution; President George Washington was inaugurated on the portico. Etching in *The Columbia Magazine*, Philadelphia (1789). Courtesy Prints & Photographs Division, Library of Congress, LC–USZ62–45577.

role became apparent when Vice President John Adams encouraged Congress to devise an official title—something like "His Excellency" or "His Elective Highness"—to be used when addressing or introducing the president. Debates over the suitability as well as the form of a title preoccupied Congress for three weeks, and the Senate ultimately agreed with Adams and resolved to call him "His Highness the President of the United States and Protector of the Rights of the Same." The more egalitarian House rejected the Senate's resolution. The Senate backed off, so Washington and his successors would simply be addressed as "the president of the United States." The argument was soon forgotten, though afterward several members of Congress derisively referred to the portly Adams as "His Rotundity."

Washington later told associates that he wished that the subject of titles had never been brought up, but in other ways he showed that he favored surrounding the presidency with a monarchical aura. The notion that the executive was more than just "one of the people" suited his personality and his own ideas about the need for strong leadership. A reserved individual, Washington never felt comfortable mingling with the public, so he set up a schedule that would uphold the dignity of his office while keeping his workload manageable. He would meet private citizens for "visits of compliment" in one-hour sessions held two afternoons each week. Men could visit with the president at formal levees, or receptions, held for one hour on Tuesday afternoons, while his wife Martha would host a public tea on Friday evenings. As president, Washington would neither return calls nor accept dinner invitations from private citizens. State dinners, held on Wednesdays, would offer invitations only to "official characters and strangers of distinction." Like the king of England, when the president traveled, even for short distances, he would ride in a fine carriage drawn by at least four horses and accompanied by an honor guard.

But President Washington also recognized his need to act as the people's servant. Congress rejected his request to serve without a salary and be reimbursed only for his expenses, as had been the practice when he commanded the army. Instead, the legislators set the president's annual salary at $25,000, a lavish sum that would not be raised for another eighty-four years. The Constitution gave the president primary responsibility for foreign relations, but in domestic matters Washington let the legislators take the initiative. As the Constitution required, he recommended issues for Congress' attention in his annual messages, but he avoided trying to dictate to the lawmakers or interfere with their deliberations. Other than consulting Madison in the tariff bill, he took no part in shaping the legislation of Congress' first session. Although the veto power gave the president a role in the lawmaking process, Washington concluded that he should use it sparingly, mainly to stop the enactment of laws that he thought violated the Constitution. Over the course of two four-year terms, he resorted to the veto only twice.

Washington's most important immediate decisions involved appointing officers to lead the executive departments and of justices to sit on the Supreme Court. The members of his cabinet would be recognized as leaders of the new government second only to the president himself, and he determined that he must select "First Characters" while balancing the claims of the most important states. Massachusetts' Henry Knox, an artillery commander in the Revolution, agreed to continue as Secretary of War, the post he had held under the Articles. Washington hoped that John Jay, the Confederation's secretary of foreign affairs, would also stay on as secretary of state. Jay, however, preferred to serve on the Supreme Court, so the president instead turned to fellow Virginian Thomas Jefferson, even though the author of the Declaration of Independence currently represented the United States as minister to France and could not occupy the position until the following spring. For the Treasury, Washington selected his former military aide, Alexander Hamilton, and for the two executive positions without departments he named Virginia's Edmund Randolph as attorney general and Massachusetts' Samuel Osgood to be postmaster general. He then appointed Jay as the first chief justice and chose five staunch Federalists—two other Northerners and three Southerners—to join Jay on the Supreme Court.

Throughout his presidency, George Washington was in charge of his administration. No one controlled him, and he made the final decisions. But during the first term, Alexander Hamilton provided the energy and direction. Well-seasoned in New York and Confederation Congress politics, Hamilton seemed better prepared than almost anyone else to take on the Union's financial troubles. He soon had the chance to display his talents. In October, the House instructed him to prepare a plan to support public credit—in other words, to make some provision for the federal debt, which would restore confidence in the Union's finances so it could borrow when necessary in the future. Virtually all American leaders agreed that the foreign debt needed to be paid back at its full value, and Hamilton handled it fairly easily: under his watch, the government would make the interest payments, then refinance the loans on better terms on the dates the principal came due. For the domestic debt, Hamilton's Report on Public Credit—presented to Congress in January 1790—offered a bold and creative solution. Instead of paying the debt, the report proposed to "fund" it—that is, to provide for the payment of interest while making provision for the debt's payment at a later date.

According to Hamilton's plan, unpaid interest on the securities issued during the Revolution would be added to the debt's principal; holders of the debt would then need to accept one of six options for payment, some in public lands, but mostly in newly issued government bonds. Most of these options reduced the interest rate on the debt from six to four percent, which would be paid annually to the bondholders. An increase in import duties, plus an excise tax on distilled liquors, would provide the money necessary to make the annual interest payments on the new certificates, while revenue from the postal service would contribute to a "sinking fund," an account that ostensibly one day would have enough to pay the securities at face value. Then, Hamilton exceeded anyone's expectations when he encouraged the federal government to "assume," or take over, the debts of the states. Money owed by the states to the central government would be credited to their accounts, but assumption would still increase the federal debt by about $25 million.

Hamilton had larger political goals in mind with his proposal than simply restoring public credit. He well knew that during the 1780s a relatively small number of opportunists had bought up the majority of government securities from their original holders, sometimes for as little as one-tenth of face value. The Constitution's ratification spurred another wave of speculation and put the debt in even fewer hands. Funding would thus provide speculators with tremendous profits on their investments. More importantly to Hamilton, it would bring the attention of wealthy and influential individuals to ensuring the survival of the new central government, if for no other reason than to get their annual interest payments. Assumption of the state debts would likewise lessen securityholders' attachment to the state governments. Tying in the interests of a newly enriched financial class would thus allow the debt to serve as what Hamilton and others called a "cement" of the Union, strengthening the central government and increasing the chances of the Constitution's long-term success.

But Hamilton also designed funding and assumption as a way to help transform the Union from a weak collection of farmers to a powerful, self-sufficient economy. Economic independence would better prepare the Union to defend itself in a hostile world. The Treasury secretary had little interest in actually paying off the debt. His goal was to restore public credit—that is, to convince creditors that the federal government could meet its financial obligations. Regular interest payments on the newly issued bonds and contributions to the sinking fund would show that the government could service its debt, creating the impression that securityholders would eventually receive payment in full. Confidence in the government's finances would thus raise the bonds' value, while money from the sinking fund could purchase the securities when necessary to stabilize their prices. Hamilton's plan would thus *monetize* the debt: the interest-bearing bonds backed by the government's credit would have value and could serve as cash in an economy with little gold or silver. Since most of the speculators were merchants in eastern port cities, Hamilton expected them to use their windfall to invest in manufacturing projects that would eventually free the Union from dependence on British goods. The wealth created in a developed American economy would likewise provide the resources necessary to develop the military forces the Union needed to protect its independence.

Hamilton's report received a mixed reaction from the House, however. Most members of Congress did not recognize its full implications. One of the ones who did was James Madison. Madison gladly worked with Hamilton to replace the Articles of Confederation, but he always expected Virginia to dominate the federal Union. Since eighty percent of the domestic debt's holders lived in Northern cities, funding would produce a tremendous boost in the wealth and influence of Northern states. The plan to devote tariff revenues to interest payments likewise meant that Hamilton intended for the United States for the present to remain commercially dependent upon Britain, the nation Madison had targeted in his discrimination proposal. At first he tried to derail support for funding by proposing to distinguish between the claims of the debts' original and current holders. Lamenting the fate of veterans who had fought for independence but then had to sell their certificates for a fraction of their worth, Madison argued that the current holders should receive payment at only the market value of their securities, which was about half of their face value. Hamilton dismissed Madison's proposal, claiming that it would not be possible to identify the original holders and that failing to pay current holders what was legally due to them would weaken public credit. Most congressmen agreed: thirty-six voted to reject adding Madison's amendment, with only thirteen—nine from Virginia—in favor of the motion.

Assumption of the debt, however, presented an opportunity to defeat Hamilton's plan or at least force a compromise. On this issue, the amount owed by their home states largely influenced the legislators' views. Massachusetts and South Carolina had the largest public debts: their representatives thus strongly favored having them taken over by the federal government. They were joined by members from New York, New Jersey, and the New England states, all of which owed less than Massachusetts or South Carolina but would nevertheless benefit from the plan. Pennsylvania's delegation was divided, while those from Maryland and Georgia, with considerably smaller debts, stood opposed. Virginia's and North Carolina's congressmen, who made up almost one-fourth of the House of Representatives, stood most adamantly against assumption. Like Maryland and Georgia, these two states had already taken care of most of their war debts. Their leaders saw no benefit in contributing to Northern states' payments, and they feared that assumption would cut too much into the sum that the federal government owed to the states for the costs of the Revolution. With such strong Southern opposition, in April the House removed assumption from the funding bill by a 31–29 vote.

Distraught over the House's decision, Hamilton knew he would have to bargain. A separate issue provided the opportunity for a deal. New York City had served as the seat of the central government since 1785, but Congress still needed to declare a permanent capital. Southern representatives wanted a more centralized location; New Englanders and South Carolinians joined New York in their support for keeping the capital in the City, while Pennsylvanians advocated returning the government to Philadelphia, the Union's effective capital during the Revolution. Several weeks after Thomas Jefferson arrived in New York in March 1790 to take office as secretary of state, he invited Hamilton and Madison to a dinner on June 20, where the three worked out a deal: Jefferson and Madison would encourage Virginians in Congress to vote for assumption, while Hamilton would persuade Northern representatives to abandon New York and accept Philadelphia as the temporary capital before moving to a new city to be established on the Potomac. Representatives from Massachusetts and South Carolina—the two states that desperately wanted assumption—then provided the crucial votes for a bill moving the capital to Philadelphia for ten years while the government built "Federal City" at a site to be selected by President Washington on the banks of the Potomac. Several Southern congressmen then changed their votes to add assumption to Hamilton's funding bill.

With funding and assumption approved, Hamilton moved on to the next stage of his plan. After recommending passage of an excise tax on the manufacture of spirits—mainly the rum produced by New England farmers and whiskey distilled on the frontier—Hamilton urged Congress to issue a twenty-year charter for a federal bank. According to Hamilton's plan, the Bank of the United States would be capitalized at $10 million, with the federal government providing $2 million and the rest raised by public stock sales. As the bank would be a private corporation with a significant government presence, the president would appoint five of its directors, with stockholders electing the other twenty. A federal bank, Hamilton explained, offered several advantages for the Union. With $10 million, the bank would hold more banking capital than all the states combined. In addition to helping collect taxes and providing an institution where the government could deposit its funds, the bank could support the Treasury with short-term loans in times of emergency. For the public, the bank would issue paper money that could serve as a national currency in a Union where gold and silver coins remained scarce. In line with Hamilton's desire to encourage economic development, the bank would also offer entrepreneurs loans for investment in manufacturing and commercial projects.

This time, Jefferson joined Madison in opposing Hamilton's initiative. After the deal trading assumption for a Southern capital, Jefferson had come to believe that Hamilton had duped him into accepting a scheme that hurt Virginia's interests. Like funding and assumption, the bank would primarily benefit Northern merchants and speculators while doing little to help Southern planters. The proposal to locate the bank in Philadelphia might so entrench the government in the Quaker City that it might never move to the Potomac, negating the major benefit Virginians thought they had gained when they swallowed assumption of the state debts. At a minimum, the bank would expand the size and scope of the federal government, possibly threatening the authority of the states. More ominously, Jefferson came to distrust the Treasury secretary's imperious manner—particularly his interference in foreign affairs, which were Jefferson's responsibility. The Virginian's firsthand observation of his fellow cabinet member convinced him that Hamilton intended to consolidate power in the central government while transforming the presidency into a monarchy, with Hamilton himself as the power behind the throne. After all, Hamilton patterned his bank after the Bank of England, whose funds the prime minister used to buy the votes of members of Parliament. Approval of Hamilton's proposal, Jefferson feared, would put a similar "engine of corruption" at the Treasury secretary's disposal.

To present a broad and principled opposition, Jefferson and Madison centered their disagreement on the charge that the bank was unconstitutional: since the Constitution did not grant Congress the power to issue corporate charters, they argued, the legislators did not have the authority to incorporate the bank. The South again provided most of the votes against a Hamilton proposal, but they could not stop the bill creating the bank from passing both chambers by comfortable margins. The constitutional issue, however, did gain President Washington's attention. The question genuinely perplexed him. He agreed with Hamilton's points on the bank's benefits for the government, but he also considered it his sworn duty to uphold the Constitution's integrity. While pondering whether to sign the bank bill, he asked Madison to prepare a veto message. Then, he asked Jefferson and Attorney General Randolph to provide for him in writing their opinions on the bank's constitutionality.

Jefferson's opinion presented the argument for what came to be known as "strict construction." According to this view, public officials must read the Constitution carefully and act only where the document clearly grants permission. Grounding his case on the Tenth Amendment, which Congress had already approved and which would soon be ratified by the states, Jefferson reminded Washington that any powers not delegated to Congress were reserved to the states and to the people. Unless the people specifically delegated a power, the lawmakers could not act without violating both the spirit and the letter of the Union's fundamental law. Attorney General Randolph's opinion reinforced Jefferson's argument for strict construction. Before making his decision, however, Washington presented the two Virginians' papers to Hamilton and asked for his opinion as well. In a report four times longer than Jefferson's, the Treasury secretary presented a case for a "broad construction" of the Constitution. Refuting the Virginians' contentions point by point, Hamilton argued that all governments had "a right to employ all the means requisite and fairly applicable" to achieve its ends, so long as its actions were neither immoral nor expressly prohibited. He particularly disagreed with Jefferson's narrow interpretation of the word "necessary," which the secretary of state claimed restricted the government to acting only where specifically authorized. According to Hamilton, in the Constitution the people had given implied as well as express powers to the government—implied powers that were constitutionally legitimate so long as they helped Congress perform its constitutionally sanctioned duties.

Hamilton's opinion satisfied Washington sufficiently to convince him to sign the bank bill into law. Disappointed with their failure to stop the bank, and fully convinced now of Hamilton's devious intentions, Jefferson and Madison began molding a more organized and effective opposition to the Treasury secretary's plans. Their efforts helped stall the final phase of Hamilton's offensive. In the Report on Manufacturers submitted to the House in December 1791, Hamilton encouraged Congress to sponsor government assistance to promote American manufacturing on a scale comparable to the industrial revolution already underway in Great Britain. Warning of the dangers presented by heavy dependence on imported goods, Hamilton contended that the development of a strong manufacturing sector would make the Union economically self-sufficient, increase its wealth, and further secure American independence. Contrary to fears that a growing industry would damage agriculture, Hamilton contended that the two activities would complement each other, for thriving factories would enrich the farmers and planters who provided raw materials and food for workers. And, since the growth in manufacturing would occur mostly in the North, the home market it created for Southern agriculture would strengthen the ties binding the Union. Hamilton concluded by proposing congressional action to lure investors into supporting manufacturing, including providing tariff protection for American-made products, exempting taxes on imported raw materials, offering bounties to reward the production of new goods, and awarding cash prizes for product improvements and new inventions.

Even though President Washington also favored economic self-sufficiency, for the most part Hamilton's proposals went nowhere. Criticism weakened potential support, while Southerners in Congress rejected Hamilton's contention that industry would benefit farmers and planters. At the same time, a sudden downturn in the securities market in the spring of 1792 preoccupied Hamilton and prevented him from pushing his latest proposals as aggressively as he had campaigned for funding and assumption and the bank. In May 1792, Congress passed a tariff law increasing the rates on goods that competed with American-made products, but most of Hamilton's other proposals were soon forgotten. But his imperious manner and his efforts to bring commercial and financial interests to the Union's support had divided the government at the highest level.

The Frontier and Foreign Relations

Despite the setback on manufacturing, the Federalists had accomplished much in the Constitution's first three years. The new government likewise made new strides to assert the Union's interests in the west. Neither Britain nor Spain displayed any more inclination to make an agreement with the Americans than they had before 1789, but treaties with the Creek and Cherokee nations temporarily quieted the southern frontier. The admission of Vermont, Kentucky, and Tennessee to the Union in 1791, 1792, and 1796 helped strengthen the frontiersmen's loyalty to the United States. In the northwest, a coalition of warriors from several nations defeated military expeditions led by General Josiah Harmar in October 1790 and by General Arthur St. Clair in November 1791. President Washington's next appointee, Anthony Wayne, spent two years training a tough and well-disciplined army, and on August 20, 1794, his thirty-five hundred men routed five hundred warriors at Fallen Timbers, a field near the Maumee River where a tornado had recently decimated a forest. By the summer of 1795, the tribes were ready to accept peace on the terms dictated by the American commander. In the Treaty of Greenville, signed on August 3, 1795, twelve nations agreed to relinquish to American settlers the lands east of the Cuyahoga River and north of the Ohio.

Events in Europe meanwhile altered American relations with the world's major powers. About the same time Federalists were organizing the new American government in 1789, King Louis XVI called together the Estates-General—a legislative assembly that had last met in 1614—an event that set in motion the French Revolution. Americans at first welcomed news of the Revolution, for these events seemed to reflect the same courageous stand for liberty that American colonists had taken thirteen years earlier. Public ardor cooled when the French Revolution veered in a radical direction. By 1792, France's internal conditions appeared to have degenerated into mob rule, and the French Republic's attacks on traditional Christianity, its mass executions of political enemies, and the January 1793 execution of Louis XVI—the king who had provided crucial aid in the War for Independence—deeply offended most Americans. Still, a large number of Americans remained sympathetic to the French cause. Over 1793 and 1794, when the French Revolution was moving into its most extreme stage, French supporters throughout the Union organized more than thirty clubs, called Democratic-Republican Societies. These societies publicly advocated sympathy for France, condemned aristocracy in all its forms, and urged the American people to take action for the cause of liberty. But overall support for the French Revolution declined, especially after French leaders recklessly plunged into widespread war, first against Austria and Prussia in April 1792, then against the Netherlands, Spain, and Britain in early 1793.

The president and his advisers recognized that the Union could gain little, and perhaps endanger its independence, if it got involved in the European conflict. In the 1778 treaty with France, though, the Union had formed a defensive military alliance that included an American promise to defend the French West Indian islands and allow French privateers—privately owned ships authorized to attack enemy vessels—to use American ports. France had declared war first and thus was the aggressor, so French leaders did not expect the United States to join the conflict. Nevertheless, they wanted American friendship and support, including permission for French ships to harbor in American ports and the denial of this privilege to France's enemies. Failure to accept the French Republic's understanding of the treaty would likely invite its hostility. But assistance to France would alienate Britain, which not only paid the tariffs that funded the American government but also maintained an ominous presence on the frontier. Britain's navy, the largest and strongest in the world, could likewise be expected to take action against American merchant ships if the Union lent any support to its enemy.

After consulting with his cabinet, President Washington issued a proclamation on April 22, 1793, announcing that the United States would maintain "friendly and impartial" relations with the belligerents while prohibiting American citizens from taking part in the war. As expected, France quickly challenged American neutrality. Edmond Genêt, the newly appointed French minister, had arrived in Charleston eleven days before President Washington issued his proclamation. The French Republic instructed Genêt to negotiate a new commercial treaty, and, to show his country's good intentions, his nation opened all French ports, including those in the West Indies, to American merchants. But France's leadership also directed Genêt to get the Union to agree to the French interpretation of the 1778 treaty. Not only should American ports be opened to French and closed to British ships, but the French government should be allowed to arm, equip, and reward American ships as privateers. France also expected the Union to "liquidate," or pay off immediately, the debt remaining from the American Revolution, while Genêt would recruit American citizens to participate in military excursions against Spanish and British territories in North America.

The enthusiastic welcome Genêt received when he arrived in Charleston convinced him that the American public favored an alliance with France. Within days he began to issue letters of marque, which authorized American ships to act as French privateers. While he traveled to Philadelphia, Democratic-Republican Societies hosted triumphant receptions in his honor, convincing him of American support. Once in the capital, he issued more letters of marque and appointed French consuls—official representatives of the French government—to judge and grant awards to the privateers for their captures. President Washington nevertheless remained committed to neutrality. Agreeing to meet with the French minister on May 18—in a room with portraits of Louis XVI and Marie Antoinette—his administration refused to pay the debt early or to provide any other direct assistance, and he insisted that Genêt respect American independence. Genêt nonetheless continued to treat the United States as a base for French privateering operations while demanding that President Washington accept the French interpretation of the 1778 treaty. But Genêt finally went too far. In July 1793, he authorized the rearming as a French privateer a captured British ship in Philadelphia's harbor. President Washington ordered the ship not to go to sea. In direct defiance, Genêt not only ordered the ship to sea but demanded that the president call a special session of Congress so the people's representatives could determine the issue.

Genêt's threat to appeal over the president to the American people had no chance of success. His demand directly insulted the president, and even Jefferson, who to this point had defended Genêt, agreed that he had crossed the lines of diplomatic propriety. With the cabinet's unanimous approval, in August Jefferson carefully worded a letter asking the French government to recall Genêt. Unknown either to Genêt or to American leaders, a new French government had already recalled Genêt; his successor, in fact, brought an order for his arrest and return to Paris for trial, where he likely faced conviction and execution. Washington saved the deposed French minister from the guillotine by granting him political asylum, and Genêt's successor, Jean Fauchet, put a halt to the proposed expeditions against the Spanish territories and stopped all privateering activities. Likewise, he agreed to accept President Washington's understanding of American neutrality, all in hope that a different approach might win American support.

While tensions with France eased, American relations with Britain deteriorated to the point that war seemed imminent. Interpreting Genêt's mission as evidence of American cooperation with its enemies, in June 1793 the British government issued an order-in-council—an order from the king through his Privy Council—imposing on the United States the "Rule of 1756," which British courts had first invoked forty years earlier during the Seven Years' War. According to this rule, Britain declared a neutral country's trade with one of Britain's enemies illegal in time of war if that trade had not been open during peacetime. Any ship involved in that trade could be seized by the British navy, and Britain would have no obligation to compensate ship captains for their losses. Since French ports were now open to Americans, the June 1793 order effectively announced that Britain would stop American grain shipments to the French West Indies. Then, in November, another order-in-council imposed a complete blockade on the French islands. That fall, the British navy captured more than 250 American vessels. Several Americans demanded war, but Hamilton instead pressed President Washington to appoint a special envoy to go to Britain to try to negotiate a settlement. Encouraged when Britain backed off from the raids in January 1794, the president agreed and sent Chief Justice John Jay to London.

Shortly after Jay sailed for England in May, President Washington faced yet another crisis, this time an uprising of American farmers in western Pennsylvania. Frontier farmers deeply resented the excise tax on whiskey that Congress had passed in 1791 to support the funding program. At twenty-five percent of the price of a gallon, this heavy tax mainly affected small farmers, who distilled whiskey from the grains they raised. Aside from serving as a common beverage at a time without reliable supplies of pure water, whiskey played an important role in the frontier economy. Since cash was scarce in the west, whiskey often served as money. Moreover, as long as trade down the rivers through New Orleans remained closed to them, the settlers' only available markets for their crops were the eastern ports, and whiskey was easier to cart overland than was raw grain. The area around Pittsburgh, where about one-fourth of all of the Union's stills were located, emerged as the center of resistance. From the fall of 1791 through the summer of 1792, public meetings in western Pennsylvania denounced the tax and called for its repeal. Meanwhile, tax collectors and those willing to pay the excise suffered harassment ranging from ridicule to being tarred and feathered.

Figure 2.2 "Washington Reviewing the Western Army at Fort Cumberland, Maryland." An artist's depiction of the army called out to suppress the Whiskey Rebellion. Oil on canvas by Frederick Kemmelmeyer (after 1795). Courtesy Metropolitan Museum of Art, New York; gift of Edgar William and Bernice Chrysler Garbis, image reference ART323107.

President Washington issued a proclamation in September 1792, denouncing defiance and reminding officials to carry out the law. The furor over Genêt's visit and the crisis with Britain soon distracted the administration, but in July 1794 a mob surrounded and attacked the home of General John Neville, whom the president had put in charge of collecting the tax in the region. Neville and his family escaped, but the crowd captured Neville's son and a federal marshal and briefly held the two hostage. Two weeks later, on August 1, a crowd of about six thousand gathered at Braddock's Field near Pittsburgh to listen to impassioned speeches calling for further resistance and threatening to burn the town. President Washington now agreed with Hamilton that a firm response was necessary. Calling out nearly thirteen thousand militia volunteers from Virginia, Maryland, New Jersey, and Pennsylvania, in early October the president himself led the army west to suppress the rebellion. Before the troops broke camp, the "rebellion" was over—the crowd had long dispersed as the farmers went back to their daily routines. The president returned to Philadelphia, but the army pressed on. Under Hamilton's oversight, the troops rounded up and interrogated about 150 suspects and hauled twenty to Philadelphia to be tried for treason. Only two of the twenty were convicted, and the president pardoned them both.

The public widely approved the president's firm response. Coming only seven years after Shays' Rebellion in Massachusetts, the Whiskey Rebellion demonstrated that the federal government—unlike the Confederation Congress—could deal effectively with an uprising. For President Washington, the uprising additionally offered an opportunity to deal with what he considered a more menacing problem. In his report to Congress about the expedition into western Pennsylvania, he blamed the uprising on the influence of "self-created societies"—a clear reference to the Democratic-Republican Societies that encouraged support for France and bitterly criticized his presidency. The societies had no connection to the uprising, but Washington's denunciation and their association with a rebellion occurred at the same time news reached American shores about the Reign of Terror's mass executions. These burdens proved too much for the societies: their membership dwindled, and by 1795 they had virtually disappeared.

In the meantime, John Jay succeeded in working out an agreement with Great Britain. When he arrived in London, Jay found British leaders increasingly preoccupied with their war with France; as a result, they proved willing to make concessions to prevent the Union from assisting their enemy. Jay's Treaty, signed in November 1794, accomplished several important gains. Britain agreed to evacuate the forts on American soil before June 1, 1796, and opened the British West Indies to American merchant ships weighing less than seventy tons—small ships that did not cross the Atlantic and hence did not compete with British merchants. Americans also gained the right to trade with British possessions in India, and the treaty established arbitration commissions to determine the border between the United States and Canada, the value of cargoes lost during Britain's recent seizure of American ships, and the amount owed to British merchants by American citizens from debts taken out before the Revolution. For his part, Jay agreed that American harbors would not serve as bases for French privateering operations while opening the harbors to British warships. But Jay also had to make some major concessions. The treaty prevented American adoption of any discriminatory duties against British trade, and Jay implicitly accepted Britain's interpretation of a neutral country's trading rights when it acknowledged Britain's right to seize a broad definition of "enemy" goods when they were being carried on American ships.

In spite of the treaty's benefits, its recognition of Britain's definition of neutral rights left American merchants subject to their onetime mother country's discretion. President Washington himself thought Jay had given up too much to gain too little, and the Senate gave the treaty barely the two-thirds majority necessary for ratification. The strength of the resistance, along with his own reservations, made the president hesitate to sign the treaty. Throughout the summer, public protests across the Union condemned the treaty, destroyed copies of the document, burned Jay in effigy, and petitioned President Washington to reject it. Ultimately, the president gave it his approval, concluding that the agreement was better than nothing. And, in spite of the initial condemnation, the popular clamor died down as the treaty proved beneficial. Britain adhered to its promise and withdrew from its American forts. Governors of Britain's West Indian colonies opened their ports to American shippers with no restrictions, and a large number of American ships entered the carrying trade, taking over for war-distracted British and French merchants the shipping of goods between their colonies and home countries. Within five years of the ratification of Jay's Treaty, American trade with the British Empire tripled, with more than ninety percent of all American commerce being conducted in American ships.

An agreement with Spain at about the same time likewise instilled confidence in the Union's future. As with Jay's Treaty, circumstances produced by the European war aided Americans in their negotiations. Spain entered the war against France as a British ally, but by the summer of 1794, Manuel de Godoy, the Spanish prime minister, planned to take his nation out of the conflict. Godoy feared that Spain's withdrawal from the alliance would consequently bring on war with Britain, and he was convinced that John Jay's trip to England was designed to produce a British-American alliance that would attack Spain's North American possessions. The Spanish leader thus notified the United States that he would begin serious talks for a treaty if the Union would send a minister to Madrid. President Washington's appointee, South Carolina's Thomas Pinckney, found Godoy eager to make an agreement. In the Treaty of San Lorenzo—signed in October 1795, and ratified by the Senate the following March—the United States gained almost everything Pinckney asked for while conceding virtually nothing. Popularly known as Pinckney's Treaty, the agreement allowed western farmers to export their goods through New Orleans and set the border separating Florida from the United States at the thirty-first parallel.

Friends of Liberty and Friends of Order

While Federalists rejoiced over the new government's accomplishments, Thomas Jefferson and James Madison moved toward open opposition to Hamilton's policies. Three days after President Washington signed the act creating the Bank of the United States, Jefferson offered Philip Freneau a clerkship in the State Department, mainly to provide him with the funds necessary to publish a newspaper to counter the influence of John Fenno's *Gazette of the United States*, a paper that regularly praised Hamilton while receiving lucrative government printing contracts. After the First Congress adjourned, Jefferson and Madison undertook a "botanizing tour" of the Hudson River Valley. The two always claimed that their only purpose in taking this tour was to see the flora and fauna, but while in New York they met with several state political leaders and likely laid the foundation for an alliance against Hamilton. The first issue of Freneau's *National Gazette* came out in October 1791, and it launched a series of vicious attacks against the Treasury secretary. Then, in May 1792, Jefferson wrote a long letter to Washington charging that Hamilton's financial program intended "to prepare the way for a change from the present republican form of government to that of a monarchy." The president appealed to both cabinet members to put their differences aside for the good of the government. Both reluctantly agreed, but as President Washington's first term neared its end, his two principal officers spoke to each other only in their official capacities.

Jefferson and Madison's dispute with Hamilton went deeper than a disagreement over policy or a clash of personalities. To be sure, they thought funding and assumption and the Bank of the United States unjustly enriched Northern merchants and speculators at public expense. They feared that keeping the Union too closely aligned with Britain not only insulted France but also contradicted the spirit of American independence. Though it had gone in a dangerous direction, the French Republic nevertheless promoted freedom and republicanism, and the French Revolution's temporary excesses still seemed preferable to the tyranny and despotism of other European nations—especially Britain. Underlying the Virginians' grievances, however, lay their conviction that Hamilton had designed his program to consolidate power away from the states into the central government so that he could transform the republic into a monarchy. Convinced that Hamilton had used his office's financial resources to buy the votes of members of Congress, Jefferson and Madison assumed that the Treasury secretary had designed his programs to control the legislative branch and eliminate the influence of the state governments, which were more responsive to the popular will. With no challenge from the states and with the legislative branch at his disposal, Hamilton could succeed in his goal to make the president an American king, with himself as the power behind the throne. Subservience to the former mother country would meanwhile return the states practically to the status of colonies, giving Hamilton access to British power against his political enemies.

Effective opposition to these schemes required the Virginians to form a political party. Like most in the Revolutionary generation, Jefferson and Madison expected a republic's leaders to act as statesmen—public servants who followed their own judgment and acted independently to promote the general welfare. Disagreements among statesmen could be expected, but when politicians set aside their own views and persistently acted together to follow the dictates of a party, most Americans presumed that they had joined together to secure their own advancement or some other self-serving interest that contradicted the public good. The severity of the threat, however, convinced Jefferson and Madison that they had to act. Factions might be undesirable and dangerous, but after Hamilton seized the initiative, they concluded that the Treasury secretary himself headed a self-interested faction. The "Republican Party," as they called it, would represent the majority against Hamilton's aristocratic cohort. As an opposition party, they could check Hamilton's efforts to consolidate power, and once they took control of the Union from the aristocrats Republicans could administer the government "in the spirit and form approved by the great body of the people." In this case, associating with a party signified not a traitorous act, but a patriotic duty.

Jefferson and Madison worked to build the Republican Party both upon criticism of administration policy and on the allegiance of established leaders dissatisfied with Hamilton's course. While Freneau's *National Gazette* hurled its broadsides against the Treasury secretary, Madison promoted resistance to Hamilton's proposals in Congress. Jefferson meanwhile used his position in the cabinet to try to counter the New Yorker's influence on President Washington. Once Congress came back into session in the fall of 1791, the Virginians quickly gained a following. Associates like House of Representatives clerk John Beckley, New York assemblyman Melancton Smith, and Virginia senators James Monroe and John Taylor sounded out members of Congress and state political leaders for their views and concerns about the Union's direction. Soon, newspapers in Philadelphia, Richmond, and New York echoed the Republicans' criticism of Hamilton. Neither Jefferson nor Madison set up or controlled these papers, and the two were disturbed when some editors included President Washington in their denunciations of monarchists. Nevertheless, they became important proponents of the Republican view and helped the opposition make its presence felt. By the spring of 1792, Republicans could count on strong support in the Southern and Middle Atlantic states, and in Congress they presented a determined, persistent, and formidable challenge to anything Hamilton advocated.

The elections scheduled for 1792 and 1793 gave Republicans the opportunity to test their strength. No one opposed George Washington's re-election in the 1792 presidential election. In fact, when the president expressed his wish to retire, Madison, Jefferson, and Hamilton all encouraged him to stay, and he was unanimously elected to a second term. Instead,

Republicans tried to replace Massachusetts' John Adams as vice president by persuading presidential electors to cast their second votes for New York governor George Clinton. Clinton's standing as a prominent onetime Antifederalist hurt his appeal, however, and the electors from every state except New York, Virginia, North Carolina, and Georgia voted for Adams so that he remained in office. More important to Republicans were the elections for representatives to the Third Congress, which would convene in December 1793. The newness of the Republicans' organization, and voters' reluctance to challenge incumbents, kept the opposition from contesting every seat, and local issues and candidates' personal qualifications would determine the outcome in most districts. Still, the results of the first census, taken in 1790, increased the number of House members from 69 to 105, and 26 of those new seats would come from the Southern and Middle Atlantic states, where Republicans already enjoyed a healthy following. Concentrating their efforts in these states, they met with more than satisfactory results. Though the views of several representatives could not be determined until they were in office, Jefferson nevertheless concluded that the contests produced "a decided majority in favor of the republican interest."

The Republican challenge compelled Hamilton and his associates to organize their supporters into their own distinct Federalist party, which, like Republicans, its adherents believed to be the only party based on principle. Contrary to Jefferson's accusations, Hamilton had not used his office to enrich himself. In fact, he resigned as secretary of the treasury at the end of January 1795, because he needed the higher income from his law practice to support his large family. Speculators and financiers benefited from his policies, but Hamilton promoted them because he thought an active government the best means of building a sound economy, strengthening the Union, and ensuring its future. His Federalist allies meanwhile saw in the French Revolution an example of the dangers presented by a freedom unrestrained by order, self-restraint, and wise leadership. For them, France had succumbed to anarchy, while Britain still presented a model of a stable and moderate form of liberty. Aside from ideological concerns, Britain remained the states' principal trading partner, and Hamilton's funding program vitally needed the money from the tariffs on British imports. France, even if not ravaged by revolution, still could not match the volume of goods and the credit provided to Americans by the British economy. To Hamilton, the Union could not risk alienating the states' onetime mother country through shortsighted support for Britain's enemy. But like other Federalists, he also feared the French hysteria's possible encouragement of violence and anarchy in America.

Beyond policy, confidence in elite rule united the administration's supporters. Holding on to traditional assumptions that the people should select public officials and leave the details of policy to them, Federalists assumed that the "rich and well-born," as Hamilton called them, alone had the wisdom and experience necessary for good government. Popular liberty had to be checked by the rule of law and reasonable judgment, as the French Revolution's mass executions, attacks on religion, and fanatical wars now clearly demonstrated. Federalists likewise interpreted Republican expressions of admiration for France's revolution as demagogic appeals designed to stir up popular passions, and the growing opposition in Congress threatened to lead the United States down the same tragic road as past republics. As the Friends of Order, Federalist leaders thought that they alone could provide the responsible guidance necessary to prevent the American republic's collapse. At first they hoped that the support of prominent individuals in the states would bring public approval to Hamilton's policies, but the opposition's growing strength in Congress compelled them to make their own attempts at party organization. Federalist newspapers emerged to defend the Friends of Order while implicating Republicans as Antifederalists and Jacobins. Leading Federalists meanwhile corresponded to organize public meetings and petition campaigns and to put forward congressional candidates to counter those advanced by Republicans.

By the beginning of President Washington's second term, Federalist and Republican leaders had laid the foundation for the competition that would characterize federal politics for the next generation. In the furor over Jay's Treaty, both parties took their case to the public for the first time. Jefferson, frustrated at his declining influence with the president, left the cabinet in December 1793, but Madison coordinated a massive outpouring of congressional denunciations and newspaper and pamphlet condemnations of the treaty, while John Beckley helped organize public protests denouncing the agreement. Federalists responded with their own speeches, publications, and public meetings while sending petitions to President Washington urging him to approve it. Though Republican efforts failed to stop the treaty, the battles further polarized the Union's leaders and set the pattern that would characterize politics for the rest of the decade. When the Fourth Congress convened in December 1795, only seven House members remained unattached to either party. The longer terms of senators and their election by state legislatures helped Federalists maintain a majority in the Senate, but in the House, Republicans continued as a strong and aggressive minority even after Federalists regained a majority in 1797.

As party conflict came to dominate the government's debates, both parties gained fairly stable followings across the Union. Principles and policy both influenced in which geographic areas the parties won their support. The South remained a solid base for Republicans, and they maintained a vigorous presence in the Middle Atlantic states. The opposition party drew the strongest support among artisans, workers, and smaller merchants in port towns, among international merchants who wanted to expand their trade in non-British ports, and in newer-settled small-farming regions less dependent on foreign exports, such as in Vermont and among Scots-Irish settlers in western Pennsylvania and South Carolina. Merchants with close ties to British traders joined financial interests as the backbone of the Federalists, while its Puritan heritage made New England the Federalists' stronghold. British commerce also contributed to the Federalists' formidable presence in the Middle Atlantic, not only among traders but among farmers who prospered from selling their produce to the British Empire. Assumption of the state's debt and the former mother country's control of the rice trade helped Federalists win support among South Carolina's low-country planters, and planters from long-settled areas in Virginia and North Carolina responded positively to the Federalists' distaste for democracy. The Washington administration's successes—especially Pinckney's Treaty— in removing foreign threats in the west helped Federalists gain a foothold elsewhere in the South, though their reluctance to support the admission of new states destroyed any following they had in Kentucky and Tennessee.

With the parties' identities and bases established, both made intense efforts to capture the presidency in 1796. Although President Washington's decisions in his second term usually favored the Federalists, most still saw him as "above party," and he remained such a towering figure that no one could challenge his re-election. But he longed to retire, and with the publication on September 19 of a Farewell Address—warning his countrymen to avoid "the baneful effects of the spirit of party"—he announced that he would not accept another term. Long before Washington publicized his decision, the parties had already begun laying plans to elect his successor. Through informal meetings and discussions, Federalists agreed in the spring that John Adams' standing as vice president made him the heir apparent, with South Carolina's Thomas Pinckney, the hero of the recent treaty with Spain, as the vice-presidential candidate. Republicans came to a quick conclusion to promote Jefferson for the presidency, even though Jefferson himself preferred Madison for the job. Since George Clinton had left the New York governor's office and reportedly suffered from illness, no obvious choice for the vice presidency emerged. Most preferred another New Yorker, Senator Aaron Burr, but an informal Republican congressional caucus held in May could not unite behind a nominee. Party leaders promoted him as the Republicans' choice, though several Southern Republicans withheld their support because they considered Burr "unsettled in his politics."

None of the candidates spoke publicly or published their thoughts about the contest. Nor, except for Burr, did any participate actively in developing campaign strategy or electioneering. The actual competition for votes proved limited. In several states where the legislature chose the electors, the state elections occurred before President Washington announced his decision to retire. In states holding popular votes, both parties promoted well-known and highly respected individuals as candidates for electors, many of whom they hoped could win without bothering to declare their presidential preference. The results from all the states seemed to return a Federalist victory. Republicans won all the votes from Georgia, Kentucky, and Tennessee, as well as all but one each from Virginia, Pennsylvania, and North Carolina. All the Republican electors voted for Jefferson, but Southern Republicans disappointed Burr when they gave him only seven votes and scattered the rest among six noncontenders. Federalists meanwhile gained the unanimous support of the five New England states plus those of New York, New Jersey, and Delaware, while district elections in Maryland gave them seven of its ten votes. If, as expected, Federalists also received the eight votes submitted by South Carolina's legislature, Adams and Pinckney would have been elected easily.

Alexander Hamilton's attempt to manipulate the outcome altered the results. Aware that he would have little influence with Adams, Hamilton tried to arrange the election of Pinckney, over whom he could have more persuasion. As soon as Federalists accepted Pinckney as a candidate, Hamilton began to urge South Carolina leaders to choose electors who would cast one vote for Pinckney and their second to someone other than Adams. Since he expected all other Federalist electors to vote for Adams and Pinckney, Hamilton argued that South Carolina could elect Pinckney to the presidency and relegate Adams to another term as vice president. New England Federalists got wind of Hamilton's scheme, so to ensure Adams' election, eighteen of the region's thirty-nine electors refused to vote for Pinckney. Then, to Hamilton's shock, South Carolina's electors ended up casting their votes for Pinckney and Jefferson, who was on good personal terms with many of the state's rice planters. As a result, the Federalist Adams won the election by only three votes over the Republican Jefferson, who now became vice president.

The Federalists' Collapse

Except for George Washington, perhaps no one had worked harder to secure American independence than John Adams. As one of the first and strongest advocates of separation, Adams' services in the Continental Congress and as a diplomat during the War for Independence had made him a hero of the Revolution. His personality, however, made him a difficult person to work with. Honest and sincere, he could also be petty, quarrelsome, and blunt, and he spoke his mind freely, usually without regard for his listeners' feelings. His extreme sensitivity to criticism produced abiding grudges, and his vanity often irritated his associates. As the new president, he took his public responsibilities very seriously, despite tensions with the party that had elected him. As vice president he had loyally supported Washington's administration, especially the neutrality proclamation and the Jay Treaty, but he shared some of the Republicans' reservations about the funding plan and the Bank of the United States. Then, shortly after the election, Adams learned about Hamilton's plot to slide Pinckney past him into the presidency. Until that point, he had always maintained good relations with Hamilton, but the effort to replace him with "such an unknown being" as Pinckney infuriated him. Convinced that Hamilton had no scruples, Adams determined that the leading Federalist would have no influence in his administration.

Adams' decision to retain Washington's cabinet unknowingly kept Hamilton's presence before him, however. Modest salaries and the requirement of long stays in Philadelphia had made cabinet appointments unattractive positions. Four men turned down the offer of secretary of war after Henry Knox resigned in January 1795. Maryland's James McHenry finally agreed to head the War Department. Similarly, five men rejected the opportunity to become secretary of state before Massachusetts' Timothy Pickering accepted the position. Political insiders considered McHenry and Pickering, as well as Treasury Secretary Oliver Wolcott, to be mediocrities. As vice president, Adams had witnessed President Washington's difficulties finding cabinet officers, and he was on good terms with McHenry, Pickering, and Wolcott, as well as Attorney General Charles Lee, so he saw no need to replace them. But unknown to Adams, Wolcott, Pickering, and especially McHenry regularly corresponded with Hamilton to seek his advice and to keep him informed about issues. The three also stood among the highest of the "High Federalists," a term coming to refer to those Federalists most disdainful of popular government and favoring close relations with Great Britain. So devoted were the cabinet officers to High Federalist ideals that, in his counsel to them, Hamilton himself often had to moderate their views.

By the time of Adams' inauguration in March 1797, deteriorating relations with France emerged as the new administration's most immediate challenge. The French Republic's latest government, the Directory, denounced the Jay Treaty as an alliance between the United States and Great Britain. In July 1796, the Directory had ordered the French navy to seize American merchant ships and confiscate cargoes headed for Britain. Before leaving office, President Washington sent Thomas Pinckney's brother, Charles Cotesworth Pinckney, to assure the French of American neutrality. When Charles Cotesworth Pinckney arrived in Paris, the Directory not only refused to meet with him but ordered him to leave the country. Federalists demanded a strong response, while Republicans promised to resist any move that might lead to war. President Adams thought a diplomatic effort could resolve the conflict, and to the High Federalists' horror he consulted with Jefferson about sending Madison to France at the head of a team of commissioners. A prominent Republican like Madison at the head of a delegation, the president reasoned, might enhance France's willingness to begin talks. The cabinet's threat to resign, and Jefferson's assurance that Madison would not accept an appointment, closed that door. Nevertheless, the president sent John Marshall, a moderate Virginia Federalist, and Elbridge Gerry, a Massachusetts Republican, to join Charles Cotesworth Pinckney in Paris and again offer to begin negotiations.

By the time the commissioners reached the French capital in October 1797, General Napoleon Bonaparte's victorious campaigns in Italy made the Directory even less inclined to deal with a minor American republic. With France now the dominant military power in Europe, the French foreign minister, Charles-Maurice de Talleyrand-Périgord, at first greeted the American commissioners and stated that he would soon contact them to begin discussions. But he never sent for them. Instead, after weeks of waiting, the commissioners received an informal visit from three French officials, who stated the conditions the Americans needed to meet before Talleyrand would receive them. Two principal points stood out: the United States must offer France a "considerable loan" in advance of any talks, and the commissioners had to pay a substantial bribe to Talleyrand and to members of the Directory. The commissioners refused to pay for the right to receive diplomatic recognition—at one meeting Charles Cotesworth Pinckney reportedly exclaimed "No! No! Not a sixpence!" They continued to talk informally with the French representatives to try to break the deadlock, but after six months, having made no progress, Pinckney and Marshall left Paris, with Gerry staying behind in case Talleyrand backed off from his demands.

President Adams initially kept quiet about the dispatches reporting the French insult. While discussing with his cabinet the possibility of declaring war, he merely notified Congress that he had given up hope for an accommodation with France. Republicans accused the president of failing to approach France in good faith, and on April 2 the House passed resolutions demanding to see the commission's reports. President Adams complied, hiding the identity of the French agents behind the labels "Messieurs X, Y and Z." The revelation produced the strongest popular outcry from Americans since the early stages of their revolution. Republican shock at France's haughty disregard for the Union was exceeded only by Federalist determination to avenge American honor. Public demonstrations condemned French arrogance and pledged support for war; "Millions for defense but not one cent for Tribute!" became the popular slogan, and crowds cheered President Adams as the symbol of American defiance. In Congress, Republican opposition dwindled as Federalists suspended all treaties with France, imposed an embargo on French trade, approved funding to fortify American harbors, and permitted American ships to retaliate against French ships that tried to capture American merchant vessels. The lawmakers also established the Department of the Navy and authorized the construction of nearly forty additional ships as well as the creation of a Provisional Army of fifty thousand that could be called into action once war was declared. Direct property taxes on slaves, land, and houses were instituted to pay for the military buildup.

Federalists also used war fever as an opportunity to silence those they considered the Union's domestic enemies. Convinced that the opposition was determined to overthrow the government, High Federalists feared that Republicans worked in league with France. A large number of recent radical British and Irish immigrants particularly disturbed them, for their hostility toward the British government made them aggressively pro-French and potentially Republican adherents. Spurred on by Maryland senator James Lloyd and South Carolina representative Robert Goodloe Harper, Congress narrowly approved four laws that collectively became known as the Alien and Sedition Acts. The Naturalization Act required immigrants to register their presence with county clerks and extended the residency requirement for citizenship from five to fourteen years. An "Act Concerning Aliens," popularly known as the Alien Friends Act, authorized the president to imprison or deport any foreign national judged "dangerous to the peace and safety of the United States," while a separate Alien Enemies Act outlined the procedure for prosecuting a person from an enemy nation who was deemed a threat during time of war. The Sedition Act, focusing on the actions of American citizens, made it punishable by fine and imprisonment to criticize the government of the United States with the intent to "defame" it or bring it "into contempt or disrepute."

Both popular revulsion at their longstanding calls for good relations with France and the threat of prosecution under the Alien and Sedition Acts now threatened the Republican Party's existence. President Adams saw no need to enforce the Alien Friends Act, and the Alien Enemies Act could not go into effect without a declaration of war. Still, the possibility of arrest or deportation induced numerous immigrants to leave, and High Federalist enforcement of the Sedition Act drove New York's two Republican newspapers out of business. Twenty-five individuals were arrested for offenses as simple as erecting a liberty pole and circulating a petition calling for the Alien and Sedition Acts' repeal. Federal officials eventually indicted fifteen Republican editors and convicted ten of seditious libel. Dispirited and fearing arrest, several leading Republican congressmen left Philadelphia. Jefferson himself spent the summer and fall at Monticello to avoid what he called the "reign of witches."

Despite the backlash, Jefferson's faith in the people's republican convictions never wavered. Convinced that Federalists had manufactured the crisis with France to strengthen their hold on power, he believed that, if Republicans could only keep up their resistance, citizens would eventually see through the Federalists' hysteria. With virtually no presence in the central government, and with the prosecution of Republican editors under the Sedition Act, the party, Jefferson and Madison concluded, could best present its protest through the states. A series of

Figure 2.3 "The Providential Detection" (1797). A Federalist cartoon depicting Thomas Jefferson attempting to burn the Constitution on the "Altar of Gallic Despotism," stopped by the American Eagle and the eye of God. Artist unknown. Courtesy American Antiquarian Society, Worcester, Massachusetts.

state declarations opposing the Federalists might compel the central government to discontinue the war hysteria; at the least, they could provide an outlet for Republican criticism of their rivals. In the fall of 1798, Jefferson and Madison each secretly drafted sets of resolutions for the Virginia and Kentucky legislatures. Promising to keep the Republican leadership's role quiet, on November 10 the Kentucky legislature approved a series of resolutions that Jefferson had written. In late December, the Republican majority in the Virginia assembly approved, over a vocal Federalist minority, a similar statement that Madison had prepared.

In turning to the state legislatures, Republican leaders backed away from the notion that the federal government was a distinct entity created by the people of all the states collectively, separate and apart from the state governments. Jefferson's resolutions for the Kentucky assembly in particular returned to the understanding that had guided the Articles of Confederation—that the Union was a compact of states—while reminding citizens that the states retained any authority not expressly delegated to the federal government. This authority, Jefferson now claimed, included the power of a state to determine for itself the constitutionality of any act of Congress. Appealing to the principle of strict construction that he had put forward against the Bank of the United States, Jefferson argued that Congress had exceeded its constitutional limitations and violated the rights of the states when it passed the Alien and Sedition Acts, for state legislatures held responsibility for laws dealing with foreign residents and with sedition. Madison disagreed with Jefferson's claim that a state had the right to nullify federal law, and he hesitated to suggest a state could trump the national government. Still, his resolutions also described the Union as an agreement among the states, and he asserted that a state could "interpose," or intervene, when the central government threatened the rights of individual citizens. Like the Kentucky Resolutions, too, the Virginia Resolutions warned that the "spirit . . . manifested by the federal government" reflected "the obvious tendency and inevitable consequence . . . to transform the present republican system of the United States, into an absolute, or at best a mixed monarchy."

Notwithstanding Madison's caution, the Kentucky and Virginia Resolutions' disunionist implications discouraged other states from responding favorably to the call for action. Legislatures in the Middle Atlantic and New England states, where Federalists either held majorities or were a strong presence, not only rejected the resolutions but defended the need for the Alien and Sedition Acts. Even strongly Republican North Carolina, Georgia, and Tennessee offered no formal response. Nevertheless, the ideals expressed in the resolutions—strict construction of the Constitution, states' rights, and resistance to the High Federalists' monarchical designs—provided a focus for the opposition's challenge. The resolutions positioned Republicans to win followers whenever the public turned against the Federalists' war measures. As Jefferson anticipated, public sentiment did start to turn, early in 1799. Few citizens had complained about new taxes or military preparations when war seemed imminent. But as months passed without conflict, the military fever cooled. The taxes especially seemed an unnecessary burden, with the "Window Tax"—the popular label for the property tax because it determined the value of houses according to the number and size of their windows—becoming a particular object of resentment. The army's expansion meanwhile stirred fears that Federalists wanted to establish a "standing army"—a permanent force of professional mercenaries that could enforce a tyrannical government's will upon its subjects.

Hostility toward the "Window Tax" spurred another apparent rebellion in Pennsylvania, this time among the German inhabitants of the eastern part of the state. Citizens held public meetings to protest the tax, while local militias were organized to prevent its collection. A federal judge ordered the arrest of the most prominent offenders in late February 1799, but when a US marshal rounded up and jailed eighteen suspects at Bethlehem, local auctioneer John Fries led a group of 140 to force the prisoners' release on March 7. Though the riot was without bloodshed, the mob broke several windows to show their displeasure. The "rebellion" quickly dissolved; Fries and his men soon regretted their outburst, and the tax assessors resumed their work. But High Federalists persuaded President Adams to declare the region in rebellion and to send a combined force of regulars and militia to restore order. A month after the incident, soldiers apprehended about sixty rebels and took them to Philadelphia for trial. Federal courts convicted Fries and two of his comrades of treason and sentenced them to be hanged. To the High Federalists' dismay, the president pardoned the trio. But long before then, the political damage had been done. With the "Principles of '98" as their rallying cry, Republicans called upon citizens to stand against the Federalists' design to create a consolidated government, supported by heavy taxes and a standing army that disregarded civil liberty.

High Federalists nevertheless expected the anticipated war with France to revive their popular support. The conflict had already begun at sea, and American successes stirred national pride. Three new frigates—the *Constellation*, the *United States*, and the *Constitution*—were launched during the summer of 1798, while the new secretary of the navy, Virginia's Benjamin Stoddert, set to work constructing more ships and commissioning private vessels to capture French vessels that threatened American merchants. In 1799 and 1800, the American navy acquitted itself well in a series of encounters with French warships that became known as a "Quasi War." Meanwhile, High Federalist entreaties persuaded a reluctant George Washington to leave retirement and accept command of the army, though he did so on the condition that President Adams appoint Alexander Hamilton a major general. All knew that Washington intended to come into active service only in case of an emergency, leaving Hamilton in actual control. Recruiting went slowly, but Hamilton laid plans to use the conflict to eliminate the Republican threat once and for all. At the same time, he began discussing with Britain a joint venture to seize Louisiana and Florida and to liberate Central and South American colonies from the control of Spain, France's ally.

But President Adams was not party to the High Federalists' plans. During the XYZ Affair, he had expected to lead the Union into war, and he firmly supported Stoddert's work building up the navy. Yet while Hamilton dreamed of military glory, the president kept open the possibility of peace. He did not expect France to invade North America, and even if it did he thought good coastal defenses and state militia support for the existing army would provide adequate protection. Sharing the popular distrust of standing armies, he saw little need for the large army that High Federalists championed, and he resented having to appoint Hamilton as its effective commander. While bickering with his cabinet over appointments, the president received evidence from Elbridge Gerry in Paris that the French government scolded Talleyrand for his treatment of the Americans and wanted to avoid war. Optimistic that a new round of talks could succeed, President Adams rejected High Federalist demands that he recommend to Congress a declaration of war. Instead, without informing his cabinet beforehand, he announced on February 18, 1799, that he would appoint William Vans Murray as the new American minister to the French republic.

The president's decision left High Federalists, in Pickering's words, "thunderstruck." Well aware that their popular support depended on continued hostility with France, he became the object of their hatred. Criticism of Murray's qualifications gave the Senate reason to reject his diplomatic appointment, while Pickering, McHenry, and Wolcott pressured the president to change his mind. But President Adams held firm, and his threat to resign if the Senate failed to approve his mission presented High Federalists with the prospect of having to deal with Jefferson as president. The Senate finally agreed to accept another three-man commission, consisting of Murray, Connecticut's Oliver Ellsworth, and North Carolina governor William R. Davie. By the time Ellsworth and Davie met up with Murray in Paris, a coup had brought Napoleon Bonaparte to power as "First Consul." Preoccupied with France's European affairs, General Bonaparte wanted to get the American distraction out of the way, so he warmly welcomed the American commissioners and instructed Talleyrand to work out a treaty. Leaving the most difficult issues unresolved for the present, in October they signed a "Convention," or temporary agreement, at Môrtefontaine, the country home of Napoleon's brother. The agreement ended the Quasi War with a French promise to respect American neutral rights and to pay for any future cargoes that might be impounded. In exchange, the United States granted to France "Most Favored Nation" status, allowing French ships to trade in American ports on the same terms as Britain.

Few Americans hailed the Convention of 1800 as a major diplomatic victory, but the agreement at least temporarily secured peace. President Adams kept the Union from rushing headlong into an unnecessary war with potentially drastic consequences. His decision also alienated him from Federalist leadership. As the 1800 election approached, the party that had elected him faced a revived opposition while finding itself divided and saddled with a standing army, repressive laws, and heavy taxes. President Adams hoped his re-election would vindicate his decision to pursue peace with France, and he had a realistic chance of winning. The decision to send another mission to Paris had won popular approval, and notwithstanding the High Federalists' disgust he still enjoyed solid support from moderates in his party. Even more than had been the case in 1796, the choice would depend less on the decisions of voters than on the dealings of political leaders. Massachusetts, Rhode Island, and Pennsylvania changed their election laws so that their legislatures would cast their state's electoral votes, leaving voters the choice of electors in only six of the sixteen states. In these circumstances, the outcome would depend less upon a candidate's popularity than upon the party's ability to secure electoral votes.

High Federalists desperately searched for a candidate to replace Adams as the Federalist nominee. Several pleaded with George Washington to leave retirement and accept a third term, but the former president refused to consider the possibility; even so, his death in December 1799 was sudden and unexpected. When no one else emerged with the prestige needed to unite the party, a caucus of Federalist congressmen in early May formally recommended Adams and Charles Cotesworth Pinckney, hero of the XYZ Affair, as candidates for president and vice president. High Federalist resistance, however, prevented the caucus from designating Adams the presidential candidate, so the meeting presented Adams and Pinckney as equally qualified to serve in either office. Publicly, High Federalists endorsed Adams, but privately they encouraged states to choose electors who would vote for Pinckney but throw their second vote to someone other than the incumbent.

New York's spring elections for the state legislature dealt Federalist prospects a severe blow. New York had cast all of its electoral votes for Adams in 1796, and Federalists had won control of the legislature in the spring of 1799. In the spring 1800 elections, Aaron Burr took control of the Republican campaign and led his party to a decisive victory that gave Republicans control of the legislature. Recognizing that New York's electoral votes now would undoubtedly go to the Republican presidential and vice-presidential nominees, President Adams concluded that his best hope of winning support elsewhere lay in distancing himself from the High Federalists. Shortly after receiving news of the New York results, the president asked for the resignations of Secretary of War McHenry and Secretary of State Pickering. When Pickering refused, claiming that he should stay in office until the end of the term, President Adams promptly fired him. Judging them as moderates who would support his presidency and strengthen the Federalist appeal in the Southern and Middle Atlantic states, the president then appointed Massachusetts' Samuel Dexter as secretary of war and named Virginia's John Marshall to head the state department. Congress meanwhile scaled the army back to its size before the 1798 crisis. For his part, Pinckney assured New England Federalists that he condoned no plot to elect him president, and he promised to accept no electoral votes unless the elector also voted for Adams.

These moves terrified High Federalists, who feared that Adams and Jefferson might join forces. But Republicans had no need for an alliance. Focused, well-organized, and determined to get Jefferson into the presidency, the Republican congressional caucus met a week after the Federalists' caucus and formally nominated Jefferson for the presidency with Burr for the vice presidency, this time as a reward for his service in New York. Republicans then launched what effectively became the first national presidential campaign. Expanding upon the "Principles of '98," Republicans charged Federalists with provoking the crisis with France so they could impose high taxes, supervise an unnecessary and costly military buildup, and attack basic freedoms through the Alien and Sedition Acts—proof, they maintained, of the Federalists' monarchical intentions. Portraying Pinckney as a mediocre political lightweight, Republicans denounced Adams for abandoning his Revolutionary principles while keeping the specter of Hamilton before voters as the author of the Federalists' designs. At the same time, they stressed the positive values that they claimed would guide Jefferson as president. Behind the scenes, Jefferson outlined what became the Republican platform in a letter to Elbridge Gerry in January 1799. Declaring himself in favor of "a government rigorously frugal and simple," the candidate pledged to support states' rights, to observe Congress' independence from the executive, to work toward paying off the federal debt, to rely on a small navy and state militia forces for the Union's defense, to promote "free commerce with all nations [and] political connections with none," and to protect the individual rights guaranteed in the Constitution.

Federalists never organized themselves as well as did Republicans, but they still conducted a formidable campaign. Moderate Federalists praised Adams for preventing war while preserving American honor. High Federalists said little about the incumbent but defended their policies while holding up Pinckney as an honorable statesman worthy of high office. Federalists united, though, when they attacked the Republican candidate's character, condemning Jefferson as a Jacobin and an atheist who would bring French radicalism to American shores and lead an all-out assault on religion and morality. Behind the scenes, party leaders spent much of their time criticizing each other. The party's rift came into the open in the fall. Furious to learn that President Adams had privately referred to him as a "foreigner" and "bastard," the West Indian and illegitimate-born Hamilton prepared a pamphlet criticizing the incumbent's "positive and serious errors of administration" and charging that he lacked "the talents adapted to the *administration* of government." Hamilton circulated his pamphlet privately among Federalist leaders, hoping that it would convince his allies to support Pinckney over Adams. Instead, they expressed shock at his bold and blunt charges. Moderates rushed to defend the president. Even High Federalists thought their champion displayed poor judgment, and, as several had feared, Hamilton's charges could not be kept quiet. Republicans managed to get hold of a copy of the pamphlet and published it in October.

Though embarrassing, Hamilton's rant had little influence on the outcome. States chose their electors at different times during the year, so no one could clearly determine the results until the last state made its decision in December. Early elections showed that Federalists would once again receive unanimous support from New England, New Jersey, and Delaware. District popular elections won them five of Maryland's ten electoral votes and four of North Carolina's twelve. Republicans carried all the electors from Virginia, New York, Georgia, Kentucky, and Tennessee, along with the remaining votes from Maryland and North Carolina. In Pennsylvania, the Federalist majority in the state senate forced Republicans in the state house to divide the state's fifteen votes and return eight Republican and seven Federalist electors. These results left the number of Federalist and Republican votes tied at sixty-five. Once again, South Carolina played the decisive role. Republicans had recently won a legislative majority, but Federalists remained a formidable presence as long as their candidate Pinckney stood as a highly regarded native son. Pinckney, however, discouraged legislators from linking the state's votes between him and Jefferson. Meanwhile, his cousin, Senator Charles Pinckney, intensely lobbied the assemblymen to support the Republican ticket and lavished upon the legislators promises for patronage appointments in a Jefferson administration. As a result, in early December South Carolina chose electors committed to vote for both Republican candidates. When Vice President Jefferson counted the electoral votes before a joint session of Congress on February 11, 1801, he and Burr each received seventy-three votes, compared to sixty-five for Adams, sixty-four for Pinckney, and one for Jay.

The election produced a close result. If any one of fourteen of the sixteen states had voted differently, the electoral college would have either re-elected Adams or returned a tie among the Federalist and Republican candidates. Nevertheless, leaders in both parties recognized that the public had turned against Federalism. Republicans now clearly enjoyed a majority among voters in Pennsylvania and New Jersey; only the Federalists' retention of Pennsylvania's senate and New Jersey's unequal representative districts prevented those states from returning all of their votes for Jefferson, which would have shifted eleven electoral votes from the Federalist to the Republican column. The congressional elections held in 1800 and 1801 revealed the popular turn even more clearly. The growing strength of the opposition in the states meant that Republicans would have a majority in the Senate when the Seventh Congress convened, while Federalists lost twenty-two seats in the House to give Republicans a thirty-vote advantage. A large majority throughout the Union thus rejected the party in power and opted to follow the course set by Republicans. Even in New England, the Federalists' supposed stronghold, Jefferson's party won seven of Massachusetts' fourteen House seats and elected both of Rhode Island's representatives.

The tie between Jefferson and Burr gave Federalists one last hope of staying in power. The decision of who would become president now went to the House of Representatives. Each state would cast one vote in the House, and the winner needed to secure a majority of the states. Since the expiring Sixth Congress would not adjourn until March 4, a House with a Federalist majority would make the choice. Republicans held the most representatives in eight state delegations, which would vote undoubtedly for Jefferson, but without the vote of one additional state he would fall one vote short of the required majority. Two states were evenly divided, but Federalists had the most representatives in six states and could deadlock the election. Some wanted to prevent the election of either Jefferson or Burr and pass a law making Secretary of State John Marshall an interim president until Congress could arrange for a special election. Most, though, expected the wily and ambitious Burr to deal with them and accept election with Federalist backing. Burr had assured Jefferson that he would defer in case of a tie, but once the results became official he remained silent, neither endorsing Jefferson's election nor withdrawing his own candidacy. Notwithstanding Hamilton's warnings that his fellow New Yorker had no principles and could not be trusted, congressional Federalists so despised Jefferson that they agreed to unite behind Burr, with the hope that at least some Republicans would join them and deny Jefferson the presidency.

Meeting for the first time in the new federal capital—recently named "Washington" in honor of the first president—the House immediately took up the presidential election. Republicans and Federalists both voted along straight party lines, with eight states for Jefferson, six for Burr, and two divided. For thirty-five ballots held over three days, the representatives remained deadlocked. Neither side gave any indication of backing down, until Federalist James A. Bayard shocked his colleagues and announced his intention to vote for Jefferson. As Delaware's only congressman, Bayard's switch would give Jefferson the ninth state he needed to win the presidency. Frustrated with Burr's silence, Bayard received assurances from Maryland representative Samuel Smith that, as president, Jefferson would keep the funding system and the navy while allowing Federalist appointees to keep their offices. Jefferson later denied that he authorized Smith to make these promises. Nevertheless, Bayard's decision resolved the crisis. After consulting with Federalist representatives from the two divided states, he agreed that he would not actually vote for Jefferson. Instead, these three state's Federalists would either miss the next ballot or submit a blank vote. These abstentions allowed Jefferson to carry Vermont and Maryland, so on the thirty-sixth ballot Jefferson won ten states. He was declared the next president on February 17, 1801.

Jefferson later referred to his party's victory as "the revolution of 1800, . . . as real a revolution in the principles of our government as that of 1776 was in its form." He might have overstated his case, but the election did produce significant change. Jefferson and Madison led a popular movement that, without violence, challenged and replaced the government's entrenched officers. Voters had not just rejected Federalists' plan to create a strong, centralized Union based upon military force and close ties to the former mother country. In this "revolution," citizens repudiated the notion that they should blindly follow their leaders. In the future, public officials would have to present themselves—rhetorically, at least—as the people's servants. Jefferson now faced the challenge of acting as the people's servant while putting a new set of ideals into practice.

Suggested Readings

Appleby, Joyce. *Capitalism and a New Social Order: The Republican Vision of the 1790s* (New York, 1984).

Banning, Lance. *The Jeffersonian Persuasion: Evolution of a Party Ideology* (Ithaca, NY, 1978).

Ben-Atar, Doron, and Barbara B. Oberg, eds. *Federalists Reconsidered* (Charlottesville, 1998).

Casto, William R. *The Supreme Court in the Early Republic: The Chief Justiceship of John Jay and Oliver Ellsworth* (Columbia, SC, 1995).

Elkins, Stanley, and Eric McKitrick. *The Age of Federalism: The Early American Republic, 1788–1800* (New York, 1993).

Estes, Todd. *The Jay Treaty Debate, Public Opinion, and the Evolution of Early American Political Culture* (Amherst, MA, 2006).

Ferling, John. *Adams vs. Jefferson: The Tumultuous Election of 1800* (New York, 2004).

Freeman, Joanne B. *Affairs of Honor: National Politics in the New Republic* (New Haven, 2001).

Hogeland, William. *The Whiskey Rebellion: George Washington, Alexander Hamilton, and the Frontier Rebels Who Challenged America's Newfound Sovereignty* (New York, 2006).

Labunski, Richard. *James Madison and the Struggle for the Bill of Rights* (New York, 2006).

Pasley, Jeffrey L. *"The Tyranny of Printers": Newspaper Politics in the Early American Republic* (Charlottesville, 2001).

Pasley, Jeffrey L., Andrew W. Robertson, and David Waldstreicher, eds. *Beyond the Founders: New Approaches to the Political History of the Early American Republic* (Chapel Hill, 2004).

Sharp, James Roger. *American Politics in the Early Republic: The New Nation in Crisis* (New Haven, 1993).

Stinchcombe, William C. *The XYZ Affair* (Westport, CT, 1981).

Watkins, William J. *Reclaiming the American Revolution: The Kentucky and Virginia Resolutions and Their Legacy* (New York, 2004).

Wood, Gordon S. *Empire of Liberty: A History of the Early Republic, 1789–1815* (New York, 2009).

III

THE JEFFERSONIAN REVOLUTION

The ceremonies began at 10:00 a.m. on March 4, 1801, but Thomas Jefferson chose to remain at Conrad and McMunn's boarding house until shortly before noon, the time scheduled for him to be sworn in as president. He wanted no formal procession to accompany him. Two military companies nevertheless paraded before the house at ten, and when he left his quarters several friends and Republican allies joined him on the short stroll to the Capitol. Cannon fire saluted his entrance into the unfinished building. As he entered the Senate chamber, Aaron Burr, who had already taken the vice presidential oath, moved so that Jefferson could take the presiding officer's chair. Then, standing with Burr on his right and Chief Justice John Marshall at his left, Jefferson read his inaugural address, aware that neither his predecessor nor the Federalist Speaker of the House was in attendance. After taking the oath of office, President Jefferson walked back to his residence to greet visitors and begin his administration until he could move into the President's House two weeks later.

Few of the roughly three hundred people attending the festivities actually heard President Jefferson's inaugural address. The new president hated giving speeches, partly because he spoke with a lisp, and on this occasion he mumbled through his text in a low, soft voice. The contents of the address nevertheless soon became well known, for the Washington *National Intelligencer* published an advanced copy that was soon reprinted in newspapers across the Union. What struck most readers was the address's moderation. After the bitter political battles of the past decade, President Jefferson called on his countrymen to recognize their common commitment to the Union and to free government. "We are all republicans," he proclaimed; "we are all federalists." But he also made it clear that his presidency would follow certain Republican principles—"a wise and frugal government," "support of the state governments in all their rights," "absolute acquiescence in the decisions of the majority," and "encouragement of agriculture, and of commerce as its handmaiden." Outlined in direct contrast to Federalist policies, this Republican doctrine guided Jefferson's presidency, successfully changed the direction of the Union, and laid the foundation for the next generation's politics. The mixed results of the Jeffersonian revolution, however, also revealed the limitations of Republican ideals.

The "Republican Tack"

President Jefferson's call for unity did not satisfy most Federalists. The views he expressed on strict construction and states' rights convinced them that the new president was an Antifederalist determined to dissolve the Union. Likewise, his well-known sympathy for the French Revolution and his association with disciples of the Enlightenment—the European intellectual movement that championed learning through observation and reason rather than revelation, tradition, and faith—persuaded them that he would bring to America the same atheistic, democratic chaos that had destroyed republicanism in France. The Federalists' hysteria distorted

President Jefferson's actual views. It was true that he trusted popular opinion more than did most of his contemporaries, and he did subscribe to the Enlightenment's devotion to science, hostility toward hereditary privilege, and acceptance of deism, the belief that a Supreme Being had created the world but never intervened in human affairs. But the Republicans' champion was not the radical his opponents feared, even though some of his extreme statements occasionally found their way into print. He entered office as a practical politician, and his administration proved more moderate than Federalists would ever concede.

Thomas Jefferson, after all, had never been an Antifederalist. He had been in France when the Philadelphia Convention wrote the Constitution, but he had supported its ratification, despite reservations about the initial absence of a bill of rights and the president's ability to serve more than one term. As president, Jefferson would not hesitate to use the powers of the office to their fullest extent. There were limits, too, to President Jefferson's "democracy." He actually seldom used the term, preferring to refer to popular government as a "republic." Like his contemporaries, he had no desire to extend political freedoms beyond the white male population. In private, he lamented slavery's detrimental affects, but he doubted African-Americans' ability to thrive as free citizens or to integrate into American society. He also had personal and political interests at stake in the institution, for he owned more than 150 slaves and depended on the slaveholding states for the bulk of the Republican Party's support. He had even less regard for women's political abilities. When Treasury Secretary Albert Gallatin had difficulty finding enough men to fill his department's numerous clerkships, President Jefferson curtly dismissed Gallatin's proposal to hire women as "an innovation for which the public is not prepared, nor am I."

He even preferred to limit participation among white males. When he referred to "the people," he mainly meant those who owned enough property to support themselves and their families through their own labors. For him, farmers—"the chosen people of God, if ever He had a chosen people," he once wrote—stood as the ideal citizens in a republic. A yeoman, or a small landowner, could produce what he needed on his own farm and did not depend on anyone for his survival. In a manufacturing society like England's—and like the one Hamilton wanted to create in the United States—the majority of the working population lived at the mercy of those who paid their wages. Independent farmers, who supported themselves with the fruits of their labor, could make decisions and vote freely in a republic without following someone else's direction. Farmers were thus "the people" whom Jefferson believed cast the Federalists from power and whose will he promised to follow. But even the yeomanry's influence had limits. President Jefferson expected voters to express their will at elections, approving or rejecting their leaders' decisions and instructing their officials as to what course to pursue. The actual governing of a republic, though, should be left to what he referred to as a "natural aristocracy," determined not by birth, hereditary wealth, or privilege, but by "virtue and talents"—education, ability, experience, and a demonstrated record of public service.

Despite the new president's moderation, Federalists correctly saw a threat in the incoming administration. President Jefferson might not try to overturn society, but he would indeed promote a different kind of union from the one that Federalists had championed in the 1790s. Through pomp, pageantry, and military strength, the Constitution's initial proponents had attempted to consolidate power in a central government that would maintain sovereignty over the states and overawe the people with the trappings of monarchy. Through Treasury Secretary Alexander Hamilton's financial program, they had tried to build up manufacturing and commerce at the expense of planters and yeomen. Now that the people had rejected the Federalists' vision, President Jefferson intended to return the central government to its original limits while instituting policies that would perpetuate the people's republican character. Representing the interests of the Union's agricultural majority, he wanted to restore the balance between state and federal authority that Federalists had tipped in favor of the central government. Moreover, he wanted to eliminate Federalism as a political force while removing any lingering "monocrat" influence in power. As he told his attorney general, he planned to "sink federalism into an abyss from which there should be no resurrection for it." In a nautical metaphor he often used, Jefferson described his purpose as returning the ship of state to "her republican tack."

This mission, the president believed, merely completed the task already initiated by the people. Though he and Burr had defeated the Federalist candidates by only eight electoral votes, the recent elections established the Republicans as the Union's overwhelming majority party. When Jefferson entered office, Republicans controlled eleven of the sixteen state governments and held two-thirds of the seats in the House of Representatives. These results demoralized Federalists, but the president and his allies wanted to make sure their opponents would never recover from their losses. Congressional Republicans maintained close contact with party leaders at home and encouraged them to maintain their organization in states where Federalists remained competitive. In Washington, Samuel Harrison Smith's *National Intelligencer* served as the administration's organ, the newspaper that unofficially announced and explained the president's decisions. Across the Union, Republican newspapers continued to publicize the Republican cause. Despite Republican denunciation of the Federalists' Sedition Act, President Jefferson encouraged state authorities to prosecute Federalist newspapers for seditious libel when they unleashed their own bitter denunciations. Federalist papers abused free speech through their lies and misrepresentations, he reasoned, so "a few prosecutions of the most prominent offenders would have a wholesome effect in restoring the integrity of the press."

Changing international conditions aided President Jefferson's efforts to change the Union's course. For almost a decade, the war between Britain, France, and their respective allies had complicated American foreign relations, as both major belligerents pressured the United States for assistance while interrupting American trade. The Jay Treaty and the Convention of Mortefontaine temporarily stopped the degradations on American shipping, but no one could tell for sure how long the respite would last. In early February 1801, however, Britain's allies concluded a separate peace with France, and after Britain's naval victory at Copenhagen in April, the powers agreed to a cease-fire and began negotiations. The resulting Treaty of Amiens would not be formally approved until March 1802, and it proved only a temporary peace. In the short term, though, peace in Europe removed the sense of urgency that underlay the intensely bitter political debates that had occurred within the United States. More importantly, peace gave President Jefferson the opportunity to start his administration without having to deal with the portentous issues that had vexed his predecessors.

The administration's first task would be to change the tone of the government. In contrast to the monarchical aura that surrounded the Federalist presidents, President Jefferson sought to promote "republican simplicity." Through the humble approach to his inauguration, he intended to convey a sense that he and other elected officials took their offices as fellow citizens—not privileged rulers—who were charged with the responsibility of serving the public. The rural conditions of Washington, DC, reinforced the modest image President Jefferson preferred. When it was agreed in 1790 that the seat of the federal government would be built on the Potomac River, everyone expected the new city to become a center of trade, commerce, and the arts. These expectations had not materialized by the time federal officials moved to Washington in the summer of 1800. About three thousand people lived across the District of Columbia, but the town contained few businesses beyond boarding houses, taverns, and services for government employees. Public buildings, including the Capitol and the President's House, remained unfinished and connected by unpaved roads. Cattle and wildlife grazed in open fields between the buildings. Politicians found Washington an uncomfortable city with a dull social life. President Jefferson himself refused to reside in the city during the summers, spending about a quarter of his presidential years at Monticello, his Virginia plantation home.

Still, the capital's simple environs discouraged the pageantry that President Jefferson believed elevated a government above the people. The president himself simplified the practices of the executive branch. The stuffy Tuesday afternoon levees came to an end. Twice a year, on New Year's Day and the Fourth of July, he hosted a public reception that any citizen could attend. Partly because of his distaste for public speaking, President Jefferson declined delivering his annual message as a speech to Congress, an event he thought reminiscent of an English monarch's speaking from the throne at the opening of Parliament. Instead, he established the custom that would prevail for the next century by sending the message in writing so it could be read in each chamber by the secretary of the Senate and the clerk of the House. When traveling in Washington, he usually rode alone on horseback; in fact, the daily rides he took for his health gave him an opportunity to talk with the village's residents. While working, he dressed casually—"neglected but not slovenly," one visitor noted. More than once, he greeted foreign dignitaries while wearing bedroom slippers. At his first state dinner, an occasion at which protocol dictated seating diplomats according to their prestige and seniority, Jefferson shocked his guests when he declared that seating would be done "pell-mell"—that is, whoever arrived at the table first would get to choose his seat.

Private dinner parties became the administration's most important social events. Other than servants and his personal secretary, Meriwether Lewis, the widower Jefferson lived alone in

Figure 3.1 "A View of the Capitol before It Was Burnt Down by the British." Shows Washington as a small, rural village at the time Thomas Jefferson's presidency began. Watercolor by William Russell Birch (c. 1800). Courtesy Prints & Photographs Division, Library of Congress, LC-DIG-ppmsca-07708.

the President's House except for occasional visits from one of his two daughters. But Jefferson hated to dine alone, so as often as five times a week he hosted a dinner for up to a dozen specially invited guests. Beyond keeping the president company, the dinners proved to have a vital political function. While Congress was in session, the president made a point of inviting every Republican member, along with some moderate Federalists, to at least one dinner, keeping careful records to make sure no one was overlooked. Seating at a round table limited private conversations, and notwithstanding "republican simplicity," Jefferson spared no expense to serve the finest wines and exquisite meals prepared by a French chef. Here, the president and his guests talked over a range of topics that included everything except contemporary politics. Through these conversations, Jefferson skillfully managed to convey to congressmen what he would like to see done, without raising concerns about his dictating his will or interfering with the independence of the legislature. The goodwill engendered at these dinners, along with the sense of common purpose among most Republicans, meant that for most of his administration Jefferson enjoyed good relations with Congress.

Jefferson also made it a priority to select competent and reliable cabinet members. Federalist resignations saved him the trouble of firing cabinet members, and the difficulties John Adams had faced from his official advisers convinced the new president to find men who would loyally support his decisions. The most important positions went to two of the most talented and influential Republicans—fellow Virginian and close friend James Madison became secretary of state, and Pennsylvania's Albert Gallatin agreed to head the Treasury Department. The appointment of Henry Dearborn as secretary of war and Levi Lincoln as attorney general, both from Massachusetts, and of Connecticut's Gideon Granger as postmaster general, provided geographical balance while strengthening the Republicans' prospects in New England. Maryland's Robert Smith, the brother of powerful Maryland congressman Samuel Smith, became secretary of the navy only after four others declined appointment. Gallatin and Madison proved President Jefferson's chief advisers. They conferred almost daily with the new president and worked closely with him to formulate Republican policy. The entire cabinet actually met infrequently, as President Jefferson followed President Washington's method of consulting with his officers individually after getting their opinions in writing. When they did meet, Gallatin and Smith increasingly argued over appropriations for the Navy Department, but on most issues the cabinet remained unified.

With a reliable cabinet and solid Republican majorities in Congress, Jefferson's administration proceeded to shift the Union's course. The Sedition Act and the Alien Friends Act, both passed as temporary measures, were allowed to expire, while the Alien Enemies Act became moot since it could be invoked only while the nation was at war. The ten prisoners awaiting trial for violating the Sedition Act received presidential pardons, and Congress reimbursed their fines with interest. On President Jefferson's recommendation, the lawmakers repealed the 1798 Naturalization Act, restoring immigrants' residency requirement for citizenship to five rather than fourteen years. Patronage proved more troublesome than President Jefferson expected. Federalists held the vast majority of presidential appointments, and President Jefferson thought most of them to be capable, though misguided, and he hesitated to dismiss competent officeholders only because he disagreed with their political opinions. Initially he planned to remove only the most obnoxious Federalists—"monocrats" who openly criticized the administration or misused their office. Political realities, though, meant he was compelled to use appointments to reward those who had helped elect him. Federalist intransigence, and pressure from Republicans who wanted their opponents rooted out of the government, likewise forced Jefferson to dismiss more appointees than he intended. Eventually he fired 109 Federalists, and two years after his inauguration Republicans held all but 130 of the 316 positions at Jefferson's discretion.

The federal debt presented the Republicans' main target. President Jefferson and Secretary Gallatin both hated the idea of a public debt, mainly because it stood at the center of what they believed to be Alexander Hamilton's plan to create an American aristocracy and corrupt the government. By the time Jefferson took office, the debt had grown to about $83 million. Despite its size, Republicans agreed it should be paid off as soon as possible. Gallatin took the lead in reforming the budget. The new Treasury secretary was one of the few in the party with the experience and business sense to understand the intricacies of Hamilton's program and to distinguish between its political aspect and its sound financial purposes. In particular, Gallatin recognized that the Bank of the United States could, if properly managed, be tremendously useful in dealing with the Union's finances. He persuaded the president to overcome his reservations and not pursue the bank's elimination. He likewise recognized the funding plan as an appropriate means of providing for the debt, so he essentially left Hamilton's structure in place while directing payments to the debt's principal, not just toward interest. He failed, however, to convince the president to delay eliminating the Federalists' internal taxes. President Jefferson feared that Republicans would get accustomed to revenue from the taxes, so despite Gallatin's concerns Congress repealed the vast majority of taxes, including the hated Whiskey excise, by early 1802.

Eliminating internal taxes made Gallatin's task especially daunting. He determined the federal debt could be paid off by 1817 if he could devote $7 million annually toward both interest and principal. Without the domestic taxes, ninety percent of the government's income depended on tariff collections, which Gallatin estimated would bring in only about $10 million a year. Attacking the debt thus required drastic cuts in the federal budget. Contrary to Republican charges, Federalists had not spent lavishly or irresponsibly when in power, so there was little room to cut domestic expenditures. Most of the cuts thus affected the diplomatic corps and military spending. At Gallatin's urging, President Jefferson closed the American legations in the Netherlands, Portugal, and Prussia, leaving missions in Britain, France, and Spain as the only permanent diplomatic presence abroad. Gallatin then cut the total annual military budget in half, to $1.9 million annually. This reduction forced Congress to reduce the army to 3,350 men, organized in three regiments but scattered across the frontier. The navy likewise was scaled back to thirteen frigates, with only six kept in active service.

Cutting the military forces fit both Secretary Gallatin's and President Jefferson's personal and political sentiments. Neither favored a strong military presence in a republic. President Jefferson in particular saw the reductions as an opportunity to reorient the Union's defenses toward what he considered a "republican" system. He approved the establishment in 1802 of the United States Military Academy at West Point, New York, to train a professional officer corps, but he wanted the army to remain small. He distrusted a large "standing army" that might back an ambitious general's desire to overthrow civilian authority, and he thought state militia companies and citizen volunteers could provide an effective defense against invasion. For the navy, he likewise preferred a fleet of small gunboats—crafts about fifty feet long, propelled by oars as well as sails, and armed with only one or two cannons—to large, expensive warships. Gunboats could patrol the American coast in peacetime, and their low cost meant the navy could expand quickly in time of war. President Jefferson's reliance on a modest military force would leave the Union in a weak position when he later faced renewed tensions with Europe. For the present, his policies contributed substantially to Gallatin's assault on the debt. Several unexpected expenses over President Jefferson's eight years in office complicated Gallatin's work, but by the end of it the Treasury secretary had reduced the debt to $57 million while accumulating a $14 million annual budget surplus.

Long before then, the ship of state seemed safely on a Republican course. Jefferson's presidency had checked Federalist influence, decreased the size of the government and the military,

Figure 3.2 "Albert Gallatin." Treasury secretary for Presidents Jefferson and Madison. Sketch by Pieter Van Huffel (1815). Courtesy Prints & Photographs Division, Library of Congress, LC-USZ62-64696.

and targeted the debt. Moreover, Republicans reduced the reach of the central government, allowing the states to resume their role as the primary authorities in citizens' lives. For most Americans, the postal service stood as the only federal presence they saw regularly. "What farmer, what mechanic, what laborer ever sees a tax-gatherer of the United States," Jefferson boasted at the end of his first term. Nevertheless, the Federalist Party presented an annoyance that persisted throughout his presidency.

Midnight Judges and Federalist Courts

Republicans had won at the polls, but Federalists controlled the Union's judiciary. Neither President Washington nor President Adams had appointed a Republican to a judicial position. Shortly before Jefferson's inauguration, Federalists took advantage of their majority in the expiring Congress to solidify their hold on the courts. While the House of Representatives argued over whether to elect Jefferson or Burr, President Adams signed the Judiciary Act of 1801, a reform that significantly altered the judicial system's structure. The act created six new circuit courts—with sixteen new jurists—to serve as appellate courts between the district court and the Supreme Court. The new tribunals would have original jurisdiction in civil cases and in cases involving crimes against the United States, and the act allowed for litigation to shift more easily from state to federal jurisdiction. Most notably, Supreme Court justices would no longer have to travel between sessions to sit with district judges on circuit courts. Since the burdens taken on by the new circuit courts presumably would reduce the higher court's work-load, the Judiciary Act of 1801 would eventually reduce the Supreme Court's membership to five, allowing a seat to remain unfilled once the next justice left.

In some ways, the 1801 Judiciary Act presented a reasonable response to serious prob-lems. The fact that justices could rule on cases twice—first on a circuit court and then on the Supreme Court—always seemed inappropriate, while the demand that justices "ride the circuit" encouraged rapid turnover on the Supreme Court and made it difficult to find com-petent jurists willing to accept appointment. Five of the court's six original justices either resigned or died during the 1790s, including John Jay, who left the chief justiceship in 1795 to become governor of New York. Nevertheless, no one could miss the political motives behind the Judiciary Act. The creation of the new circuit courts allowed President Adams to appoint sixteen new Federal judges, and the reduction of the Supreme Court's size would deny the incoming Jefferson the opportunity to appoint a Republican justice until at least two vacan-cies occurred. Similarly, a separate District of Columbia act, approved a week before Jefferson's inauguration, authorized the president to appoint as many justices of the peace for the district as he thought necessary. President Adams quickly nominated forty-two justices, along with the several judges, attorneys, and marshals provided for in the act, all of whom the Senate quickly confirmed. Then, to replace the recently resigned Oliver Ellsworth as chief justice, President Adams appointed John Marshall, the moderate Federalist who, though Jefferson's distant cousin, shared a mutual hostility with the new president.

Rumors that President Adams stayed up well into his last night in office filling out com-missions produced the name "Midnight Judges" to describe the late appointments. The label stretched the truth—the president submitted the name of the last appointee to Congress at midday—but Republicans nevertheless condemned the Judiciary and District of Columbia Acts as crass political maneuvers. President Jefferson especially considered the "Midnight" appointments a personal affront from his former friend; he immediately recalled the attorneys, marshals, and justices of the peace, reduced the number of offices, and filled them with his own appointees. Similarly, he instructed Madison to withhold four justice of the peace com-missions that John Marshall—ironically, Madison's predecessor as secretary of state—had failed to deliver before leaving office. The judgeships presented a more difficult problem. The Con-stitution stated that judges were appointed to life terms and could not be removed unless they criminally abused their powers. As a result, the president could not simply dismiss and replace Federalist judges, no matter how arrogant or aristocratic they might behave. Still, Republicans expected their opponents to use their influence on the courts to try to thwart their reforms. These fears seemed confirmed when the District of Columbia's circuit court attempted to indict *National Intelligencer* editor Samuel H. Smith for slander when the Washington paper printed an editorial critical of the Federalist judiciary.

Several Republicans argued in favor of repealing the 1801 Judiciary Act, which would abol-ish the new circuit courts, to get some Federalists off the bench. Jefferson hesitated to sup-port this move, unsure whether Congress could constitutionally deprive judges of their life appointments once they had been duly appointed and confirmed. A decision from Chief Justice Marshall's court convinced Jefferson to overcome his doubts. Led by William Marbury, the four Federalists from whom Secretary Madison was withholding justice of the peace com-missions asked the Supreme Court to grant a writ of mandamus, a court order that would compel Madison to give them the commissions. When the court convened in December 1801, it granted a motion directing Madison to explain why he had not delivered the commissions. President Jefferson was furious with what he saw as the court's attempt to direct the execu-tive branch. With his endorsement, Congress repealed the Judiciary Act in March 1802. Seven weeks later, the Republican majority completed a new Judiciary Act that restored the same basic court structure set up in 1789. The Supreme Court would continue to have six members, and justices had to resume the demands of circuit riding, a practice that would continue for the next sixty-seven years.

Republicans suspected that their elimination of the circuit judgeships might give the Supreme Court an opportunity to declare unconstitutional the 1801 Judiciary Act's repeal. To delay that possibility, Congress passed another law delaying the court's next session until February 1803. Marshall actually had no desire to provoke a showdown with Congress or the president, but he did see an opportunity to enhance the court's prestige through an assertion of judicial review—that is, the power of the courts to determine the constitutionality of laws. The delegates at the Philadelphia Convention had discussed the principle of judicial review, but they did not specifically include the power in the Constitution. Marshall and other Federalists firmly believed the courts should have the final say in determining constitutionality, but several Republicans disagreed, arguing that the Tenth Amendment reserved to the states and to the people "powers not delegated to the United States." Several agreed with Jefferson that each branch of the federal government should decide constitutional questions on its own, subject to the voters' will. Marshall well knew that Jefferson would ignore a controversial assertion of judicial review, and since the court had no authority to enforce its decisions, a direct confrontation with Republicans would only weaken it.

Marshall concluded that he could invoke judicial review—and embarrass the administration in a way Republicans could not oppose—in the case filed by the four Federalists who were denied their justice of the peace commissions. When the court finally convened in February 1803, the chief justice announced the decision in the case of *Marbury v. Madison*: The court could not grant the petitioners' request, and the four would not receive their commissions. But though the outcome pleased Republicans, its reasoning confounded them. In the majority opinion, which Marshall wrote himself, the court acknowledged that Marbury and the other three Federalists had a legal right to their offices: Since the president had signed their commissions and the Senate had confirmed their nominations, they had been duly appointed to their positions. But after implicitly scolding Madison and Jefferson for their failure to carry out the law, the chief justice concluded that the court could not legally grant the plaintiff's request: The four had asked for a writ of mandamus, and the Constitution had not authorized the court to issue these writs. The section of the Judiciary Act of 1789 conferring that power was thus unconstitutional, and the court could make this determination because, Marshall declared, "It is emphatically the province and duty of the judicial department to say what the law is."

Republicans rejected Marshall's argument, and disputes about judicial review continued long afterward. Nevertheless, by invalidating a portion of the 1789 Judiciary Act—the only time it would overturn an act of Congress until 1858—the court aggressively proclaimed its authority to determine constitutionality in a way its opponents could not challenge. Despite Marshall's lectures, the decision gave the administration the result President Jefferson wanted. Six days later, the chief justice further perplexed Republicans when he announced the court's decision in *Stuart v. Laird*, which affirmed the constitutionality of the repeal of the 1801 Judiciary Act. High Federalists expressed frustration with Marshall's apparent timidity, but his decisions ultimately strengthened the court's authority and thus the central government. Though he never again challenged a federal law, under Marshall's leadership the court several times emphasized the Union's supremacy by using judicial review to invalidate state laws.

Marbury v. Madison and *Stuart v. Laird* came at a time when Republicans launched their own offensive against Federalist judges. The Pennsylvania legislature's successful impeachment and conviction of state judge Alexander Addison in January 1803 convinced congressional leaders that they could impeach the most obnoxious Federal jurists. The behavior of New Hampshire district judge John Pickering provided a case that might establish a precedent. Pickering had once been a highly regarded attorney, but since George Washington had appointed him to the bench in 1795, either senility or disease had afflicted his mind. Alcoholism, along with his openly Federalist sentiments, likewise compounded his increasingly erratic and incompetent performance in the courtroom. In one case, he completely disregarded procedure in order to side with an accused Federalist against Republican prosecutors. Jefferson referred Pickering's behavior to the House in February 1803, with a reminder that "the Constitution has confided a power of instituting proceedings of redress." Actually, the Constitution authorized the impeachment of federal officials, including judges, only for "treason, bribery, or other high crimes and misdemeanors," which most understood did not include incompetence. Nevertheless, in a straight party vote, the House approved a series of articles of impeachment that focused on Pickering's misbehavior. The close of the session prevented the Senate from taking up Pickering's case until March 1804, but after a two-week trial the senators convicted Pickering and removed him from his post.

Republicans next targeted Associate Supreme Court Justice Samuel Chase, one of the highest of the High Federalists. As a Maryland delegate to the Second Continental Congress, Chase had signed the Declaration of Independence, but since 1776 his outspoken and abrasive personality had involved him in numerous controversies. President Washington had appointed him to the court in 1796 only because no other qualified candidate was willing to serve, and Republicans despised him for his harsh rulings in the trials of John Fries for his "rebellion" and of Thomas Cooper and James Callender for violating the Sedition Act. In 1800, Chase refused to dismiss a grand jury until a prosecutor exhausted his investigation into seditious libel accusations against a Republican editor; more recently, he had denounced the repeal of the 1801 Judiciary Act in a charge to another grand jury, predicting that "our Republican Constitution will sink into a mobocracy—the worst of all possible governments." Though Chase had committed no "high crimes and misdemeanors," on the day of Pickering's conviction the House approved eight articles of impeachment against Chase. These articles focused on Chase's rulings and political convictions, and most Republicans remained confident that John Pickering's removal would justify a broad reading of the Constitution's impeachment provisions in Chase's trial as well.

This time, though, the Senate trial went badly for Republicans. Virginia congressman John Randolph, the Republicans' unofficial leader in the House, wrote the impeachment articles so broadly that, as Chase's defenders pointed out, a justice could be removed for merely making a mistake. When the trial began in February 1805, Randolph led the prosecution and relied more on oratorical appeals than on a strong legal case. Chase's able defense team meanwhile stressed that, no matter how obnoxious his actions or opinions, the justice had not committed an impeachable offense. Presiding over the trial, Vice President Aaron Burr, whom the administration had largely isolated, emphasized procedure over politics. Several Republican senators, moreover, concluded that removing Chase solely on the basis of his political views would indeed threaten the independence of the judicial branch. Most Republicans voted to convict Chase, but enough broke with the party to keep any of the articles from receiving the two-thirds vote necessary for Chase's removal. Five articles, in fact, failed to secure even a simple majority.

Chase's conviction would have opened the door to more impeachments. Marshall correctly suspected that he would have been Republicans' next victim. Instead, Chase's acquittal established the principle that crimes, not political views, provided the only grounds for impeachment. Nevertheless, time eventually gave Republicans the opportunity to reduce the Federalists' influence on the bench. Before the end of his presidency, Jefferson replaced three retiring Supreme Court justices. Other than in the judicial branch, Federalists presented no serious political threat to Republican ascendancy. Several prominent Federalists retired after

Jefferson's election, convinced that radical democracy and its excesses had triumphed. Some tried to keep up the fight. Alexander Hamilton proposed reviving the party's fortunes through the organization of a "Christian Constitutional Society" to mobilize citizens against Jefferson's presumed atheism, while Massachusetts' Timothy Pickering entered the Senate in 1803 and became the most visible figure in the "Essex Junto," a group of Federalist extremists determined to resist all Republican measures. Younger aspirants, such as Massachusetts' Harrison Gray Otis, South Carolina's John Rutledge and Robert Goodloe Harper, and Delaware's James A. Bayard, tried to match the Republicans' popular appeal through organization and mass campaigning, including setting up cheap newspapers that presented the Federalist case to the common folk. Likewise, through the organization of Washington Benevolent Societies, Federalists combined electioneering and charitable work while reminding voters of their party's association with the popular first president.

These efforts did little. President Jefferson's moderation made Federalist warnings about Republican radicalism seem little more than delusional rants. Peace with Europe and the administration's successes meanwhile raised the president's popularity to a level almost as high as Washington's a decade earlier. Federalism remained strong in New England—where long-recognized leaders, trade ties with Britain, and the endorsement of the established Congregational and Presbyterian churches provided bases for continued resistance. The party also presented a respectable but clear minority in the Middle Atlantic states and in Maryland. Elsewhere, Federalists were reduced to a handful of adherents, with small pockets of support in the South and West. The midterm elections revealed the party's declining fortunes. When the Eighth Congress convened in December 1803, Federalists could claim only 39 seats in a House that expanded to 141 members. In the Senate, Republicans increased their majority to 25–9. Notwithstanding the Federalists' presence in the courts, by the middle of his first term Jefferson's desire to "eradicate" Federalism seemed well on the way to fulfillment.

An Empire of Liberty

Restoring the Union to its "Republican tack" involved more than limiting Federalist influence. Throughout his presidency, Jefferson undertook several positive actions to further what he called an "Empire of Liberty"—that is, a union of free, landholding farmers expanding across North America. As long as farmers—the ideal republican citizens—made up the majority of the male population, President Jefferson believed, the United States would remain a republic. If future population growth outpaced the expansion of US territory, there would not be enough land for each man to support himself and his family, and citizens would have to take jobs in factories and workshops making "luxuries" for the wealthy. Manufacturing would displace agriculture's dominance, and the majority of Americans would find themselves in poverty and dependent upon their employers. Aggressive promotion of agriculture and commerce could delay this fate, so Jefferson's administration concentrated on securing the frontier for farmers while encouraging trade as an outlet for their produce. Small-scale artisans and farmers' "household manufactures"—coarse goods made in their homes—could provide the Union's basic, necessary products. Otherwise, Jefferson admonished, "let our workshops remain in Europe."

President Jefferson's hopes for the Union's future directly contrasted with Alexander Hamilton's vision. Federalists wanted to use western lands as a national asset, selling the land at high prices to bring crucial income to the government. Rapid and chaotic occupation of the west would squander the land sales' potentially high revenues, and the isolated and backward settlements that resulted would undoubtedly expand Republican support. To promote stable, well-organized communities that understood the need for order, Congress passed a Land Act in 1796 that set the minimum price of public lands at $2 an acre and stipulated that it could be bought only in 640-acre parcels. Since few people could afford the $1,280 in cash required upfront to purchase a parcel, only wealthy individuals or land speculating companies could buy the land, both of which would likely sell their holdings to actual settlers in smaller parcels at a higher price per acre. The Land Act's terms proved too restrictive; after a few years of sluggish sales, the lawmakers passed another Land Act in 1800, which reduced the smallest amount purchasable to 320 acres. It also allowed purchases by credit, with one-fourth of the total due at the time of purchase and the remainder payable over the next four years.

Despite the Federalists' intentions, the west continued to be settled, fueled by the Union's rapid population growth. The 1800 census showed that the population had grown to more than five million, a thirty-five percent increase since 1790. Most who headed to the frontier simply squatted on government or speculators' lands and waited for an owner to challenge their occupation. Enough moved into Ohio that the territory became the seventeenth state in 1803. Farther west, a group of settlements around an old French trading post at Vincennes lay in the area that Congress had designated as the Indiana Territory in 1800. In the South, several communities stood at the Muscle Shoals region on the south bend of the Tennessee River, and after 1798 American soldiers occupied the Spanish fortress at Natchez on the Mississippi.

Once in power, Republicans worked to open more of these lands for settlement. The Native presence prevented pioneers from entering either the northern portion of the Indiana Territory or Georgia's western lands, which extended to the Mississippi. To open these areas, President Jefferson appointed several agents to try to persuade Natives to adopt settled agriculture, embrace "civilization," and trade their hunting grounds for lands farther west. Through bribery, intimidation, and encouraging tribal leaders' indebtedness to American traders, Jefferson's agents eventually secured more than fifty land-cession agreements, though Natives' reluctance to part with their tribal lands still limited white Americans' western presence outside of the Ohio, Cumberland, and Tennessee valleys. Nevertheless, Congress made it easier for actual settlers to buy their lands. A new Land Act passed in 1804 reduced the minimum purchase to 160 acres, with a down payment of $80. Secretary Madison, Secretary Gallatin, and Attorney General Lincoln meanwhile negotiated a convention with Georgia in April 1802 to give the United States the title to Georgia's southwestern lands, which Congress in 1798 had designated the Mississippi Territory. In exchange for the land, the United States paid Georgia $1.25 million and agreed to extinguish Native titles in the region—even though the government had agreed in 1791 to "solemnly guarantee" the Cherokee nation's lands in Georgia.

Early in his presidency, Jefferson also demonstrated his willingness to use presidential authority to defend American trade overseas. Since gaining independence in 1783, the United States annually paid a large tribute to the dey of Algiers and the pasha of Tripoli to keep their pirates from raiding American ships in the Mediterranean. Jefferson had long opposed these payments, convinced that a show of strength would force the North African states to back down. About the time Jefferson took office, the brother of the pasha of Tripoli seized the throne. Needing cash, the new pasha demanded a higher payment from the Americans. When President Jefferson refused, the pasha declared war. The president responded by sending four frigates to the Mediterranean with orders to protect American ships and to destroy any hostile vessel, thus beginning what became known as the Tripolitan War.

President Jefferson expected the American ships to reduce the pasha's fleet quickly and inexpensively, but like most wars, the conflict lasted longer than expected. Commodore Richard Dale combined the American ships with a Swedish naval force to impose a blockade on Tripoli, which convinced other Barbary leaders to stay out of the conflict. The blockade could not completely isolate the pasha's ships, however, so a second fleet under the command of Edward Preble in 1802 bombarded the city. Preble's force suffered a major loss in October 1803, when the frigate *Philadelphia* sailed too close to the coast, ran aground, and was captured. A daring raid led by Lieutenant Stephen Decatur destroyed the *Philadelphia* in February 1804 before the pasha could sell it to Britain or France, though its sixty crew members remained captives. Finally, in the spring of 1805, General William Eaton, the former American consul to Tunis, organized a force of American marines and Arab, Greek, and Berber mercenaries to capture the coastal town of Derne. The conquest convinced the pasha to sue for peace. The resulting treaty, completed in June 1805, secured the pasha's agreement to halt his pirates' harassment of American commerce in exchange for $60,000 ransom for the *Philadelphia*'s crew and $5,000 for the right to establish an American consulate in Tripoli.

By that time, a potential crisis had already produced President Jefferson's most important diplomatic achievement. Britain's possession of Canada to the north presented a threat to American security, but the southern and western borders appeared safe as long as Spain held the three other territories that bordered the Union: West Florida (the region east of New Orleans between the Mississippi and the Perdido Rivers), East Florida (the peninsula east of the Perdido), and Louisiana (the vast, vaguely defined region west of the Mississippi). Though Spain once stood as one of Europe's most powerful nations, recent wars showed that Spain's strength had declined. Its colonies in the Caribbean and in Central and South America still made it a force in the western hemisphere, but it could maintain only a small presence in Louisiana and the Floridas. President Jefferson expected these territories one day to become American possessions as the rapidly growing American population filled their lands with American citizens. During Jefferson's first summer in office, however, it came to light that in the secret Treaty of San Ildefonso signed in 1800, France had agreed to conquer Tuscany and give its throne to the Duke of Parma and his Spanish wife; in exchange, Spain would transfer Louisiana to France.

The prospect of French control of Louisiana greatly alarmed President Jefferson. Any sympathy he held for the French Republic had disappeared when Napoleon Bonaparte established himself as a dictator. Having shaped France into the world's strongest military force, Napoleon seemed intent on extending his dominion, and Louisiana's acquisition indicated his desire to assert his authority in the new world. At a minimum, Napoleon could be expected to send an occupation force to New Orleans. A French presence there would block American expansion westward and subject the vital port to the whims of French diplomacy. More ominously, the transfer of Louisiana placed the United States between colonies of Europe's two most formidable enemies. Though the two nations were currently at peace, most Americans expected France's war with Britain to resume soon. When that happened, Americans could anticipate a British conquest of Louisiana, and then the former colonies would be surrounded. Any of these scenarios threatened the Union's security and compromised its independence. The dangers of the French presence seemed realized when, in October 1802, the Spanish *intendant* in Louisiana—in direct violation of the 1795 Treaty of San Lorenzo—revoked the Americans' right of deposit in New Orleans, apparently in preparation for France's occupation of the territory.

Jefferson expressed American displeasure to Louis André Pichon, the French *chargé* in Washington, and instructed the Union's minister in Paris, Robert Livingston, to hint that France's possession of Louisiana might force the United States into an alliance with Britain. But Jefferson recognized France to be a more formidable foe than Algiers, so he hoped to find a diplomatic solution. Hoping his bluff might compel Napoleon to reconsider his arrangement with Spain, in January 1803 the president appointed his friend James Monroe to join Livingston with an offer to buy New Orleans and West Florida for up to $10 million. Before Monroe arrived in Paris, however, the dictator had already decided to abandon his vision of a North American empire. Napoleon had intended to reassert French control over its sugar colonies in the Caribbean, with Louisiana supplying food for the colonies' slave populations. However, the expedition he sent to subdue a rebellion in Saint-Domingue, the country's largest colony, failed miserably and met a bloody end. Now, needing cash for the war he knew would soon resume with Britain and recognizing that he could not hold Louisiana against an enemy invasion, Napoleon instructed France's foreign minister to offer Louisiana to the United States for $15 million—only $5 million more than Monroe was to offer for New Orleans alone.

Though France's offer exceeded their instructions, Livingston and Monroe realized that a delay might give Napoleon time to change his mind, so they quickly accepted his offer without waiting for President Jefferson's approval. Once they completed the negotiations in May, however, the president enthusiastically accepted the agreement. The public then widely praised President Jefferson for peacefully resolving the diplomatic crisis and for gaining a potentially bountiful territory for American use. The deal's only drawback was that it would expand the federal debt. Although $3.75 million of the purchase price would be covered by the general government's assumption of American citizens' claims against the French government for the merchant ships seized during the 1790s, the remainder required an issue of government bonds. Constitutional issues surrounding the purchase also bothered President Jefferson, for nowhere did the Constitution authorize the acquisition of new lands. To alleviate his concerns, he drafted an amendment that would retroactively approve the purchase. His advisers persuaded him that the president's authority to make treaties included the power to acquire new territories, however, so he never sent the amendment to the Senate, which ratified the agreement in October.

His constitutional reservations put to rest, President Jefferson moved quickly to consolidate the Louisiana Purchase. Spain vehemently protested the sale: France had never delivered Tuscany as promised, it argued, so Spain still possessed Louisiana. Moreover, in the Treaty of San Ildefonso, Napoleon promised he would not transfer Louisiana to any other country. Nevertheless, Secretary of State Madison brushed aside complaints from Spanish minister Don Carlos de Casa Yrujo while Jefferson sent additional troops to the Mississippi Territory. Faced with this resolve, the Spaniards backed off, and Americans marched into New Orleans in December. Jefferson then tried to gain control of West Florida, where several rivers that flowed through the Union emptied into the Gulf of Mexico. Claiming that the Louisiana Purchase included West Florida, President Jefferson sent Monroe to Madrid to insist on Spain's yielding the territory, again hinting at a British alliance should Spain refuse. Congress meanwhile passed a Mobile Act in 1804 that authorized the president to establish a customs district in West Florida. When Spain held firm, Jefferson offered Napoleon $2 million if he would pressure Spain to cede the Floridas to the United States. The French emperor demanded more money for his services, though, while Spain strengthened its military presence on the American border. For much of Jefferson's second term, the two nations seemed on the verge of war. Complications with other European powers forced both nations to proceed cautiously; despite President Jefferson's desire for the region, West Florida remained in Spanish hands when he left office.

President Jefferson's frustrations with West Florida did not slow the Union in establishing control over its new lands. In 1804 Congress established the Orleans Territory in the area south of the thirty-third parallel, including New Orleans and most of the region's non-Native inhabitants; the remainder to the north became the Louisiana Territory, with its capital at Saint Louis. President Jefferson meanwhile arranged for an exploratory expedition west of the Mississippi. Long a champion of advancing natural science, even before the Louisiana Purchase he had pushed for an excursion to gain information about the west's geology and its plant and animal life. Now that the Union had a claim to the region, the mission would help secure it for the Union through mapping unknown lands, determining the routes of the Missouri River and its tributaries, and establishing trade with Native peoples now under foreign influence.

Spain had rebuffed President Jefferson's request for permission to explore the lands, but once Louisiana became an American possession, his former private secretary, Captain Meriwether Lewis, joined Captain William Clark to command an expedition that headed up the Missouri River in May 1804. Lewis and Clark's "Corps of Discovery," as their unit came to be known, crossed the Rocky Mountains and reached the Pacific Ocean before returning to Saint Louis in September 1806. The excursion lost only one man and brought back a treasure trove of information about the land, life, and peoples of the West.

Jefferson hoped that similar exploratory excursions to the Southwest beyond the Red River might strengthen his claim that Texas was also included as part of the Louisiana Territory purchased from Spain. General James Wilkinson, the governor of the Louisiana Territory, thus sent Lieutenant Zebulon Pike on two missions, one north to find the source of the Mississippi River and another southwest to find the headwaters of the Arkansas and Red Rivers. The European presence in North America, however, prevented these ventures from repeating Lewis and Clark's success. Pike's first mission left Saint Louis in the fall of 1805 and spent several months looking for the Mississippi's origin, but he could not proceed when they came upon several forts in lands Britain claimed were part of Canada. Thomas Freemon and William Dunbar led a company across the Red River in May 1806, but they were forced to turn back in July when confronted by a Spanish force. Pike's second expedition met the same fate as Freemon's and Dunbar's mission. After spending seven months exploring the mountains in northern Mexico, Pike and his men were captured by a Spanish army and held for four months. Pike's expeditions still significantly advanced the mapping of lands previously unknown to Americans, but the frustrated excursions convinced President Jefferson to accept the Red River as Louisiana's western boundary.

The Louisiana Purchase's popularity, the administration's overall success, and the Federalists' weakness assured Republicans that Jefferson would face no serious challenge to his re-election in 1804. Publicly, the president remained silent about his candidacy; privately, he dropped hints in January of the election year that he would not refuse another term. Republicans had already taken precautions to avoid the confusion that nearly cost him the office four years earlier. In December 1803, Congress passed a constitutional amendment directing presidential electors to cast one vote each for president and vice president, rather than two votes for president. The revised method would prevent an electoral college tie between party nominees like the one between Jefferson and Burr in 1800. The necessary thirteen states completed the Twelfth Amendment's ratification by September 1804, well in time for the election. Long before then, on February 25, Republican congressmen met in caucus formally to nominate Jefferson for a second term. But the caucus refused to re-nominate Burr. In fact, the incumbent received no votes, and the caucus chose retiring New York governor George Clinton to replace Burr as the Republicans' vice-presidential candidate.

Burr's refusal four years earlier to withdraw from the presidential election in Jefferson's favor had destroyed his credibility among Republicans. Once in office, President Jefferson kept Burr at a distance and, until the vice president presided over the trial of Samuel Chase, followed few of his patronage recommendations. Burr's isolation, along with his reputation as a political maverick, gave some Federalists hope that he might aid their plan to escape a Union dominated by their enemies. Timothy Pickering and his Essex Junto secretly encouraged a plot to get the New England states to secede; cooperation with Burr's New York would enhance the scheme's prospects for success and create a stronger confederacy that might convince Britain's maritime Canadian colonies to join. To stir up popular hostility between North and South, Federalists persuaded the Massachusetts legislature to pass resolutions calling for the elimination of the Constitution's three-fifths clause and for slavery's prohibition in the Louisiana Territory. Then, they sounded out Burr to see whether he might lead New York out of the Union. Though the vice president's replies were elusive and noncommittal, New York Federalists endorsed Burr as their candidate in the April 1804 gubernatorial election.

To Pickering's dismay, the Essex Junto's plot never caught on. With the Union at peace and prosperous, New England voters displayed little resentment toward Virginia's Republicans, despite their association with slavery. Most Federalists opposed calls for secession, and several party leaders opposed dealing with Burr. Alexander Hamilton, in fact, vehemently denounced Burr's candidacy and went to great lengths to discredit the vice president. Republicans easily defeated Burr in the election, but the loss doomed more than the secession plot. Hamilton's rhetoric infuriated Burr, and once the results were in, the vice president challenged the former Treasury secretary to a duel. Meeting at Weehawken, New Jersey, on July 11, Burr shot and killed the Federalists' champion.

The loss of their central figure further demoralized Federalists. Party leaders made no arrangements for a congressional caucus or any other formal method to nominate candidates. In the spring, Federalist newspapers put forward South Carolina's Charles Cotesworth Pinckney and New York's Rufus King as their presidential and vice-presidential nominees, but beyond bitter denunciations of the incumbent, Federalists presented only a token campaign. Most Federalist rhetoric reflected frustration more than a serious attempt to win. Amid the usual charges against Jefferson's "radicalism" and "atheism," opposition editors picked up a charge from disgruntled Republican editor James Callender to attack the president's character. Callender turned against Jefferson when the president refused to appoint him as Richmond's postmaster. To retaliate, Callender's Richmond *Recorder* charged that Jefferson had fathered several children with Sally Hemings, a slave at Monticello. Jefferson never responded to Callender's attacks, either privately or in public, though a 1998 study comparing the DNA of Hemings' descendants with samples from the Jefferson family indicates the charge was likely true. Republicans and voters nevertheless dismissed the accusation, and in the election Jefferson carried every state except Connecticut and Delaware. Republicans meanwhile increased their congressional majorities to 116–25 in the House and 27–7 in the Senate.

Ironically, Federalist weakness began to reveal cracks in Republican unity. In many states, the absence of serious opposition produced factional divisions in the party for control of state politics. The most serious divisions appeared in New York. Aaron Burr's recent dalliance with Federalism showed the dangers of fragmentation. New York's two major Republican factions, the Clintonians and the Livingstons, managed to come together to defeat Burr in 1804, but in Pennsylvania Federalist support helped re-elect Governor Thomas McKean in 1805 after the Republican majority rejected McKean because of his patronage decisions and his refusal to support a reform of the state's courts. Similar tensions simmered among Republicans in Rhode Island, Delaware, and Virginia, and the administration feared that the divisions might lead to the formation of a third national party to challenge Republican leadership.

The frustrations of several Southern Republican congressmen reinforced these concerns. Members like House Speaker Nathaniel Macon, John Randolph of Virginia, and Joseph H. Nicholson of Maryland firmly believed in states' rights and strict construction, and they expressed disappointment with President Jefferson's apparent compromises with centralization and Federalism, such as his retention of the Bank of the United States. Randolph became particularly infuriated with party moderates when the Senate refused to approve his case in the impeachment of Justice Chase. He likewise denounced the president's attempt to bribe Napoleon for help securing West Florida, and for more than a month his obstruction delayed the appropriation of the funds the president needed. In April 1806 he proclaimed himself in open opposition to the president, labeling those who joined him as *Tertium Quids*—the Latin term for a "third something"—between Republicans and Federalists. Randolph's third party never gained a widespread following. His insistence on ideological purity prevented either faction in New York or Pennsylvania from joining with him, while various divisions on specific issues likewise kept dissenters from uniting across state lines. His ranting speeches and erratic behavior further isolated potential allies, and the Quid faction in Congress consisted of only a handful of representatives. Jefferson tried to woo them back, but he eventually appointed Nicholson to a district judgeship to get him out of Congress and accepted Macon's replacement as House speaker.

Other Southern Republicans, though, also expressed concern over the administration's course. In his second inaugural address, Jefferson called for government funding to construct "rivers, canals, manufactures, education, and other grand objects." To pay for these projects, the president recommended a constitutional amendment that would authorize distributing federal revenues to the states. Congress instead authorized funds in 1806 to build a road from Cumberland, Maryland, to Wheeling, Virginia, on the Ohio River, which became the foundation for a National Road across the center of the Union. The next year, the Senate asked Secretary Gallatin to prepare a comprehensive report on roads and canals. The subsequent "Report on Transportation," submitted in 1808, proposed for the federal government to fund and construct a vast network of "internal improvements" east of the Mississippi. Jefferson himself expressed little interest in Gallatin's proposals, so the dissenters mainly blamed Madison and Gallatin for trying to persuade the president to abandon his state-rights principles. These "Old Republicans," as the Southern extremists came to be known, continued to support the administration but pledged to work against Madison's election as Jefferson's successor, which Jefferson desired and most Republicans expected. Along with the Quids and the various state factions, they at first presented mostly an annoyance to the administration. Over time, though, the dissenters complicated President Jefferson's efforts to deal with the problems and frustrations of his second term.

Conspiracy and Crisis

Much of the frustration of President Jefferson's second administration stemmed from circumstances beyond his control. In some cases, his own decisions compounded his troubles. Possibly, he unwittingly assisted in the early stages of a conspiracy involving his first vice president. Rejected for another term, defeated in his bid to become New York's governor, and, after his duel with Hamilton, under indictment for murder in both New York and New Jersey, Aaron Burr turned his attention to the lands recently acquired from France. After his deadly encounter with Hamilton, Burr returned to Washington, where one of his last responsibilities as vice president would be to preside over Justice Samuel Chase's impeachment trial. Apparently to gain Burr's assistance, President Jefferson agreed to appoint several of Burr's associates to choice positions in the new territories. Most significantly, the governorship of Louisiana went to Burr's long-time friend James Wilkinson, the commanding general of the army. Jefferson brushed aside criticism for appointing a military officer to a civil position, noting that the governor's main task would be to defend the sparsely populated region. But unknown to Jefferson, Wilkinson acted as a paid agent for Spanish colonial officials, providing information on American military strategy as well as offering suggestions on how to counter the Union's western expansion. Also unknown to the president, the general and the vice president might have been laying plans for the western territories' separation from the United States.

The exact objectives of Burr's scheme remain unclear. Burr always maintained that his chief purpose was to develop lands he purchased in 1806 in the Orleans Territory while raising a military force to defend the west in case of a war with Spain. Later testimony and various documents suggest that he planned to lead an invasion of Mexico, the northern portion of Spain's colonial empire. Rumors circulated that he intended to lead the states west of the Appalachians out of the Union to form his own empire. Most likely he planned to coordinate an excursion against Mexico with an uprising against American authority in New Orleans. William C.C. Claiborne, governor of the Orleans Territory, faced strong opposition from American speculators and from French refugees who had fled either Napoleon or the slave rebellion in Saint-Domingue. The dissenters demanded immediate statehood so they could get control of the area through a state government. Since President Jefferson's demands for West Florida made a war with Spain probable, Burr could raise support for a volunteer army, ostensibly in support of the Union but mainly to assist the dissidents in a coup in New Orleans. With financial and naval assistance from Britain, he and Wilkinson could then conquer Mexico—not for the Union, but to create their own domain.

During Burr's last few weeks in office, he sounded out western politicians to gauge their interest, and he and Wilkinson copied maps of the west. The vice president also met with British minister Anthony Merry, who approved the plan and promised to encourage his government's endorsement. Then, once his term expired in March, Burr headed for New Orleans by way of Pittsburgh, Cincinnati, Louisville, Lexington, Nashville, and Natchez, meeting with local leaders about the possibility of raising an army. To most he revealed little of his true intentions, stressing instead the need for an attack on Mexico when the expected war with Spain came. After talking with dissidents in New Orleans, Burr returned to Washington, where in November he met with Jefferson several times over dinner. Neither left a record of their conversations, but the president perhaps knew of the plan to invade Mexico while unaware of Burr's more grandiose designs. But any conspiracy Burr had planned soon unraveled. From Jefferson, Burr most likely learned that the administration would attempt to bargain with Napoleon for Florida, making war with Spain unlikely. At the same time, Merry informed him that the British government rejected the plot and would provide no assistance.

For the next several months, Burr tried to salvage his project until Spain's decision to occupy Texas in May 1806 revived the prospect of war that he needed. President Jefferson ordered General Wilkinson to take his army south and to hold the Sabine River as the Orleans Territory's western boundary. Since Spanish troops had already crossed the river, war seemed imminent. Burr notified his comrades in July that the time had come to launch their plan: Burr would go west to raise his army, rendezvous with Wilkinson's troops at Natchez, and lead their combined armies toward New Orleans. Whatever their scheme, Wilkinson had already concluded that he needed to betray Burr to protect himself, likely recognizing that carrying out the plot would only reveal his duplicity to the American government. Rumors of Burr's intentions circulated throughout the west, and the general delayed taking his army south for four months, giving the Spanish time to retreat across the Sabine. When the general did move south, he worked out a truce with the Spanish commander to recognize disputed territory as "neutral ground." Then, he notified the president of Burr's plot, stressing that a rebellion in New Orleans was to "be made an auxiliary step to the main design of attacking Mexico"—and that, contrary to rumors, Wilkinson himself had no role in the conspiracy. Moving his army to New Orleans, Wilkinson ordered Burr's arrest while apprehending Burr's associates in the city.

Jefferson had heard earlier reports of Burr's apparent scheme, but Wilkinson's report forced him to act. In November the president issued a proclamation warning westerners against supporting an unauthorized attack on Spanish possessions, and in January 1807 he proclaimed Burr guilty of treason when he notified Congress of the conspiracy. Burr meanwhile moved through the west, unaware of Wilkinson's betrayal. While one of his followers, an Irish immigrant named Harman Blennerhassett, gathered men and supplies on his island in the Ohio River, a Federalist district attorney in Lexington ordered Burr arrested for planning an illegal military operation. A grand jury dismissed the case, but the arrest and delay damaged the former vice president's credibility. Once President Jefferson's November proclamation reached the frontier, the western leaders who had once welcomed Burr now kept their distance. Ohio's governor ordered the seizure of the supplies on Blennerhassett's Island. Blennerhassett and about thirty men slipped away and joined with Burr's small force at Jeffersonville in the Indiana Territory, but when Burr's "army" of about sixty men reached Natchez, they learned of Wilkinson's treachery. The troops surrendered to the Mississippi Territory's acting governor; Burr himself fled but was apprehended near Mobile in February on his way to board a ship to Europe.

Because Blennerhassett's Island lay in Virginia's judicial district, Burr's captors took him to Richmond for trial. Furious with Burr's duplicity, Jefferson actively worked to secure Burr's conviction for treason, a charge that could result in his execution. The president had already proclaimed his belief in Burr's guilt; behind the scenes, he helped gather evidence for the prosecution while publicly defending the questionable conduct of the government's star witness, the less-than-honorable Wilkinson. But Jefferson met a formidable adversary in Chief Justice Marshall, whose circuit court responsibilities made him the presiding judge at Burr's trial. Marshall honored a defense motion to subpoena President Jefferson to testify before a grand jury about documents implicating Wilkinson's guilt. The president ignored the order, but at the trial the chief justice ruled that merely planning or assembling men failed to satisfy the Constitution's definition of treason: an "overt act" against the government that could be confirmed by two witnesses. The prosecutors presented a strong circumstantial case, but the inability to prove an "overt act" meant they could not meet Marshall's high standard of what constituted treason. Although predisposed to find Burr guilty, on September 1, 1807, the jury returned a verdict of "not proved," which Marshall officially recorded as "not guilty."

Disappointed with the failure to secure Burr's conviction, President Jefferson sent the trial's proceedings to Congress with a hint that it could provide grounds for Marshall's impeachment. A crisis in the Union's foreign relations, however, distracted Republicans from going after the chief justice. As expected, France and Britain resumed their war in 1803. The hostilities once again presented an opportunity for Americans to prosper: Farmers could expect high prices for grain and cotton sales to the belligerents, while merchants could make tremendous profit from carrying Caribbean colonial produce to their mother countries. Trade with Europe did expand dramatically, even though Britain declared a blockade of all French ports and again invoked its Rule of 1756, which prohibited wartime trade between a neutral nation and a British enemy if the nations had not conducted that trade in peacetime. Since 1800, British officials had quietly tolerated the American carrying trade, so long as merchant ships first carried goods to an American port then reloaded cargoes onto another ship for transportation to their final destination. Soon after President Jefferson's second term began, however, the commercial provisions in Jay's Treaty expired, leaving the Union with no trade agreement with Britain. Then, in July 1805, a British admiralty court ruled in the case of the impounded American ship *Essex* that a "broken voyage" no longer exempted a neutral vessel from the Rule of 1756.

In the months following the announcement of the *Essex* decision, Britain captured more than sixty American merchant ships. The renewed aggression accompanied an expansion of Britain's long-standing and more offensive practice of impressing sailors from American crews. Harsh conditions, poor pay, and the horrors of battle limited the number of volunteers in the British navy, so commanders had long relied on press gangs to kidnap British subjects and force them into service. Many seamen would desert while in American ports, and some would later sign on to work on merchant vessels. American authorities recognized British captains' right to search for deserters on American ships while in port, but since the 1790s several British warships had stopped American ships at sea, not only to apprehend deserters but also to impress American citizens into the British navy. The practice seemed particularly galling, partly because Britain refused to acknowledge their subjects' naturalization as American citizens, but also because impressed sailors—unlike merchants, who could appeal to British admiralty courts for compensation for their losses—had no legal recourse for their fate. Like their commanders, who haughtily dismissed American captains' complaints, the British government paid little attention to diplomats' protests. The British navy had already impressed thousands of American crewmen since 1793, and with the resumption of war British seizures only intensified.

The war with Tripoli had shown that President Jefferson would use force to defend the Union's rights at sea. But Jefferson recognized that either Britain or France presented a greater challenge than did the Barbary pirates, especially since Gallatin's budget cuts had reduced the army and the navy to the point where neither could seriously threaten the European powers. The president hoped, too, that commercial pressure might avoid war while protecting American interests. Forty years earlier, in the 1760s, agreements among the American colonies to cut off trade with the mother country had forced Britain to concede to colonial demands. Now, Jefferson reasoned, the Union might likewise use its economic resources to force the belligerents to respect its neutral status. As an agricultural people, Americans provided vital food resources to both belligerents; the carrying trade likewise helped both powers get important products from their colonies. Britain's economy meanwhile depended on its sale of goods that Jefferson described as "luxuries," which he believed Americans could easily sacrifice. Cutting off the Union's imports or exports could thus severely damage the belligerents' economies while having only a minor impact on Americans' fortunes. The mere threat of a boycott might be enough to compel Britain and France to stop their harassment of American merchants and to respect American neutral rights. But if the Union did actually close its trade, the policy would at least keep American ships and sailors at home, preventing their capture and impressment.

The threat of losing American trade seemed an even more powerful weapon when the European conflict entered a new phase in late 1805. On October 21, Admiral Horatio Nelson's British fleet virtually destroyed the combined French and Spanish navies at the battle of Trafalgar off the coast of Spain in the Mediterranean. Six weeks later, Napoleon's army defeated an Austrian force at the Battle of Austerlitz, making France the unrivaled military machine on the continent. Since neither power wanted to fight against its enemy's strength, both turned to cutting off trade to starve the other off in a war of attrition. Napoleon attempted to institute what became known as the Continental System, which would exclude Britain from commerce while developing France as the principal supplier of Europe's manufactured goods. To implement the Continental System, he issued the Berlin Decree on November 21, 1806, declaring a blockade on the British Isles and forbidding any European nation under French influence from importing British goods. Britain retaliated with a series of orders-in-council that tightened Britain's blockade of France and even further restricted European trade with neutral countries, especially the United States. With each power attempting to cripple the other's economy, President Jefferson hoped that both sides would have an even greater need for American trade and would gladly respect American merchants in order to secure the Union's assistance.

President Jefferson hesitated to impose trade restrictions, since the policy might provoke an aggressive response that could undermine his efforts to acquire West Florida. Instead, he wanted to keep the threat of a boycott as a background for the negotiations conducted by James Monroe, whom he had sent to London following an unsuccessful mission in Madrid. Several Republicans in Congress nevertheless pushed for immediate action. One faction, led by Maryland senator Samuel Smith, the brother of the secretary of the navy, pressed for a naval buildup so the Union could negotiate from a position of strength. This plan gained support after an incident in New York harbor on April 1: H.M.S. *Leander* fired a warning shot to indicate its intention to search an American merchant vessel, but the shot accidentally hit the ship and killed a crewman. President Jefferson ordered the *Leander* to leave American waters and demanded its captain be court-martialed. Still, the president hoped to negotiate an agreement, fearing that Smith's overly aggressive stance might provoke a strong response from Britain. To his relief, Congress ultimately rejected the senator's demands and instead in April 1806 passed a Non-Importation Act, which prohibited the importation of all but the most important British goods. To give negotiations a chance, the lawmakers immediately suspended the act's implementation until the following November. As a concession to Senator Smith's supporters, however, President Jefferson agreed to appoint William Pinckney, a Maryland Federalist, to join Monroe at the talks in London.

By the time Pinckney arrived in London in August, the administration's moderation seemed on the verge of success. Madison's instructions to Pinckney and Monroe stressed impressment as the Union's principal grievance. The two were to secure severe restrictions on the practice while asking for compensation for American ships seized since the *Essex* decision. Charles James Fox, Britain's recently appointed foreign minister and a longtime American sympathizer, refused to make any concessions on impressment, but he apologized for the *Leander* incident and promised to investigate its captain's conduct. After Fox's death in September, British representatives proved willing to concede resumption of American merchants' "broken voyages," to grant the Union most-favored-nation status, and to prohibit the stopping of unarmed ships within five miles of the American coast. Monroe's experience in Paris had persuaded him that President Jefferson would accept a good treaty, even if it did not conform to their instructions, so he and Pinckney agreed to renounce imposing commercial restrictions on Britain for the next ten years. Convinced they had made the best bargain possible, the two signed the treaty on December 31, certain that they had secured peace. To their dismay, however, the president found the treaty unacceptable. Not only did it fail to address impressment, which increasingly symbolized Britain's disregard for American neutral rights, the treaty's renunciation of commercial restrictions bargained away the Union's ability to use its chief diplomatic weapon. The president rejected it without bothering to send it to the Senate.

Over the next several months, Britain's hardening attitude confirmed President Jefferson's suspicions and brought Anglo-American relations to a crisis. In Norfolk, Virginia, several British sailors jumped ship and enlisted in the US Navy. Captain Salusbury P. Humphreys, the commander of H.M.S. *Leopard*, learned that several of the deserters were serving on U.S.S. *Chesapeake*, so on June 22, 1807, the *Leopard* hailed the *Chesapeake* as it left port, demanding permission to inspect its crew. The *Chesapeake's* commander, Captain James Barron, refused Humphreys' request, but the *Leopard* then opened fire, killing three sailors and wounding eighteen others. The crippled ship could return only a single shot and had no choice but to yield. The *Leopard's* boarding party then seized three Americans and one Briton. Tried for desertion in Halifax, the three Americans were sentenced to receive five hundred lashes and the British subject was hanged.

The unprovoked assault in American waters outraged the public. Stopping a merchant ship, although it was disturbing, could be justified by international law; attacking a warship was an act of aggression that appeared to reveal Britain's complete disregard for American independence. Protest meetings and newspaper editorials demanded war to avenge American honor. Nevertheless, President Jefferson once again hesitated. He agreed that the affront demanded a strong response, but he also recognized that American armed forces remained unprepared for war. Instead of calling an emergency session of Congress, Jefferson recalled all American ships to port and issued an order barring British ships from American waters. Madison meanwhile launched a formal protest with the British government and again demanded an end to impressment. George Canning, Britain's new foreign minister, disavowed the attacks and promised to investigate the conduct of the *Leopard's* captain as well as his superior officer, while naval officials commuted the sentences of the three Americans taken in the *Chesapeake* incident before releasing them. But Canning refused to retreat on impressment, and Britain tightened even further its efforts to curtail American shipping. In November, a new order-in-council required any neutral ship trading with a European nation to stop and pay a duty in a British port before completing its journey. Napoleon's response, the Milan Decree of December 1807, subjected to French seizure any ship that acquiesced in the recent British order. Any American merchant vessel, regardless of its destination, was now open to capture and forfeiture.

By the fall, President Jefferson seemed ready for war. But public sentiment had cooled since the *Chesapeake* incident, and now he doubted whether a declaration of war could pass Congress. The time had come, he concluded, to implement economic coercion. The Non-importation Act, which had been in effect since November 1806, had already eliminated the importation of several British goods. Now, after Congress convened in December 1807, the president moved to expand commercial retaliation by recommending the imposition of an embargo on the sale of American products to all foreign nations. According to the proposal, no American ship could participate in foreign trade, and no American goods could leave the United States. The ban would halt the attacks on American merchant ships, while the prohibition of exports would supposedly hurt Britain, presumably the nation most dependent on American supplies. President Jefferson hoped that the harm to Britain's war effort might also compel France to adopt a more conciliatory stance toward American shipping and perhaps persuade Napoleon to assist in his efforts to acquire Florida. Prohibiting trade with all nations, moreover, would keep both Britain and France from acquiring American products through a third party. With few alternatives, Congress approved the Embargo Act after only four days of debate. After the president signed the act into law on December 22, American ships could not travel to foreign ports unless they received special permission from Jefferson himself.

Though President Jefferson never adequately explained the policy's intentions, the public at first generally supported his embargo. Nations often imposed an embargo before declaring war, and most expected the cessation of trade to last only a short time. But the American economy depended on foreign trade more than President Jefferson realized. By the spring of 1808, the prohibition of exports sent the economy into a depression. With foreign markets eliminated and some importations permitted, prices and property values collapsed, while capital drained from the country. Popular protests condemned the "Dambargo" and ridiculed the "cursed Ograbme"—*embargo* spelled backward—as the source of the Union's woes. As the protests increased, President Jefferson became more convinced that the embargo could succeed only if the government intensified its enforcement. Congress passed several additional acts to close loopholes left unaddressed in the original law, imposing severe penalties on violators. Treasury Secretary Gallatin loyally tried to carry out the laws' provisions, even though he had argued against the policy, but President Jefferson personally reviewed and mostly denied requests from captains for permission to clear port. Federalists gleefully noted how a Republican president now used the army as a police force and interfered in citizens' lives more than ever expected by his opponents. A more stinging rebuke came when William Johnson, President Jefferson's first appointee to the Supreme Court, ruled that the president had overstepped his legal authority when he ordered Charleston's customs collector to deny clearance for a ship that had met all the legal requirements for taking a load of rice and cotton to Baltimore.

None of the resistance weakened Jefferson's resolve. But he had miscalculated the European powers' response. The war had already closed most of France's Atlantic commerce, and since Napoleon now controlled the European continent, he no longer needed American supplies. In fact, the emperor sarcastically claimed he would help enforce the American embargo when in April 1808 he issued the Bayonne Decree, ordering the seizure of any American ship in a European harbor. The embargo did negatively affect Britain, where bread prices increased due to the stoppage of American grain shipments, while sales of goods to the Union

Figure 3.3 "The Happy Effects of that Grand Systom [sic] of Shutting Ports against the English!!" British cartoon showing Jefferson defending the embargo from complaints against its economic consequences. Etching by George Cruickshank, published by Walker and Cornhull (1808). Courtesy Prints & Photographs Division, Library of Congress, LC-USZ62-121460.

decreased. Still, the Nonimportation Act permitted British shipments of woolen cloth, cotton cloth, and iron, the products Americans imported most heavily. Revolutions in Central and South America meanwhile opened Spain's Latin American colonies to British merchants, helping them make up the losses from the American trade. Despite Jefferson's determination, enough goods were smuggled out of the Union to weaken the embargo's effects. Whatever the embargo's impact, the British were too determined to defeat Napoleon to accede to American demands. Ironically, one of the embargo's main effects was to encourage capital investment in manufacturing, promoting the type of self-sufficiency Hamilton's Federalists desired. But to Jefferson's horror, his political opponents became the embargo's chief benefactors. Focusing on the policy's unpopularity, in the 1808 elections Federalists doubled their number in the House of Representatives.

Republicans remained the Union's dominant party. Despite the Federalists' modest revival, the minority still only held 48 of 142 House seats. And, despite public disapproval of the embargo, James Madison safely won the 1808 election and would succeed Jefferson as president. Worn down by the frustrations of his second term, President Jefferson looked forward to retirement. Until the date arrived for Madison's inauguration, the Republicans' champion remained committed to enforcing the embargo, believing it would eventually force Britain to give in to American demands. But he realized his political limits, and he offered no resistance when on March 1, 1809, only three days before the end of his presidency, Congress repealed the Embargo Act.

Though his last major policy failed, President Jefferson had accomplished much during his eight years in office. His administration could not completely dismantle the structure his

Federalist predecessors had built, but with him at the helm Republicans significantly reduced the size and influence of the central government, restored the states' pre-eminence in domestic affairs, defended the Union's honor in war, added and explored a vast new territory, and dramatically reduced the Union's debt. Over the next generation, Jeffersonian Republican principles became national ideals. Still, Republican policies left the Union weak in a hostile world. The international difficulties President Jefferson had faced would continue to plague his successor. Eventually, they presented the young Union with its most serious challenge.

Suggested Readings

Allison, Robert J. *The Crescent Obscured: The United States and the Muslim World, 1776–1815* (Chicago, 1995).

Ben-Atar, Doron S. *The Origins of Jeffersonian Commercial Policy and Diplomacy* (New York, 1993).

Cogliano, Francis. *Thomas Jefferson: Reputation and Legacy* (Charlottesville, 2006).

Gordon-Reed, Annette. *Thomas Jefferson and Sally Hemings: An American Controversy* (Charlottesville, 1997).

Kaplan, Lawrence S. *Thomas Jefferson: Westward the Course of Empire* (Wilmington, DE, 1998).

Kastor, Peter J. *The Nation's Crucible: The Louisiana Purchase and the Creation of America* (New Haven, 2004).

Kukla, Jon. *Mr. Jefferson's Women* (New York, 2007).

McCoy, Drew R. *The Elusive Republic: Political Economy in Jeffersonian America* (Chapel Hill, 1980).

McDonald, Forrest. *The Presidency of Thomas Jefferson* (Lawrence, KS, 1976).

Miller, John Chester. *The Wolf by the Ears: Thomas Jefferson and Slavery* (New York, 1977).

Onuf, Peter S., ed. *Jeffersonian Legacies* (Charlottesville, 1993).

Sloan, Herbert E. *Principle and Interest: Thomas Jefferson and the Problem of Debt* (New York, 1995).

Spivak, Burton. *Jefferson's English Crisis: Commerce, Embargo, and the Republican Revolution* (Charlottesville, 1979).

Tucker, Robert W., and David C. Henderson. *Empire of Liberty: The Statecraft of Thomas Jefferson* (New York, 1990).

Wallace, Anthony F. C. *Jefferson and the Indians: The Tragic Fate of the First Americans* (Cambridge, MA, 1999).

IV

THE UNION IN PERIL

No one played a greater role in creating the US Constitution than James Madison. His work as an adviser to President Washington, as leader of the Democratic-Republican opposition, and as secretary of state under President Jefferson made him one of the central figures in the founding of the federal government. Still, he never gained the popularity or the personal following of the giants of his era. Even though he had taken a leading role in establishing the Republican Party, many considered him Thomas Jefferson's protégé. His inauguration as the fourth president did little to dispel this notion. In a ten-minute inaugural address, President Madison reiterated the Republican principles that President Jefferson had announced eight years earlier and concluded with an acknowledgment of his predecessor's "exalted talents." At that evening's ball, Jefferson beamed so happily that Margaret Bayard Smith, the wife of Maryland's senior senator, observed that "a father never loved a son more than he loves Mr. Madison." The new president himself seemed uncomfortable with the affair, appearing "spiritless and exhausted" and telling one visitor that he preferred to be home in bed. Attendants expressed more interest in the new, young, and vivacious first lady than in the president. Seventeen years younger than her husband, Dolly Payne Madison charmed the guests with her social grace and outgoing manner, with Smith approvingly noting that she "looked a queen" in her Parisian gown.

Notwithstanding his wife's allure, Madison entered the presidency in a weak position at a critical time. The embargo he had championed had failed to force Great Britain to respect American maritime rights, and the tensions among Republicans that President Jefferson had smoothed over now stood ready to challenge the new president's authority. Over the next eight years, President Madison would never gain the reputation of a strong and decisive leader who could unite his party. Yet despite a potentially disastrous war, a threat of secession, and a seemingly inconclusive peace, the Union emerged from Madison's presidency stronger, more unified, and with a greater sense of nationalism than Americans had expressed since 1776. President Madison committed some errors, but good fortune and his effective leadership allowed him to retire with more popular approval than President Jefferson. More significantly, the Union he had worked so hard to create escaped many of the threats it had faced since the Revolution, and he left it in a position to become the dominant North American nation.

A New Captain at the Helm

Thomas Jefferson's influence helped carry Madison into the presidency. When he announced his intention to retire in November 1807, President Jefferson gave no formal announcement of his preference for a successor, but privately no one doubted his desire for Secretary of State Madison's election. A caucus of congressional Republicans nominated the secretary of state on January 23, 1808, and endorsed incumbent George Clinton for another term as vice president. Not all Republicans accepted President Jefferson's wishes. New Yorkers particularly resented watching another Virginian ascend to the presidency while one of their own remained in the second spot. DeWitt Clinton, the vice president's nephew and a prominent New York politician, wanted the office, but George Clinton's years of service compelled him to promote his uncle's elevation to the presidency, despite his age and poor health. Quids and Southern "Old Republicans" meanwhile denounced Madison as an apostate who had led President Jefferson away from pure Republican principles. They instead promoted Virginian James Monroe, who still resented Madison and Jefferson for rejecting the treaty he negotiated with Britain in 1806. Neither Monroe nor Clinton took any steps to halt the movements promoting their candidacies. Neither challenger could gain enough Republican support to win, but Federalist backing might carry either to victory or at least prevent Madison from gaining a majority in the electoral college, which would leave the choice to the House of Representatives.

Although the embargo's effects worsened through the year, the rival candidates failed to derail Madison's election. In fact, the embargo actually strengthened Madison's claims, for the prospect of a Federalist revival emphasized the need for Republican unity. Monroe never gained much support outside of Virginia, where he still remained the second choice, but President Jefferson effectively destroyed Monroe's chances when he submitted Madison's diplomatic correspondence to Congress to deflect charges that the secretary of state had mishandled negotiations with Britain. Clinton kept open the possibility of his serving in either office, but eventually he had to repudiate his supporters' diatribes against Madison to ensure his own election to at least the vice presidency. Once Federalists realized the limits of Clinton's following among Republicans, they abandoned any thought of endorsing him and instead again re-nominated their candidates from 1804, Charles Cotesworth Pinckney and Rufus King. Federalist condemnation of the embargo and accusations of Republican subservience to France proved unable to counter the Republican majority. Six New York electors remained loyal to Clinton, while Pinckney and King carried Delaware and four of the five New England states. Nevertheless, Madison carried the remaining 122 votes to win a comfortable majority in the electoral college.

The challenges reflected widespread uncertainty about Madison. Mainstream Republicans expressed little enthusiasm for the new president. A brilliant political theorist, Madison won praise for his dedication and hard work, but his thin, low voice and his tendency to remain silent in large gatherings gave him a reputation for being cold, bookish, and standoffish. His physical appearance contrasted sharply with President Washington's robust physique and also with the tall and lanky President Jefferson. At five-foot-four and barely one hundred pounds, he would be the shortest person ever to serve as president. He looked much younger than his fifty-seven years, and he suffered from what one biographer labeled "epileptoid hysteria," which caused seizures similar to those of epilepsy. Never comfortable with popular politics, he did little to cultivate a following, and as president he seldom left the grounds of the President's Mansion while in Washington. In small gatherings, he displayed a warm and friendly personality, and after his evening wine he frequently entertained guests with anecdotes that one visitor described as the "habitual smut" common among Virginia planters. Lacking President Jefferson's stature and persuasiveness, however, he never earned the reverence his predecessor enjoyed among Republicans. His strong belief in the separation of powers, moreover, joined his distaste for intrigue to restrain him from trying to manage the legislative branch. Many thought the presidency would overwhelm Madison. Others expected him to be little more than President Jefferson's puppet.

Aware of President Madison's weakness, several Republicans defied his leadership even before the inauguration. The new president wanted Treasury Secretary Albert Gallatin to replace him as secretary of state. Old Republicans distrusted Gallatin as much as they did the new president, but the main opposition to Gallatin's promotion came from a corps of senators who came to be known as the "Malcontents," or "Invisibles," which included Virginia's William B. Giles, Pennsylvania's Michael Leib, and Maryland's Samuel Smith. This faction had tepidly supported Madison's election, but they despised the Swiss-born Gallatin, partly due to personal conflicts, partly due to resentment at his accomplishments, but also because the Treasury secretary refused to go along with their patronage demands and their calls for increased spending for military preparations. Fearing that the Malcontents might persuade the Senate to reject the appointment, President Madison decided to have Gallatin continue as Treasury secretary, where he would not need Senate confirmation. In an attempt to conciliate his opponents, he offered the State Department to Robert Smith, President Jefferson's secretary of the navy and Senator Smith's brother.

The Malcontents' obstruction saddled President Madison with a mediocre cabinet. Gallatin stood out as the most intelligent, able, and responsible official, and he remained the president' closest adviser. Smith, however, already had a reputation for laziness and incompetence. He never developed a rapport with President Madison and proved a nonentity at a time when foreign relations proved the Union's most pressing concern. In fact, President Madison ended up having to act as his own secretary of state, often writing diplomatic papers for Smith to sign. Animosity between Gallatin and Smith meanwhile discouraged President Madison from holding meetings with his entire cabinet unless absolutely necessary, and he continued President Jefferson's practice of dealing with his officers mainly through written requests and private sessions. Other than Delaware's Cesar Rodney, who had become attorney general in 1807 and agreed to stay on for the new administration, the president's other official advisers provided little service. Both Massachusetts' William Eustis, who became secretary of war, and South Carolina's Paul Hamilton, the new secretary of the navy, were selected mainly to give the cabinet geographical balance. Neither had much experience in the area now under his charge.

His bland reputation and uninspiring cabinet notwithstanding, President Madison proved a competent executive. He assumed the decisions of his administration for himself, seldom seeking President Jefferson's advice or counsel, and despite charges of drift and indecision, his reputation for honesty, sincerity, and wisdom helped retain the following of most Republicans. Dolly Madison's efforts likewise aided her husband's political standing. The charming and vibrant socialite always enjoyed more popularity than the president, and she moved the executive branch away from the austerity of President Jefferson's "republican simplicity" to create a lively Washington social scene. With President Madison's encouragement, the new First Lady oversaw the renovation of the executive mansion into a fine and elegant home. In the revamped quarters, Dolly replaced President Jefferson's small, intimate dinners with weekly feasts for up to thirty guests a time. On Wednesday evenings she hosted receptions—popularly called "Mrs. Madison's Crush" because of the large number of guests—that became the highlight of the capital's social activities. President Madison remained uncomfortable in crowds but dutifully attended the "Crush" to make himself available to the guests, while Dolly consciously used her personality and social graces to help create goodwill toward her husband.

In general, President Madison's policies upheld the ideals of President Jefferson's "wise and frugal government," which emphasized respecting the rights of the states while acting effectively in areas under federal authority. Eliminating the debt continued to stand as the highest priority, while the administration remained committed to securing control over North American lands for future generations of farmers. Soon after he took office, a new development in European affairs allowed President Madison to accomplish a goal that long eluded President Jefferson. In 1808, Napoleon Bonaparte deposed King Charles IV of Spain so he could place his brother Joseph Bonaparte on the throne. Napoleon's coup provoked a rebellion that would eventually contribute to his own downfall, but more immediately it left most of Spain's New

World colonies with no direction. American inhabitants in the western portion of West Florida took advantage of the uncertainty. In September 1810 they proclaimed West Florida an independent republic, sponsored a military expedition that captured the Spanish fortress at Baton Rouge, and sent a request to President Madison for annexation to the United States. The president immediately issued a proclamation reiterating the American claim to the area as part of the Louisiana Purchase and ordered William C.C. Claiborne, the governor of the Orleans Territory, to take possession of the region.

Claiborne's army moved into the territory in December and met little resistance. The Spanish governor reinforced his position at Mobile, a fort on West Florida's principal harbor, but by early 1811 the majority of the colony's residents—most of whom were American émigrés—acquiesced in the American occupation. Congress attached the area between the Mississippi and the Pearl Rivers to the Orleans Territory, which was admitted to the Union in April 1812 as the state of Louisiana. The remainder of the region, between the Pearl and Perdido Rivers with Mobile at its center, was designated part of the Mississippi Territory. Though Mobile remained in Spanish hands, the occupation of West Florida proved the highlight of President Madison's first term. The Union's continuing difficulties with Britain and France dominated his attention, and like President Jefferson before him, he failed to find a peaceful solution to the challenges from either European power. The apparent inability of republican principles to provide an answer only compounded his frustration.

The Road to War

The protracted European war remained the primary source of the Union's troubles. As part of its blockade on French trade, Britain's orders-in-council required American merchants to pay a licensing fee at a British port before trading on the European continent. The British navy likewise continued to insist on its right to impress seamen on American ships on the high seas. France's Berlin and Milan decrees meanwhile subjected any American ship trading with Britain to capture. The smaller and weaker French navy seemed less of a threat, but raids on American merchants in the summer of 1807 showed that France could seize as many ships as could its enemy. The insult that the powers presented to the young Union proved especially galling, for both simply used force against the United States at will and arrogantly disregarded American trading rights as a neutral nation. The British government's haughty treatment particularly offended Americans, for the former mother country's interference with American trade often seemed designed more to eliminate a potential commercial rival than to weaken Napoleon's empire. British ships routinely patrolled American shores as if they were still Britain's property.

Madison long championed economic coercion as a means of compelling France and especially Britain to respect American demands. Once the embargo failed, though, no clear alternative presented itself. For the moment, economic coercion remained in effect. On the same day Congress repealed the embargo, the lawmakers approved a Non-Intercourse Act, which continued to prohibit commerce with Britain and France but offered to restore trade with either if it would stop harassing American shipping and repeal its offensive policies. Few expected this act to have much effect; since Britain and France remained the Union's largest trading partners, the reopening of American ports to other nations' ships offered only limited relief for the economic depression. Also, once a ship left an American port, there seemed no way to prevent its captain from gaining a quick profit from illegally trading with one of the belligerents. The embargo indicated that the United States needed British or French trade more than the powers needed American goods, and non-intercourse offered little hope of coercing either nation. The economic leverage on which Republican leaders had long relied appeared a dead end.

The new president hoped negotiations could work out an agreement to guarantee American rights peacefully, but increasingly his administration appeared to face a choice between submission and war. Neither Britain nor France seemed interested in discussions unless the United States accepted restrictions on American commerce. Since Britain controlled the high seas, submission effectively meant accepting that nation's orders-in-council while permitting Britain to continue impressing American sailors. That might reduce the depredations on American ships, but it would also compromise American independence to the point that would practically return the United States to the status of British colonies—and virtually admit that the republican experiment had failed, since a government based upon the consent of the people had proven unable to defend its rights among the community of nations. But war also presented an undesirable alternative. The Union stood less prepared for a military conflict than it had been immediately after the *Chesapeake* affair two years earlier, and expensive war preparations would derail efforts to pay the debt but still require taxes to pay for a standing army and an expanded naval force like those the Federalists had implemented, and Republicans condemned, a decade earlier. These efforts still might not work, for the Union would find itself in a fight with one—or both—of the strongest military forces in the world.

Both submission and war found adherents among President Madison's rivals. On both ends of the political spectrum, the extremes preferred submission. Federalists, especially those from areas of New England heavily dependent on trade with Britain, saw France as the greatest threat to order and civilization and favored keeping close ties with the former mother country, even if it meant accepting British restrictions. They blamed the entire controversy on President Jefferson's and President Madison's presumed Anglophobia and supposed desire to align the United States with France. Old Republicans disagreed with Federalists on virtually every other issue, but in this case they agreed that the presidents' obstinacy had caused the Union's international problems. Rather than openly side with Britain, they rejected the argument that the government had a responsibility to protect American merchants, contending instead that captains should arm their ships at their own expense. Clintonians and Malcontent Republicans meanwhile called for a military buildup, including an expansion of the army, a naval buildup, and reinforcement of coastal defenses. Few demanded an immediate war, but they believed that a show of strength would more likely produce British concessions while leaving the country prepared for war if talks proved unproductive. In the meantime, they wanted to arm merchant vessels and order warships to escort and protect American traders from British or French assaults.

Military preparations cost money, so for the present President Madison held off from advocating an expansion of either the army or the navy. He recognized that the failure of negotiations could force the Union into a war, but he rejected any move toward submission. He determined, too, that, if war should come, the enemy should be Britain. The president had long abandoned optimistic notions about French republicanism, especially with Napoleon ravaging Europe, but he knew that a war against both powers at the same time would be suicidal. France, moreover, no longer had any significant presence in the western hemisphere, making a war against the continental power impractical. On the other hand, the United States could fight Britain in Canada as well as on the high seas. Impressment, especially with the British navy patrolling off American shores, likewise made Britain's policies more directly offensive and also more likely to incite the public hostility necessary to fight. President Madison tried to secure concessions from both powers, determined to give diplomacy every opportunity to avert a war, but his administration approached Britain as the greatest offender.

Shortly after his inauguration, the new president's faith in negotiations seemed vindicated. Britain's representative in Washington, thirty-year-old David M. Erskine, had already served in the United States for several years. Married to an American, Erskine sympathized with his wife's homeland, and he had developed a good relationship with Madison when he was secretary of state. Fearing that a declaration of war would follow the embargo, Erskine persuaded British foreign secretary George Canning to approve discussions for a new treaty. Canning authorized Erskine to settle the *Chesapeake* incident, but he stipulated the government would repeal the orders-in-council only if the United States agreed to allow Britain to trade duty-free in American ports, to close American trade to France, to cease its opposition to the Rule of 1756, and to allow the British navy to seize American ships that were illegally trading with France. The young diplomat knew that Canning's conditions would only offend American leaders, so he ignored them and instead worked out a generous deal that he thought he could persuade his government to accept. Concluded in mid-April 1809, the Erskine Agreement stipulated that Britain would pay reparations for the *Chesapeake* affair and repeal the orders-in-council by the following June if the United States reopened its trade with Britain.

President Madison reasoned that the Erskine Agreement met the conditions set in the Non-Intercourse Act, so on April 19 he issued a proclamation announcing the resumption of the British trade on June 10. Across the Union, Americans cheered the agreement as an honorable end to the dispute. But the celebration proved premature. In July, word came that the British government rejected Erskine's arrangement because he had violated his instructions. More ominously, the disgraced minister would be replaced by Francis James Jackson, a diplomat known for his haughty presumption of British superiority and his impatience with weaker nations. Regretfully, President Madison issued another proclamation in August reinstating non-intercourse with Britain. Talks with Jackson in the fall proved fruitless. The new British minister had nothing to offer beyond the terms Canning originally gave to Erskine, and his arrogance—reinforced by his frequent meetings with Federalists, who assured him of President Madison's incompetence and unpopularity—caused the president and the secretary of state to stop formal meetings and communicate with Jackson only in writing. When Jackson accused President Madison of having tricked Erskine into his agreement, the president demanded his recall. Once again, American relations with Britain came to an impasse.

British inflexibility pushed President Madison toward an aggressive stance. When Congress convened in the fall, he wanted to promote an expansion of both the army and the navy. He backed off, however, when Secretary Gallatin threatened to resign rather than oversee an increase in military expenses and an unbalanced budget during peacetime. Gallatin meanwhile drafted a law in a new effort to use the Union's trade as an economic weapon. Introduced into Congress by Nathaniel Macon, who was once again on good terms with Republican leaders, Gallatin's proposal would permit American ships to trade with any port and would allow the importation of British and French goods if they were brought to the United States by Americans. The prohibition against British and French vessels' entry into American harbors would continue, but the law offered to reopen trade with either belligerent if it would respect American neutral rights. The House approved "Macon's Bill Number One," as the measure came to be known, but criticism in the Senate ranged from charges that it was too hostile to charges that it was too submissive. Senate amendments changed the original proposal so much that the law became known as "Macon's Bill Number Two." Most importantly, the final version shifted the law's potential attraction. Approved in May 1810, the act re-opened trade with Britain and France and promised to re-impose an embargo on one of the belligerents if the other would repeal its restrictions on American commerce.

The reopening of trade provided some economic relief, but few expected Macon's Bill to have much effect on either power. President Madison himself had little regard for the act. To his surprise, in the late summer it appeared to present an opportunity to break the diplomatic stalemate. In September, he received from John Armstrong, the American representative in France, a letter that Napoleon had dictated to his foreign minister, the Duc de Cadore. The

Cadore letter stated that the French dictator would consider the Berlin and Milan decrees repealed as of November 1 provided that the United States "cause their rights to be respected by the English." Napoleon's condition could be interpreted in a variety of ways, and President Madison probably doubted the emperor's intention to halt French seizures of American merchant ships. Nevertheless, after careful consideration, he chose to accept the Cadore Letter as a declaration of a change in French policy, reasoning that the threat of again losing trade while Americans traded with France might compel Britain to repeal its orders-in-council. If Britain continued its stubbornness, the temporary accommodation with Napoleon would allow the administration to concentrate its intention on Britain and reduce the prospects of a war against both powers at once. Thus, on November 2, President Madison issued a proclamation reinstating the embargo against Britain.

As President Madison likely expected, the proclamation produced no change in British policy. From London, American minister William Pinkney reported that the government rejected the Cadore Letter as evidence that Napoleon had repealed the French decrees. British officials, in fact, largely ignored Pinkney's presence, convincing the frustrated minister to return home in February 1811, which left the United States without an official diplomatic presence. In the meantime, the British navy continued to patrol off American shores. In May, U.S.S. *President* fired at H.M.S. *Little Belt* near the entrance of New York harbor. The circumstances provoking the encounter remain unclear, but the incident presented a clear sign that Britain had no intention of backing down. Reports soon showed that Napoleon likewise had no intention of respecting American rights. French assaults on American merchant ships continued, and word came that, on the same day he issued the Cadore Letter, Napoleon had ordered extortionate tariff increases on continental trade as well as the sale of recently seized American ships. In the opinion of President Madison's critics, the cagey French emperor had used his letter to take advantage of a naïve president. Rumors of Secretary of State Smith's vehement private denunciations of the president's decision indicated a serious division within the government. The *Little Belt* incident stimulated patriotism and reminded Americans that Britain remained the Union's main antagonist, but to many the administration seemed unable to keep up with the realities of international diplomacy.

The administration reached its low point when Congress took up a bill to renew the charter of the Bank of the United States, which was due to expire on March 4, 1811. Twenty years earlier, Madison had opposed the bank's initial charter, but now he agreed with Gallatin on the bank's utility and accepted its constitutionality. Believing that as president he should not interfere in congressional deliberations, President Madison stayed out of the debate, but Gallatin actively championed the bank's cause. Federalists and several mainstream Republicans favored the recharter bill, but Old Republicans continued to insist that Congress had no authority to charter a corporation. Clintonians and Malcontents meanwhile charged it with mismanagement and foreign control. Opponents sealed the recharter's fate when they spread a rumor that Madison still opposed the bank. In late January the House of Representatives voted 65–64 to postpone the bank bill indefinitely, a move that effectively killed the proposal. A month later, a Senate vote on a similar bill produced a 17–17 tie, but Vice President George Clinton cast the deciding vote against recharter. The result forced the bank to close its doors, eliminating a crucial financial institution on the eve of a war while again indicating that the government lacked effective leadership.

The bank's demise compelled President Madison to take bold action to reassert control of his administration. Distraught with Congress's decision, Gallatin submitted his resignation as secretary of the Treasury. President Madison, though, refused Gallatin's resignation; instead, he fired Secretary of State Robert Smith and offered the State Department to his estranged associate, James Monroe. Monroe had recently won election as governor of Virginia, but he accepted the cabinet position after receiving assurances from Madison that "free consultation and mutual concession" would guide their deliberations. Assuming the office on April 1 after Congress had adjourned, the appointment replaced the incompetent and disloyal Smith with an able diplomat while effectively undercutting much of the criticism of Madison's presidency. John Randolph and the Quids saw Monroe's willingness to join the administration as a betrayal, but Monroe's eagerness to vindicate the agreement with Britain that President Jefferson and President Madison, as secretary of state, had rejected four years earlier deflected charges that Madison's Anglophobia produced the difficulties with Britain. Respect for Monroe's ability meanwhile prevented Malcontents from criticizing his appointment too harshly, notwithstanding their close association with Smith. The deposed secretary's rejection of President Madison's offer of a diplomatic post in Russia, along with his publication of a vituperative pamphlet denouncing his dismissal, only convinced the public of the wisdom of President Madison's decision. When the Senate reconvened in the fall, it confirmed Monroe's appointment in a unanimous vote.

Monroe came to office confident he could work out an agreement with Britain. The arrival in July of Britain's new minister, Augustus John Foster, dashed his hopes. From his earlier service as part of Britain's diplomatic delegation, Foster knew President Madison well; the two had a good relationship, and Foster conducted himself more graciously than had Francis James Jackson. Nevertheless, he followed his instructions and demanded more proof than the Cadore Letter to show that France had repealed its decrees. In fact, British policy hardened. Foster could offer compensation for the damages to U.S.S. *Chesapeake* only after the United States accepted responsibility for the *Little Belt* incident, and his government presented a stern protest against the recent American occupation of the West Florida territory. Foster's stance convinced the new secretary of state of what the president had already realized: Britain would treat the American states as colonial dependencies as long as its war with France continued. With no sign that the war would end soon, President Madison and Secretary Monroe began to move the Union toward war. On July 24, the president issued a proclamation calling Congress to convene on November 4, a month earlier than scheduled, and began preparing a message recommending military preparations.

In the meantime, he sent Joel Barlow as a special envoy to France to try to work out an agreement, or at least to delay a confrontation with Napoleon until the Union had worked out its troubles with Britain. Reports of Native unrest in the West assisted the president's determination to focus attention on Britain. Already embittered by their dependence on American and European goods and bordered by hostile tribes to their west, the northern tribes strongly resented the cession treaties negotiated by President Jefferson's agents because they required Natives to yield even more lands to encroaching American settlers. The agents received their share of the blame, but Natives particularly directed their hatred toward the "annuity chiefs"—many of questionable authority—who had signed away the lands in exchange for gifts and bribes. In several tribes, the discontent coincided with the emergence of revival or "rebirth" movements, in which charismatic leaders preached the rejection of white culture and a return to traditional ways. Among the Shawnee, the man known as Tenskwatawa, or "the Prophet," explicitly combined calls for renewal with angry condemnations of the Americans. Tenskwatawa's brother, the warrior Tecumseh, had less interest in spiritual matters, but he saw in Tenskwatawa's message a way to unite the various Native nations in an alliance that could prevent further cessions and perhaps push the Americans back across the Ohio River.

William Henry Harrison, the governor of the Indiana Territory, kept close watch on Tecumseh's movements. Like most on the frontier, Harrison suspected that British officials were encouraging Natives to fight American expansion. In September 1809 he completed the Treaty of Fort Wayne with chiefs of the Delaware, Potawatomie, Miami, and Eel River tribes. Again in exchange for substantial payments, the chiefs agreed to cede three million prime acres in present-day central Indiana for about two cents an acre. Appalled by this agreement, Tecumseh contended that individual tribes could not cede the western lands because the Nations held them in common, and he demanded that Harrison repudiate the treaty. Despite the warrior's threat to kill the offending chiefs, Harrison stood by the agreement. British commanders in Canada refused to support Tecumseh's call for war, so the Shawnee chief headed south to try to gain more allies. When he learned about Tecumseh's absence, Harrison led a combined force of about a thousand regulars and Kentucky and Indiana militia out of the territorial capital at Vincennes toward Prophet's Town, Tecumseh's home base near the confluence of Tippecanoe Creek and the Wabash River. Harrison intended to demonstrate American resolve by demanding that Tenskwatawa hand over the perpetrators of recent raids on frontier settlements. But, while Harrison's men were camped near the settlement on the evening of November 6, 1811, Tenskwatawa sent six hundred braves to attack them. Though taken by surprise, the Americans managed to hold off the attack. The next day, they proceeded to Prophet's Town and burned the abandoned settlement.

President Madison accepted Harrison's heroic account and proclaimed the "Battle of Tippecanoe" a major victory. The clash compelled Natives to abandon the northeastern portion of the Indiana Territory, but settlers who moved into the area still faced the constant threat of Native attack. Even before the encounter, the threat of renewed hostilities strengthened Southern and Western resolution for war against Britain. Canadian officials actually wanted peace and discouraged Tecumseh's alliance, but the discovery of British-made weapons at Prophet's Town seemed to confirm the British were backing the Shawnee leaders. Western and Southern farmers likewise blamed continuing low prices for their produce on British seizures of American merchant ships. Popular support for war spread across the frontier. Public meetings throughout these regions called on President Madison to stand firm against British harassment, and in the congressional elections in late 1810 through 1811, pro-war candidates demanded an invasion of Canada to remove the British threat and preserve the Union's honor. When the Twelfth Congress convened in November 1811, twenty-eight new Southern and Western House members—including South Carolina's John C. Calhoun, Tennessee's Felix Grundy, and Kentucky's Henry Clay—promoted the conflict so vehemently that their opponents labeled them "War Hawks."

The War Hawks provided President Madison with vital backing as he moved the Union toward war. Gallatin's reluctance persuaded the president to tone down his message to the new Congress, but after reviewing the failure of negotiations he recommended expanding the army, raising a volunteer corps, increasing the supply of munitions, and raising the tariff. War Hawks endorsed President Madison's proposals, and as Speaker of the House, Henry Clay used his authority to pack important committees with pro-war members. Departing from the tradition that the Speaker act impartially, Clay so boldly advocated war that many considered *him*, rather than the president, to be the Republicans' leader. But President Madison was determined to give Britain one last opportunity. In January 1812, the House Foreign Affairs Committee approved a report proposing legislation to implement the president's recommendations. President Madison ordered the news be sent to Britain on U.S.S. *Hornet*, a fast dispatch ship, and he would await the *Hornet*'s return in the spring before recommending a declaration of war. He did not expect the news to change anything, but when war came, no one could doubt that he had exhausted every opportunity to preserve the peace. In the meantime, the Union prepared itself for a fight. Expecting Britain to present an unsatisfactory response, in April Congress approved a ninety-day embargo on all trade as a signal of the Union's determination to declare war.

The *Hornet*'s return to New York on May 19 ended any hopes for a peaceful and honorable settlement. In its official response to American military preparations, Britain offered to share the income from its licensing fee on continental trade but otherwise made no concessions. With no alternatives remaining, President Madison on June 1 submitted a message to Congress recommending a declaration of war, explaining that impressment, the orders-in-council, and the Native hostilities in the west provided clear evidence of Britain's long-standing hostility toward the United States. Congress approved the declaration after three weeks of debate, but the vote reflected the Union's divisions. Federalists and Old Republicans continued to reject any need for war, while Clintonians and Malcontents demanded another attempt at negotiation, this time with military preparations to back American demands. In the end, less than two-thirds of either chamber approved of war, with the House voting 79–49 and the Senate 19–13 in favor of the declaration.

News from Europe further complicated American resolve, for in late July, Americans learned that an economic recession had convinced a new British government to repeal the orders-in-council. After reviewing the reports, President Madison nevertheless decided to proceed with war. Britain still maintained it had the right to restrict American commerce at will and indicated it might re-impose the orders-in-council the next spring. The continued impressment of American sailors meanwhile remained a symbol of British disregard for the Union's neutral rights. War thus remained necessary, Republicans insisted, to protect American honor and to demonstrate its standing as an independent nation. After years of uncertainty, the Union dove into the war it had long sought to avoid. Unfortunately, it was a conflict for which it would prove ill-prepared.

"Mr. Madison's War"

American strategy in any war against Britain seemed obvious: The United States should invade and conquer Canada. Not only was the colony close, it appeared vulnerable. The loyalty of its five hundred thousand inhabitants appeared questionable. Descendants of French settlers dominated Lower Canada—the eastern portion of the colony, north of the Saint Lawrence and Ottawa Rivers—while American migrants made up two-thirds of the population in Upper Canada, the area west of the Ottawa and north of the Great Lakes. Britain stationed only seven thousand troops in both provinces, and the war against Napoleon would prevent reinforcements. American officials thus reasoned that possessing Canada should bring the war to a quick end: It would remove foreign support from hostile northwestern Natives while depriving Britain of a region it had developed into a food supplier for its West Indian sugar colonies. President Madison could then use Canada as a bargaining chip in peace negotiations, and if Britain proved uncooperative the United States could hold the region and deny Britain its North American base. In either case, Republican leaders expected the possession of Canada to be all that was necessary to succeed.

Republican confidence, though, overlooked the Union military's ill-prepared state. President Madison hoped to rely on short-term volunteers and militia troops, but Congress instead voted to expand the existing army to thirty-five thousand for five years' service and to leave the organization of volunteers to the states. As President Madison feared, the long-term commitment required of soldiers hampered recruitment. As a result, the Union entered the conflict with fewer than twelve thousand soldiers. Finding enough troops would remain a challenge throughout the war. The army's leadership meanwhile inspired little confidence. Unimaginative old men staffed the highest command positions; most had little combat experience, and many of them had not seen action since the Revolution almost forty years earlier. President Jefferson's promotion of ineffective gunboats, along with Gallatin's cost-cutting, had left the navy with only seventeen ships. Neither Secretary of War William Eustis nor Secretary of the Navy Paul Hamilton had demonstrated competence in their posts. After the death of the Bank of the United States and Congress' refusal to approve new taxes, Gallatin tried to pay for the war with high-interest loans from state and local banks, but the shortage of funds eventually forced him to issue Treasury notes—short-term interest-bearing notes that, though not legal tender, citizens could use to pay taxes or buy public lands.

The American weaknesses revealed themselves once the fighting began. General Henry Dearborn, the former secretary of war, now assumed a field command and designed a plan for a three-pronged invasion of Upper Canada. Dearborn himself would lead the main thrust toward Montreal from Lake Champlain, while offensives from Fort Detroit in the Michigan Territory and from Fort Niagara in western New York would distract and divide the enemy. British defenses, however, proved more formidable than Dearborn expected. Though outnumbered, General Isaac Brock, the commander of the British forces, had been in Canada for a decade and long planned for a potential American invasion. Tecumseh's confederation supplemented his troops, and British ships controlled the Great Lakes. But an early disaster in the west showed that poor leadership, more than British resistance, would thwart Dearborn's plan. General William Hull led an army across the Detroit River on July 12, but he scampered back to the fort when he learned that Britain had captured the small American garrison at Fort Mackinac at the strait between Lake Michigan and Lake Huron. Once back at Detroit, Hull ordered 130 soldiers and civilians to evacuate Fort Dearborn near Chicago, but five hundred Potawatomie Indians attacked and killed eighty-five of the refugees on August 15. Before he learned about the massacre, though, Hull panicked. Surrounded by a British and Indian force of about thirteen hundred, he surrendered the fort and its twenty-five hundred men on August 16.

Furious with Hull's surrender, President Madison ordered William H. Harrison—now major general in addition to Indiana's territorial governor—to retake Detroit. After recruiting an army of sixty-five hundred, Harrison relieved Fort Wayne from a Native siege in September and over the next three months conducted a series of raids on Native settlements that solidified American control over the lands south of the Michigan territory. The onset of winter forced him to postpone a move against Detroit, though not before he sent General James Winchester with 850 men to the rapids of the Miami River. Once there, Harrison ordered Winchester to hold his position and concentrate on keeping his army together. Instead, Winchester marched his army toward Frenchtown on the River Raisin in southeastern Michigan. Failing to dislodge a larger British force, Winchester surrendered his men on January 21, 1813. A band of Wyandotte Indians massacred between thirty to sixty wounded Americans who were left in the town when the British moved out. "Remember the Raisin" became a rallying cry that strengthened American resolve in the west. The region remained on the defensive, however, and continued reversals there convinced even the most optimistic Republicans that the war would not go as anticipated.

While Harrison stabilized the west, the planned invasions to the east faltered. An offensive on the Niagara peninsula was supposed to coincide with Hull's march from the west, but slow recruiting and bitter bickering between Stephen Van Rensselaer and Alexander Smyth, the commanding generals in western New York, delayed any movement until weeks after Hull's surrender. Van Rensselaer finally ordered six thousand men to cross the Niagara River in October in an effort to seize Queenston. British defenses held the town, even though they were vastly outnumbered, and even though British commander Brock was killed in the battle. The New York militia then refused to leave American territory, preventing Van Rensselaer from providing reinforcement. As a result, the Americans remaining at Queenston had no choice but to surrender. The fiasco compelled Van Rensselaer to resign, and Smyth planned to restore American honor with an assault on Fort Erie, located across the river from Buffalo. Beyond issuing boastful proclamations, Smyth did little to prepare his men for the campaign. After a confused and chaotic river crossing on December 1, Smyth followed his subordinate officers' advice and called off the assault.

The main offensive farther east produced an even less glorious result. General Dearborn established his headquarters near Albany, but when he heard about the repeal of the orders-in-council he worked out an armistice with George Prevost, Canada's governor-general. The armistice convinced Dearborn there was no need to recruit an army, while Prevost sent soldiers to assist in the capture of Detroit and the defense of the Niagara region. Once President Madison rejected the agreement, Dearborn wasted several weeks touring New England to raise troops and to inspect coastal defenses. Finally, by the fall he had amassed an army of more than six thousand. Moving his force to Plattsburgh on Lake Champlain, Dearborn and his men set out for Montreal on November 19. Several militia units again refused to leave American soil, and the army met resistance from nineteen hundred Britons at the Lacolle River. The Americans managed to capture a blockhouse, but in the confusion of the ensuing skirmish they ended up firing on each other, wounding some of their own men. Anticipating that British defenses would get stronger as they neared Montreal, and underwhelmed with his army's performance, Dearborn called off the invasion after only four days.

In sharp contrast to the setbacks on land, the navy won several victories in the war's early stage. The American fleet was only a fraction of the size of the British navy, but American ships were well-built and commanded by able seamen, many of whom had gained valuable combat

Figure 4.1 "Action between USS *Constitution* and HMS *Guerriere*, 19 August 1812" by Anton Otto Fischer (date unknown). Depicts a major American victory during the War of 1812, though naval historians believe this painting actually represents the *Constitution*'s battle against H.M.S. *Java*. Oil painting on canvas. Courtesy of Navy Art Collection, Naval History and Heritage Command, NH 48472-KN.

experience in the Tripolitan War or the Quasi War with France. American captains thus welcomed direct, one-on-one encounters with their British counterparts. U.S.S. *Constitution* first demonstrated the Union's naval prowess in August, when the forty-four-gun frigate captured and burned H.M.S. *Guerrière* about 750 miles east of Boston. In the five months following the *Guerrière's* seizure, American ships defeated six other British warships on the high seas, including H.M.S. *Tara's* destruction in December by the *Constitution*—now nicknamed "Old Ironsides," from reports that enemy cannonballs merely bounced of its hull—and U.S.S. *United States'* capture of H.M.S. *Macedonian*, which was refitted and incorporated into the American navy. The navy likewise seized more than fifty British merchant ships, while American privateers took several hundred more enemy traders. The British navy's capture of three ships—the *Wasp, Nautilus,* and *Vixen*—presented a sobering reminder of British sea power, but the American naval successes stunned British leaders, made the involved captains national heroes, and helped sustain morale after the humiliating losses on the Canadian border.

Still, the setbacks on land embarrassed the administration and gave Clintonians and Malcontents a hope of replacing President Madison. In May 1812, the Republican congressional caucus dutifully endorsed the president for another term. Vice President Clinton had died in April, and Massachusetts' Elbridge Gerry agreed to serve as vice president. Eleven days after the caucus, the New York legislature nominated DeWitt Clinton. This time, Federalist support made a Republican challenger a formidable contender. Federalists outside the northeast hesitated to sacrifice their principles to support a Republican, but New England Federalists actively promoted Clinton. Although a meeting of Federalist leaders held in New York in September failed to give Clinton a national Federalist endorsement, his supporters waged an aggressive campaign against Virginia dominance. Their criticism of the decision for war and its inept prosecution made the election a referendum on the conflict. Still, Clinton carried only his home state of New York along with New Jersey and four New England states. Republican loyalty and continuing distrust of Federalism helped President Madison carry the South and West plus Vermont. The outcome nevertheless remained uncertain until Pennsylvania's voters gave the Virginian the state's twenty-five votes in late October. Though Republicans remained in power, Madison's 128–89 electoral college majority proved the closest result since 1800. The ensuing congressional elections likewise reflected the public's growing discontent, as Federalists nearly doubled their number in the House of Representatives.

Once re-elected, President Madison accepted Hamilton's and Eustis' resignations and installed Pennsylvania's William Jones as secretary of the navy and New York's John Armstrong as secretary of war. Armstrong immediately began identifying younger, more able commanders while designing plans for a new assault on Canada. Federalist and Malcontent demands to debate the war's origins complicated relations with Congress, but the lawmakers nevertheless voted to expand the army to fifty-seven thousand, to increase the soldiers' pay, and to construct sixteen new ships for patrolling the high seas and several smaller crafts for fighting on the Great Lakes. A $16 million loan and the issuance of an additional $5 million in Treasury notes were to pay for the expansion, and, in late July 1813, Republicans finally consented to a direct tax on land, a duty on salt, and a series of excise taxes. President Madison meanwhile kept open any opportunity to bring the war to a quick end. A "Seamen's Act," passed in February at the president's behest, sought to remove Britain's justification for impressment by proposing to prohibit foreign subjects from serving on American ships if Britain would renounce its right to search neutral vessels. Soon after signing the act, the president received word from John Quincy Adams, the American minister in Russia, that the tsar's government was offering to mediate a settlement between the United States and Britain. Madison eagerly assumed that Britain would accept the offer, and he sent Albert Gallatin and James A. Bayard, to join Adams in Saint Petersburg for negotiations.

Until Britain responded to the Russian offer, however, the fighting would have to continue. The campaigns in 1813 brought the Union some successes, the most important being the American recovery in the west. Although the expiration of volunteer and militia enlistments reduced General Harrison's army to about a thousand, Harrison managed to hold off British and Native attacks on Fort Meigs and Fort Stephenson in Ohio in May and July. In the meantime, Captain Oliver H. Perry oversaw the construction of a fleet of ships at Presque Isle, the present-day site of Erie, Pennsylvania. On September 10, Perry's ships defeated the British flotilla to give the Union undisputed control of Lake Erie. Two weeks later, Harrison's army—reinforced to forty-five hundred with new recruits and militia units—moved into the Michigan Territory and reoccupied Detroit, as well as Fort Malden in Canada, after British troops evacuated these posts. Harrison then pursued the enemy and on October 5 delivered a crushing blow to the combined British-Native force at Moraviantown, near the Thames River. Casualties were light at the Battle of the Thames, as the encounter came to be known, but Americans captured more than six hundred British troops. Among the dead was the Shawnee chief Tecumseh, whose death ended his Indian confederation and severely weakened Native resistance. Though Harrison returned to Detroit after the battle, his victory ended any further threat of British aggression in the west.

Fighting in the east left the Union more vulnerable. Armstrong's plan called for a series of attacks on British defenses around Lake Ontario as preludes to an assault on Montreal. Like his subordinate Perry, Commodore Isaac Chauncey oversaw the construction of a small fleet of ships at Sackett's Harbor, on the lake's eastern shore. The cautious Chauncey wanted to avoid directly confronting the British fleet, so he joined with General Dearborn to persuade Armstrong to let them launch the first attack, not at the principal British naval base at Kingston, but at York, a secondary base at the present-day site of Toronto. In late April, Chauncey's ships conveyed seventeen hundred troops across the lake to York, where the men defeated a smaller British and Native force. The explosion of a magazine at the garrison killed nearly three hundred Americans, including General Zebulon Pike, and the soldiers burned the town in retaliation for what they thought was an act of sabotage. Abandoning York, Americans under New York militia General Jacob Brown held off a similar British attack on Sackett's Harbor in May. Later that month, General Winfield Scott's forty-five hundred men captured Fort George, compelling Britain's evacuation of three other forts in the Niagara region. The British regrouped to defeat American troops at Stoney Creek on June 5, however, and their Native allies ambushed an American force at Beaver Dams on June 24.

The losses on the Niagara frontier convinced Armstrong to remove Dearborn as the commander of American operations in the east. Command now fell to General James Wilkinson, whom Armstrong had ordered to Sackett's Harbor after his imperious manner, mismanagement of his army, and now-known connections to Spanish officials destroyed his credibility in the southwest. Wilkinson likewise inspired little confidence among his new subordinates. Perhaps no one despised him more than General Wade Hampton, the commander of American troops at Plattsburgh who served as Wilkinson's second-in-command in the east. Wilkinson's leisurely journey from New Orleans delayed any operations until October. Since Britain had reinforced Kingston in the meantime, Armstrong ordered Wilkinson to lead his seven thousand men toward Montreal on the north side of the Saint Lawrence while Hampton's four thousand men headed for the town from the south. But a smaller British force held off Hampton's troops near the Chateaugay River on October 26. Disheartened by a report that Wilkinson had ordered the construction of winter quarters, Hampton called off his invasion and returned to Plattsburgh. Wilkinson meanwhile hesitated to move, spending most of his time trying to get a statement from Armstrong absolving the general of any responsibility in case the invasion failed. When he finally ordered an attack at Crysler's

Farm on November 11, his troops suffered such a humiliating defeat that Wilkinson likewise retreated.

As 1813 came to an end, the tide of the war seemed to be turning against the Union. British strength on Lake Ontario forced General George McClure to abandon Fort George in December; this was followed by the capture of Fort Niagara and a series of raids on the New York frontier that included the burning of Buffalo. Naval victories, which had stirred American hopes in 1812, now occurred less frequently as Britain imposed a blockade on the American coast. The loss in June of U.S.S. *Chesapeake*—the same warship that had been attacked off the Virginia coast six years earlier—proved discouraging enough, but the war's effects on the home front likewise began to hit the public hard. In raids along the Virginia, Maryland, and North Carolina coast, the British destroyed property and stole food and supplies. Commanders of these raids offered to grant freedom to any slaves who provided assistance, raising American fears that the enemy intended to provoke a widespread slave rebellion. British ships eventually carried away more than four thousand slaves, six hundred of whom were organized into a Corps of Colonial Marines that joined the raids and later fought alongside the redcoats in regular operations. The black soldiers' efficiency and effectiveness impressed British officers, while their eagerness to exact vengeance terrified their former masters. The blockade meanwhile created shortages across the Union, tripling or even quadrupling commodity prices, while the reduction in trade dramatically reduced tariff revenue. The loss of revenue compelled Congress to approve another $25 million loan and an additional $10 million in Treasury notes, adding further to inflation and economic instability.

President Madison did receive some hopeful news in January 1814. Britain rejected Russian mediation, but its leaders were willing to begin direct negotiations for peace. Eagerly accepting the offer, President Madison sent Jonathan Russell and House Speaker Henry Clay to join Adams, Gallatin, and Bayard on the American diplomatic team. But more ominous reports also came from Europe. Napoleon's decision to invade Russia in June 1812 had proven disastrous. The French emperor lost two-thirds of his six hundred thousand soldiers not only in battles, but also due to disease, heat, starvation, and desertion. Counterattacks by the tsar's armies drove out the invader out of Russia before the end of the year. At the same time, British assistance helped Spanish rebels chase a French army out of the Iberian Peninsula. Napoleon tried to regroup in central Europe, but in October 1813 a combined Russian, Austrian, and Prussian force defeated his troops at Leipzig. Limping back to Paris with only a few thousand men, the French dictator abdicated in April 1814. American leaders had expected the European war to go on for several more years, but the conflict's sudden end meant that Britain could now devote its full attention to its dispute in North America. Despite Britain's agreement to begin peace talks, the transfer of veteran fighters to America also indicated that British leaders intended to punish the Union for provoking a distracting and needless war.

Given these challenges, American forces acquitted themselves well in the 1814 campaign. The soldiers had gained valuable experience in the war's first two years, and new, younger generals, including Jacob Brown, George Izard, Edmund P. Gaines, and especially Winfield Scott, provided effective training and inspired a sense of professionalism among the troops. Control of Lake Erie likewise assured the Union's hold on the west while providing a base from which the Americans could conduct their own operations. Now anticipating a British invasion, the administration was determined to proceed with its own offensive. In May, seven hundred Americans raided and burned Port Dover on Lake Erie's northern shore, and in July Brown took thirty-five hundred men and seized Fort Erie, across the mouth of the Niagara River from Buffalo. Heading for Fort George at the river's northern end, Brown's army defeated a British force near the Chippewa River. Commodore Chauncey's reluctance to bring his fleet across Lake Ontario kept Brown from getting reinforcements, however, and, in the war's most intense fighting, on July 25 a larger British force repulsed the Americans at Lundy's Lane near Niagara Falls. Brown and Scott were both wounded in the battle, and, with the enemy well-entrenched, Brown reluctantly ordered his men to return to Fort Erie. Nevertheless, the American army under General Gaines repelled the British effort to retake the fort, holding off two direct assaults in August and September.

Americans also fended off the major British offensive to the east. After Wilkinson fumbled another move toward Montreal in March, British troops captured Fort Oswego in western New York in early May. Over the summer, Britain occupied about a hundred miles of Massachusetts' Maine district, east of the Penobscot River, and in late August, General George Prevost led ten thousand men toward Lake Champlain. Prevost planned a joint land-sea operation designed to gain control of the lake and capture the American base at Plattsburgh on its western shore. The general thought it might serve as a bargaining chip to force American concessions in the peace negotiations, and Plattsburgh appeared particularly vulnerable. General Izard had well fortified the town, but Secretary of War Armstrong ordered him to take four thousand men to reinforce Sackett's Harbor. The British fleet on the lake likewise outnumbered the ships that Lieutenant Thomas Macdonough had constructed at Vergennes, Vermont. Macdonough skillfully placed his ships to counter the British advantages, however, and when the attack came on September 11, Macdonough's ships not only defeated the British squadron but also captured four enemy vessels. Meanwhile, General Alexander Macomb's four thousand men held off Prevost's simultaneous attack on Plattsburgh. Though casualties were light, Prevost feared that the fleet's loss on the lake would cut his supply lines, and the increasing number of desertions among his troops convinced him to withdraw.

A major embarrassment farther south overshadowed the successes on Lake Champlain and at Plattsburgh, however. As a diversion to assist Prevost's invasion, forty-five hundred Britons under General Robert Ross landed on August 19 at Benedict, Maryland, only thirty-three miles from Washington. Despite President Madison's urgings, Armstrong had left Washington undefended for most of the war, and he realized his mistake too late to protect the city. A makeshift army of five hundred regulars and a few thousand Maryland militiamen attempted to stop Ross's men on August 24 at Bladensburg, but so many Americans ran away from their posts that the rout popularly became known as the "Bladensburg Races." Federal officials evacuated the capital only hours before Ross's men entered. After the general and his staff dined at the President's Mansion on the meal prepared for President Madison and guests, Ross ordered the burning of all public buildings. Leaving the city the next day, the British met stronger resistance at Baltimore, where Senator Samuel Smith had overseen the city's defenses. A frontal assault at North Point on September 12 pushed back the American line, but the British suffered heavy casualties, including General Ross, who was killed by a sniper's bullet. The losses convinced British commanders to attempt a naval bombardment on Fort McHenry, which guarded Baltimore harbor. The overnight attack on September 13 and 14 inflicted only minimal damage, however, and the invading force withdrew.

Despite the British offensives' overall failure, the burning of Washington cast a shadow across the Union. The nation seemed at its lowest point since the early stages of the Revolution, and public support for the administration declined dramatically. In addition to apparent military incompetence, an embargo imposed in December 1813 to stop trade with the enemy heightened economic shortages, and the severe reduction in tariff revenue would cause the government to default on its payment of the federal debt in November 1814. President Madison nevertheless worked quickly to revive the federal presence. Returning to Washington only two days after the British had left, he set to work in the former residence of the French minister and issued a call for Congress to meet in a special session in September. The lawmakers met in the Patent Office and the Post Office and rejected a proposal to move

the capital permanently to "a safer place." They then refused to approve the president's proposals to raise additional troops through a draft and to create a new national bank, but they eventually increased the bounty for new recruits and allowed the president to raise forty thousand
more volunteers. In the meantime, the president dismissed Armstrong, and James Monroe,
acting as both secretary of war and secretary of state, began to lay plans for the next year's
military operations. In spite of the embarrassment to the national capital, the army had held
firm in 1814. Still, the Union remained in a weak position, and it would not likely withstand
a sustained British invasion.

Fortunately, Britain had no intention of launching another invasion. In fact, the completion
of a peace treaty ended the war before any more campaigns could begin. With the conclusion
of the European conflict, both nations agreed to move the talks from their original location
at Gothenburg, Sweden, to Ghent, in Belgium. British leaders nevertheless delayed beginning
the talks until August 1814 because they expected that year's military operations to humiliate
the Union to the point that British officials could dictate the terms of the peace. By that time,
British officials were also meeting with representatives of the European powers at the Congress of Vienna, which opened in November to re-establish order on the continent following
the collapse of Napoleon's empire. Britain thus sent its best diplomats to Austria, leaving the
American team to deal with three second-rate representatives whose blustering eventually
required their government to oversee their deliberations. In contrast, John Quincy Adams, who
headed the American delegation, already had years of diplomatic experience, and Bayard, Russell, and especially Gallatin and Clay were all intelligent and perceptive politicians. The Madison administration's decision to drop the demand that Britain repudiate impressment—which
became an obsolete issue with the end of the European war—likewise made the delegation's
task easier.

The British representatives nevertheless opened the conference with unacceptable demands.
Their initial proposal centered on the creation of a Native "buffer state" in the west, situated
according to the boundaries set by the Union's treaty imposed on the northwestern tribes at
Greeneville in 1795. Rejecting this plan outright, the American delegation instead proposed a
settlement based on the principle of *status quo antebellum*—"as things stood before the war"—
which would restore to each nation any territory lost during the war. Surprised by the Americans' firmness, the Britons backed off but insisted on the principle of *uti possidetis*—"keep what
you have"—so they could retain eastern Maine, Fort Niagara, and some posts captured in the
west. The Americans again rejected this proposal, and their threat to leave the negotiations
coincided with news of British setbacks on Lake Champlain and at Baltimore. Bickering at
Vienna likewise revived the prospect of war in Europe and convinced British officials to terminate the American conflict as quickly as possible. Signed on December 24, 1814, the Treaty
of Ghent implemented *status quo antebellum*, required both nations to recognize the boundaries of Native nations as they stood in 1811, and provided for commissions that would later
settle the boundary between the United States and Canada. The treaty made no mention of
the issues that started the war, but both governments eagerly welcomed the peace. The Senate
unanimously ratified the agreement in February 1815.

The war for which President Madison had seen no alternative produced mixed results. The
military conflict could at best be described a stalemate. Notwithstanding some impressive
naval victories, the army experienced several embarrassing losses, and the Union suffered the
humiliation of having its capital burned. The economy was in shambles, and the war's costs
had tripled the federal debt that Republicans so desperately worked to eliminate. Still, the
United States emerged with its borders intact and had won the European powers' grudging
respect. With the conclusion of peace, reflection on the successes of 1814 encouraged a sense
of national pride across the Union. And a major battle—fought, ironically, after the peace treaty

had been signed—not only convinced Americans that they had won, but also helped eliminate the Republicans' political rivals.

The Hartford Convention and the Battle of New Orleans

As the war dragged on, Federalist opposition to Republican leadership had only intensified. Throughout the Union, Federalists charged that Madison's administration had bungled relations with Britain and provoked a conflict in order to assist France in the European war. Rejecting Republican claims that patriotism required them to support the war, Federalists insisted that they could best serve the Union by bringing it to an end. Their meager presence made Federalism a minor annoyance in the South and West, but in the Middle Atlantic and especially the New England states their dissent proved troublesome. Shortly after Congress declared war, Republican mobs in Baltimore destroyed a Federalist press, severely beat several dissenters—including former Virginia governor Henry "Light Horse Harry" Lee—and murdered a Revolutionary War veteran. President Madison refused to cede to calls for a sedition law, but the savagery of the Baltimore riots opened Republicans to charges of intolerance. Rumors meanwhile circulated that New England Federalists actively aided the enemy. Stephen Decatur, captain of the *United States*, complained that flashing blue lights on the coast sent a signal to British patrols that prevented his squadron from escaping New London, Connecticut, raising even more suspicions about the intentions of the "Blue Light Federalists." Few assisted the British directly, though New England merchants continued to trade with their British counterparts as the British navy initially exempted the region from the blockade. Federalist

Figure 4.2 "The Hartford Convention or Leap or No Leap." This Republican cartoon depicts Rhode Island and Massachusetts dragging Connecticut into the arms of King George III while Federalist leader Timothy Pickering prays for the success of "this great leap." Etching by William Charles (c. 1814). Courtesy Prints & Photographs Division, Library of Congress, LC-USZC4-12748.

governors in Massachusetts, Connecticut, and Rhode Island meanwhile invoked states'-rights arguments to deny administration requests to supplement the army with their states' organized and better-trained militia regiments.

For Massachusetts Federalists, the war was the last straw. Tired of subservience in a Union dominated by the South and West, protest meetings denounced the war and advocated a separate peace, with some openly calling for withdrawal from the United States. Extremists urged Governor Caleb Strong to call a convention of the northeastern states to demand changes to the Constitution, backed by the threat of secession. Governor Strong and other state party leaders hesitated to open themselves to charges of disunion. To mainstream Federalists, the war was more of a party issue than a sectional dispute, and the fact of the Union's potential markets for New England's developing manufacturing sector outweighed the war's annoyances. Congressional approval in December 1813 of an embargo to stop New England's trade with the enemy allowed Massachusetts radicals to make the 1814 state elections a referendum on a convention. The embargo's repeal in April and the beginning of peace negotiations temporarily dampened dissent, but Britain's occupation of eastern Maine, the extension of its blockade, and raids on the New England coast brought the war directly to the Federalists' stronghold. Fearing that secessionists might take extreme measures, moderate Federalists now took up demands for a convention as a way to promote the region's defenses.

The Massachusetts legislature in October finally issued the call for a New England convention, but to avoid the appearance of Massachusetts dominance, twenty-six delegates from the five New England states met in Hartford, Connecticut, from December 15, 1814, through January 5, 1815. Republicans watched the proceedings carefully, with Secretary of War Monroe stationing troops in Albany in case the convention attempted secession. Despite administration fears and extremists' hopes, the meeting proved anticlimactic. Moderates dominated the proceedings. Complaining that Republicans had failed in their duty to respect New England, former Massachusetts congressman Harrison Gray Otis drafted the convention's report and kept its focus on defense. The report's final version asserted state control over the militia while recommending that the states pre-empt collection of federal taxes to use the money for the states' protection. The delegates also encouraged the states to "interpose" their authority against proposals to enlist those younger than eighteen and to draft citizens into the army. As a concession to extremist demands, the report proposed seven constitutional amendments that would weaken Republican and Virginia dominance, including abolition of the three-fifths clause, limiting a president to one term, prohibiting consecutive presidents from the same state, and requiring a two-thirds vote of Congress to declare war, restrict foreign trade, or admit new states. After appointing three commissioners to present the report to President Madison, the delegates adjourned but agreed to meet again in June if the federal government failed to respond to their demands.

On their way to Washington, the commissioners learned of a smashing American victory in the southwest—a victory that made the convention's demands seem treasonous. The Southern frontier had remained quiet in the early stages of the war. Spain maintained a tenuous presence in fortresses at Mobile and Pensacola. Though allied with Britain in the European war, Spain technically remained neutral in the North American conflict, and the civil war that Napoleon had provoked in 1808 prevented Spain from providing Britain with substantial assistance. Nevertheless, President Madison saw an opportunity to solidify American authority in West Florida while taking the region east of the Perdido River. Spain's presumed assistance to southwestern Native tribes justified seizing the Florida territories, he reasoned, so in early 1813 two thousand Tennessee militiamen under General Andrew Jackson had marched to Natchez to undertake an assault, probably against the Spanish-held Mobile.

The early setbacks in the northwest—especially the River Raisin Massacre—distracted the president from the operation, and Congress refused to authorize the expedition. General Wilkinson ordered Jackson to dismiss his men when they reached Natchez, but Wilkinson's lobbying convinced Secretary of War Armstrong to give him the honor of seizing Mobile in April. Wilkinson met no resistance, but it otherwise appeared that the war would have little effect on the South.

During the summer of 1813, however, an internal division within the Creek nation allowed the Union to solidify control over the southwest. During his 1811 visit to the South, Tecumseh failed to convince the Southern tribes to join his confederation, but he found a willing audience among younger Creek warriors, who resented both American encroachment on their lands and their older leaders' fears of a war with the Union. Several "Red Sticks"—so called because their bright red war clubs signified their alliance with the Shawnee confederation—contributed to the northern campaigns and participated in the River Raisin Massacre. When young warriors murdered several whites near the Duck River in Tennessee, the older chiefs' demand for their capture and execution effectively served as a declaration of civil war. After several skirmishes, the older chiefs appealed for help from Benjamin Hawkins, their agent from the US government. At Hawkins' urging, a Mississippi militia unit in July attacked a band of Red Sticks at Burnt Corn, about eighty miles north of Pensacola, after the natives had picked up supplies at the Spanish fort. In retaliation, the hostile Creeks in August attacked and killed 250 Americans, including women and children, at Fort Mims, a stockade located about forty miles north of Mobile.

The Fort Mims massacre sent panic through the southwest. The Tennessee legislature again called out twenty-five hundred men, and under Jackson they defeated the Red Sticks at Tallushatchee and Talladega in November. Low supplies prevented Jackson from following up and moving into the heart of Creek territory, and many of his troops threatened to abandon him because they had volunteered for the aborted East Florida invasion and claimed that their year of service had expired. Jackson nevertheless persuaded Tennessee's governor not to call off the excursion, and reinforcements from Tennessee volunteers and a regular army regiment eventually brought his force to nearly four thousand. Moving into the Creek nation in January 1814, Jackson fought two inconclusive battles at Emuckfau and Enotachopco Creek, but aided by friendly Creeks his men dealt the Red Sticks a devastating blow at Horseshoe Bend on the Tallapoosa River on March 27, killing more than eight hundred Creek warriors. After the battle, President Madison appointed Jackson a major general in the regular army and authorized him to negotiate a peace. The resulting agreement reflected the general's distrust of any Native. Completed in August, the Treaty of Fort Jackson forced not only Red Sticks but also friendly Creeks to give up half of all Creek lands, including one-fifth of Georgia and three-fifths of what would later become Alabama.

While concluding the treaty, Jackson turned his attention to a greater threat. The general expected Britain to attack the Gulf Coast, so after completing the Fort Jackson treaty he marched a thousand men to Mobile. His hunch proved correct. As part of its 1814 operations, British admiral Alexander Cochrane proposed a plan to capture New Orleans, the Union's principal Southern city and the key to controlling the Mississippi Valley. The British government first approved the plan as a diversion to support the northern operations, but after the European war ended, the high command saw an opportunity for a larger and more decisive offensive. In a preliminary move, in early August one hundred British marines occupied Fort Barrancas, which guarded Pensacola in Spanish Florida. Anticipating that Mobile would be the next target, Jackson strengthened and reinforced Fort Bowyer, a poorly constructed outpost designed to guard Mobile Bay. The improved defenses helped repel an undermanned British attack on September 12, while the bay's shallow waters prevented the British ships from effectively bombarding the fortress. Hearing no direct orders from Washington, and reinforced by volunteers, regulars, and Chickasaw and Choctaw warriors, Jackson took his 4,100-man force into Spanish Florida in early November and seized Pensacola on November 7. Outnumbered and caught by surprise, the British troops abandoned and destroyed Fort Barrancas before Jackson could attack it.

With Pensacola neutralized, Jackson returned to Mobile, where he received a letter from James Monroe forbidding him to move against Spanish neutrality. But Monroe's letter also reported that Britain had ordered a large force to Jamaica to prepare for an attack on New Orleans. Jackson still suspected Mobile would be the principal target, but rumors and intelligence from the Caribbean confirmed Monroe's report and convinced him to direct his attention to the Crescent City. Taking two thousand of his men, Jackson arrived in New Orleans on December 2 and immediately set to work building the city's defenses. Reinforcements from Louisiana, Kentucky, and Tennessee militias, along with Jackson's willingness to accept the services of New Orleans' free black battalion and of Jean Lafitte's Baratarian pirates—a notorious band of outlaws—eventually swelled his army to more than four thousand. The arrival of an advance force of sixteen hundred Britons across Lake Borgne indicated that the enemy would approach New Orleans from the south. Jackson's army attacked on the evening of December 23, and though the Britons held their ground, they faced constant harassment for several days both from American snipers and from two gunboats on the Mississippi. Jackson meanwhile pulled back to set up his main defensive line across the Plains de Chalmette, a narrow track of dry land among the swamps that surrounded the city and which now appeared to be the enemy's planned route.

Figure 4.3 "A Correct View of the Battle near the City of New Orleans, on the Eighth of January 1815." A print celebrating the American victory, depicting the death of British commander General Edward Pakenham in the foreground. Engraving by Francisco Scacki (1815–1820). Courtesy Prints & Photographs Division, Library of Congress, LC-DIG-pga-03275.

Jackson's troops were outnumbered, but overconfidence and a series of mishaps produced a resounding American victory. General Edward Pakenham, the commander of the British force, arrived on the front on December 26 with an additional four thousand men, but his decision to wait for reinforcements allowed the Americans to complete construction of a defensive line. After a botched attempt to bombard the Americans on January 1, 1815, Pakenham decided to launch a major offensive on January 8. His plan called for a regiment under Colonel William Thornton to cross the Mississippi before dawn, capture an American battery on the west bank, and turn the battery's guns against the right side of the American line while Pakenham led the main force in a frontal assault. However, the river's unexpectedly heavy current drove Thornton's troops a mile and half farther downriver than planned, delaying their attack until mid-morning. They easily seized their target, but Pakenham had proceeded with his assault as planned, despite a heavy morning fog. Conveniently, the fog lifted right before the marchers reached the American line. Without the expected distraction on their flank, Pakenham's confused men were mowed down by Jackson's cannons. Pakenham himself was killed, and his two immediate subordinates suffered serious wounds before the next in command finally called off the slaughter. In a mere thirty minutes, the British suffered nearly three hundred killed, more than twelve hundred wounded, and about five hundred captured, compared to Jackson's mere six killed and seven wounded.

The Battle of New Orleans occurred almost three weeks after the signing of the Treaty of Ghent, but it nevertheless had a significant impact on the Union's development. Britain had always upheld Spain's claim that Napoleon had no right to sell the Louisiana Territory to the United States. Had Pakenham's army captured the city, Britain would probably have held on to it, notwithstanding the Treaty's *status quo antebellum* principle. In fact, the general had brought with him a commission naming him governor of Louisiana as well as a proclamation declaring British sovereignty in the territory on behalf of Spain. At a minimum, the conquest of New Orleans could have prolonged the war. At worst, it could have provided a base for further British operations up the Mississippi and left the Union surrounded by hostile British and Spanish colonies. Instead, the victory secured the Louisiana Purchase and its important port as American possessions, opening the continent to further American expansion.

More immediately, the triumph reinforced the sense of nationalism prevailing across the Union. American patriotism in 1815 reached a level stronger than any since at least 1798 and probably since 1775. When news of the British rout reached Washington in early February, crowds poured into the streets for spontaneous demonstrations and parades praising the success of American arms. Similar celebrations broke out in other towns and communities, many of them singing the words of "The Star-Spangled Banner," a poem Francis Scott Key wrote after the bombardment at Baltimore and set to the tune of an English drinking song called "Anacreon in Heaven." Jackson immediately became a national hero. For years, his countrymen commemorated the eighth of January as a second independence day. Recollection of the victories at Plattsburgh and Lake Champlain likewise stimulated pride in American military prowess, while President Madison's publication of documents relating British arrogance during the peace negotiations heightened national unity. By the time news of the Treaty of Ghent arrived, Americans had convinced themselves that they had won the war. They were sure that they had shown how a republic of citizen-soldiers could defend their rights and independence against a corrupt aristocratic power, even though that power had defeated Europe's greatest military force.

Final resolution of the lingering conflict with the Barbary States further heightened national confidence. Since signing the treaties concluding the First Barbary War in 1805, pirates from the North African principalities still occasionally captured American merchant ships and enslaved their crews. With the United States at war, the pirates took advantage of the Union's distraction to increase their seizures. The dey of Algiers acted particularly obnoxiously, telling a negotiator his plan was "to increase, not to diminish the number of my American slaves." Furious, President Madison was determined to deal with the problem as soon as the war with Britain had ended. Two weeks after the Senate ratified the Treaty of Ghent, the president ordered Stephen Decatur to lead a ten-ship squadron to the Mediterranean. The Second Barbary War, or Algerine War, proved a quick affair. Before arriving at Algiers on June 28, 1815, Decatur's fleet captured two Algerian warships, taking five hundred prisoners. Once in the port, his display of American naval strength compelled a newly enthroned dey to accept a treaty returning American prisoners and recognizing American trading rights in the Mediterranean without requiring tribute. Similar treaties with Tunis and Tripoli in July and August solidified Decatur's status as a hero while demonstrating once again that the Union could defend itself among the community of nations.

Ironically, the Federalist Party ended up the major casualty of the new nationalist spirit. The party of Washington, Hamilton, Adams, and Marshall long championed a centralized Union with a strong, active government. But Federalists were never comfortable with the emerging expectation of popular input in public affairs. Notwithstanding younger partisans' efforts to adopt Republican campaign methods, the party in opposition had mainly become known for its bitter and vindictive criticism of Republican leadership. Although moderate Federalists had successfully derailed extremist demands, the party's opposition to the war with Britain allowed Republicans to label the Hartford Convention as the "Blue Lights'" first step toward secession and disunion. News of the victory at New Orleans and the completion of an honorable peace made any questioning of the war seem the height of treason. Outside of the northeast, the Federalist presence virtually disappeared. Even in New England, Federalist support declined to the point that by the 1820s the party had become a clear minority.

The Union had survived its worst crisis to date. Madison's administration avoided a devastating defeat, and good fortune allowed Republicans not only to claim victory but also to accomplish their long-standing goal of eliminating the Federalist threat. Well aware that they had narrowly avoided disaster, President Madison and Secretary Monroe—his presumed successor—moved for legislation to strengthen the Union and to help the republic achieve its apparent national destiny. But as they moved forward, the agricultural republic of small farmers and planters that President Jefferson had envisioned was already transforming into a complex modern society. These changes would challenge the assumptions at the foundation of Jefferson's republicanism. They would also destroy the Republicans' newfound unity while generating sectional interests that would endanger the Union's existence.

Suggested Readings

Banner, James M. Jr. *To the Hartford Convention: The Federalists and the Origins of Party Politics in Massachusetts, 1789–1815* (New York, 1970).

Buel, Richard Jr. *America on the Brink: How the Political Struggle over the War of 1812 Almost Destroyed the Young Republic* (New York, 2005).

Dowd, Gregory Evans. *A Spirited Resistance: The North American Indian Struggle for Unity, 1745–1815* (Baltimore, 1992).

Egan, Clifford L. *Neither Peace nor War: Franco-American Relations, 1803–1812* (Baton Rouge, 1983).

Hickey, Donald R. *The War of 1812: A Forgotten Conflict* (Urbana, IL, 1989).

Jortner, Adam. *The Gods of Prophetstown: The Battle of Tippecanoe and the Holy War for the American Frontier* (New York, 2011).

McCoy, Drew R. *The Last of the Fathers: James Madison and the Republican Legacy* (Cambridge, UK, 1989).

McMichael, F. Andrew. *Atlantic Loyalties: Americans in Spanish West Florida, 1785–1810* (Athens, GA, 2008).

Owsley, Frank L. Jr. *Struggle for the Borderlands: The Creek War and the Battle of New Orleans* (Tuscaloosa, AL, 1981).

Remini, Robert V. *The Battle of New Orleans* (New York, 1999).

Smith, Gene Allen. *The Slaves' Gamble: Choosing Sides in the War of 1812* (New York, 2013).

Stagg, J.C.A. *Mr. Madison's War: Politics, Diplomacy, and Warfare in the Early Republic* (Princeton, 1983).

Taylor, Alan. *The Internal Enemy: Slavery and War in Virginia, 1772–1832* (New York, 2013).

Watts, Steven. *The Republic Reborn: War and the Making of Liberal America, 1790–1820* (Baltimore, 1987).

V

NATIONAL TRENDS AND SECTIONAL TENSIONS

The outcome of the War of 1812 stimulated a deep national pride, a belief that Americans constituted a common people created by the Declaration of Independence. Ten years later, Americans further celebrated their nation's accomplishments when they honored their "Jubilee" on July 4, 1826, the Declaration's fiftieth anniversary. The unofficial celebration actually began two years earlier, with the arrival in New York of the Marquis de Lafayette, the French nobleman who had volunteered his services to the Continental Army. Making his first visit to America in forty years, Lafayette spent thirteen months touring the Union, and Americans so heartily cheered the champion of liberty in feasts and celebrations that the occasions planned to observe the "Fiftieth Fourth" seemed anticlimactic. Nevertheless, President John Quincy Adams oversaw the ceremonies in Washington, and virtually every community hosted an event to praise the departed patriots who had preserved American liberty. Within weeks of the jubilee, Americans learned that former presidents John Adams and Thomas Jefferson—two of the last surviving signers of the Declaration—died within hours of each other on the Fourth. For most, the timing of the Revolutionary heroes' passing went beyond coincidence: It signified God's divine approval of the young Union's progress.

Americans emerged from the fiftieth anniversary confident of the Union's future. At the same time, many expressed anxiety. All recognized that the Union was rapidly changing. Many of the changes opened opportunities and made wealth available for ambitious young white men. Change also strengthened the ties that bound the states together, promoting the national spirit expressed in the celebration of both the war and the national jubilee. But it also brought unsettling trends. Americans increasingly became dependent for their livelihoods on buying and selling, rather than self-sufficiency or their neighbors. Economic growth meanwhile began to divide society into classes that seemed to have less and less in common with each other. Most significantly, perhaps, development exacerbated sectional differences, which both paralleled and pulled against the national spirit. Greater wealth and economic strength stimulated optimism, but challenges clearly lay ahead, with potential clashes over slavery already the most troubling concern.

Growing into a Nation

The political map of North America displayed the Union's most obvious changes. The War of 1812 had weakened or eliminated Native resistance to American expansion east of the Mississippi, and white settlers poured into lands northwest of the Ohio River and south of Tennessee. Within four years of the Treaty of Ghent, four new states—Indiana, Mississippi, Illinois, and Alabama—had more than enough people to gain admission to the Union. An agreement with Britain in 1818 set the forty-ninth parallel as the boundary with Canada while permitting both Britain and the United States to occupy the Oregon Territory, the huge but lightly populated region in the Pacific Northwest. The next year, a treaty with Spain acquired East Florida while confirming American possession of the Louisiana Territory. Missouri's application for admission as a slave state in 1819 set off a firestorm over the relative number of slave and free states. Linking Maine's admission with Missouri's partly resolved the crisis, and for the next twenty years Congressional leaders maintained sectional balance by pairing a slave state's admission with the admittance of a free state. Arkansas statehood in 1836 was soon followed by Michigan's in 1837. Florida and Texas both joined the Union in 1845, but the admission of Iowa and Wisconsin maintained the balance while bringing the total number of states by 1848 to thirty.

The rapidly growing population filled the new states and territories. The first federal census in 1790 had counted just under four million people in the Union, not including Natives. Sixty years later, the population had grown to more than twenty-three million, increasing about one-third each decade and doubling every twenty-three years. Almost eighty percent of the growth came from natural increase—that is, the number of births each year exceeding the number of deaths. The large number of births made the population a young one. In 1850, about seventy percent of Americans were under thirty, with nineteen the median age. The expanding and youthful population put increasing demands on the declining amount of available land in the original states. Thousands of people moved west to try their fortunes on the frontier, and by mid-century more than half of native-born whites lived outside the state of their birth. Usually settlers moved into lands most directly accessible in the west. New Englanders tended to move into western New York or northern Ohio, from which future generations would migrate to the Great Lakes region and the northern parts of Indiana and Illinois. Restless souls from the Middle Atlantic and Chesapeake states more often moved into the southern part of the western states, into Kentucky and Tennessee, and to the northern portions of Mississippi and Alabama. Virginians, South Carolinians, and Georgians meanwhile provided the main sources for the peopling of the southwestern states, from Alabama through Louisiana.

Immigration provided another important source for population growth. The Revolution and the European wars slowed the flow of immigrants, but the number of newcomers picked up following the War of 1812. During the 1820s, more than 128,000 immigrants entered the Union, with another 588,000 coming in the 1830s. Economic depression in the late 1830s and early 1840s again hampered immigration, but after mid-decade it resumed at an astonishing pace. During the 1840s, the number of migrants exceeded 1,713,000—more than had come to North America in the previous 250 years. By 1850, foreign-born inhabitants made up 9.5 percent of the total population. Many newcomers still came from Britain, but a higher proportion—thirty percent in the 1830s—came from central Europe's German states. The largest number, though, came from Ireland, with the Irish making up forty-four percent of immigrants in the 1830s and almost half in the 1840s. Unlike the Scots-Irish Presbyterians from Northern Ireland who had settled during the colonial era, Irish immigrants now consisted mostly of Roman Catholic settlers from southern Ireland, and with large numbers of German Catholics they made Catholicism for the first time a notable presence in the Union.

Immigrants could be found throughout the Union. More than half of the newcomers settled in New York, Pennsylvania, or Ohio, and a majority actually lived in rural areas with old-stock "Native" Americans—descendants of white Western Europeans whose ancestry in North America went back several generations. But many moved into the cities, where they joined those moving in from the country to create a substantial urban population. In 1790, only five percent of the Union's population lived in towns that the census described as "cities." Many of that year's "urban" dwellers actually lived in what modern Americans would consider small towns, as the census defined a "city" as a community with more than twenty-five hundred inhabitants. New York stood as the largest city in 1790, with a population of 33,131, whereas

Philadelphia—the largest town in colonial America—ranked a close second with 28,522. By 1850, the proportion of urban residents had risen to fifteen percent, and a greater proportion now lived in larger cities more like modern metropolitan areas. New York's population had swelled to 515,547, and Baltimore's 169,054 and Boston's 136,881 surpassed Philadelphia's 121,376 among the Union's largest cities. New Orleans and Cincinnati also had more than 100,000 inhabitants. Sixteen other cities had more people than lived in New York in 1790, and nearly sixty percent of urban dwellers lived in cities with more than twenty-five thousand residents.

Immigrants came to America mainly because they saw opportunities for a better life than they experienced in their native countries, for the Union's economy likewise grew rapidly in these years. Sparse and unreliable records make it impossible to measure the exact extent of the expansion, but increases in the value of American exports from $20 million in 1790 to $144 million in 1850—an increase of more than six hundred percent—indicates the impressive expansion in the Union's production. Over the same period, the value of goods imported into the Union expanded more than seven hundred fifty percent, from $23.8 million to $180.5 million. Personal income per capita meanwhile by the 1840s had doubled from the Revolutionary era.

Agriculture, the principal occupation for most Americans, provided the source of much of the economy's expansion. As population growth brought more lands under cultivation, farming continued to be hard work. At the beginning of the nineteenth century, farmers used the same methods that their European ancestors had used for hundreds of years. Following the War of 1812, new technology saved labor, expanded yields, and produced more food for sale at home or abroad. In upstate New York, Jethro Wood developed an affordable cast-iron plow, making it easier for farmers to till their lands, and in 1837 John Deere, an Illinois blacksmith, produced a steel plow that could cut through the tough soil and clay of the western prairie. Horse-powered hoes, iron harrows, and threshers became available during the 1820s and 1830s, and in 1831 the Virginian Cyrus McCormick followed up on his father's initial designs and successfully developed a horse-drawn mechanical reaper. McCormick's reaper allowed a farmer to harvest ten to twelve acres of wheat in a day—a phenomenal increase over the one-half to three-quarters acre per day that could be harvested with a scythe. The use of new tools and the cultivation of new lands exponentially increased production on the Union's farms. The 1850 census showed that American farmers produced more than one hundred million bushels of wheat and almost six hundred million bushels of corn.

Shortly after the Revolution, a new crop emerged as the Union's major product. During the colonial era, Americans produced only a little cotton. In the mid-eighteenth century, British manufacturers developed a technology that could quickly spin cotton fibers into yarn, which workers could then weave into a soft, comfortable fabric. Natural and technological obstructions, though, kept Americans from meeting the British demand for a reliable cotton supply. Rice planters found that the high-quality, long-staple "sea island" cotton grew well on the islands along the South Carolina and Georgia coast, but sea island cotton's long growing season limited how much they could produce. Farmers on the mainland meanwhile could grow ample amounts of the stronger but lesser quality "upland" cotton, but the sticky seeds that teemed through the bolls of the upland cotton required an entire day's work to remove the seeds from just one pound of the fiber.

Cotton's prospects changed in 1793 when Eli Whitney, a young Yale graduate working as a tutor on a Georgia plantation, developed the cotton "gin" (short for "engine"). Whitney's machine made it possible to remove the seeds from upland cotton without damaging the fibers. Using a gin, a single laborer could now remove the seeds from fifty pounds of cotton in a day. Almost overnight, cotton became the South's most lucrative crop. By 1815, Southern planters and farmers produced sixty times more cotton than they had in 1790. As production spread westward, the "Black Belt" region across central Georgia, Alabama, and Mississippi—so called because of its dark, rich soil, and because of the region's large number of slaves—became the world's leading cotton producer, growing more than sixty percent of the world's supply by the 1840s. Cotton likewise became the Union's principal export. Three-quarters of the cotton produced in the South was shipped abroad, mostly to Britain, and between 1820 and 1850 cotton made up anywhere from thirty percent to sixty percent of all of the American products exported.

Much of the money that cotton exports brought aided the growth of the Union's first significant manufacturing sector. British laws had discouraged manufacturing in Britain's American colonies, to prevent the development of industries that might compete with British firms. Colonists still produced some of what they needed through "household manufactures"—that is, making basic products on farms or in small shops. Several farmers possessed spinning wheels or churns or had fashioned plows and hoes from what was available. Most communities had small mills to grind flour into wheat, cut lumber, or transform cowhide into leather, while blacksmiths, carpenters, and cobblers provided the iron and wooden products and the shoes that farmers could not provide for themselves. In larger port towns, other skilled artisans—craftsmen who knew how to make finished products from raw materials—set up shops to make basic goods for the public and luxuries for the wealthy. Still, the traditional methods that artisans used limited the number of items that they could produce, and most Americans preferred the cheaper British goods. Aside from iron mines in Pennsylvania and shipbuilding yards along the Atlantic coast—an industry that benefited British as well as American merchants—no significant manufacturing businesses existed in the American colonies. In its first decades of independence, the new Union remained dependent on Britain for finished goods.

A few homegrown industries emerged in the years immediately following the Revolution. In 1789, Oliver Evans, a Delaware wheelwright, received the first federal patent for his self-automated flour mill, a machine that allowed one man to process three hundred bushels of wheat in an hour. In the same year, Samuel Slater left England for New York and brought with him the knowledge of how to build the water frame, the machine used in British factories for quickly and efficiently spinning cotton fibers into yarn. British law prohibited exporting British manufacturing technology to potential competitors, but Slater memorized the machine's construction while working in a factory, and he managed to escape England by concealing his identity. Once in America, Slater formed a partnership with William Almy and Moses Brown to set up a factory in Pawtucket, Rhode Island, for the production of cotton yarn. The yarn still had to be "put out"—that is, taken to local homes where farmers could weave it into cloth—but several other spinning mills soon emerged. Treasury Secretary Albert Gallatin counted about fifty American yarn-spinning mills in 1810.

Gallatin and his fellow Republicans had rejected Alexander Hamilton's plan to promote industry through federal assistance. Ironically, Thomas Jefferson's embargo and the War of 1812 boosted manufacturing by reducing British imports and temporarily discouraging merchants from investments in the trans-Atlantic trade. Like Samuel Slater's spinning mills, the largest and best-known establishment to emerge also imitated British industry. While visiting England in 1810, New England merchant Francis Lowell learned how to construct a power loom, a machine that could weave cotton yarn into cloth. Upon his return, he joined with several other merchants to form the Boston Manufacturing Company, which used Lowell's recollections to establish a cotton mill in Waltham, Massachusetts, in 1814. Set up along the fall line of the Charles River, the Waltham plant brought under one roof the entire cotton manufacturing process, from spinning to weaving to printing. The success of the Waltham plant led the company to construct a second, larger mill in 1822 in East Chelmsford, which the investors renamed "Lowell" after their founder died. By 1850, the "Lowell Mills" included fifty-two factories that employed more than ten thousand workers across eastern Massachusetts and southern New Hampshire. Americans still imported British cotton goods, but American producers had captured a large share of the domestic market and actually competed with British cotton manufacturers in foreign trade.

Only a few industries followed the Lowell Mills' example to start out as factories—large mechanized establishments with hired managers supervising labor. Workshops—owned by artisan craftsmen who still worked alongside their journeymen and apprentices—still produced most manufactured goods. Some expanded production through the "putting out" system, while others relied on traditional methods to make goods by hand. Artisans expanded their production, though, by dividing the labor among workers: rather than training apprentices or coaching journeymen on the entire process of making a good, each would repeatedly perform only one or two steps of the production process. The division of labor exponentially increased how many goods the laborers could produce in one day. Workshops, especially in the boot and shoe, hat, farm tool, and ironware industries, increased their production by assigning workers specific tasks and helped the Union approach self-sufficiency in these products as well as in textiles and leather, paper, and glass products. Gradually, artisans replaced their apprentices with unskilled workers, while journeymen had to use their training to find work as skilled employees. Master craftsmen meanwhile took on the character of business managers—and their children as absentee owners—as workshops increasingly transformed into factories.

American manufacturers also pioneered the development of tools for making manufactured goods while devising machine tools like lathes, milling machines, and gear cutters that helped make the machines that made finished goods in factories. After inventing the cotton gin, for example, Eli Whitney worked to develop instruments that could cut such precision that he could apply the concept of interchangeable parts to gun manufacturing. Whitney never achieved the extent of interchangeability he desired, but his efforts inspired Simeon North's invention of a milling machine that measured and cut so exactly that North himself became a major producer of firearms. By the 1830s, North and Chauncey Jerome had applied the concept of interchangeable parts to the mass production of clocks, watches, and locks. New machinery like Elias Howe's sewing machine, patented in 1846, further advanced textile production, while the woodworking machines, Colt revolvers, and McCormick reapers displayed in 1851 at London's "Crystal Palace" Exhibition so impressed British industrialists that they referred to the use of tools, machines, and interchangeable parts as the "American System of Manufacturing."

Manufactured goods made up less than ten percent of the Union's exports before 1850. Americans still imported more goods than they exported, and in the 1840s farming remained the principal occupation for two-thirds of the labor force. Nevertheless, by then American manufacturers provided most of the Union's basic necessities. Most imports now consisted of tropical commodities, high-grade textiles, and similar luxuries. Meanwhile, new methods of moving people, goods, and information produced what historians refer to as "revolutions" in transportation and communication. Following the Revolution, modes of travel across the Union remained primitive. Colonial roads either followed Native trails or were constructed by local communities, with little thought to a "system" or network that could unite the colony. The roads' haphazard layout and poor quality severely constricted travel. George Washington needed nine days to go from Northern Virginia to Philadelphia for his inauguration. Even thirty-six years later, news of Andrew Jackson's victory in New Orleans took a month to reach the Union's capital. Ships helped shorten journeys along the coast, while rivers provided highways into the interior and allowed farmers to float their produce downstream. But the difficulty of rowing or sailing upriver countered the rivers' advantages, and natural debris and shallow passages often obstructed downstream travel. Western farmers sent their wheat and corn on rafts or flatboats down the Mississippi River and its tributaries to New Orleans, but then they would sell their crafts for lumber and walk hundreds of miles home rather than fight the river's current. The trip by river from Pittsburgh to New Orleans took four to six weeks, but the walk back could take as long as four months.

Steamboats helped Americans master the rivers. British and French engineers had experimented with ways to use Scotsman James Watt's steam engine to power a boat that could travel against a river's current. Building on these efforts, Virginia's James Rumsey and Pennsylvania's John Fitch ran early versions of paddle-driven steamers on the Potomac and Delaware Rivers in the mid-1780s. Robert Fulton first demonstrated the steamboat's commercial potential in 1807 when he began regular passenger service on the Hudson River on the *North River Steamboat*, which he later renamed the *Clermont*. Fulton's craft cut the travel time along the 150 miles between New York City and Albany from several days to thirty-two hours. Entrepreneurs soon built similar boats for their own routes on rivers across the Union, dramatically reducing both travel time and the costs of going against the currents. The trip from New Orleans to Louisville, for example, now took eight days rather than ninety, cutting shipping costs by ninety percent. By the 1840s, steam-powered "riverboats" had become the main method for long-distance passenger travel, especially in the West, with more than 550 steamboats sailing on the western rivers.

Governments meanwhile took steps toward improving overland travel. Congress funded the construction of several "post roads" to assist in the delivery of the mail as well as a "National Road," known as the "Cumberland Road," that could provide a direct route west through the Appalachians. Begun at Cumberland, Maryland, in 1811, the National Road reached the Ohio River in 1818 and by 1839 stretched to Vandalia, Illinois. Conflicting ideologies and interests made the federal government's role in constructing "internal improvements" a major political issue. Few, though, questioned the authority of the states in improving infrastructure. State legislatures granted corporate charters to hundreds of private companies to clear rivers, construct

Figure 5.1 "The 'Clermont,' 1807." Robert Fulton's steamboat opened the first regular travel service on the Hudson River between Albany and New York City. Illustration in *The Steam Engine and Its Inventors: A Historical Sketch*, by Robert L. Galloway (1881). Courtesy Prints & Photographs Division, Library of Congress, LC-USZ62-110382.

bridges, and build "turnpike" roads, so called because owners would erect a rotating gate or "turnpike" across the road and charge a toll for its use. In the late 1830s, legislatures began to approve "general incorporation" laws; rather than require a specific law to grant a charter to each new corporation, these laws allowed a company to receive a charter once it met a set of guidelines. Several states meanwhile provided financial assistance through purchasing a company's stock or issuing bonds, especially as companies turned to building wooden "plank" roads or "macadamized" roads, paved with a mixture of stones and cement designed by the Scottish engineer John McAdam.

States also turned their attention to the construction of canals, which could transport goods more quickly than roads. The completion of the Erie Canal in New York in 1825 kicked off a "canal craze" across the Union. Championed by Governor DeWitt Clinton and paid for by the legislature, the canal took eight years to finish. Once completed, "Clinton's folly" connected Albany to Buffalo on Lake Erie 364 miles to the west, opening up the state's western lands and tying the vast farmlands around the Great Lakes to international markets through New York City. The canal cut the cost of shipping one ton of goods from Buffalo to New York City from nineteen cents to less than three cents per mile. The wealth and population growth that followed the canal's opening inspired other states to follow New York's example. Pennsylvania tried to rival New York's accomplishment by constructing the Main Line Canal, which when finished in 1834 connected Pittsburgh and Philadelphia across 395 mountainous miles. The Main Line never provided much competition for New York, partly because Ohio, Indiana, and Illinois built their own canals to connect their farmlands to the Great Lakes. By 1840 more than thirty-three hundred miles of canals cut across the Union, with more than half of the costs paid by state governments. Like the Main Line, none matched the Erie Canal's success, but canals became a principal means for thousands of farmers and manufacturers to ship their goods to their markets.

Just as the "Canal Age" reached its height, the states shifted their attention to railroad construction. As with steamboats, English engineers had tried since the late eighteenth century to use a steam engine to power cars to run on rails. The cost and technological challenges involved delayed the development of a workable long-distance train until 1825, but once railroads proved effective, Americans acted quickly to build their own lines. Construction began on the Baltimore and Ohio Railroad on July 4, 1828, with ninety-one-year-old Charles Carroll of Carrollton—the last surviving signer of the Declaration of Independence—on hand to break the ground. Two years later, the route's first thirteen miles opened for passenger service. In the meantime, the South Carolina Canal and Railroad Company began building a route to divert cotton shipments from the Savannah River to the port at Charleston. Opened in October 1833, the Charleston and Hamburg line stood as the longest railroad in the world, at 136 miles. Despite higher costs, the railroads' faster speeds—and the fact that, unlike canals, they could operate in cold weather—persuaded investors of their advantages. By 1840, Americans had constructed the same number of miles of railroad track as they had dug in canals, but ten years later the nearly eighty-nine hundred miles of track far outstripped the thirty-seven hundred miles of canals.

Improvements in transportation facilities increased interaction among Americans and stimulated demand for information. Newspapers thus flourished across the Union. Most colonial port towns produced at least a weekly or biweekly paper, but technological developments in the early nineteenth century helped expand the number of presses so that even frontier towns could have their own paper. Hundreds of papers proved short-lived, but effective editing, population growth, and the vital aid that papers provided for political causes allowed hundreds more to succeed. By the 1830s, there were more than twelve hundred papers across the Union, and Richard March Hoe's development of a rotary press in 1843 made daily editions possible in most cities. Virtually all of these papers were large sheets folded into four pages, with advertisements dominating the front and back, and with editorials, news stories, and items of interest on pages two and three. Correspondents sometimes provided news from larger cities. More often, editors agreed to "exchanges" with printers in other towns and states, swapping free copies of their issues—which could be mailed to other editors at no charge—and using material from the exchanges in their own papers. Through the papers, readers gained greater awareness about national and international conditions as well as the concerns facing their fellow citizens in states that only recently seemed as distant as foreign countries.

Samuel F.B. Morse's invention of an electromagnetic telegraph further quickened the speed of news across long distances. The Yale-educated son of a prominent Federalist and Congregationalist minister, Morse enjoyed a reputation as an accomplished painter when personal tragedy drove him to search for a faster method of conveying messages. While in Washington in 1825 to paint the Marquis de Lafayette's portrait, he received word of his wife's precarious condition after delivering their third child; she died before he could return to their home in Connecticut. Over the next decade, Morse built on the work of several scientists to develop a device that could send electronic pulses across a single wire, along with a "code" of dots and dashes that signified the letters of the alphabet. Congress approved $30,000 in 1843 to test Morse's telegraph by establishing lines connecting Washington with Baltimore. Though incomplete, the telegraph proved its utility in May 1844 when it conveyed the news of Henry Clay's presidential nomination seventy-five minutes before a train from Baltimore brought confirmation of the report. Three weeks later, Washington politicians followed regular updates sent on the completed line from the Democratic National Convention. Despite the success, federal officials declined to establish further lines, but private investors provided the funds needed to connect Washington to both Chicago and New Orleans by 1848. Two years later, more than ten thousand miles of telegraph wire hung across the Union, and knowledge of telegraph operation and of the "Morse Code" became valuable skills for aspiring young men.

Improvements in transportation and easier availability of information, like the growth of the economy, subtly but significantly affected Americans' lives. In a process that historians have called the "Market Revolution," Americans gradually shifted their activities away from a focus on subsistence production—that is, concentrating first on securing the food, shelter, and clothing necessary for the family's survival and selling only surplus goods for money needed to buy a few products. Instead, they increasingly focused on producing for a market, specializing in producing a few goods or services and using the cash brought in to buy necessities. Americans never completely depended on either subsistence or market production: Even in the colonial era, farmers sold at least some of their surplus, and by the mid-nineteenth century most still consumed much of what they grew on their own lands. Still, the market slowly played a greater role in Americans' lives, and specialization and market production both dramatically helped expand the nation's wealth and improve the overall standard of living. As early as the 1830s, families throughout the Union could fill their houses with items like stoves, kitchen utensils, carpets, "fancy chairs," clocks, and mirrors and pictures to hang on once-barren walls. In the 1840s, glass jars and tin cans allowed customers to buy preserved fruits and vegetables and bread at local general stores. Over the next decade, traditional "household manufactures" practiced by small farmers had all but disappeared, and the economy's impressive gains made the average American wealthier than his counterparts in Western Europe.

Greater reliance on the market, though, also brought greater uncertainty. As barter and swapping goods and services became less common, a bad harvest now presented farmers with the prospect of destitution. Dependence on distant strangers' buying and selling brought more reliance on credit. To meet the demand for money, state-chartered banks issued paper notes to make the buying and selling of goods easier. Two major financial panics—one in 1819, another in 1837—revealed the perils of collapsing commodity prices while creditors demanded immediate payment for loans, but even in good times paper money could become worthless because an issuing bank had gone out of business. Most significantly, not all Americans benefited equally from the economy's growth. The richest Americans gained a greater share of the wealth. By the 1840s, the wealthiest five percent of all families owned about seventy percent of all property, and the word "millionaire" came into popular use. The number of property-less families meanwhile increased, with many finding themselves in poverty. The worst conditions could be found in the cities, where thousands lived in destitution in crime-filled neighborhoods like New York's "Five Points," which the English novelist Charles Dickens—no stranger to the poor—described in 1842 as "reeking everywhere with dirt and filth." In rural areas, population growth often exceeded available lands, forcing many to become permanent farm laborers or to seek jobs in the cities. The frontier offered a new start for those with the resources for a move, but the poor usually could not afford the supplies and travel costs necessary.

Nevertheless, material progress convinced white Americans that their Union was a "land of opportunity," an "open" society in which a person's work and personal responsibility determined his social standing and his family's comfort. Success, measured in terms of wealth, was believed attainable by anyone who set his mind to it and took advantages of the opportunities present. In a rapidly expanding economy, thousands of young men indeed rose from poorer circumstances to respectability and importance. Abraham Lincoln, the son of a poor Kentucky farmer, attended school for only eighteen months, but through his own reading, study, and hard work he became a successful lawyer. Similarly, his political rival Stephen A. Douglas appeared destined to the life of a cabinetmaker, but determination gained him a college education before he embarked on his own successful legal career. A few, such as the shipping and railroad magnate Cornelius Vanderbilt, managed to accumulate massive fortunes. Examples like these convinced Americans that their free republican institutions made advancement available for anybody. Unlike the rigid social rankings and restrictions of European aristocracies, Americans presumed their social inequalities to be temporary, with nothing preventing deserving young men from attaining prosperity. The wealthy meanwhile often enjoyed admiration as "self-made men"—as long as they avoided extravagance and aristocratic presumptions, acknowledging that they could lose their fortunes as easily as the ambitious could rise to prominence.

The economy was neither as stable nor as open as popular ideals would have it. Social mobility likewise proved far less open than widely assumed. For every Lincoln, Douglas, and Vanderbilt, many others failed, and the vast majority of people remained in the social rank into which they were born. Still, the overall increase in wealth and the appearance of new conveniences sustained the belief that the Union was indeed a land of opportunity. Increasingly, Americans celebrated their land as a nation that was more free, more prosperous, and better than any other in the world.

The Marshall and Taney Courts

Almost an afterthought in the Union's earliest years, the Supreme Court played a crucial role in promoting both federal authority and economic growth. The court's emergence as an influential branch of the federal government resulted mainly from the work of John Marshall, its fourth chief justice. Prior to his appointment in 1801, the court stood as an overlooked institution that most considered of only minor importance. Uncertainty over the court's exact role gave it little to do. The Constitution failed to outline its specific duties; Pierre Charles L'Enfant, the architect who designed the City of Washington, failed to provide a building for the court, leaving it with no place to meet until the House gave up one of its committee rooms. Even after Congress passed the Judicial Act of 1789, the justices sat for a year and a half before hearing their first case. In its first dozen years, the court heard only sixty-three cases. Its decision in *Chisholm v. Georgia* (1793) proved the only case of any significance, for it led to the ratification in 1795 of the Constitution's eleventh amendment, which prohibited citizens from using the federal courts to sue a state government.

The physical demands involved in the Judiciary Act's requirement that justices "ride the circuit"—traveling to hear appeals while the Supreme Court was not in session—meanwhile made service on the court undesirable. Prior to Marshall's appointment, thirteen different men had sat in the court's six seats. Marshall himself turned down President Adams' offer to make him an associate justice in 1798, and President Adams appointed him chief justice only after his first two choices turned down the position. Most Federalists expressed disappointment with President Adams' decision. The Federalist majority in the lame-duck session of the Senate in fact delayed Marshall's confirmation for a week, and the party accepted his appointment only after it became clear that the president would not appoint Alexander Hamilton's preference, New Jersey's William Paterson. But Marshall far exceeded the Federalists' expectations. Taking his seat in February 1801, he presided over the court for thirty-four years, the longest tenure of any chief justice and the second longest of any justice in the court's history. More importantly, his direction transformed the tribunal into a powerful body that many recognized as the final authority in determining the meaning of the law.

To enhance the court's prestige, Marshall worked to effectively unite the justices so the court could speak with one voice. Initially, the justices followed the English practice of having each prepare and read his own opinion on a case. In Marshall's view, the various principles outlined in multiple opinions undercut a decision's impact on the law, so he used his warm and affable personality to persuade his fellow justices to allow him to present a single opinion—usually written by the chief justice himself—that would represent the court's official position. In his first four years as head of the court, Marshall wrote twenty-four of its twenty-six decisions. By 1810, he had written eighty-six percent of the court's majority opinions; none of his colleagues presented a dissenting view, and only one had presented a separate opinion. As Marshall expected, the reading of a single opinion when issuing a decision strengthened the court's claim to speak as the constitutionally sanctioned authority on the interpretation of the law.

Marshall's Federalist colleagues easily acquiesced in his leadership. Bushrod Washington, the first president's nephew, was recognized for his first-rate legal mind, and he fully supported Marshall's objectives. The court's other Federalists had neither the ability nor the initiative to present any serious challenges. But Marshall managed to preserve the court's unity even when resignations and deaths brought the appointment of Republican justices. Thomas Jefferson expected his first Supreme Court appointee, South Carolina's William Johnson, to counter Marshall's influence, and Johnson eventually did produce more independent opinions than any of his colleagues, with most of them in dissent. It turned out, though, that he agreed with the chief justice's nationalist vision and his understanding of the court's role, and he either supported or, if he had reservations, refused to challenge the court's most important decisions. Massachusetts' Joseph Story, whom President Madison appointed following Samuel Chase's death in 1811, had served in Congress as a loyal Republican, but he soon emerged as one of Marshall's closest allies. The youngest person ever named to the Supreme Court at age thirty-two, Story had already established a reputation as one of the Union's leading legal scholars, and his research and knowledge of precedent cases gave greater weight to the court's actions. After 1811, of the original Federalist members only Marshall and Washington remained, and Republican appointees more often filed individual opinions. Nevertheless, Marshall remained the court's dominant figure.

Marshall recognized that he needed more than unity to enhance the court's status. Moving in 1809 to its permanent quarters in the basement of the Capitol, underneath the Senate

Figure 5.2 "John Marshall." Portrait by Robert Matthew Sully (1829–1830). Courtesy Prints & Photographs
Division, Library of Congress, LC-DIG-det-4a26555.

chamber, the chief justice recognized that enhancing the court's prestige remained an uphill
battle. He had the political sense to know how far he could push the court's claims. His
written opinions anticipated its critics' arguments while presenting the court's decision with
sound legal reasoning, leaving opponents with little means of mounting a challenge. Most
notably, the 1803 *Marbury v. Madison* decision significantly strengthened the court's claim to

judicial review in determining the constitutionality of congressional acts—despite Republican rejections—by giving the Jefferson administration the outcome that it wanted. After *Marbury v. Madison*, the court would not reject another congressional act until 1858. Instead, its major decisions focused on invalidating *state* laws that threatened federal authority. The chief justice understood the Constitution as the American people's grant of power to the federal government, and the court's role was to interpret the document so that the government would have the power it needed to act. Through this approach, the Marshall Court upheld the "supreme law of the land" to enhance central authority against state claims. In a sense, the Marshall Court put into effect the federal veto over state laws that the Constitutional Convention had rejected in 1787.

Marshall's court first invalidated a state law with its decision in the case of *Fletcher v. Peck* (1810). In 1795, the Georgia legislature sold thirty-five million acres in the Yazoo region that later became part of the state of Mississippi. Georgians protested the legislature's action because speculators had bribed the lawmakers to secure the deal. The next year, a newly elected legislature rescinded the act selling the land. Those who had purchased land from the speculators challenged the repeal, and the Marshall Court upheld the original sale because its recension violated the Constitution's "contract clause," which prohibited a state from impairing any legal contract. Six years later, in *Martin v. Hunter's Lessee* (1816), a complicated case that also involved land titles, the court rejected the Virginia Court of Appeals' refusal to follow an earlier Supreme Court decision that voided a state law. A Virginia law contradicted the 1794 treaty with Great Britain, the court concluded; more importantly, Joseph Story's opinion for the majority argued conclusively that the court's authority to review constitutional issues included ruling on state court decisions. Then, in *Cohens v. Virginia* (1821), which began when Virginia officials arrested two brothers for violating a state law that prohibited selling lottery tickets, the court rejected Virginia's claim that the Supreme Court could not review the case. Marshall's opinion declared that the federal court would decide for itself which state cases it would hear—even though its decision upheld the state law because the congressional act authorizing the lottery tickets' sale applied only to the District of Columbia.

Marshall's boldest statement for national authority came in his decision in the case of *McCulloch v. Maryland* (1819). After Congress chartered a second Bank of the United States in 1816, seven legislatures imposed heavy taxes on "foreign" banks in efforts to keep the bank's branches out of their states. Maryland brought the suit against the bank's Baltimore branch when James William McCulloch, its cashier, refused to pay the state's tax. In the case, Marshall rejected Maryland's claim of state sovereignty: In the powers granted to it by the Constitution, he reasoned, the federal government was supreme because it represented *all* the people, not just the people of a particular state. Then, using the same principle that Alexander Hamilton used to defend the first Bank of the United States twenty-eight years earlier, Marshall broadly interpreted the "necessary and proper" clause to mean that Congress could undertake whatever action it deemed appropriate, so long as it was not clearly prohibited, to perform its responsibilities as specified in the Constitution. Congress thus had the constitutional authority to charter the bank because it was responsible for the Union's finances, and since "the power to tax involves the power to destroy," a state could not impose a tax that might impede or obstruct a federal institution from performing its responsibilities. Otherwise, Marshall concluded, the Constitution's statement that congressional acts were the "supreme law of the land" became an "empty and unmeaning declamation."

Through its confirmation of the doctrine of implied powers, *McCulloch v. Maryland* gave the federal government legal sanction to do whatever it considered necessary to achieve its constitutionally sanctioned ends. The case also encouraged the Union's economic expansion. Not only did the court explicitly authorize the national bank's legality, but by assuring the federal government's supremacy it supported the stable and centralized legal environment necessary to promote investment in new money-making ventures. Other Supreme Court decisions likewise favored economic development. *Fletcher v. Peck* had already demonstrated that a state legislature could not change a legally binding contract. In *Dartmouth College v. Woodward*, issued a month before *McCulloch v. Maryland* in 1819, the court extended the principle by concluding that the Constitution's "contract clause" involved public as well as private contracts—that is, a legislature could not modify or dissolve a charter that it had issued to a private corporation, protecting from government interference hundreds of banks, internal improvement, and manufacturing companies at the economy's forefront. Another 1819 decision, *Sturges v. Crowninshield*, allowed states to pass bankruptcy laws until Congress took up the responsibility. In *Gibbons v. Ogden* (1824), the court invalidated a New York state monopoly initially granted to Robert Fulton and broadly interpreted the Constitution's "commerce clause," which gave Congress the power to regulate interstate trade. States could regulate trade within their boundaries, Marshall reasoned, but federal law would take precedence over state law, with the court determining how far federal authority extended.

Marshall's accomplishments eventually provoked resistance. Not all accepted the court's assertion of judicial review, as presidents—especially Andrew Jackson—and numerous members of Congress maintained that each branch of the federal government should decide the constitutionality of congressional acts for itself. Large numbers of citizens likewise rejected the court's judicial nationalism and aggressively asserted the states' pre-eminence. The most vocal challenge came from Spencer Roane, president of the Virginia Court of Appeals—and the jurist whom Thomas Jefferson had wanted to appoint as chief justice if he could have secured Marshall's impeachment. In June 1819, Roane attacked Marshall's sweeping decisions in four essays published in the *Richmond Enquirer* under the pseudonym "Hampden." Roane charged that Marshall's reasoning was designed "to give a Carte Blanche to our federal rulers, and to obliterate the state governments, forever, from our political system"; instead, he contended, the Union represented a compact among the states, which had given power to the central government. The strength of Roane's arguments compelled Marshall to respond personally in a series of nine essays, published anonymously in the *Alexandria Gazette* under the name "Friend of the Constitution," which defended the court's decisions and reasserted Marshall's belief that the Constitution represented "the people of the United States . . . adopting a government for the whole nation." Still, the Virginia Assembly passed resolutions condemning the Supreme Court and instructing its congressional representatives to propose Constitutional amendments limiting its power. Congress never approved the proposed amendments, but the states' rights "compact" theory of the Union would long persist as a counter to the court's nationalism.

Marshall died in July 1835, and states' rights advocates expected his successor, Maryland's Roger B. Taney, to take the court in a less centralizing direction. Taney gained his appointment because he had been one of President Andrew Jackson's chief lieutenants in forming the Democratic Party, which Jackson himself declared would not "confound the powers" that the states had "reserved to themselves with those they have granted to the Confederacy." Jackson, in fact, had the opportunity to remake the court. Besides Taney, he appointed five justices, including two to fill the new seats created when the Judicial Reorganization Act of 1837 increased the number of justices from seven to nine. Frequent turnover and the appointment of cantankerous personalities prevented Taney from enjoying the unity that Marshall had achieved, but Taney's court indeed showed greater respect for state authority. One of his early decisions, *Briscoe v. Commonwealth Bank of Kentucky* (1837), ruled that the Constitution did not prohibit state banks from issuing currency. Starting with *New York v. Miln* (1839), a decision that upheld a state law requiring ship captains to provide information on passengers coming into New York City, for the next two decades the court significantly advanced acceptance of the states' *police power*—that is, the power to regulate behavior and to promote the health, welfare, and morals of its citizens.

Nevertheless, Taney's court actually continued Marshall's promotion of both national authority and economic progress. Taney had begun his political career as a Federalist and, like Marshall, agreed that the Constitution represented the national people's grant of power to a government. With the support of his colleagues, he showed that the Democrats' respect for states' rights could co-exist with a belief in a permanent Union fully empowered to achieve its constitutional ends. The court's reasoning in several decisions likewise helped modify the law so that it better supported commercial development. Taney's first major decision, *Charles River Bridge v. Warren Bridge* (1837), rejected the Charles River Bridge Company's claim that the Massachusetts legislature implicitly granted the company a monopoly. Taney ruled that a monopoly could not be implied, observing that transportation monopolies would discourage new technologies like the canals and railroads that were sprouting up across the Union. Two years later, in *Bank of Augusta v. Earle*, Taney ruled that a corporation chartered in one state could operate in other states unless state laws specifically prohibited "foreign" corporations from doing business within its boundaries. Then, in *Swift v. Tyson* (1842), Justice Story, with Taney's approval, announced the court's unanimous decision that federal courts were not subject to state court decisions when deciding commercial questions, laying the foundation for the development of a national commercial common law.

The Marshall and Taney courts provided the legal foundation for an active central government that could lead a nation. It also provided the legal conditions needed in a dynamic economy. Ironically, the court furthered national authority at the same time that economic changes heightened regional differences pulling against the centralizing trends.

Foundations of Sectionalism

While the Supreme Court promoted national development, expansion and development encouraged Americans to see the Union as composed of distinct Northeastern, Western, and Southern regions, each with unique interests and outlooks. The New England and Middle Atlantic sections of the colonial era formed the Northeast as it gradually became the Union's manufacturing center. The strength of the region's commerce in the colonial era provided the foundation for industrial development. Urban merchants had capital available for investment, and the risks involved in trans-Atlantic voyages encouraged many to put their capital behind new, experimental ventures. Likewise, craftsmen and "all purpose" artisans in port towns made the crude implements that advanced early industry, while the declining availability of eastern land drove farmers' sons and daughters to look for work in towns and factories. By the 1840s, manufacturing production joined trade at the center of the Northeast's economy; within another decade, the majority of the region's labor force had abandoned agriculture. Agriculture remained important to the region; as late as 1850, Pennsylvania and New York ranked among the top three states in wheat production. Rather than ship their goods abroad, though, farmers increasingly devoted their attention to vegetables, dairy products, and beef that they could sell with grains to feed the young men and women who left their fields to take jobs in workshops and factories.

The move toward manufacturing stimulated rapid urban growth in the Northeast. The old colonial port towns, including New York and Boston but especially Philadelphia and Baltimore, provided homes for several new industries, but smaller and new towns also grew as they became manufacturing centers. Lynn, Massachusetts, for example, had been a struggling New England village, but by 1850 it had become the Union's leading shoe-producing center, with more than fourteen thousand inhabitants. Several towns grew up around the factories of the Lowell Mills, which had been set up in rural areas along rivers to provide power for machines, while in newer settled areas like along the Erie Canal, boomtowns like Rochester, Utica, and Troy provided services for canal travelers and processed goods for the rural population. Immigrants contributed to the growth, but, before the 1840s, city populations mainly grew due to Americans relocating from the country. No matter what a city's background or the laborers' origins, the rapid expansion in shops and businesses, and the need for workers to live within walking distance of their jobs, made the Northeast the Union's most urbanized region. By 1850, more than one-third of the Northeast's population lived in cities; nineteen of the Union's thirty-two largest cities were located in the northeast, and Northeastern cities contained sixty-five percent of the nation's urban population.

Manufacturing expansion profoundly affected Northeastern society. In the colonial era, master craftsmen followed the traditions brought from Europe and passed on their skills to apprentices—boys who would live for years with a master craftsman in order to learn his skill—while providing guidance to journeymen—young men who had finished their apprenticeships but needed more experience or lacked the money to open their own shops. Journeymen and apprentices lived in their master's home and under his oversight, while masters worked alongside their employees, with the amount of work to be done determining the length and intensity of the workday. The need to expand production and the consequent shift toward factories dramatically altered these arrangements. Whether using machines or simply dividing tasks among workers, business owners increasingly lived away from the workplace and employed managers and clerks to oversee production. Semi-skilled and unskilled workers gradually replaced journeymen and apprentices, and laborers worked by the clock, performing the same repetitive tasks in twelve-to-fourteen-hour shifts. Employers now had less contact with their workers and no longer assumed responsibility for their activities beyond working hours. Laborers meanwhile faced intense and strictly regimented workdays, but their free time was now their own.

Separating employees from employers' oversight moved manufacturing regions toward societies based on social classes, founded partly on wealth but also on the type of labor a person performed. In the colonial era and the Union's first generations, the wealthy frequently interacted with their less prosperous neighbors in community and social activities. As a market-based economy grew, employers and employees increasingly had less to do with each other outside of the workplace, as people tended to spend their time with those who shared their economic status. By the 1830s, the foundations at least of class-based residential neighborhoods had emerged in most industrial towns, with the different classes displaying distinct outlooks, values, and ideals. Business owners joined merchants and large landowners to form an elite class that established private clubs and participated in exclusive social activities. Managers, clerks, and bookkeepers joined small shopkeepers, doctors, and lawyers in a middle class, characterized by labor based more on their intellectual than their physical abilities. Middle-class residents provided the membership for most churches while joining societies that espoused the virtues of thrift, sobriety, and personal responsibility. Workers meanwhile resided in working-class districts, relieving the tensions of their tedious workdays in taverns and boisterous theaters. In larger cities, working-class residents often formed gangs and engaged in violence that seemed the antithesis of middle-class respectability.

The prospect of a class-based society disturbed many Americans. A society with such a deep chasm between rich and poor presented the antithesis of a successful republic, and many feared that the United States might follow the course of Britain, where a small number of wealthy capitalists controlled and exploited an impoverished and ignorant mass of industrial workers. Manchester and Birmingham, the center of Britain's cotton and iron industries—filthy cities filled with impoverished laborers where industrialization appeared to have reached its most advanced stages—especially stood as warnings of the degradation that might accompany American industry. A few entrepreneurs hoped to avoid these ills when setting up their plants. Samuel Slater, for instance, hired families to work in his spinning mills. The Boston Manufacturing Company made a concerted effort to avoid a working class in its cotton mills by hiring mostly young women, usually between the ages of sixteen and thirty. To be sure, the lower wages paid to women kept labor costs down, and the operatives expected the women to be more reliable workers than men. Still, they presumed that women recruited from rural New England farms would work for only a few years before they left to marry. They could then be replaced with other farmers' daughters, who would likewise work for only a short time.

To make the "Lowell Girls'" time in the factories seem a positive experience, the company housed employees in dormitories, overseen by a "house mother" who enforced strict regulations on behavior. The company likewise provided church services, classes, lectures, libraries, and other "wholesome" activities designed to "improve" the women as they prepared for marriage and motherhood. Very quickly, the Lowell Girls became an international phenomenon. European visitors made pilgrimages to the mills to witness their unique manufacturing and labor system, while Americans celebrated the company for seemingly finding a way to enjoy the benefits of industry without its negative consequences. Since the mills paid two to three times as much as single women could earn as domestic laborers or seamstresses, thousands took the jobs and participated in the off-hours activities. From 1840 until 1845, one group published stories, poems, and essays written by their co-workers in a monthly periodical they entitled the *Lowell Offering*.

The reality of work in the mills, though, proved far from idyllic. The long hours and tedious work paralleled that of other industrial workers, and exhausted women found little privacy in the communal life in the dormitories, where as many as six shared a room. Women spent an average of five years in the factories, but a large number stayed for longer periods, preferring their wages and their relative independence to the restraints of marriage and domesticity. To the operators' horror, by the 1830s the "girls" were expressing their interests and grievances as industrial workers. In February 1834, several led a strike in response to a wage cut. Another strike in October 1836 followed an increase in rents at the boarding houses. In both instances, managers simply fired the strike leaders. By the early 1840s, though, more protests demanded limiting the workday to ten hours, and in 1845, women workers formed a union, the Lowell Female Reform Association. The mills' expansion eventually compelled the operators to hire more male Irish immigrants to meet the demand for labor. Women still dominated the workforce for the next forty years, but long before then, the company's efforts to provide paternal care and avoid the emergence of a permanent working class had become a quaint memory.

The problems facing the Lowell Girls reflected the challenges facing workers in most Northeastern industries. Employers set wages and the length of the workday with no input from their employees, who could be dismissed at will. Low pay, long hours, and frequent periods of unemployment became typical. Journeymen especially resisted what they recognized as the degradation of both their work and their status. Instead of gaining the respected positions in their communities they had once expected as independent shopkeepers, they saw themselves reduced to the status of permanent wage-earners, dependent on their employers and without the means to raise themselves one day to achieve respectability. Increasingly, the term "journeyman" itself came to refer to a worker with some technical skills, as opposed to an artisan who had completed his apprenticeship, while "mechanic" continued to refer to a skilled craftsman but became less associated with a shopkeeper than a general skilled worker.

Several workers concluded they could redress their grievances only through collective action. In some larger cities, journeymen formed trade unions to promote their interests and to organize strikes for better pay and conditions. Business owners challenged the legality of the unions. In 1806, a Pennsylvania state court dealt workers a blow when it declared Philadelphia shoemakers "guilty of a combination to raise their wages." Organization nevertheless continued, and in the mid-1820s and mid-1830s several strikes met mixed success. Increasingly, protestors expanded their demands from wages and work hours to include free public education for their children and abolishing imprisonment as a punishment for debt. In 1829, "Working Men's" parties in Philadelphia and New York elected laborers to several local offices. Philadelphia's Mechanics' Union of Trade Associations, organized in 1827, and New York's General Trades' Union, formed in 1833, represented the first attempts to create unions that united workers across different industries and represented labor as a class with its own distinct interests. In 1834, a handful of activists from several Northeastern cities attempted to form a National Trades' Union; Philadelphia workers won a ten-hour day in 1835 after successfully holding a "general strike" involving journeymen in several trades. Over the next two years printers, carpenters, weavers, and shoemakers formed their own "national" unions across the Northeast.

Most workers, though, grudgingly accepted the new conditions, trusting that America's standing as a "land of opportunity" might allow them to work their way into better circumstances. Several factors meanwhile limited the effectiveness of cross-trade and national unions, including the conflicting interests among workers in different industries, disagreements on tactics, workers' reluctance, and their religious and occupational suspicions of each other. The economic depression that followed the Panic of 1837 put a temporary end to most labor organization, as workers had to struggle for any employment they could get. After President Martin Van Buren issued an executive order in 1840 limiting the workday on public projects to ten hours, protests in private industries focused on the demand for a ten-hour day. Labor activity likewise gained a major boost in 1842, when Massachusetts chief justice Lemuel Shaw ruled in the case of *Commonwealth v. Hunt* that unions were legal organizations and that workers had the right to strike for a closed shop, which would mean employers could hire only union members. But as the number of immigrants increased in the 1840s, ethnic tensions further divided workers: "Old stock" Americans distrusted the foreign and predominantly Catholic newcomers, while migrants themselves brought with them the resentments against other groups that long prevailed in Europe. The continuing reluctance of many employees to see themselves as part of a distinct, permanent "class" likewise hindered efforts to unite workers among various industries. Still, despite the doubts and fears of those in better circumstances, the Northeast's manufacturing districts continued to move toward a society founded upon deeply divided classes.

West of the Appalachians, farming remained most people's central activity. Rapid growth and fertile soils transformed the area north of the Ohio River into the Union's agricultural heartland, populated with small farmers focusing on producing food crops and livestock. By 1850, twenty percent of the Union's population lived in the states carved out of the Northwest Territory. Ohio ranked as the third most populous state with almost two million inhabitants, and Ohio, Indiana, and Illinois stood among the four leading states in corn production. Western farmers acquired their lands through the federal government's generous land policies. The Land Act of 1800 required investors who bought public land to purchase at least 320 acres at a minimum of $2 an acre, though buyers could put up one-fourth of the price as a down payment and pay the balance within three years. As part of the Jeffersonian Republicans' reforms, Congress in 1804 reduced the minimum number of acres that could be purchased from 320 to 160—more than enough for a decent small farm. In response to the Panic of 1819, Congress in 1820 required purchasers to pay up front and in cash, but it reduced the minimum purchase to 80 acres and lowered the minimum price from $2 per acre to $1.25. Another law, in 1832, further reduced the smallest purchase of a tract to forty acres.

Small parcels at low minimum prices did not necessarily make the land affordable. After surveying a tract, the federal government would open a land office in a district and auction the lands starting at the minimum price. Many settlers refused to wait for the surveys, instead "squatting" on public lands and setting up farms in hope of gaining the necessary funds before the land office opened. In several communities, squatters formed "claim associations" to defend one another's holdings, including showing up at auctions to discourage bids against a squatter. Speculators nevertheless ended up purchasing most of the lands. Many were men of modest means who planned to live on part of their purchase and sell the remainder, but whether an absentee owner or a resident, speculators who found their lands occupied either had to evict squatters or work out arrangements for them to purchase their holdings. Improvements that squatters had made complicated these dealings, as occupants often cleared forests, put up buildings and fences, and plowed fields: Squatters wanted compensation for their labor and property, while speculators demanded full payment for farms that squatters had made more valuable. States generally resolved the conflicts with laws protecting squatters' rights in the improvements, and Congress greatly assisted their claims when it passed a Pre-emption Act in 1841. This law gave squatters the right to purchase up to 160 acres at the minimum price before a tract became available to the public.

Settlers in the southern sections of Ohio, Indiana, and Illinois had usually migrated from the upper South across the Ohio River. Popularly the Southern migrants became known as "Butternuts," due to the yellowish-brown color of their homespun clothes that were dyed in butternut juice. In contrast, migrants from New England and New York populated the northern portions of the west through Michigan and Wisconsin, forming what they called "Greater New England" or the "Universal Yankee Nation." No matter their origin, the pioneers who settled the Old Northwest moved as quickly as possible toward growing surplus crops for sale. As commercial farming expanded, farmers added different crops like fruits and vegetables to make the most out of an area's particular climate. Certain regions gained national renown for the quality of their goods. Ohio, for one, became a center of pork production; cattle-raising became an Illinois specialty, and eastern Ohio farmers rivaled western New York farmers for their production of cheese and dairy goods.

Commerce also contributed to the emergence of several major Western cities. Only Cincinnati, with more than 115,000 inhabitants in 1850, approached the size of the Union's largest cities on the Atlantic coast. Still, by mid-century, five cities west of the Appalachians to the Mississippi had populations of more than forty thousand—larger than the population of New York when it was the Union's largest city in 1790. Ten cities had more than ten thousand inhabitants each. Most impressively, the western cities emerged virtually overnight. Unlike in the East, where the colonial population base provided the foundation for urban growth, Western cities sprang from small villages or military posts, or out of the wilderness in what had only recently been Native lands. Cincinnati grew up around Fort Washington and had only seven hundred people in 1790. Saint Louis, established as a French outpost in 1763, likewise had several hundred inhabitants when the United States acquired Louisiana in 1803, but by 1850 it emerged as a city of 77,860. The village around Fort Detroit that had 1,442 people in 1820 had transformed by 1850 into a city of 21,019. Chicago, incorporated in 1833 with only 350 inhabitants, had almost thirty thousand people by 1850, while the fur-trading post at Milwaukee saw its population explode from only seventeen hundred in 1840 to more than twenty thousand just a decade later.

Western cities thrived mainly because they served the needs of the region's farmers. Western farm products tended to spoil quickly, so the most important commercial centers rose up at river junctions or similar locations where goods could be collected for quick shipment.

Pittsburgh, for example, lay where the Monongahela and Allegheny Rivers joined to form the Ohio, while much of Cincinnati's growth was attributable to its location at the end of the Miami and Erie Canal, which connected the Great Lakes to the Ohio River. The cities also housed numerous businesses for processing farm goods for easier shipment and sale. Flour mills emerged as important urban establishments; Cincinnati widely became known as "Porkopolis" because of the prevalence of its slaughter houses, while Chicago, located where the Illinois and Michigan Canal reached Lake Michigan, gained a similar reputation for its beef. Western cities likewise provided manufactured goods for the farm population. A few larger plants could be found; Cyrus McCormick in 1847 chose Chicago, rather than his native Virginia, as the location for the factory to make his grain-harvesting machine. The vast majority, though, remained small operations employing a modest number of workers. Manufacturing production remained far behind the levels reached in the Northeast, but the west made great strides toward self-sufficiency. The appearance of labor organizations and occasional strikes meanwhile indicated that the West's cities were moving toward the same type of class-based society that increasingly characterized the East.

Rural values remained dominant in the West, but in many ways the Northeast and the West appeared to follow converging paths. Diversification and development characterized these sections' economies as they experienced the early stages of a transformation that within the next century would make the United States the world's leading industrial power. Despite labor strife and the emergence of social classes, the belief remained strong among Northerners that they lived in an open society that offered equal opportunities to all white men. As fewer men relied on land ownership and small farming for their livelihood, clerks and others in middle-class positions considered their working for businesses owned and managed by others as a new form of independence, as their salaries offered financial security and protection from the market economy's fluctuations. For many, wage labor came to be explained as a temporary stage in which young men earned the money they needed to buy their own farms or open their own shops. Most workers actually remained wage laborers for the rest of their working lives, but whether part of the middle, working, or even upper classes, Northeasterners and Westerners emphasized that all men stood free and independent and could sell their goods to customers or their services to employers on a free market. "Free labor," in fact, became for Northerners the key to progress and prosperity, and one's social status, they assumed, depended primarily on his or her own abilities and efforts.

The South appeared headed in a different direction. As in the West, agriculture remained dominant, but the warmer climate and longer growing season allowed Southern planters to focus on large-scale cultivation of market crops for sale either at home or abroad. Tobacco production expanded from Virginia and North Carolina westward into Kentucky and northern Tennessee, while planters continued to grow rice along the South Carolina and Georgia coast. Rice as well as sugar also became cash crops along the lower Mississippi, and hemp for manufacturing rope emerged as the vital crop in the Bluegrass region of Kentucky. Cotton, though, quickly emerged as the region's dominant crop, the "king" that defined the Southern economy. Most cotton was raised in the "Black Belt" region across Georgia, Alabama, and Mississippi, but production of the fiber actually stretched westward from South Carolina to Louisiana and Texas and moved northward into western Tennessee and Arkansas. Like the South's other market goods, cotton was a labor-intensive crop that needed constant care and attention to make sure it grew successfully. As a result, planters depended heavily on slaves to serve as their labor force.

As in the colonial era, the plantation—that is, a large farm with hundreds of acres worked by a large number of resident laborers—maximized production of cotton, tobacco, and other market crops. The plantation, in fact, became the symbol of the South, especially as planters with substantial holdings in land and slaves rose to prominent positions in society and politics. Few plantations, though, approached the vast estates of legend. In fact, plantations were the minority among Southern farms, and most white Southerners did not own slaves. The 1850 census showed that only twenty-eight percent of white families in the slave states owned slaves, with only 1,733 individuals out of more than six million whites owning more than one hundred. Among slaveowners, only eleven percent—less than one percent of the total white population—owned more than twenty, the number commonly understood to qualify a family as belonging to the large planter ranks. Sixteen percent of owners possessed between ten and twenty slaves to stand as smaller planters, while half of the owners owned fewer than five. The majority of slaves actually lived on large plantations, and a significant portion of the white population depended heavily on slave labor. Most white Southerners, though, had only an indirect connection to the institution of slavery.

Large landholdings and bound labor may have encouraged planters to see themselves as a European-style aristocracy, and the persistence of a strong, traditional code of honor—including occasional duels to settle "matters of honor" long after the practice died out in the North and in western Europe—seemed to reinforce the South's image as an "old world" surviving in a new land. Lower South cotton planters, though, were actually better described as self-made men. Often rising from common backgrounds, they worked hard and used good business sense to organize their plantations to grow as much cotton and gain as much money as they could. Hired overseers managed the slaves on large plantations, while "drivers"—usually slaves

Figure 5.3 "The First Cotton-Gin." This image from the post–Civil War era probably reflects the antebellum period more than it does the gin's early use. Drawing by William Sheppard (1869). Courtesy Prints & Photographs Division, Library of Congress, LC-USZ62-103801.

themselves—prodded workers through the long days in the fields. Smaller planters more often oversaw their bondsmen themselves, while slaveowning "yeomen"—an English term for land-owning small farmers that remained in use in the South—worked alongside the few slaves they possessed. Nonslaveholders meanwhile continued to practice a form of "semi-subsistence" agriculture, concentrating on food production for their family's use and devoting maybe a few acres to cotton or tobacco to sell for cash. Some regions, such as Middle Tennessee and Virginia's Shenandoah Valley, resembled the West and prospered from producing food and raising livestock. But for most in small-farming regions, especially the mountains and hills ranging from western North Carolina to the northern portions of the Black Belt states, market production remained a secondary concern.

Planters and nonslaveholding yeomen largely lived in different worlds. Slaveowners on average held ten times as much wealth as nonslaveholders, and their focus on market crops drew their attention to national issues and international markets. Small farmers' lives centered more on their local community, where they relied heavily on their neighbors for barter and mutual support. Different living standards, interests, and outlooks created a tense social environment. Planters tended to look down on the ragged and often illiterate yeomen, while small farmers often resented slaveholders' snobbish pretentions. Several circumstances eased the strains: Family ties often bound planters and yeomen together, and the political system forced ambitious planters to downplay their advantages and to demonstrate physical strength, common sense, and plain manners to win nonslaveholders' votes. Some small farmers hoped that good fortune might give them an opportunity to join the ranks of slaveholders, though rising slave prices made that prospect increasingly less likely. Race, however, proved the most powerful unifying force. Yeoman farmers might dislike slavery, but they recognized that divisions among whites might tempt the slaves to rebel. Southern politicians meanwhile reassured nonslaveowners of their worth by preaching that slavery's presence guaranteed white equality, arguing that a poor white man would never have to work or take direction from the rich because they would always be recognized as superior to slaves.

Racism thus helped unite the white South despite slavery's divisive effects, and, as the Union's principal export, cotton brought in much of the capital that would fuel national economic development. But, ironically, slavery and market crops also hindered the South's economic progress. For one, the international demand for cotton discouraged the emergence of a significant merchant class, the class with the money and entrepreneurial outlook that invested in manufacturing in the North. Local *factors*, or brokers, connected planters to Northeastern shipping companies that would take the cotton to the Northeast or to England and bring manufactured goods back directly to the planters. Reliance on slave labor, and small farmers' relative isolation from the markets, likewise prevented the growth of a large wage-earning group that could have bought locally manufactured goods. As a result, the need for local industry to provide necessities remained small. The prospects of success from cotton planting, too, often absorbed cash that might have been invested in economic development. Good prices could persuade any successful artisan, professional, factor, or small planter to buy land and slaves to go into cotton planting, rather than put it into seemingly riskier ventures like manufacturing establishments or internal improvements.

To be sure, several industries did emerge in the South. Aside from the persistence of small-scale workshops and grist and saw mills, there were several iron foundries throughout the region, the most notable being the Tredegar Iron Works set up near Richmond, Virginia, in 1841. Richmond and central Virginia also became the prime location for processing tobacco into snuff, cigars, and plug chewing tobacco, and Alabama's Daniel Pratt and South Carolina's William Gregg set up mills to encourage Southerners to manufacture cotton textiles themselves. By the 1840s, Southerners provided twenty percent of the nation's capital invested in manufacturing, and businessmen had adapted slave labor to mining; to textile, iron, and rope production; and to tobacco and lumber processing. The slave states produced $171 million in manufactured goods in 1850. By then, if it had existed as a separate nation, the South would have stood among the world's largest economies. By then, too, a middle class of white-collar workers and professionals had become a significant presence in Southern cities. Though middle-class Southerners upheld slavery, they otherwise expressed a similar outlook to their Northern counterparts and pressured the region's planters to support more investment in commercial development and social reforms such as public schools.

Still, Southern manufacturing lagged far behind Northern production. Southerners contributed only seventeen percent of the nation's industrial production in 1850, and almost half of the region's manufacturing could be found in Maryland, Kentucky, and Missouri—states that were increasingly becoming more like the Northeast and the West than the South. Despite the presence of a middle class, the South's slower urban growth reflected continuing rural dominance. Only New Orleans, the vital port near the mouth of the Mississippi with 116,375 people in 1850, rivaled the size of the Northeastern cities. Washington, DC, Richmond, and the coastal towns of Charleston, Savannah, and Mobile, had populations ranging between twenty thousand and forty-three thousand, which generally lagged behind the impressive growth of the Western cities. Most Southern cities contained populations of fewer than ten thousand, and only fourteen percent of the Union's urban dwellers lived in the South. A larger urban population might have provided the customers needed to help small farmers move deeper into market production and stimulate economic activity. Improved transportation systems also could have promoted manufacturing. Given the region's network of rivers, however, there was little reason to dig canals, and Southerners invested less frequently in railroads, leaving the slave states—half of the Union's total—with less than half of the nation's railroad tracks in 1850. While the Southern economy thus grew in wealth and size, it grew without developing, remaining a "colonial" economy that produced raw materials for export but was dependent on imports for its manufactured goods.

Planters, of course, saw no problem with cotton's dominance. Some worried about the region's economic disparities and the lack of industry, but Southern whites usually regarded agriculture as the source of their section's strength. Like Thomas Jefferson, Southerners held on to the belief that farming provided the foundation of individual independence, since each man supposedly provided all of his family's needs through his own labor and depended on no one else for wages or support. Likewise, although values like thrift, sobriety, and personal integrity increasingly became prevalent in the North's commercially developed regions, Southerners more often held on to traditional notions about the importance of courage, bravery, and above all maintaining the respect of one's peers, even to the point of putting one's life at risk over the slightest perceived insult. Despite slavery's persistence, Southerners remained convinced that they stood as the heirs of the Revolution. At the same time, they became increasingly concerned about the ways that slavery distinguished their region from the rest of the Union.

Slavery and Union

In the Union's early years, slavery only occasionally became a divisive issue. The desire to preserve the Union proved a strong motivation to moderate opinions on the institution. Northern whites expressed a general distaste for slavery, though as their states moved toward abolition, most Northerners expressed little concern for African Americans living in bondage. They likewise recognized slavery's importance to the South and accepted its existence—so long as it remained distant from them and so long as their connection to it remained minimal. Southern leaders proclaimed their dislike for slavery and expressed hope that eventually they could eliminate it, but they insisted that Southerners alone should determine slavery's fate. The widespread acceptance of slavery as a "necessary evil" provided the basis for what historians describe as a "federal consensus" that guided politicians when dealing with slavery-related issues. Southerners publicly admitted that slavery contradicted republican ideals and acknowledged that someday in the distant future, when they could remove freed slaves from their society, the institution should be abolished. In the meantime, Northerners recognized slavery as a "Southern" problem that should be dealt with by the state governments. Under no circumstances, whites nationally agreed, should the federal government interfere with slavery in the South.

The federal consensus rested on the assumption that slavery was in decline. The rise of cotton and the plantation economy's expansion westward, however, revived the institution, as the invention of the cotton gin promised to make slave labor viable for generations to come. Virginia and Maryland planters who had worried about their large slave populations could now sell their "surplus" slaves to the cotton frontier. At the same time, the prospect of a massive rebellion like that begun in 1791 in the French colony of Saint-Domingue, on the island of Hispaniola, terrified white Southerners. Inspired partly by the French Revolution's calls for "liberty, equality, and fraternity," that rebellion had led to the establishment of the Republic of Haiti in 1804; refugees from the island brought to American shores stories of the bloody atrocities and horrible reprisals that the rebels committed as they overthrew their masters. The Haitian Rebellion reminded Southerners that emancipation had never before been achieved peacefully. The slave Gabriel's unsuccessful rebellion in Richmond in 1800, as well as an uprising of two hundred Louisiana slaves in 1811, kept alive fears that a similar catastrophe might happen in America. Sensitive that any proposal that hinted against slavery might provoke an uprising—and with a deepening economic commitment to bound labor—Southerners became more adamant in their demand that outsiders avoid any statement or action that might undermine state authority over the institution of slavery.

Some Southerners insisted that Congress reject discussion of any issue relating to slavery, since congressional action might be understood as an acknowledgment of the federal government's power to act against it. Most held back from this extreme position, for in the Union's first years Northern antislavery sentiment seemed only a minor threat. Instead, the consensus on the Union's importance, and the influence of Southern officeholders, kept the federal government firmly behind the slaveholders' rights. Despite pride in the Union's claim to stand as an example of liberty, American diplomats pressed Britain for compensation for bondsmen lost during the Revolution and in the War of 1812; likewise, they demanded agreements with Britain and Spain to extradite fugitives who had escaped to Canada or to a Spanish colony—demands that Britain, Spain, and later Mexico rejected. The Washington administration sent $700,000 to help French planters in their effort to put down the rebellion in Saint-Domingue. Once the rebels controlled the colony, President Adams reopened trade and expressed a willingness to negotiate with the rebellion's leaders, but President Jefferson halted the talks, refused to recognize Haitian independence, and suspended commerce with the black republic. These policies reassured Southerners of the Union's fidelity while notifying the international community that the American encouragement of liberty did not extend to slave uprisings.

Congressional approval of a Fugitive Slave Act in 1793 most visibly demonstrated the federal commitment to uphold slavery. The Constitution stated that a "person held to Service or Labor in one State" would not become free if he or she escaped to a state that had abolished slavery; instead, a fugitive slave was to "be delivered up" once an owner claimed his property. The Constitution's writers probably expected state officials to "deliver" runaways, but a specific case led Congress to set federal guidelines for fugitives' recovery. In November 1788, a Pennsylvania court indicted three Virginians for kidnapping a free African American whom they claimed was a fugitive slave. Virginia governor Beverly Randolph refused to extradite the three, and Pennsylvania governor Thomas Mifflin referred the matter to President Washington in July 1791. The president in turn submitted Mifflin's information to Congress. The resulting law, passed in February 1793, had the support of representatives from free states as well as those from slave states. The act mainly set out the responsibilities for state governors when handing over criminals, but it also outlined the process for the recovery of escaped slaves. Once an owner or the owner's agent apprehended a suspect, the person would be brought to a federal judge or a local magistrate who would review evidence—written or oral—that the person was a fugitive. If satisfied, the judge was to issue a "certificate of removal" allowing the claimant to take the slave out of the state. Anyone interfering with the process could be sued for up to $500.

Notwithstanding its commitment to slaveowners' rights, the federal government followed through with plans to outlaw slave importations. The Constitution forbade the prohibition of slave importations before January 1, 1808. As that date approached, President Jefferson reminded Congress of the restriction's coming expiration, and in March 1807, the lawmakers approved a bill banning American participation in the Atlantic slave trade after the next January 1. The act failed to eliminate all slave importations—over the next fifty years, possibly as many as fifty thousand slaves were smuggled into Southern ports—but it significantly reduced the number of new slaves that might have been brought to the Union. Slave merchants continued to ship blacks from Africa to colonies in the western hemisphere, but federal authorities worked to suppress American involvement. American ships patrolled the Caribbean and the coast of Africa to intercept traders, and Congress in 1820 declared participation in the slave trade to be piracy, a crime punishable by death. Reluctance to allow the British navy to search American ships defeated an 1824 treaty with Britain for joint cooperation in suppressing the trade. Still, by the 1830s American and British efforts had significantly reduced American involvement. Few by this time expected the prohibition of importations to serve as the first step toward abolition, as many once believed, but it restricted the slave population's growth and reflected a national agreement to limit the institution's presence.

Several issues involving slavery nevertheless irritated relations between free and slave states. Especially during the War of 1812, Federalists criticized the Constitution's three-fifths clause, which counted three-fifths of the slave population to determine the slave states' representation in the House of Representatives, as the source of Republican power in the federal government and, consequently, the Union's involvement in what seemed to Federalists a disastrous war. The war's satisfactory outcome disgraced Federalists, but northern Republican factions picked up the charge as a way to challenge Southern dominance of their party. As the cotton economy spread across the South, many suspected that slaveholders were extending their influence into the North. Agents representing planters came to the Middle Atlantic to buy slaves to take south before they reached the age that state laws stipulated for them to be freed. Others came to look for fugitives, and some seemed eager to claim as fugitives or kidnap free African Americans so they could be forced into bondage. Southerners in turn became more defensive. Demanding more federal protection, Southern representatives in 1818 pushed Congress to debate a new Fugitive Slave Act that would require Northern state officials to assist in the transfer of fugitives. The proposed law would also allow Southern judges to issue removal certificates that Northern judges would be bound to respect. Both chambers approved the act, but it ultimately failed because senators and representatives could not agree on its final version.

Concerns about slavery's strain on the Union contributed to the formation of "The Society for the Colonization of Free People of Color of America," or, as it became known, the American Colonization Society (ACS). Following up on a proposal from Virginia Federalist Charles Fenton Mercer, several prominent Northerners and Southerners met in Washington in

December 1816 to create an organization to raise funds for transporting free African Americans to a new settlement in West Africa. Colonizationalists like Mercer believed the ACS could solve the racial "problem" used to justify slavery by removing free blacks following their emancipation. Some slaveowners, though, openly acknowledged that African-American emigration could strengthen slavery through the removal of free blacks' "evil" influence and example. The vagueness of the ACS's message broadened its appeal. Chapters were formed in every state, and though it enjoyed less popularity in the lower South, slaveholders throughout the Union gave the ACS their support. Several state legislatures provided financial assistance, and a $100,000 grant from Congress helped the ACS in 1821 establish an African settlement that organizers named Liberia, with Monrovia—named for the American president—as its capital. Over the next forty years, the ACS would send to Liberia almost eleven thousand African Americans—most of them manumitted slaves. Though the Liberian legislature declared its independence in 1847, the black republic long remained under American protection.

Still, for many in the North, slavery's westward expansion reflected its increasing strength. The free states accepted the institution's existence in Kentucky, Tennessee, and the southwest because these states had been carved out of eastern slave states. Most Americans expected climate, soil conditions, and geography to restrict the growth of the plantation economy that needed slave labor, so Northerners tolerated slavery's expansion as long as it remained within its "natural limits," with the Ohio River as the geographic boundary between free and slave regions. Despite the prohibition of slavery in the Northwest Ordinance of 1787, however, Southern migrants took slaves across the Ohio into the Northwest Territory, and territorial governments upheld the institution. Ohio and Indiana formally outlawed slavery when they gained statehood in 1803 and 1816, but when Illinois entered the Union in 1818, its constitution only prohibited bringing new slaves and recognized slaves already in the state as "involuntary servants." Five years later, pro-slavery Illinoisans demanded a new constitution to make Illinois a slave state. The referendum for a constitutional convention was defeated mainly through the work of Governor Edward Coles, who had served as President Madison's personal secretary and had left Virginia to free his slaves. Nevertheless, the prospect of a slave state beyond slavery's "natural limits," along with Southern agents' purchasing of Northern slaves scheduled to be emancipated and their kidnapping of free blacks, provided Northerners with sufficient evidence to convince them that slavery, far from declining, seemed to be on the rise.

Resentments over slavery's expansion thus simmered long before Missouri's 1819 application for admission as a slave state provoked the most serious threat to the Union's existence since the 1780s. Despite the bitterness of the Missouri debates, the compromise that politicians worked out gained popular support as a fair settlement that subordinated sectional interests for the persistence of the Union. Still, slavery remained a sensitive topic that threatened to become divisive. Most free state whites still expressed strongly racist views, and Southerners continued to describe slavery as a "necessary evil." But after the Missouri Crisis, there was a gnawing sense that the Union contained divergent sections that might not be able to coexist. Northerners could tolerate slavery's existence as long as it remained contained in the South, and many hoped that the American Colonization Society could take the first steps toward its elimination. But Southerners made clear they would defend their right to determine slavery's future for themselves, and beginning in the 1830s, some argued that the institution should be understood not as a "necessary evil," but as a positive good.

The Union that Americans celebrated during the 1826 "Jubilee" had changed dramatically since its founding. Expansion had made the United States the dominant presence in North America. Booming agriculture and burgeoning industry lay the foundation for America's emergence as an economic power. Development brought social changes that increasingly divided Americans into distinct classes, while contrasting economic and labor systems appeared to be creating divergent cultures in the North and South. Nevertheless, the Union's transformation encouraged Americans to see their country as a nation, as one people that existed before the Constitution gave them a government. Nationalism meant that the Union was permanent and the bulwark of their freedom. Most agreed when President Andrew Jackson declared in 1833 that "Without union our independence and liberty would never have been achieved; without union they never can be maintained." Three years earlier, Massachusetts senator Daniel Webster—one of Jackson's political foes—expressed the same sentiment more succinctly when he proclaimed: "Liberty *and* Union, now and forever, one and inseparable!"

Not all Americans agreed with these sentiments. In fact, Webster's declaration came in response to South Carolina senator Robert Y. Hayne's assertion that the Union represented a compact among the states and that the states had the duty to protect individual liberty from encroaching federal power. For Hayne and other Southern leaders, protecting liberty through states' rights increasingly meant protecting their human property. Most Americans continued to see the federal and state governments as equals, fully empowered to accomplish distinct responsibilities. But sectional rifts increasingly threatened to bring state and federal authority into conflict. Moral and cultural developments likewise made it more difficult for Northerners and Southerners to cooperate on slavery. Despite the growing nationalism, the Constitution's recognition of state power provided a fault line where sectional resentments could threaten to divide the Union.

Suggested Readings

Balleisen, Edward J. *Navigating Failure: Bankruptcy and Commercial Society in Antebellum America* (Chapel Hill, 2001).

Baptist, Edward E. *The Half Has Never Been Told: Slavery and the Making of American Capitalism* (New York, 2014).

Blumin, Stuart M. *The Emergence of the Middle Class: Social Experience in the American City, 1760–1900* (Cambridge, UK, 1989).

Burin, Eric. *Slavery and the Peculiar Solution: A History of the American Colonization Society* (Gainesville, FL, 2005).

Burstein, Andrew. *America's Jubilee, July 4, 1826: A Generation Remembers the Revolution after Fifty Years of Independence* (New York, 2001).

Clark, Christopher. *Social Change in America: From the Revolution to the Civil War* (Chicago, 2006).

Faragher, John Mack. *Sugar Creek: Life on the Illinois Prairie* (New Haven, 1986).

Hobson, Charles E. *The Great Chief Justice: John Marshall and the Rule of Law* (Lawrence, KS, 1996).

John, Richard R. *Spreading the News: The American Postal System from Franklin to Morse* (Cambridge, MA, 1995).

Johnson, Walter. *River of Dark Dreams: Slavery and Empire in the Cotton Kingdom* (Cambridge, MA, 2013).

Kornblith, Gary J. *Slavery and Sectional Strife in the Early American Republic, 1776–1821* (Lanham, MD, 2009).

Larkin, Jack. *The Reshaping of Everyday Life, 1790–1840* (New York, 1988).

Larson, John Lauritz. *The Market Revolution in America: Liberty, Ambition, and the Eclipse of the Common Good* (Cambridge, UK, 2009).

Mason, Matthew. *Slavery and Politics in the Early American Republic* (Chapel Hill, 2006).

Newmyer, R. Kent. *The Supreme Court under Marshall and Taney* (Arlington Heights, IL, 1968).

Novak, William J. *The People's Welfare: Law and Regulation in Nineteenth-Century America* (Chapel Hill, 1996).

Taylor, George Rogers. *The Transportation Revolution, 1815–1860* (New York, 1951).

Wells, Jonathan Daniel. *The Origins of the Southern Middle Class, 1800–1861* (Chapel Hill, 2004).

VI

REVIVING AND REFORMING
THE UNION

New England Federalists regularly charged Thomas Jefferson with atheism. Actually, Jefferson accepted the existence of a "Great Creator" and the moral teachings of Jesus. But he rejected biblical accounts of miracles and Christian claims of divine intervention in human affairs, arguing that "priestcraft" and "kingcraft" had corrupted the "pure Christianity of Christ." He also believed that a person's religion should stand as a matter of conscience, not a matter of state, and he drafted Virginia's law to end state support for the Anglican Church. The Baptist Association of Danbury, Connecticut, lauded him as a champion for religious liberty in 1801 in the congratulatory address it sent to the newly elected president. Danbury's Baptists could worship openly, but since they still had to pay taxes to support the established Congregational Church, their letter complained that they experienced their privileges as "favors granted" rather than "inalienable rights." Jefferson's reply recalled "with solemn reverence" that the Constitution's first amendment prohibited Congress from passing laws establishing a national religion, "thus building a wall of separation between Church & State."

Connecticut would disestablish its church seventeen years later, and for later generations Jefferson's "wall of separation" metaphor became a core principle in constitutional thought. But to Jefferson's dismay—and the Baptists' delight—religious freedom took the Union in a different direction than the third president expected. The enlightened rationalism that the third president thought would prevail in the Union instead lost adherents. Conversely, religious revivals swept across the states, convincing thousands that God had chosen America to be His "New Israel." Faith underlay a strong conviction that moral reform could purify their society, as believers joined with skeptics to promote the improvement of individuals and institutions. For millions, self-control provided the key to a successful and well-meaning life; for some, withdrawing to form a perfect society offered the solution. Like economic and social change, revivalism and reform fostered the belief that Americans belonged to a national community that transcended loyalties to the states. They also highlighted the tensions over slavery that threatened national unity. Whether dedicating themselves to God, to righting social wrongs, or to creating their world anew, revivals and reform movements offered Americans a way of restoring a sense of order in a nation that, to many, seemed to be changing too fast.

The Second Great Awakening

Jefferson, the Danbury Baptists, and virtually every white American grew up in a culture heavily influenced by the Judeo-Christian tradition. Protestant versions of Christianity dominated the European nations from which their colonial ancestors had come, so most Americans accepted the existence of a God who controlled nature and human affairs and expressed Himself in the Trinity—that is, as a Heavenly Father; as Jesus the Son, who had lived among men and through His death reconciled followers to the Father; and as the Holy Spirit, which represented the continuing presence of God on Earth. Most accepted Christianity's basic moral and ethical teachings as well as the Bible as God's word. The English colonies had supported religion's influence in society through public prayers and public proclamations declaring days of fasting or thanksgiving. Most colonies had also provided financial and legal support for an officially established church. The Church of England, or Anglican Church, had enjoyed government backing in New York and the colonies south of Pennsylvania, while New England's Puritan origins had made the Congregational Church the established faith in Massachusetts, New Hampshire, and Connecticut. Only Rhode Island, Pennsylvania, Delaware, and New Jersey had officially allowed religious freedom, though these colonies still required belief in God.

Established churches and a common Protestant heritage had not guaranteed religious unity. In New England, disagreements over ministerial appointments led several Congregational churches, mostly in Connecticut, to form a Presbyterian system, in which boards of elders oversaw local church affairs. Elsewhere, the need to attract settlers convinced colonial founders to grant toleration to migrants of other faiths. As a result, several small sects could be found across the continent, with the largest tolerated churches usually populated by non-English migrants. The Scottish-dominated version of Presbyterian prevailed among the Scots-Irish descendants in the western portions of the Middle Atlantic and Southern colonies, just as followers of Lutheran or Reformed churches dominated German communities. Roman Catholics and Dutch Reformed believers remained influential minorities in Maryland and New York. The proliferation of churches, though, did not translate into widespread devotion. A series of revivals known as the "Great Awakening" shook up New England and the Middle Colonies in the 1730s and 1740s, but in the next generation Christianity's influence seemed to wane, as fewer people attended church or paid much attention to spiritual affairs. Americans emerged from the Revolution as a Christian people, but more by tradition than by devotion.

Much of the churches' troubles derived from the establishments' own self-assurance. With state support, neither Anglicans nor Congregationalists had much incentive to win converts or to serve their congregants. Increasingly college-educated ministers centered their Sunday services upon reading sermons designed more as theological treatises than as inspirational or instructional messages. Growing acceptance of the rationalist ideas of the Enlightenment increased the distance between clergy and laymen. Enlightenment principles rejected divine revelation as the source of truth, relying instead on observation of facts, scientific experimentation, and human reason. In several churches, ministers subtly moved their sermons away from a presumption of the Bible's divine inspiration while presenting God as a reasonable, benevolent Father who had designed the universe but seldom, if ever, had performed miracles. Rationalism's influence in New England eventually led several Congregational churches to reject the Trinity and proclaim themselves Unitarians, who honored Jesus as the great teacher and redeemer but denied His divinity. A more secular version of rationalism persisted among elites and urban artisans, with many—including most of the Union's founders—openly subscribing to deism, the belief that a Supreme Being had created the world and established "natural law" to guide it but never intervened in or paid much attention to human affairs.

Rationalism's expanding influence contributed to the Great Awakening's outbursts. The revival spirit that cut across several colonies helped expand a sense of devotion among the common people and in many instances challenged the authority of the established churches, both for their failure to provide spiritual guidance and for their ministers' departure from traditional beliefs. By the time of the Revolution, the Awakening's revivals had ceased, especially as the disruptions caused by the war further distracted the public from religious affairs. The rebellion's emphasis on individual liberty led to calls for religious freedom and resulted in the Anglican Church's disestablishment in New York and the South. The Puritan heritage, widespread membership, and political preferment allowed New England's "Congregational

Standing Order" to hang on for another generation. Eventually Anglicans joined with Baptists and Jeffersonian Republicans to end state support for the Federalist-dominated Congregational establishments in Connecticut in 1818 and New Hampshire in 1819, leaving Massachusetts the only state with an official church until voters in 1833 eliminated support for its Congregational Standing Order. Even in New England, though, churches throughout the Union emerged from the Revolution with minimal influence on society. Though maybe half of the population regularly attended services, by the 1790s less than ten percent of Americans formally belonged to a church.

By that decade, though, stirrings among several sects indicated that another series of revivals had already begun. Since the 1760s, a small number of Anglicans had followed the regimen of devotional activities designed by the clergyman John Wesley. In 1771, Wesley sent Francis Asbury to America to promote adherence to his spiritual "method." Wesley's well-known Tory leanings initially limited Asbury's success, but his more than sixty missionary tours eventually brought thousands of adherents into the Methodist Episcopal Church. Similarly, a handful of Baptist churches had emerged throughout the eighteenth century, mostly in New England and Virginia, both from Congregationalists and English Puritans who concluded that adult baptism represented a visual demonstration of a person's decision to follow Christ. Meanwhile, on the Kentucky frontier, Presbyterian ministers like James McGready began gaining larger followings at their "communion services"—outdoor meetings in which a series of sermons surrounded observance of the "Lord's Supper" ritual. The growth of all three denominations in the 1790s foreshadowed a wider outbreak of revivals and conversions that came after 1800 in a movement that Americans would refer to as a "Second Great Awakening."

A communion service held at Cane Ridge, in northeastern Kentucky, kicked off this Awakening. In August 1801, Barton W. Stone, one of McGready's converts, organized a communion service that attracted a crowd estimated at between ten and twenty thousand. Numerous local Baptists and Methodists joined Stone's fellow Presbyterians at the event, which turned from a three-day meeting into a weeklong series of sermons, fasting, prayers, conversions, and strange behaviors that adherents believed to reveal a dramatic outpouring of the Holy Spirit. Participants uncontrollably sang, danced, laughed, fell down unconscious or in a kind of trance, rolled around on the ground, or partook in a "barking exercise"—excessively grunting and jerking, sometimes while snarling and crawling on all fours like a hound to "tree the Devil." After Cane Ridge, similar revivals broke out across the West and the South, especially in frontier areas, but revivalism likewise moved eastward into the original states. Few matched the size or intensity of the initial Kentucky revival, but afterward "camp meetings" became regular events, characterized by powerful preaching, emotional testimonials and conversions, and the singing of new, popular gospel hymns. With hundreds held each year, camp meetings brought thousands of followers into the Presbyterian, Baptist, and Methodist folds.

Revivalists won followers through preaching an *evangelical* gospel, so named from the Greek term for "good news." As in traditional Christianity, evangelicals stressed a person's redemption from sin through belief that Christ was the Son of God, and that His death paid the penalty for human sins. Whereas the established faiths assured members that church membership and following its moral teachings fulfilled one's religious responsibilities, evangelicals maintained that a conversion experience marked the central experience in a Christian's life. Conversion came at a deeply felt emotional moment when a person repented of sins and dedicated his or her life to God. Through this experience, the convert avoided damnation and underwent a spiritual "rebirth" that transformed the believer's life, which he or she would now devote to serving God through prayer, righteous living, and spreading the gospel message. In sharp contrast to the traditional churches' hierarchy and authoritarianism, the evangelical faiths also stressed the common believers' dignity before God and laymen's control of church affairs.

Devoted to the Bible as the sole source of religious truth, they maintained that conversion was available to anyone who could read the Word or hear the message. Likewise, a person's "calling" and preaching ability, rather than formal education, provided the only qualification necessary for the ministry.

Evangelicalism's emotional excesses and potentially rebellious implications appeared threatening to the traditional churches. In 1784, Asbury and Thomas Coke organized the American Methodist Episcopal Church in Baltimore, setting up "general conferences" headed by bishops who would appoint "circuit riders"—traveling ministers who would hold camp meetings anywhere they could in a district. Among Presbyterians, arguments over emotional conversions and popular outbursts divided the church's general assembly in 1837 into "Old School" and "New School" factions. The Baptists' emphasis on congregational independence prevented a centralized organization, and disagreement on different doctrinal points divided the church into several small sects. Still, the majority of Baptists formed a "General Mission Convention" in 1814 to coordinate missionary efforts, though the Baptists' expansion came mainly through the work of "farmer preachers"—common men whose calling led them to preach and start congregations when they moved into new areas. The Baptist message spread, especially among the rural poor. Methodists likewise tended to win converts from poorer folk while also gaining support from modest farmers and urban workers. Within a generation, the two denominations had become the Union's largest, with Methodists claiming about 2.7 million adherents by 1850 and Baptists about 1.6 million. The Presbyterian Church meanwhile claimed more than six

Figure 6.1 "Religious Camp Meeting: An Old-Time Camp Meeting." An artist's depiction of the revivals common on the frontier during the Second Great Awakening. Watercolor on paper by J. Maze Burbank (1839). Courtesy New Bedford Whaling Museum, New Bedford, Massachusetts; number 1910.1.2.

hundred thousand members, bringing close to seventy percent of all American Protestants into one of the three major churches.

Although mostly associated with the South and West, revivalism also affected Puritan descendants in the Northeast. During the 1790s, Congregational and Presbyterian ministers redoubled their efforts to produce renewals of faith in several towns. The major revival occurred on the Yale University campus at New Haven, Connecticut. Concerned over the popularity of deism among students, Timothy Dwight, Yale's president since 1795, began a four-year series of sermons in 1801 designed to restore confidence in Christianity's basic tenets. At first Dwight's messages produced few results, but a revival in 1802 converted a third of the college's 225 students. Many of the converts entered the ministry and promoted similar revivals throughout New England, New York, and the Northwest. The northern outbursts seldom matched the emotional intensity of those in the South and West. Assured that emotional responses could not produce well-grounded conversions, ministers expressed confidence that "calm" revivals would avoid ridicule and win nonbelievers' respect. Still, the Yale revival kicked off a renewed sense of devotion among New England's traditional churches that made evangelicalism as important to Northeastern society as it was elsewhere.

The Northeast's best-known and most effective revivalist never attended college. Born in Connecticut in 1792, Charles Grandison Finney rejected Christianity as a young man. After reading the Bible to assist his legal studies and to strengthen his friendly arguments with the local Presbyterian minister, he experienced a dramatic conversion on October 10, 1821, and immediately embarked on a preaching career. Over the next forty years, Finney gained renown as an itinerant minister for producing revivals, from the Northwestern frontier to the east coast's urban centers. Finney's charisma, athletic frame, and handsome appearance made him a popular speaker. With no formal training, he preached without notes, wore a business suit rather than a clerical robe, and peppered his sermons with illustrations from everyday life. Moreover, he developed techniques designed to prod potential converts into making the right decision. In public prayers, he called individuals by name to ask for their conversion; he encouraged women to testify publicly in services, arranging for those thought to be wavering to sit in the "anxious bench"—usually located in the front row—where he could appeal to them directly; and he ended sermons with an "invitation" enticing sinners to come forward to repent. His greatest success came at Rochester, New York, where from September 1830, through March 1831, his preaching won hundreds of converts and gained for the city a reputation for spiritual renewal second only to Cane Ridge.

Other revivalists quickly adopted Finney's techniques, and several forces contributed to promote revivalism's success. The evangelical message of redemption and self-worth undoubtedly appealed to many people, regardless of their circumstances. Living in a nominally Christian culture, many converts had received religious instruction in their youth and returned to the faith as adults. The revivalists' popular approach and new religious style struck a chord with listeners, while the new social conditions in the rapidly changing Union made many Americans ripe for the revivalists' harvest. Ministers took advantage of the new transportation facilities to spread the gospel. As printing technology advanced, religious publications proliferated, with each denomination producing several publications. For many people on the frontier, revivalism provided a source of release from both hard work and isolation. In new rural settlements and small towns like those in the "Burned-Over District"—the term Finney used to describe the region along the Erie Canal because of the fervor of revivals he conducted there during the late 1820s—joining a church provided an anchor of institutional stability when many traditional institutions had broken down or were being re-formed. Church membership also provided a community that gave frontiersmen and new town dwellers a sense of place and fellowship among like-minded persons. Women in particular responded to the revivalists' appeal, as their behind-the-scenes work provided rewarding responsibilities and leadership experience unavailable in other areas.

For many, too, revivalism offered a way of regaining a sense of order in a society seemingly out of control. Especially in the small manufacturing towns in the Northeast, businessmen and professionals lived fairly close to the growing working class and worried about their inability to regulate their employees' raucous behavior. As a result, Finney's preaching attracted mostly middle-class followers, who were attracted to Christianity's teachings on self-control, sober living, honesty, integrity, and hard work. Revivalism offered an opportunity to fill society with morally responsible individuals who would one day have to account for their sins before God. Many employers would hire only church members, convinced that Christian virtues characterized reliable workers. Journeyman craftsmen made up almost half of the new church members in the "Burned-Over District," as many recognized that conversion could get them secure employment. Similarly, revivalism made little headway in the Northeast's largest cities until after the beginning of the depression in 1837, when workers in New York and Philadelphia concluded that Christianity offered both an edge when looking for a job and a way to take control of their lives in the more regimented industrial society.

Regardless of the reasons for conversions, the Second Great Awakening profoundly impacted American Christianity's practices and beliefs. The emphasis on individual transformation, the equality of believers, and lay participation in services encouraged a more egalitarian and democratic form of the faith. Clergymen could no longer claim respect as a separate and distinct caste based upon their education and training. Instead, a minister's heartfelt conversion and conviction—displayed in his conduct and sermons—demonstrated the necessary qualifications for leadership. Churches also dismissed tradition as a basis for authority. Charging that Roman Catholic leaders had corrupted the "true" church soon after the age of Christ's apostles, evangelicals stressed that believers could now read the Bible for themselves to discover the answers to religious questions. Ministers meanwhile sought to discern in Scripture a New Testament pattern to restore the practices of the pure, "primitive" church. In primitivism's most extreme expression, Presbyterians Barton W. Stone and Thomas and Alexander Campbell led separate movements calling for believers to identify themselves simply as "Christians," with "no creed but the Bible." Uniting their efforts in 1830, the Stone-Campbell movement formed the Disciples of Christ, a new denomination that claimed more than 200,000 followers by 1850. Most evangelicals remained in the larger churches, but each denomination placed greater emphasis on biblical, rather than historical or traditional, foundations for their beliefs and practices.

The Awakening also marked an important theological shift in American Protestantism. During the colonial era, churches mostly followed the teachings of the sixteenth-century Swiss reformer John Calvin, who contended that God revealed Himself only to a predestined "elect" that He had chosen before the foundation of the world. By the time of the Second Great Awakening, individual opportunity and the belief in equality had undermined Calvinism's cultural foundations, and revivalists either implicitly or explicitly preached a gospel based on Arminianism, a term from the Latin form of the last name of the Dutch theologian Jacob Hermannson. Arminian thought stressed that God had given humans free will and that salvation came when a person decided to dedicate his life to Christ. Revivals could be produced through persuading individuals to change their lives; once the believer received salvation, he could avoid sin and honor God through his performance of good works. Methodists and Disciples openly embraced Arminian tenets, but the challenges to the long-held Calvinist theology disturbed many members of churches in the Puritan tradition. Outside of a few sects, most Baptists joined Congregationalists to describe themselves as Calvinists while in practice promoting an Arminian gospel. Presbyterian revivalists accepted Nathaniel Taylor's "New Haven" or "New School" theology to argue that "original sin" referred to individual failure rather than to the predestined human condition. Still, "Cumberland Presbyterians" in Kentucky and Tennessee in 1829 formed a separate denomination that openly advocated Arminian views.

The emphasis on individuals' actions likewise produced a shift in Protestant views on millennialism, the belief that the end of time would bring a thousand-year reign of Christianity in a world of peace, prosperity, and brotherhood. American Christians had traditionally accepted *pre-millennialism*, which held that, after a prophesied period of tribulation and persecution of His followers, Christ would return to begin the millennium and rule Himself in a Heaven on Earth. As the Second Great Awakening progressed, believers increasingly expressed their acceptance of *post-millennialism*, the belief that Christianity would expand and transform the world to bring about a long period of peace and prosperity before Christ returned at the end of time. The wave of conversions—along with the economy's expanding wealth, the development of new technologies and conveniences, and the widespread belief in the Union's secular mission as the land of liberty—convinced many that the millennial age was at hand. Post-millennialism, too, fit well with Arminianism's emphasis on the individual's role in accepting and expanding the faith. Since human efforts could produce more conversions and improve their world, many concluded that preaching and good works could bring on the millennium and hasten Christ's second coming.

The followers of William Miller, a Baptist minister from New York, revealed the power of millennial beliefs. Miller grew up a deist but experienced his conversion while a soldier at the Battle of Plattsburgh in the War of 1812. While studying for the ministry, he convinced himself that the "cleansing" of "the sanctuary" prophesied in the Old Testament Book of Daniel referred to the Second Coming. In conjunction with other biblical passages, he calculated that the "Advent" would occur by March 21, 1843. Within a decade after he started preaching in 1831, Miller gained more than twenty-five thousand followers. Thousands quit their jobs or refused to harvest their crops, in anticipation of the millennium's beginning. Evangelicals and even nonbelievers who doubted Miller nevertheless watched with anticipation. When the year passed without Christ's return, one follower recalculated Miller's reasoning using the Jewish calendar and concluded the Second Coming would actually occur on October 22, 1844. After that date likewise came and went with no sighting of Jesus, most of Miller's followers abandoned him. Core adherents remained firm, maintaining that the "cleansing" actually occurred in heaven in preparation for Christ's imminent return, and they shifted their attention to arguing that Scripture directed Christians to worship on Saturday rather than Sunday. Soon they were competing for converts as Seventh-Day Adventists.

Few others identified a specific date for the Second Coming. In a moment of excitement, Finney predicted that, if Christians fully applied themselves, they could bring on Christ's return within three years, but he soon backed off this prediction. By the mid-1840s, the coming kingdom of God seemed more distant. The wave of revivals slowed, especially as the expanding economy allowed a new generation of Methodists and Baptists to move into the middle class; anxious for respectability, many now shied away from the radical, emotional, and anti-intellectual traits of their parents' revivals. Many Americans meanwhile resisted the evangelicals' appeal. Anglicans reorganized into the Episcopal Church in 1784 and by 1850 had the following of only three percent of churchgoers, but the church had recovered from its English heritage and the loss of state support to maintain a strong following among wealthy Southerners. Large numbers of German and especially Irish immigrants after 1830 helped make the Roman Catholic Church the third largest church in the Union. The revival spirit had more influence among German Protestants, though most remained adherents of a Lutheran church that largely avoided evangelicalism's influence. In addition, many Americans refused to accept any faith. A significant minority expressed strong skepticism of Christian claims, while others simply rejected the faith on account of indifference.

Nevertheless, Christianity remained a powerful cultural influence. Probably more than one-third of all Americans were active church members, and estimates indicate that more than forty percent of all Americans sympathized with the evangelical outlook. Despite constant bickering on minor theological points, the churches united to promote the belief that the Union represented God's chosen nation, a people whose free institutions and pure religion would usher in the millennium. Nonbelievers recognized the importance of faith to its adherents and seldom challenged its public presence. At the same time, the churches' emphasis on individual conversion and right behavior both reflected and reinforced a wider desire to improve oneself and the larger society.

The Reform Impulse

In the Northeast especially, revivalism went beyond saving souls to include improving conditions in the world. Evangelicals like Lyman Beecher—a Yale graduate second only to Finney as the Northeast's leading revivalist—feared that disestablishing New England's Congregational Church would destroy morality in their states. The social changes accompanying urbanization and manufacturing expansion convinced the pious as well as skeptics that society stood on the verge of collapse. Irreverent behavior in urban working-class and poorer districts seemed particularly disturbing. Crime seemed to dominate the cities, and adult and juvenile gangs roamed districts rife with poverty, drunkenness, and gambling. More than 130 urban riots broke out from the 1810s through the 1830s, and the growing numbers of prostitutes and brothels reflected a wider breakdown of traditional morality. Among rural inhabitants, fights and lynching remained common, with dueling persisting in the South. Inspired by a sense of Christian duty and with a hope of bringing on the millennium, ministers reasoned that changing individuals' behavior presented the best way to improve social conditions. Many with secular motives shared a desire to encourage improvement, and they agreed that the key lay in reforming individuals. Their efforts met with mixed success, but the intensity of their efforts made the reform impulse even more widespread than religious revivalism.

Reformers addressed the Union's social ills mainly through "voluntary associations"—private groups organized to draw attention to problems and to propose remedies for them. Several interdenominational organizations in the Northeast formed what ministers called the "Evangelical United Front." Clergymen like Beecher provided clerical leadership for much of the "Benevolent Empire," which mainly sought to spread the gospel through assisting those in need, while wealthy laymen like New York entrepreneurs Arthur and Lewis Tappan provided funding. Several denominations formed local organizations to send missionaries to the western frontier; eventually the largest state groups united to form the American Home Missionary Society in 1826. Reports from missionaries of the conditions they confronted stirred the devout to form new associations to address specific problems. The American Bible Society, formed in 1816, and the American Tract Society, organized nine years later, printed religious literature with the goal of making them available to every family in the Union. The American Sunday School Union, organized in 1824, established schools in rural regions to impart Christian lessons. Charles Finney's wife Lydia helped found the Female Moral Reform Society in 1839 to bring women out of prostitution, and several local societies offered medical care, set up orphanages, and distributed food to the poor.

Christian reformers overreached, though, when they promoted observance of Sunday as a national holy day. American Protestants long respected the first day of the week as the "Christian Sabbath," a day devoted to worship, prayer, and spiritual concerns. In 1810, Congress passed a law requiring post offices to remain open on Sunday, regardless of local laws requiring businesses to close on the Sabbath. Because most postmasters also kept stores, the Sunday mail law meant that, on the "Lord's Day," churches in small communities now had to compete with bustling centers of activity. To evangelicals, the government encouraged the increasingly common practice of "Sabbath-breaking," so Beecher, Lewis Tappan, and Josiah Bissell formed the General Union for Promoting the Observance of the Christian Sabbath to petition Congress to end Sunday mails. Bissell meanwhile formed the "Pioneer Line" to show that a transportation company could prosper without doing business on Sundays.

The efforts of the "Sabbatarians" had little impact. Unable to secure a mail contract, the Pioneer Line went out of business within a year. Tappan and Bissell called for boycotts of businesses that operated on Sundays, but as Beecher feared, their demand only alienated the public. The petition effort's only impact was to make Kentucky senator Richard M. Johnson—a practicing Baptist—a national figure for his powerful report to Congress defending the separation of church and state.

The evangelicals' war against alcohol proved much more successful, making the temperance cause the Union's most popular reform. Drinks like wine, beer, whiskey, and hard cider were well established as part of American culture at meals, for relaxation, and on special occasions. Farmers usually distilled much of their corn into whiskey—partly because it would be easier to transport over a long distance, but also because they considered it a healthier beverage than their water. Artisans meanwhile often shared drinks during the workday with their journeymen and apprentices. Churches condemned drunkenness but not alcohol itself, and ministers as well as devout congregants enjoyed drinking as much as the unfaithful. Americans of all social ranks drank a lot; by 1825, the average person over age fifteen drank about seven gallons of alcohol a year. By that time, drunkenness appeared to have become more prevalent, and drinking became closely associated with unemployment, idleness, crime, and domestic abuse. Many young men appeared to drink their lives away. With hard liquor seeming to flow mostly among the poor and immigrants, factory and workshop owners came to see liquor as a disruptive force that kept their workers from performing responsibly and efficiently.

As with missionary efforts, local societies first took action against alcohol, calling for its members to practice temperance—that is, moderation in drinking and avoidance of distilled beverages and drunkenness. Lyman Beecher issued the call for a national organization during a series of anti-alcohol sermons that he preached in the fall of 1825. In February 1826, Beecher and fifteen fellow crusaders met in Boston to create the American Society for the Promotion of Temperance, better known as the American Temperance Society. Under the leadership of Reverend Justin Edwards, the ATS distributed literature and sponsored lectures promoting sobriety and condemning drunkenness as the path to ruin and eternal damnation. Relying on "moral suasion" to convince Americans to give up drinking, temperance advocates compiled statistics to show alcoholism's association with crime, poverty, poor health, and insanity. Initially the movement emphasized only giving up hard liquor and practicing moderation with less-pungent beverages like beer and wine, but increasingly temperance came to mean total abstinence from any alcoholic drink. When the ATS reorganized as the American Temperance Union in 1836, the organization required members to sign a pledge promising to abstain from any alcohol, with many declaring that henceforth they would drink only cold water. Those who signed the pledge were to place a small "T" next to their signatures, showing their commitment to the temperance movement and identifying them as "teetotalers."

More than other reforms in the "Benevolent Empire," the American Temperance Society gained a wide following in every region of the Union. By 1834, more than five thousand chapters existed across the states, and an estimated two million individuals took the Temperance Union's teetotal pledge. Countless others never joined but renounced alcohol nonetheless. Urban workers went beyond the ATU's appeals to form their own organization that encouraged both avoiding drunkenness and the rehabilitation of confirmed drunkards. According to legend, six hard-drinking workers attended a temperance lecture in Baltimore on April 2, 1840, intending to ridicule the proceedings. Instead, the message persuaded them to reform their lives and give up drinking. Eager to spread their new faith, the six formed the Washington Temperance Society, named in honor of the first president. Stressing the practical benefits of sobriety, the "Washingtonians" presented a more secular message than did the ATU and featured testimonials from ex-drunkards who had transformed themselves through temperance. Within three years of its founding, the organization had gained more than 500,000 members, most in larger urban centers, where religious reformers usually had less influence.

The temperance campaign proved remarkably effective. By the late 1840s, the average amount of alcohol consumed by those over age fifteen had declined to less than two gallons a year. When "moral suasion" appeared to have reached everyone it could, some temperance advocates concluded that government alone could rid the Union of the evils of strong drink. Several states approved local-option laws that allowed town and county authorities to restrict drinking. In 1838 and 1839, the legislatures in Massachusetts and Mississippi both approved laws prohibiting selling distilled spirits in small portions, which would prevent selling hard liquors as drinks and make the beverages too expensive for the poor. In Maine, Portland merchant Neal Dow worked tirelessly for total prohibition to counter the poverty and despair he witnessed in his home town. His efforts resulted in an 1851 act that outlawed the sale of all alcoholic beverages except for "medicinal, mechanical, or manufacturing purposes." Within four years, twelve other states, including New York and all New England states, had passed their

Figure 6.2 "The Drunkard's Progress. From the First Glass to the Grave." Depicts the temperance movement's view on the dangers of alcohol. Lithograph by Nathaniel Currier (1846). Courtesy Prints & Photographs Division, Library of Congress, LC-DIG-ppmsca-32719.

134

own "Maine Laws." Political opposition from immigrant voters, along with many temperance men's doubts about the effectiveness of prohibition, led to the quick repeal of most of the Maine Laws, but debates over restrictions on alcohol would continue for several generations.

Other reformers also concluded that state action could accomplish their ends. Assuming that reforming society required changing individuals' behavior, government power provided the opportunity to reach those most in need or most resistant to moral appeals. Through the establishment of *asylums*—a term based on the Greek word for "haven"—the government could provide the necessary environment for indigents and deviants to learn how to become productive and responsible citizens. Blaming laziness and character flaws for poverty among the "able poor"—unemployed men, as opposed to the "deserving poor" like helpless widows and orphans—local governments in the early 1820s began to require indigents to move into almshouses or workhouses and moved away from providing "outdoor relief"—the traditional delivery of food, fuel, and a small amount of cash directly to the homes of the poor. In the "poorhouses," inmates received food and shelter, but they also had to follow strict, regimented schedules and accept labor requirements that were designed to instill the living skills and work ethic necessary for them to become self-sufficient. Similarly, when dealing with children who had lost their parents, communities less often apprenticed or "farmed out" wards to reluctant relatives, instead constructing orphanages where they could learn thrift, industry, and personal responsibility.

Reformers likewise believed that asylums could sharply reduce crime. In the colonial era, authorities carried out justice swiftly through punishments like locking offenders in stocks, whipping or branding them, or execution by hanging. Reformers concluded that criminal behavior, like poverty, resulted from personal flaws, probably brought on through poor home conditions and a lack of family guidance when young. Confident that changed circumstances could reform even the most hardened criminal, reformers advocated "penitentiaries," institutions where inmates could live in positive environments to develop responsible characteristics. The first penitentiaries, built in New York at Auburn in 1816 and in Ossining, or "Sing Sing," in 1825, required prisoners to work and observe scheduled prayers. Communication with other inmates was strictly prohibited, partly to limit the spread of criminal influences but mainly to force offenders to reflect and eventually become "penitent" for their crimes. Philadelphia's Eastern State Penitentiary, built in 1829, went even farther, with inmates living and working in solitary confinement with no exposure to other prisoners. Over the next generation, reformers debated the relative merits of the "Auburn" system as opposed to the "Pennsylvania" system, but by 1850 most states had constructed their own penitentiaries. Cities meanwhile set up "Houses of Refuge" for abandoned and abused orphans, to provide the parental guidance necessary to steer delinquents away from a life of crime.

Some reformers insisted that asylums could liberate even those suffering from physical and mental disabilities. The blind, deaf, and "dumb"—the common term for those who could not speak—were long considered helpless and permanently afflicted, but reformers contended that, as with criminals and the poor, a supportive environment could transform them into contributing members of society. The Hartford Asylum for the Education and Instruction of the Deaf and Dumb, established in 1817 by Thomas H. Gallaudet and Laurent Clerc, became a model for institutions in other states, as did the school for the blind that Dr. Samuel Gridley Howe set up in Boston in 1832. In 1833, Samuel B. Woodward accepted the post of superintendent of Massachusetts' Worcester "Lunatic Asylum," the first state hospital devoted to the treatment of the mentally ill. Most mentally ill persons nevertheless remained jailed with criminals, in appalling conditions. After learning of these conditions, Dorothea Dix, a Massachusetts teacher, prepared a report for the state legislature that graphically described the brutal treatment of insane inmates. Her portrayal of the patients' horrible experiences persuaded lawmakers to

Figure 6.3 "Eastern State Penitentiary." Though surrounded by rural farmland when opened in 1829, Pennsylvania's first penitentiary was located only a mile and a half from Center City Philadelphia. Hand-colored engraving by C. Burton (1831). Courtesy of Eastern State Penitentiary Historic Site.

expand the size of the state hospital, and Dix spent the next decade traveling the Union to promote better treatment of the mentally ill. Often the first woman to speak before a state's legislature, Dix succeeded in convincing her hearers to set up mental hospitals throughout the Union.

The asylum movement swept across the Union, but in the long run the results proved disappointing. Schools did teach important skills to the disabled while advancing new methods of dealing with the loss of speech, eyesight, and hearing. Dix's campaign improved living conditions for the mentally ill, and though Woodward's claims about patient recovery were often exaggerated, a significant portion of the Worcester asylum's patients were able to return to mainstream society. Still, the reformers' conviction that they could redeem any person through changing the environment, instilling proper virtues, and shaping character proved unrealistic. Most mental disabilities remained beyond the reach of science. Prisoners resisted rehabilitation, compelling authorities to impose harsher punishments. As costs increased, legislatures often failed to provide sufficient funds to support the asylums, leaving them dirty, overcrowded, and unable to supply sufficient food. A few reformers remained hopeful, but by the 1850s most had given up on asylums' rehabilitating potential. Instead, poorhouses, prisons, houses of refuge, and mental hospitals assumed "custodial" roles, becoming institutions in which society housed its "undesirables."

More promising state action came through the promotion of public schools. Americans entered the nineteenth century among the most literate people in the world. Three-quarters of white adults could at least sign their name. Wealthy families hired tutors or sent their children to private academies, while middle-class, rural, and poorer Americans learned basic skills from family members, in apprenticeships, or at urban "Dame Schools," where parents could leave their children during the workday. After the Revolution, states helped fund "district" and "field" schools—one-room, one-grade schools for which parents would hire a teacher to offer instruction to children of any age. These schools seldom went beyond the "Three R's"—reading, writing, and arithmetic—and their quality varied widely. They were sometimes taught by college graduates, but often the instructors knew barely more than did their pupils; terms were always short, and many locations never bothered to set up a school. The conviction that a republic needed an educated citizenry, along with the desire to control the crime and social disorder that accompanied economic expansion, convinced many people of the need for schools as a means of maintaining a stable society. Evangelicals and social conservatives concluded that proper instruction could promote morality and responsible citizenship. Manufacturers hoped that schools could instill the discipline and skills they wanted for an efficient labor force, while labor organizations demanded schools as a means of offering a better life for workers' children.

Reformers concluded that a centralized state administration could best improve schools' quality while making them socially useful. Massachusetts created the first state-directed system in 1837, with Horace Mann as the first secretary of the state board of education. In more than a decade of service, Mann oversaw the construction of new schools across the state, lengthened the school year, and implemented a statewide common curriculum, with separate grades determined by both age and ability. A Unitarian, Mann believed that education could promote moral as well as intellectual development, so he encouraged Bible reading in classes yet prohibited teaching the views of any particular denomination. His efforts to develop teaching as a respectable profession led to the establishment in 1839 of the state's first "normal" school—a college devoted to training teachers. Likewise, his conviction that schools should offer opportunity to all, regardless of social rank or background, led him to promote high schools that could provide the more advanced study usually available only to the elite. Older teachers, a number of parents, Catholics who resented the schools' use of the Protestant Bible, and taxpayers without children resisted Mann's reforms. Nevertheless, the passage of a mandatory attendance law in 1852 marked the state's acceptance of his program.

By the 1850s, the Northeastern and Western states had implemented several of Mann's reforms. Field schools remained the main form of public education in the South, where the plantation-based economy and largely rural societies weakened interest in most reforms besides temperance. The urban middle class provided the bulk of support for the reform impulse, and their efforts had a long legacy. The demand for prohibition laws would remain significant for the rest of the century, while asylums and public schools became central institutions in American society. Many nineteenth-century Americans, though, concluded that changing others' behavior could not produce reform. For some, reform started with improving oneself. For others, it meant withdrawing from the republic altogether.

Individuals and Communities

Confident that success, or at least a better life, awaited any young white man who simply took advantage of the opportunities before him, Americans championed self-improvement as equally valuable to society as religious revivals and the reform impulse. Even before Massachusetts implemented Mann's reforms, people throughout the Union recognized education as the key to accomplishment. The common schools, if available at all, emphasized only the fundamentals, so ambitious young men often devoted their spare time to reading whatever they could get their hands on. Local literary and debating clubs provided the opportunity to discuss the ideas in their books and argue about contemporary issues. Numerous towns set up libraries and constructed town halls called *lyceums*—named after Aristotle's school in ancient Athens—for local and traveling speakers and artists to present lectures, dramatic performances, and concerts. Horace Mann, William Andrus Alcott, Samuel Gridley Howe, and the historian Jared Sparks all participated in the lyceum circuit. Ralph Waldo Emerson, recognized as one of the era's most original writers, polished his essays as lyceum lectures before their publication. Printers meanwhile published etiquette guides and self-help manuals to instruct readers on how to transform themselves into refined, respectable, and knowledgeable citizens.

Good health seemed as important as intellectual development in achieving a satisfying life. Revivalists concluded that physical health reflected a person's spiritual condition. Believing that strong Christians could better battle Satan and aid the onset of the millennium, several advocated strengthening the body through work and proclaimed physical activity almost as important a responsibility as studying Scripture. In 1826, Andover Seminary in Massachusetts—founded in 1807 when orthodox Calvinists left Harvard after the college appointed a Unitarian as professor of divinity—admonished students to spend time away from their studies to make boxes, cabinets, and other small carpentry goods. The apparent improvement in the students' health soon led other seminaries to adopt optional work programs. In 1830 Theodore Dwight Weld and Lewis Tappan formed the Society for the Promotion of Manual Labor in Literary Institutions to promote the benefits of work to other schools. At western New York's Oneida Institute, a Presbyterian seminary founded in 1827 under Charles Finney's influence, students made work projects part of the curriculum, as a way to encourage social cooperation. The shift to desk jobs in manufacturing likewise led to a proliferation of manuals prescribing exercise and outlining healthy lifestyles for middle-class men.

When illness struck, Americans usually relied on folk remedies like poultices and herbal medicines. Some followed the new homeopathic approach imported from Germany, which emphasized finding the right natural drug for an ailment. Doctors denounced these methods as quackery and slowly moved toward establishing professional standards with the establishment of the American Medical Association in 1847. Still, the primitive nature of "professional" medicine—which included blistering, bloodletting, and prescribing mercury-based calomel as a "purgative"—drove many to follow the course prescribed by the Presbyterian minister Sylvester Graham. Graham took an interest in health in 1830 when he became a lecturer for the Pennsylvania Society for Discouraging the Use of Ardent Spirits. After an 1832 epidemic of cholera—a potentially fatal intestinal disease characterized by severe vomiting and diarrhea—he became convinced that the proper care of the stomach offered the key to good health. Dissenting from the widespread belief that hearty eating built up a person's constitution, Graham advocated avoiding not only alcohol but also meats, spicy foods, and any beverage other than cold water. Limiting the diet to fruits and vegetables, coarse-grained breads, and a few dairy products, Graham went on to prescribe a general regimen for healthy living that included exercise, wearing loose-fitting clothing, keeping rooms and houses well ventilated, regular bathing in cold water, teeth-brushing, and abstaining from sex.

Graham himself suffered a tragic end. His wife—perhaps from frustration—rejected his teachings and tempted him with rich, lavish, meaty meals. Eventually he suffered a nervous breakdown and died after an extended illness in 1851. His legacy, though, long outlived him. Later generations remember him for his "Graham Bread"—a whole-grain mixture that became the basis for the graham cracker—which he devised to supplement his recommended diet. Contemporaries denounced Graham as a lunatic, but numerous prominent reformers and revivalists became devoted "Grahamites." In 1837, Graham's followers played a leading role in the founding of the American Physiological Society in Boston. The society's president, William Andrus Alcott, wrote more than one hundred books and pamphlets advocating Graham's bland diet and providing advice on a wide variety of topics, including exercise, manners, friendship, sex, and education. Alcott's ability to popularize Graham's ideas made him the Union's lead-ing health advocate, while another Grahamite, Mary Gove Nichols, became the most visible proponent of *hydropathy*—the belief that drinking and bathing in cold water promoted fitness and provided a cure for most illnesses. As in Europe, spas and baths located at springs and other natural water sources became popular expensive retreats for people suffering from various maladies. In New York and Boston, meanwhile, numerous "Graham boarding houses" opened to allow visitors to practice Graham's regimens while away from home.

Other Americans found "scientific" guidance though *phrenology*, the belief that the size and shape of the skull reflected a person's intelligence as well as particular personality traits. The German physician Franz Joseph Gall in 1796 mapped out thirty-seven sections of the brain that he concluded generated specific "faculties" or characteristics, including self-esteem, hope, cautiousness, friendship, destructiveness, acquisitiveness, and "amativeness," or sexual desire. Gall reasoned that the size of each section presumably represented the strength of that characteristic, so measuring the size and shape of the skull could reveal much about an individual's quali-ties. In 1832, Gall's student Johann Gaspar Spurzheim came to America to spread the word about his mentor's findings. Though he died only two months after his arrival, Spurzheim's charisma—and the attention his public autopsy received—persuaded many that phrenology offered the key to self-awareness. The brothers Orson and Lorenzo Fowler soon emerged as phrenology's chief American proponents, publishing the *American Phrenological Journal* and establishing offices in New York, Boston, and Philadelphia that organized lectures, founded museums for displaying skulls, and sold models that outlined the brain's faculties. "Practical" phrenologists meanwhile offered "readings" of the skull to help clients identify their strengths and to learn where they needed to improve. Employers often required a reading before hir-ing workers. Some couples even visited phrenologists to determine their compatibility for marriage.

The phrenology craze faded by the 1850s, but the desire for self-improvement remained strong across society. Still, some Americans concluded that humans could gain self-fulfillment not through molding themselves to the existing culture, but by remaking the world altogether. With plenty of open land available across the continent, visionaries made several attempts to create new, better societies constructed according to their ideals. They found willing par-ticipants among those looking for new experiences, along with the dissatisfied who wanted to withdraw from mainstream society. More than one hundred "communal utopias" formed across the Union during the first half of the nineteenth century. Most proved short-lived; a few continued for generations, and all reflected the wider desire to get a sense of control in a society going through profound changes.

Several communities originated from Europeans' concerns over the rise of class distinc-tions and the materialism prevalent in commercially based manufacturing societies. The Welsh reformer Robert Owen, who had gained a fortune in Britain's cotton industry, undertook the first experiment in "utopian socialism." Unlike most successful industrialists, Owen took a sincere interest in the lives of his employees and provided good working and living condi-tions, schools for workers' children, and reasonable responses to his employees' concerns. The accomplishments he achieved at his mill town at New Lanark, Scotland, convinced Owen that a transformed environment—rather than a revived heart—best promoted productive and meaningful lives. When a severe depression hit Britain's economy after 1815, Owen advocated replacing the existing system of relief for the poor with the construction of villages much like New Lanark, with five hundred to fifteen hundred inhabitants living in dormitories and working to support themselves. Owen's ideas gained little attention in his homeland, but in late 1824 he received an offer to buy the land and buildings of the Harmony Society, a German sect that had moved to southwestern Indiana to flee religious persecution. The "Rappites"—so called for their leader, George Rapp—had decided to move their settlement to Pennsylvania, so Owen quickly agreed to buy their land and buildings and set out to create an ideal community in America.

Arriving in New York in November 1824, Owen christened his project "New Harmony" and invited anyone interested to join. Several forces soon undermined his vision. The community began operations in May 1825 with about eight hundred settlers, but the buildings provided housing for only seven hundred. Owen himself never developed more detailed plans than those he had outlined in Britain, and he spent most of 1825 away publicizing the community rather than overseeing its operations. Many residents believed in Owen's vision, but a majority came for land or work, with little interest in utopian schemes. Instead of harmony, disorganization and factional squabbles characterized the settlement. Owen expected the residents to sell farm produce and divide the profits among all members, with more going to those who provided the most labor. Several members, however, avoided work; virtually everyone complained about their meager daily allowances, and those who did work protested over the small credits they received for their labor. Women resented being exclusively assigned domestic chores, despite Owen's declarations in favor of gender equality. The founder's atheism and denunciation of traditional marriage likewise disturbed the inhabitants while damaging New Harmony's public image. Three reorganizations in four months in early 1826 brought little change and no profits. Facing legal challenges and losing most of his personal fortune, Owen abandoned the project in May 1827. Most settlers also left, though a handful set up private farms and eventually purchased the land.

Despite New Harmony's failure, nineteen other Owenite communities were founded across the Union in the 1840s. The most notable venture attempted to implement an antislavery program devised by the Scottish radical Frances "Fanny" Wright. Popularly known as a champion of liberty, Wright accompanied the Marquis de Lafayette on his 1824 tour of the Union. After the Frenchman's return to Europe, Wright's visit to New York inspired her to develop a community where slaves could work to earn the money necessary to purchase their freedom. When Congress ignored her call for land and funds, she purchased two thousand acres about fourteen miles northeast of Memphis, Tennessee, and settled nine adult slaves, along with several children, at "Nashoba" to put her plan into effect. Yet Nashoba met the same fate as New Harmony. Slaveholders distrusted an antislavery project in their neighborhood, while Wright spent more time trying to raise funds than overseeing the settlement. At lyceum lectures, she increasingly devoted less attention to Nashoba than to voicing her more extreme views, which distracted her from the community's needs while weakening its public approval. Proclaiming herself the "Priestess of Beelzebub," her denunciations of Christianity and advocacy of "free love"—sexual activity outside of marriage—brought condemnations of Nashoba as "one great brothel." The inexperienced overseer she left in charge of the settlement meanwhile proved incompetent and managed it poorly. With Nashoba clearly failing, Wright abandoned the experiment in 1828, though she did arrange to liberate its slaves in Haiti.

The ideas of French social theorist Charles Fourier presented a more promising way to create a utopia. Fourier proposed to organize communities called *phalanxes*, a term that referred to an ancient Greek military formation in which heavily armed soldiers marched together closely. According to Fourier, a phalanx should have 1,620 inhabitants living in a *phalanstery*, a large building with a central hall for "quiet activities." Two lateral wings would provide space for workshops and for social gatherings. Residents' work responsibilities would rotate, with profits distributed according to the amount of labor contributed. Work schedules were to allow ample time for inhabitants to enjoy themselves and pursue their own interests. Other than an abortive attempt to establish a phalanx outside of Paris, Europeans largely ignored Fourier's proposals. However, Albert Brisbane, the son of a wealthy New York storekeeper, met Fourier in 1833 and afterward devoted his life to popularizing the Frenchman's teachings. In 1840, Brisbane published *The Social Destiny of Man*, a collection of his mentor's writings that provided simplified explanations while toning down Fourier's more outlandish ideas, including his contention that animals would live peacefully in phalanxes while humans would develop "long and useful tails." *The Social Destiny of Man* sold well, and New York *Tribune* editor Horace Greeley allowed Brisbane to promote Fourierism further through a regular column in his paper.

Popular interest soon led to attempts to establish Fourierist communities. By 1843, there were twenty-eight phalansteries across the Union, located mostly in Northern states but with one in Texas. The best known, Brook Farm near Boston, began as Unitarian minister George Ripley's project to create a community that combined work with intellectual pursuits. The North American Phalanx, in Monmouth County, New Jersey, became a showcase for Fourierism because of its apparent success and its proximity to New York City. All the American phalanxes, though, faced immediate difficulties because they were much smaller than the communities Fourier had described. Despite the support of prominent New England writers like Nathaniel Hawthorne, Henry David Thoreau, and Margaret Fuller, Brook Farm at its height had only seventy members. The North American phalanx—the largest—never had more than 150 residents. All, too, experienced financial challenges and suffered from members' declining support. Brisbane meanwhile could not completely suppress knowledge of Fourier's attacks on capitalism and his advocacy of sexual liberation, and public interest in phalanxes rapidly declined. Deeply in debt, Brook Farm dissolved in 1846 after experiencing both a smallpox epidemic and a fire. The North American persisted until 1854 but likewise dissolved after its own devastating fire. By then, the enthusiasm behind Fourierism had faded even among its adherents. Greeley offered a $12,000 loan to help rebuild the North American community, but its members expressed little interest in continuing the project.

Utopian socialist communities most often failed because they were poorly organized and because the majority of their members lacked a commitment to the survival of the community. Weak leadership and a democratic expectation of equal participation in making decisions likewise led to factional squabbles. Members of religious communities, on the other hand, believed that they were establishing heaven on earth, and the prospect of carrying out a divine mission gave them the determination needed to sustain their ventures. In addition, they usually took shape under the direction of powerful, charismatic leaders for whom followers proved willing to make whatever sacrifice necessary. The sense of God's presence and the fellowship of like-minded believers provided many religious separatists with an anchor amid the far-reaching changes that were reshaping American society.

One of the most prominent religious separatist groups came from England. The "United Society of Believers in Christ's Second Appearing" followed the teachings of Ann Lee Stanley, a Quaker who proclaimed herself the second incarnation of Christ. Stanley and eight followers gained more disciples after migrating to New York in 1774. After her death ten years later, Joseph Meacham organized Lee's followers into a self-sufficient separate community at Mount Lebanon, New York. There they established a routine of living in simplicity, working in silence, and restraining their emotions until releasing themselves in frenzied worship services that were characterized by singing, mystical experiences, speaking in otherworldly "tongues," and marching together in a regimented ritual known as "the dance"—giving the sect its popular name "Shakers." Women joined men in leadership roles, and, in accordance with Stanley's teachings, Shakers prohibited sexual intercourse, contending that procreation was unnecessary because the millennium had begun. Without children of their own, Shakers relied on adoption and conversion to expand their membership. They gained numerous adherents from men and especially women who had been awakened in the revivals but ultimately found the evangelical churches unsatisfying. The number of converts led to the formation of other Shaker settlements. By the mid-1820s, more than four thousand Shakers dwelled in nineteen villages that stretched from New England to Ohio and Kentucky in the west.

Sexual relations played a dramatically different role at the Oneida community. While preparing himself for the ministry, John Humphrey Noyes concluded that Christians could attain a state of perfection, in which they no longer sinned. Believing that he achieved this state on February 20, 1834, Noyes likewise reasoned that perfect Christians held all things in common—including each other. In a system of "complex marriage," intercourse between any sanctified man and woman not only became permissible but gained recognition as a "joyful act of fellowship." When Vermont officials threatened to indict him for adultery, Noyes and forty-five followers moved in 1848 to Oneida in the "Burned-Over District," where for nearly thirty years they were largely ignored by New York authorities. The few outsiders who knew about Oneida's "communism in love" denounced its libertinism, but Noyes actually regulated the community's "sexual transactions." Potential partners approached each other through a third party, and community leaders kept detailed records of consummations. Eventually, Noyes' tendency to reserve for himself the honor of serving as "first husband" for young women aggravated his followers. Years later, he would flee to Canada to avoid charges of statutory rape. At its height, though, the Oneida settlement contained more than three hundred members and stood as the most prosperous of the era's separatist communities, enjoying a reputation for manufacturing animal traps, silk garments, and the silver flatware for which it is still known.

The most successful separatist group emerged with the development of a distinctly American variant of Christianity. The Latter-Day Saints originated from a series of visions experienced by Joseph Smith, one of eight children in a failed farming family living near the Erie Canal.

Figure 6.4 "Shakers near Lebanon State of New York, Their Mode of Worship." Shakers maintained gender segregation even when performing the "dance" that gave them their popular name. Engraving, artist unknown (c. 1830). Courtesy Prints & Photographs Division, Library of Congress, LC-USZ62-13659.

To help the family earn money, Smith helped local farmers find lost belongings and determine locations for wells using "seer stones," a New England folk practice. In the mid-1820s, Smith reported receiving revelations from an angel named Moroni, who directed him to find buried at a local hill some golden plates, on which was written in "reformed Egyptian" hieroglyphics a lost book of scripture. Using two seer stones, "Urim" and "Thummim," Smith translated the plates into English before Moroni returned them and the seer stones to Heaven. The resulting "Book of Mormon" contained both religious instructions and the story of an ancient people who had migrated to North America, received their own visitation from Christ, and engaged in a series of conflicts like those in the Old Testament. In the final war, the evil Lamanites—the ancestors of Natives—had extinguished the once-God-fearing Nephites. The last of the Nephites—Mormon and his son Moroni—recorded the experiences and teachings on the golden plates, which they buried in 384 A.D. so a future prophet could re-establish God's North American kingdom in the "latter days."

Within a few months of *The Book of Mormon*'s publication in 1830, more than forty followers acknowledged Smith to be a prophet of God. Missionary efforts over the next decade rapidly expanded the church's following to include converts from as far away as Britain and Scandinavia. In January 1831, Smith and his followers established an earthly "City of Holiness" at Kirtland, Ohio, where one convert, Sidney Rigdon, led a small Christian community that converted to Mormonism with him. Kirtland's financial collapse in 1837 forced Smith and six hundred followers to move to Independence, Missouri, where efforts to minister to Natives had established a second Mormon center. The church's rapid growth, attempts to convert Natives, and inclusion of free African Americans drew attacks by local vigilante groups. Mormon reprisals produced a virtual war in 1838 that resulted in Smith's arrest and sentencing to death. Smith managed to escape, and with his followers—now numbering around ten thousand—he established another City of Holiness at Nauvoo in western Illinois. Eventually, Mormons clashed with "gentiles" in Illinois as well, sparked both by Smith's increasing megalomania and by the church's adoption of polygamy. A rioting mob killed Smith and his brother on June 27, 1844. Brigham Young soon emerged as the church's new leader, and from 1847 to 1848 he oversaw its "exodus" to a new holy city beside the Great Salt Lake in modern Utah, then part of northern Mexico.

Shakers, Oneida's inhabitants, and Mormons formed only a few of the numerous religious communities spread across the Union. Numerous pietistic sects had, like the Harmony Society, left Europe to escape persecution, but groups emerging from American culture ranged from a Christian Universalist utopia at Hopedale, Massachusetts, to the "Kingdom of Matthias," led by a sickly New York carpenter who had anointed himself a prophet. Neither the religious nor secular communities had much impact on mainstream society. Nor did most of the more radical expressions of reform, like the American Pacifists' call to secure world peace through renouncing individual violence. One radical reform movement, though, aggravated the tensions already present over the Union's most divisive institution.

Abolitionists

Though most white Americans disliked slavery, few took action against it. Those who did usually supported the American Colonization Society's approach, which stressed gradual emancipation, compensation for slave owners, and removing freed slaves from American shores. Some activists, often living in the Upper South, worked to keep the issue before the public. In 1820, Elihu Embree, a Quaker living in Jonesborough, Tennessee, published about fifty issues of an antislavery newspaper entitled *The Emancipator*. After Embree's death, Benjamin Lundy revived and published the paper in Baltimore from 1824 until 1839 under the title *The Genius of Universal Emancipation.* Both Embree and Lundy based their challenges on the colonization-ists' calls for gradualism and compensation, but most Americans still ignored the antislavery message. Convinced that slavery's sudden end would devastate Southern society, and that African Americans could not coexist with whites as social equals, Northerners and Southerners continued to treat slavery as a "necessary evil" that would, in some unexplained way, simply disappear at some point in the future.

Antislavery veered sharply in a new direction on January 1, 1831, when William Lloyd Garrison published the first issue of *The Liberator.* Raised in poverty, Garrison learned the printing trade as an apprentice in Newburyport, Massachusetts, and in 1828, at age twenty-three, he began co-editing *The Genius of Universal Emancipation* with Benjamin Lundy. Public indifference to the antislavery message convinced him that only a more direct, confrontational approach could challenge the institution's hold. His interaction with free African Americans likewise showed him that they had little interest in colonization while dispelling any fears he had about a biracial society. Garrison expressed these views in aggressive editorials that slowly alienated him from Lundy, and in 1830 he served seven weeks in jail for seditious libel after accusing a Newburyport merchant of participating in the slave trade. Following his release, he returned to Boston to start a paper dedicated to slavery's immediate abolition. In *The Liberator's* first issue, Garrison stated clearly his determination not to be ignored. Publicly recanting moderate antislavery as "a sentiment so full of timidity, injustice and absurdity," he pledged to be "as harsh as truth, and as uncompromising as justice." "I am in earnest," he pledged; "I will not equivocate—I will not excuse—I will not retreat a single inch—AND I WILL BE HEARD."

The Liberator's declaration reflected Garrison's passion and inspired others to take action against both Northern public apathy and slavery's apparently growing strength. For abolitionists, slavery presented more than a social, political, or economic problem: It was a sin, a moral evil in the sight of God, and it needed to be dealt with immediately. Calls for "gradualism," abolitionists charged, merely allowed the Union's greatest failing to persist indefinitely; although it might not be possible to eliminate the institution overnight, the nation should enact at once the first serious steps to bring about its end. Compensating owners for emancipated slaves they denounced as rewarding "manstealers" for their crime; instead, slaveholders and non-slaveholders alike needed to repent of their ownership of humans and their toleration of cruelty. Likewise, abolitionists rejected colonization and called upon white Americans to abandon racial prejudice and support education and training to incorporate African Americans as equals in a color-blind society. Not all abolitionists shared the depth of Garrison's commitment to racial equality, and the movement remained vague about the specific measures needed to abolish slavery. Still, abolitionists were united on the goal of "immediatism"—slavery's immediate end, regardless of the consequences—and relied on moral suasion as the best means of accomplishing this end.

African Americans in the Northeast enthusiastically applauded the call for immediatism. Free blacks, in fact, made up more than three-fourths of the roughly three thousand readers who subscribed to *The Liberator.* The abolitionist appeal also gained the adherence of several reform activists and revival ministers. Arthur and Lewis Tappan came to regard abolishing slavery as the Union's most pressing need, while Charles G. Finney and Lyman Beecher expressed sympathy for the cause. Quakers, with a long-standing tradition against slavery, likewise voiced their support, as did many New England Unitarians. With this reception, Garrison and sixty-one other abolitionists, including four women and three African Americans, formed the American Anti-Slavery Society (AASS) in Philadelphia in December 1833. The AASS focused on distributing antislavery literature, holding rallies, and using whatever means available to produce "the abolition of slavery by the spirit of repentance" while securing to the "colored population . . . all the rights and privileges which belong to them as men and as Americans." Local AASS chapters soon formed throughout the Northeast and westward through "Greater New England" in the northern portions of the middle and western states, especially western New York and northeastern Ohio. Even a few Southerners accepted the abolitionist message, including Alabama planter James G. Birney, Kentuckians Cassius M. Clay and John Fee, and the sisters Sarah and Angelina Grimké from Charleston.

The vast majority of Americans in the North and South, however, rejected the abolitionists' call. The handful of Southern converts usually came from Quaker or evangelical backgrounds that predisposed them to reject slavery. Otherwise, white Southerners vehemently condemned antislavery activists. Even Southern Baptists and Methodists, whose evangelical faith had once encouraged them to accept African Americans as equals, now defended slavery and racial hierarchy as their churches became more socially respectable. Denouncing abolitionism as fanatical and dangerous, Southerners generally expressed confidence that Northerners would recognize the impracticality of abolitionists' appeal. Otherwise, they feared, moral denunciations might inspire slaves to rise up against their masters. Only recently, in 1829, David Walker, a free black in Boston, had written *Appeal to the Coloured Citizens of the World*, a pamphlet that encouraged African Americans to resort to violence if necessary to secure their freedom. Walker died shortly afterward, but in August 1831 the slave Nat Turner led an uprising in Southampton County, Virginia, that killed nearly sixty whites. Turner's rebellion, coming as it did a mere eight months after *The Liberator*'s first issue, convinced Southerners that agitation over slavery would only produce a bloody race war.

Southern legislators responded to abolitionism with laws prohibiting the possession or distribution of antislavery literature. Several Southerners rejected charges of slavery's immorality, claiming that it was actually a "positive good," a beneficial institution that made Southern society superior to the North. Proslavery spokesmen, including William and Mary professor Thomas Dew and South Carolina politician John C. Calhoun, continued to stress slavery's benefits as a form of race control, but now they asserted that slavery placed African Americans in the laboring and service roles for which they were "naturally" suited. Slavery "civilized" Africans, defenders claimed; great civilizations like ancient Greece and Rome had relied on slavery, and now it freed whites from menial labor so they had time for greater accomplishments. Proslavery advocates likewise argued that slavery promoted white equality: Unlike in the class-riven society developing in the manufacturing Northeast, Southern poor whites would never have to depend on the wealthy for work and wages. Southern ministers meanwhile rejected the charge that slavery contradicted Christian principles. Bondage brought the Gospel to the heathen, they claimed, and the Bible not only never condemned slavery but instead regulated slaves' treatment and encouraged them to serve their masters well. The "necessary evil" view remained strong in the South. Still, the proslavery cause gained strength through the 1830s and 1840s and reassured Southern whites of slavery's morality as they resisted abolitionists' offensive.

Northern whites dismissed the proslavery case, but they likewise gave abolitionism a hostile reception. Calls for equality deeply offended whites' sense of racial superiority, and many feared that emancipated slaves would migrate to the North, where they would incite racial conflict and compete with workers for jobs. Merchants and politicians recognized that antislavery activism threatened both their trade ties with the South and the peace of the Union. When mobs incited riots in Northern cities and attacked antislavery spokesmen, local leaders whom abolitionists denounced as "gentlemen of property and standing" offered no protection. In the summer of 1834, mobs in New York City and Philadelphia destroyed Lewis Tappan's home and rampaged through African-American neighborhoods. Garrison himself faced a possible lynching on October 21, 1835; he escaped only when Boston authorities jailed him to protect him from his assailants. At Lane Seminary, a school founded in Cincinnati to train revivalist ministers for the Presbyterian Church, Theodore Dwight Weld converted the majority of his fellow students to abolitionism. When hostility from the local population compelled trustees to disband the school's antislavery society in 1834, Weld and forty other students withdrew to establish Oberlin College in northeastern Ohio as the Union's first integrated college. Violence against abolitionists nevertheless persisted. Elijah P. Lovejoy paid the ultimate price in November 1837 when a rioter shot him in Alton, Illinois, while a crowd destroyed the printing press he had brought to the town to publish an antislavery newspaper.

Notwithstanding public hostility, abolitionists soon provoked national controversies that gained them Northern sympathy. Southern laws and the potential for violent retribution made it dangerous for abolitionist spokesmen to travel or speak in the South. To counter this resistance, Lewis Tappan proposed to mail antislavery pamphlets to slaveowners throughout the South, with the hope that at least some would read the tracts and accept abolitionist gospel. Over the next year, the AASS printed more than one million copies of tracts for distribution in the South. But the mailings produced a bigger uproar than anyone expected. When the pamphlets arrived in Charleston on July 29, 1835, a mob stole them from the post office and used them to start a bonfire that burned effigies of William Lloyd Garrison and Arthur Tappan, Lewis' brother and himself a prominent abolitionist. Five Southern state legislatures approved resolutions calling upon Northern states to silence abolitionists, while citizens in Virginia and South Carolina demanded the extradition of AASS leaders to stand trial for attempting to incite insurrection. Postmaster Amos Kendall meanwhile permitted Southern postmasters to intercept the antislavery pamphlets before their delivery, despite the postal service's legal responsibility to deliver the mail. In December, President Andrew Jackson's annual message to Congress echoed the call to stop abolitionist activities while recommending a federal law to prohibit sending "incendiary" publications through the mail.

At the same time as the postal campaign, abolitionists flooded the national legislature with petitions to take action against slavery. Moderate activists had long petitioned Congress to eliminate slavery in areas clearly under federal authority, including the District of Columbia, military posts, and territories. As a custom, the clerk would read petitions aloud before the House of Representatives, which would then vote immediately to "table" those dealing with antislavery—that is, the members would "postpone" discussion of the petition until a later date, which in practice meant they would ignore it. Abolitionists reasoned that a deluge of petitions could publicize their cause, getting those who signed them to commit to immediatism. The reading of such a large number of petitions—through 1835 the House received more than thirty thousand—threatened to delay the legislature's business, and the petitions' wording frequently included moral denunciations that insulted slaveholding representatives. Northern representatives expressed little sympathy for abolitionists, but a proposal to reject antislavery petitions threatened a long-standing right and sparked a heated six-week debate. Ultimately, enough Northern representatives accepted Southern concerns to pass what became known as the "Gag Rule": From 1836 until the rule's repeal in 1844, the House would accept antislavery petitions but table them immediately, without having them read or included in the House's proceedings.

The backlash to the postal and petition campaigns helped abolitionists gain grudging Northern support, for many who rejected immediate emancipation regarded efforts to silence antislavery activism as an attack on free speech. Through 1835, the number of AASS chapters doubled, and by 1838 abolitionists had submitted more than four hundred thousand petitions to Congress. More importantly, several Northern politicians took up the charge that a "slave power" violated white Northerners' liberties through its demand for special protection of their property. The need to renew the Gag Rule at the beginning of each congressional session allowed former president John Quincy Adams—now representing a Massachusetts district and resentful toward slaveholders for denying him a second term—to provoke angry debates, often approaching violence, when he ridiculed Southern fears and branded Northern colleagues who supported the Gag Rule as the "slave power's" tools. The agitation revived Adams' reputation in the North while bringing death threats from the South. Over the next few years, the election of more explicitly abolitionist representatives, such as New York's Seth M. Gates, Vermont's William Slade, and Ohio's Joshua Giddings, gave antislavery a vocal presence in Washington.

Still, abolitionists grew frustrated at the backlash and the popular rejection of immediatism. Resistance drove Garrison and a core of radicals to more extreme demands. For these abolitionists, ending slavery came to represent merely the first step in the Union's transformation into a truly equal and just nation. *The Liberator* always promoted causes like women's rights, pacifism, and even anarchism, but in the aftermath of the postal and petition campaigns, "Garrisonians" proclaimed each cause as important as antislavery. Radicals likewise insisted that abolitionists withdraw from all institutions tainted by slavery, an action that they expected to challenge others to take action while ensuring their own moral purity. Garrison himself denounced ministers who would not condemn slavery as a sin. Likewise, although he favored activism as a means of pricking the public's conscience, Garrison refused to vote in a "corrupt" political system that tolerated and protected slavery and inequality. By the early 1840s, Garrison concluded that the Constitution should be rejected as a proslavery document, and he called upon Northerners to secede from the Union. At rallies, he proclaimed that there should be "no compromise with slavery, no union with slaveholders." Quoting the Old Testament book of Isaiah, he condemned the Constitution as "a covenant with death" and "an agreement with Hell."

The Garrisonians' radical shift disturbed more moderate abolitionists, including the Tappans and Theodore Weld. Moderates wanted to keep the movement focused on ending slavery, and they recognized that the Garrisonians' attacks on clerical authority and biblical literalism, their refusal to participate in politics, and their open disrespect for the Constitution only alienated potential followers. The promotion of women's rights particularly concerned moderates. Women played important roles in organizing local antislavery activities, but radical encouragement of Sarah and Angelina Grimké's 1837 lecture tour through New England contradicted the prevailing sentiment that women should remain silent and under male authority. When Garrisonians elected the outspoken feminist Abby Kelley to the American Anti-Slavery Society's executive committee in July 1840, moderates withdrew to form the American and Foreign Anti-Slavery Society (AFASS), which would present slavery as abolitionism's primary issue while avoiding the Garrisonians' extremism. Representing the movement's majority, moderates hoped AFASS's more restrained approach might persuade churches to condemn slavery as a violation of the New Testament's teaching on the brotherhood of all men. Likewise, they encouraged abolitionists to vote for politicians who were committed to opposing slavery, which could help hasten the end of the institution.

Violence against abolitionists largely subsided by 1840, but Northern indifference to slavery limited the new organization's effectiveness. Despite moderate appeals, mainstream ministers continued to treat slavery as a civil rather than a moral issue. None of the major Christian denominations publicly proclaimed slavery a sin. Abolitionists' votes helped elect some antislavery candidates, but with such a small number they could make little headway against the dominant political parties. Several moderates concluded that the movement might gain more visibility through a separate, single-issue third party. As the 1840 presidential election approached, a "National Convention of Friends of Immediate Emancipation" met in Albany, New York, in April to nominate the Southern convert James G. Birney for president, with Pennsylvania Quaker Thomas Earle for vice president. The "Liberty Party" convention then approved a platform promising to outlaw slavery in the District of Columbia, to abolish the interstate slave trade, and to prevent the admission of any new slave states to the Union. With little time to organize an effective campaign, Birney's supporters expected their candidate to fare poorly. The Liberty Party nominee won fewer than 7,500 votes, less than one half of one percent of the total across the free states.

Still, abolitionists gained valuable experience in the 1840 campaign, and after the election the Liberty Party's prospects seemed brighter. Several events brought slavery-related issues to the forefront of the public's attention. In March 1841, the Supreme Court issued its decision in the case of *United States v. Amistad*. Thirty-eight Africans had taken over a Spanish ship, the *Amistad*, and tried to sail it to Africa. The Coast Guard seized the ship off the coast of Long Island, and President Martin Van Buren's administration backed the Spanish government's demand to return the Africans because as slaves they were Spanish property. The court, however, freed them and ordered their return to Africa on the grounds that they had been enslaved illegally. Later in 1841, the federal government demanded the return of 135 slaves who had reached the Bahamas after taking over the *Creole*, a brig transporting them from Hampton Roads, Virginia, to New Orleans. British officials in the colony rejected the American appeals and ultimately freed the rebels. In 1842, though, the Supreme Court upheld the federal government's responsibility to assist in the recovery of escaped slaves in *Prigg v. Pennsylvania*, which invalidated the "personal liberty laws" that several free state legislatures had passed to allow local officials to obstruct execution of the 1793 Fugitive Slave Act. Most importantly, in 1843 President John Tyler began negotiations for the annexation of Texas, a huge slaveholding region that would strengthen slavery's presence in the Union.

Many Northerners expressed anger over the *Prigg* decision and the move to annex Texas. They displayed little concern for the fate of African Americans working on Southern plantations, but they condemned slavery as economically backward and socially undesirable. Federal officials' apparent determination to uphold slaveowners' rights likewise stoked fears that the "slave power" enjoyed too much influence on the central government. More free state residents now proved willing to take a firmer stand. The largest denominations still would not condemn slavery, but controversies involving the institution divided the Methodist Church in 1844 and the Baptist General Convention in 1845. More citizens, too, proved willing to express their displeasure by voting for the Liberty Party. Again nominating Birney for the presidency, with former Democratic representative Thomas Morris as his running mate, the party launched an earlier and better-organized presidential campaign in 1844 and increased Birney's vote eightfold, to more than sixty-two thousand. Though this result represented only three percent of the free state total, the Liberty Party's increased visibility and growing attention to slavery-related issues convinced a new generation of abolitionists, including Illinois' Owen Lovejoy, Ohio's Salmon P. Chase, and Massachusetts' Charles Sumner, to channel their antislavery efforts through politics. Their work would lay the foundation for the explosive battles over slavery that would dominate the next decade.

Though abolitionists remained outside of the mainstream, they fit well in an America that had changed significantly since the Revolution. The religious condemnation of slavery reflected Christianity's importance as a cultural force, and their plea to their countrymen to right moral wrongs paralleled other reformers' attempts to purify their world. Like the economic and social developments that produced them, religious revivals and social reforms strengthened the belief that Americans constituted one people, a nation that transcended state lines. Northern resistance to abolitionism revealed the limits of revivalism and the power of the desire for national unity. As national loyalty reached its heights following the War of 1812, the growing antislavery sentiment demonstrated that nationalism rested on an unstable foundation.

Suggested Readings

Abzug, Robert H. *Cosmos Crumbling: American Reform and the Religious Imagination* (New York, 1994).

Boylan, Anne M. *Sunday School: The Formation of an American Institution, 1790–1880* (New Haven, 1989).

Bushman, Richard L. *Joseph Smith and the Beginnings of Mormonism* (Urbana, IL, 1984).

Guarneri, Carl J. *The Utopian Alternative: Fourierism in Nineteenth-Century America* (Ithaca, NY, 1991).

Hanley, Mark Y. *Beyond a Christian Commonwealth: The Protestant Quarrel with the American Republic, 1830–1860* (Chapel Hill, 1994).

Hatch, Nathan O. *The Democratization of American Christianity* (New Haven, 1989).

Hirsch, Adam Jay. *The Rise of the Penitentiary: Prisons and Punishment in Early America* (New Haven, 1992).

Laurie, Bruce. *Beyond Garrison: Antislavery and Social Reform* (Cambridge, UK, 2005).

Lazerow, Jama. *Religion and the Working Class in Antebellum America* (Washington, DC, 1995).

Mintz, Steven. *Moralists and Modernizers: America's Pre–Civil War Reformers* (Baltimore, 1995).

Noll, Mark A. *America's God: From Jonathan Edwards to Abraham Lincoln* (New York, 2003).

Numbers, Ronald L., and Jonathan M. Butler. *The Disappointed: Millerism and Millenarianism in the Nineteenth Century* (Bloomington, IN, 1987).

Pegram, Thomas R. *Battling Demon Rum: The Struggle for a Dry America, 1800–1933* (Chicago, 1998).

Porterfield, Amanda. *Conceived in Doubt: Religion and Politics in the New American Nation* (Chicago, 2012).

Ragosta, John. *Religious Freedom: Jefferson's Legacy, America's Creed* (Charlottesville, 2013).

Spurlock, John C. *Free Love: Marriage and Middle-Class Radicalism in America, 1825–1860* (New York, 1988).

Stein, Stephen. *The Shaker Experience in America: A History of the United Society of Believers* (New Haven, 1992).

Walters, Kerry S. *Rational Infidels: The American Deists* (Amherst, NY, 1992).

Walters, Ronald G. *American Reformers, 1815–1860* (New York, 1997).

Wigger, John H. *Taking Heaven by Storm: Methodism and the Rise of Popular Christianity in America* (Urbana, IL, 1998).

VII

A WHITE MAN'S NATION

The twenty-five-year-old Frenchman Alexis de Tocqueville arrived in Newport, Rhode Island, on April 2, 1831. With his friend Gustave de Beaumont—like Tocqueville, a low-level official in the French government—Tocqueville had persuaded the government of King Louis Philippe to grant permission to the two to study the American penal system. As instructed, Tocqueville and Beaumont visited all the major penitentiaries in the United States, and upon their return they prepared a report recommending reforms to improve France's prisons. Tocqueville and Beaumont had arranged their trip mainly so they could see the American republics for themselves. During their nearly ten months in North America, they observed residents' ways of life and talked to hundreds of men and women; like other foreign visitors, once he returned home, Tocqueville published a book explaining his impressions of the American people.

Tocqueville's two-volume work stood out from other visitors' accounts for the depth of its perceptions about American society. What most impressed him he indicated in the title of his work: *Democracy in America*. "Among the novel objects that attracted my attention during my stay in the United States," he began, "nothing struck me more forcibly than the general equality of condition among the people." Tocqueville recognized that some were better off than others. By "equality of condition," he referred to the absence of rigid distinctions that separated nobles from commoners in Europe and persisted even in post-Revolutionary France. American culture had indeed come to regard all adult white males as equals, regardless of wealth, occupation, or education. Every man, Americans believed, should have an equal opportunity to succeed, regardless of background. Each, too, belonged to the "sovereign" people, who not only provided the foundation of political authority but actually seemed to rule the nation. These convictions grew with an expansion of democratic values and practices during the first quarter of the nineteenth century. But as democracy expanded to include all white men, Americans drew sharper racial distinctions that expelled African and Native Americans from membership in society. Attitudes about gender meanwhile significantly altered women's roles while severely limiting their public contributions.

The Rise of Democracy

The Revolution first sparked the American democratic sentiment. Appeals to defending the people's liberty convinced some that "the people" themselves should rule. Participation in the military and on extralegal local committees gave small farmers and artisans political experience that in the colonial era had been reserved to their social betters. Democratic expectations influenced most of the first state constitutions. Several states reduced the long-standing property requirement for voting. Three eliminated property restrictions altogether, and in Pennsylvania, frontier farmers and Philadelphia artisans created nearly a direct democracy in the state's 1776 constitution. In these and other states, representatives from humble backgrounds more often won election to the newly expanded legislatures. Despite these developments, most Americans remained uncomfortable with actual government "by" the people. Revolutionary leaders had intended to establish representative republics that would be governed by law and led, with popular consent, by the wisest and best in society. *Democracy*, on the other hand, remained mostly associated with mob rule and anarchy—an unstable and unjust system that would ultimately lead to violence and result in a dictatorship. As popular influence in public affairs increased, Revolutionary Americans considered the democratic element as only a part of their republics of property-owning men. Even in Pennsylvania, opponents succeeded in revising the 1776 constitution so that after 1790 the government resembled other states' systems, with a governor and similar checks on the popular will.

A large number of Americans likewise continued to support property requirements on voting. In several states, owning a sufficient amount of land remained a condition for holding political office. Possession of property seemed to provide the best way of identifying those with a "stake" in society; that is, since laws and government decisions would most affect their property, owners could be expected to take a deeper interest in public affairs than those without land. Property also provided a way of identifying those who should be considered heads of household. Those who owned a farm or shop large enough to support their families were thought to be the appropriate voters, because they enjoyed the independence necessary for one to make decisions uninfluenced by an employer or a master. Household heads, too, assumedly represented everyone living in their homes, including women, children, slaves, and hired laborers. Because farmhands and journeymen craftsmen had to rely for their living on their employers or "masters," expanding the vote to those without property, Americans thought, would only increase the influence of those with the largest households, who would simply instruct their dependents on how to vote.

Despite the Revolution, political practices remained more influenced by assumptions left over from the colonial era than by democratic ideals. Overall, Americans paid more attention to affairs of state and proved more likely to participate in local elections. Voter turnout nevertheless remained erratic, as apathy, bad weather, or the inconvenience of traveling long distances often kept the number of voters low. Several states continued the practice of *viva voce* voting, in which voters publicly declared their choice before the candidates and his friends and neighbors. Elections thus usually served more as exercises of communal solidarity than as expressions of a "sovereign people." Although Americans now considered all white men equal before the law, most elected officials still came from the local elite, and many voters continued to believe that those in society's upper ranks, distinguished by their wealth, education, and respectability, had a responsibility to provide leadership. Planters, merchants, professionals, and other men of means regarded civil service an obligation of their status. Aspirants might openly solicit votes more often after the Revolution, but many followed the colonial-era practice of subtly making known their "availability" while demonstrating refined characteristics that made them worthy of consideration. Campaigning usually involved visiting and talking personally with voters—without mentioning the upcoming election—and candidates often "treated" the voters—hosting a public reception, with lavish amounts of liquor, to demonstrate a gentleman's elite status.

Gradually, the idea of popular rule breached the walls of tradition, and democratic values gained the strength necessary to transform American politics and culture. For one, political confrontation worked to further acceptance of democracy. The Republican Party's challenge to the Federalists, its claims to represent "the people," and the adoption of the name "Democratic-Republicans" furthered acceptance of democracy—even though, ironically, Thomas Jefferson and James Madison both wanted the states to remain republics of property-owning voters. Within the states, a new generation of political leaders emerged shortly after the turn of the century to push for popular reforms—partly from ideological conviction, but also as a political strategy, since expanding suffrage could provide the votes they needed to defeat their opponents. Republicans in New England in particular denounced Federalist elitism as part of their campaigns to win elections, while in states like New York and New Jersey, factions within the Republican party used suffrage reform as an issue against the party's more conservative and traditional leaders. In several Southern states, proponents of democracy claimed that extending the vote would help unite white men, which would ensure non-slaveholders' cooperation in defending slavery and keeping the slave population under stricter control.

More subtle social and cultural changes also furthered democratic notions. Those who fought in the Revolution had grown up with the colonial era's acceptance of elite leadership, but their children and grandchildren came to maturity in an environment with fewer reservations about "the people's" ability to rule. As the Revolutionary generation passed away, generations with fewer fears about an enlarged, non-propertied electorate became the majority. Economic changes meanwhile slowly shifted farm laborers and journeymen craftsmen from a "master's" subordinates to hired employees responsible for themselves. Defenders of tradition could no longer claim that household heads represented the interests of their property-less dependents, especially as opportunities for success seemed increasingly available to all men. Perhaps most importantly, many came to see military service as equally valid as property ownership as a way of demonstrating one's "stake" in society. Particularly after the difficulty recruiting soldiers for the War of 1812, democratic advocates demanded suffrage reforms, on the principle that men should not be asked to fight for a republic in which they could not vote. By the 1820s, traditional beliefs that voting should be reserved for financially independent citizens gave way to recognizing as a voter any man who demonstrated his membership in society through taxpaying or military service. Over the next two decades, most abandoned even these modest restrictions, believing voting stood as a right that belonged to all adult white men.

Legal changes moved most states closer to putting democracy into practice. Western states saw the vote as an enticement to lure new settlers. Starting with Kentucky in 1792, new states entered the Union with no property requirements. The original thirteen meanwhile revised their state constitutions to reduce or eliminate restrictions. By 1830, only eight of the twenty-four states still had a property requirement in place. Two decades later, only Virginia and North Carolina required most voters to own land; New York required African-American voters to own property, Rhode Island applied the restriction only to foreign-born men, and a residency requirement exempted the vast majority of South Carolinians from a fifty-acre requirement on newcomers. New state constitutions likewise increased voters' responsibilities. By 1850, every state except South Carolina provided for a popular election to select the governor, and in most, the voters now chose state officers and local officials. Legislatures also moved to give citizens the power to select the states' presidential electors. Most adopted a *general ticket system*, in which supporters of presidential aspirants would nominate a list of electors committed to a candidate; whichever nominee won the statewide election would then receive all of the state's votes in the electoral college. Twelve states adopted the general ticket system by 1824, and after 1832 only South Carolina reserved the choice of electors to the state legislature.

The democratic spirit's impact went beyond lowering voter restrictions and holding more elections. Changing cultural expressions celebrated the common folk as the "sovereign people" whose contributions and worth distinguished the United States from any other nation. Wealth, education, and privilege—the onetime signs of status and leadership—now were condemned as the trappings of weakness and aristocracy, while the common laborer, whether farmer or craftsman, received praise as the ideal citizen in a republic. Mainstream Americans described the Union as a classless society, in which no one man stood better than another and with each having the same influence as any other. The respectful titles "Mr.," "Mrs.," and "Miss"— shortened forms of "master" and "mistress" and once reserved for the privileged—became the standard form of address for white adults. The buckled shoes, knee breeches, cocked hats, and powdered wigs of the colonial elite became antiquated; middling and poorer sorts as well as the wealthy more often dressed in the short coats and long pants that British and American manufacturing made more easily available. Men of all social ranks likewise preferred short hair instead of their fathers' and grandfathers' longer locks and queues—tied or braided hair hanging down the back. Stagecoaches and steamboats meanwhile made no class distinctions and crammed travelers from all backgrounds into uncomfortable accommodations.

Open rebellions in Rhode Island and New York showed that Americans expected democratic aspirations to remain within the confines of the law. Long after the Revolution, Rhode Island retained as its constitution the colonial charter that King Charles II granted in 1663. The charter required voters to own land worth at least $134 or to pay at least $7 in rents each year, and by the 1830s, this qualification disenfranchised more than half of the state's men. Manufacturing expansion brought a significant influx of Irish and French-Canadian workers to Providence, but disfranchisement and disproportionate representation in the legislature kept the state under the control of the rural counties in the southern portion of the state. Caught up in the democratic spirit, Thomas Dorr, a Harvard-educated lawyer and legislator, formed the Democratic Constitutionalist Party in 1834 to demand a new state constitution. At first the party gained little attention, but the economic crisis of the late 1830s brought the support

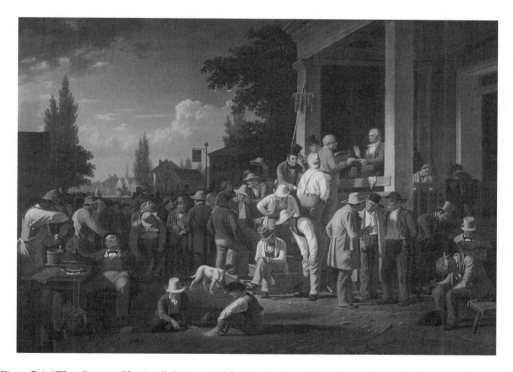

Figure 7.1 "The County Election." George Caleb Bingham's painting shows how elections served as social events that encouraged a sense of equality among white men. Oil on canvas (1852). Courtesy Saint Louis Art Museum, Gift of Bank of America, Object Number: 44:2001.

of workers and sympathetic reformers, which allowed Dorr to transform the weak third party into the broader-based Rhode Island Suffrage Association. To forestall radical action, the legislature summoned a constitutional convention, but the Suffrage Association nevertheless went ahead with its own plan for elections—with all men participating—for delegates to a separate convention to meet in October 1841. The extralegal "People's Convention" then produced a constitution that would reapportion the legislature while giving the vote to all white men. The official "Landholder's Convention" meanwhile reaffirmed the 1663 charter with a constitution that made only minimal changes.

In the state's official referendum, legal voters soundly rejected the "Landholder's Constitution," while the "Dorrites" claimed that more than fourteen thousand turned out for their election to ratify the "People's Constitution." Another round of extralegal elections, in April 1842, chose a new state legislature, with Dorr as governor. The official state government, though, enacted a series of repressive laws—called the "Algerine Laws," likening them to the tyrannical dey of Algiers—that ordered harsh punishment for anyone associated with the rebellion. Governor Samuel King arrested several members of the "People's" legislature and requested President John Tyler's help in suppressing the rebellion. Dorr himself fled the state, and when he returned with a small army of supporters, state officials easily drove back their assault on a federal arsenal. Another official convention meanwhile revised the "Landholders' Constitution" to give Providence a larger presence in the legislature. To divide Dorr's supporters, the convention exempted American-born residents from the property requirement for voting but left the restriction on the foreign-born. Voters ratified the changes in November 1842, and with native-born workers appeased and a legitimate government firmly in place, the uprising quickly subsided. Dorr himself served a year of hard labor for treason.

In a similar uprising in New York, strained economic circumstances drove tenants on the estates of the state's "Manor Lords" to challenge their landlords' traditional, seemingly aristocratic privileges. The need to attract settlers had convinced the colonial Manor Lords to grant their tenants several major concessions, including the right to vote and ownership of improvements on their lands. Most tenants worked on farms with long-term or life leases, and landlords retained some of the manorial rights they received when granted their estates, including deferential treatment and work requirements from their renters. After the Revolution, several Manor Lords sold their holdings to their tenants, but the traditional system persisted in the counties around Albany. For a while, relations between landlords and tenants remained stable, mainly because the Manor Lords remained tolerant when farmers could not pay their rents. After 1800, division of estates among the landlords' sons reduced their size and compelled the younger generation of landlords to insist on annual rent payments to maintain their income. Then, after the Erie Canal opened in 1825, the flood of wheat imports from the west undercut the prices of the tenants' crops. Many farmers shifted to wool production, but especially after the Panic of 1837, the greater challenge of paying rents joined with the growing national democratic spirit to increase the tenants' resentment of the Manor Lords' aristocratic pretensions.

Direct challenges followed the death of Stephen Van Rensselaer III in January 1839. Known among his tenants as the "Good Patroon," Van Rensselaer owned the largest estate, which included more than 400,000 acres in two counties, but in his will he directed the collection of almost $400,000 in back rents to pay off his substantial debts. When his heirs rejected appeals for lenience, Van Rensselaer's tenants refused to pay any rents, organized to resist collectors, and demanded the right to purchase their farms. The protest soon spread to other estates. Young men, dressed as Natives, harassed rent collectors and local officials while intimidating tenants who were reluctant to comply. Several state officials, including Governors William Seward and Silas Wright, expressed sympathy for the tenants' goals, but the antirenters' challenge to property rights and the sanctity of contracts complicated finding an acceptable response to their demands. The outbreak of violence meanwhile cost the tenants support, especially after August 1845, when a demonstration resulted in the death of a deputy sheriff. By the mid-1840s, the improving economy toned down the protests. Still, the tenants' influence as a powerful voting bloc compelled a state constitutional convention in 1846 to prohibit manorial leases and long-term leases lasting more than twelve years. Over the next two decades, the remaining Manor Lords gradually sold their holdings to the tenants.

Both the "Dorr War" and the "Anti-Rent War" revealed the boundaries of the democratic impulse. Americans, believing that popular rule should remain within the confines of the law, displayed little tolerance for violent social revolution. Voters channeled their political impulses into existing political institutions, and democratic expectations dramatically altered the way Americans understood and practiced their politics. Calls for "popular sovereignty"—once thought to refer only to the people as the source of political authority—increasingly justified the notion that "the people's will," determined by the majority of voters in an election, actually directed the government. Those dissatisfied with an election's result were expected to appeal to the "sober second thought of the people" to correct the decision in the next contest. As state legislatures set up more polling places, easier access to the polls and politicians' efforts to "get out the vote" significantly increased voter turnout across the Union. States likewise switched from *viva voce* voting to the secret ballot, and elections became raucous events. For some, the flow of alcohol, crowds cheering on or heckling candidates, and individuals' gambling on the outcome belied the assumption that a reasonable, "virtuous" people governed itself. Nevertheless, the regular cycle of campaign events, public speaking, and candidate debates became major public affairs. Participating in politics became a principal form of entertainment especially in rural farm communities with few other distractions.

Aspirants for office likewise changed their approach. Americans still expected presidential nominees to stay in the background and let others promote their claims, but candidates for local offices or for Congress aggressively worked for any votes they could get. No longer presenting themselves as coming from the best social standing, candidates downplayed their wealth or education and instead portrayed themselves as "one of the people" while labeling their opponents as "aristocrats." Many times, candidates for the same position traveled together across a district, county, or state—often sharing the same bed at night—to engage in extensive debates that often lasted for several hours. Less often, too, did candidates come from the traditional ruling elite. Officeholders usually did have significantly more wealth than the average American, but no longer were the wealthy expected to participate in political affairs as part of their social standing. Many of the richest Americans withdrew from politics, considering it a degenerate business beneath their dignity. At the same time, the political system offered young men from humble circumstances a way of making a name for themselves. By the 1830s, politics had effectively become a profession, a career path in which ambitious men skillfully worked at winning elections and carrying out "the people's will." Many never served in elective office but found their calling as party managers, campaigners, and operatives—popularly referred to as "wire-pullers"—people behind the scenes who played an increasingly critical role in directing political affairs.

The democratic transformation culminated with the emergence of the Second Party System, in which two effective organizations engaged in what Americans expected to become a lasting persistent struggle for the right to implement the will of the people. With larger and more loyal followings than Federalists and Republicans had gained, two-party competition appeared by the late 1830s to have become a permanent fixture in American politics. By that time, too, the term "democracy" had become largely synonymous with "republic." Popular interest and participation in elections and widespread white manhood suffrage meanwhile provided a strong foundation for the pervasive belief that the Union stood as the world's most democratic nation. Democracy, though, remained restricted to white men. As state constitutions eliminated property rights, some inserted the word "white" to make it clear who should and who should not be recognized as members of the political community. Ironically, Americans who most fervently championed a white man's democracy insisted on the exclusion of nonwhites and women.

From Assimilation to Removal

At the end of the War of 1812, Native nations east of the Mississippi River still seemed formidable. In the South, Cherokee lands covered northwestern Georgia and spilled over into Alabama and Tennessee; the Creek nation occupied most of eastern Alabama; the Chickasaws and Choctaws possessed much of Mississippi, and the Seminoles lived in northern and central Florida. To the north, Iroquois tribes still dominated much of western New York and eastern Ohio, while several smaller, more decentralized nations claimed lands in the northwest, including the Shawnee and Miami in northern Ohio and Indiana, the Winnebago and Potawatomie in Michigan, and the Fox and Sauk nations in northern Illinois and Wisconsin. Though they looked impressive on the map, the war had left the nations in a weak position. More than a century of warfare and European diseases had reduced the eastern Native population to around 125,000. Goods brought through trade with Americans and Europeans made life easier in some ways, but it also brought dependence on potential enemies who coveted their lands. The nations had no desire to give up any more territory, but the failures of Tecumseh's confederacy and of the Creek War demonstrated the futility of military resistance. After the Battle of New Orleans, Spanish weakness and the withdrawal of British assistance deprived Natives of allies who had once helped them challenge American expansion.

Since George Washington's presidency, the federal government dealt with Natives by loosely following a policy of "civilization" or "assimilation." "Civilization" approached Natives as morally responsible beings, with the same intellectual and physical capabilities as whites, but at a "savage" hunting and subsistence level of existence through which white Americans and their European ancestors had already passed. From this understanding, promoting Natives' economic and cultural advancement offered the best way of securing peace. Federal agents sent to Native nations thus offered tools, domestic animals, and instructions on how to practice settled farming, hand manufacturing, and "civilized" living. After 1812, the government allowed the American Board of Commissioners for Foreign Missions, an interdenominational organization founded in Boston, to send missionaries to try to convert Natives to Christianity and to establish schools that could provide an English-based education. Washington's administration assumed that Natives would remain separate peoples, but Thomas Jefferson and his successors thought "civilization" could eventually result in Natives' incorporation into American society. Progress would take several generations, it was assumed, but Native culture would eventually become identical to Americans' way of life. At that point, the United States could recognize them as citizens and absorb or "assimilate" them into the Union.

Natives responded to American overtures by adopting what would benefit them. Before the war, tribes usually welcomed American agents, and they sometimes ceded lands in order to acquire supplies, pay off debts to merchants, and secure gifts and cash payments. After 1815, "Progressive" factions in many tribes—often led by chiefs of mixed Native and white parentage—recognized their weakness and embraced "civilization" as their people's best hope for protection. The small Northwestern nations proved most resistant to change, though the Iroquois nation gradually moved away from hunting to emphasize farming. The South's "Five Civilized Tribes" rapidly adopted many features of American life; resistance persisted within each nation, but Creeks and Cherokees especially raised new food crops—including cotton, grown by slaves and sold to Southern factors—learned crafts like metalworking and carpentry, set up taverns and stores, and more often wore western-style clothes. "Progressives" learned to speak, read, and write in English, and the Cherokee silversmith Sequoyah in 1821 completed a syllabary—a kind of alphabet—that made it possible to read and write in the Cherokee language. Sequoyah's system spread rapidly among his people, and in 1828 Elias Boudinot began publishing the *Cherokee Phoenix*, a newspaper printed in both English and Cherokee.

Even "Progressive" Natives selectively chose which aspects of "civilization" they would adopt. Most welcomed missionaries and their schools, but relatively few converted to Christianity, holding on to traditional beliefs as a way to retain their sense of separation and distinction as their daily lives became more like those of white Americans. Similarly, the nations continued to consider their lands as possessions of the entire tribe and rejected American encouragement to divide tracts into individually owned family farms. Through these means, Natives subverted the government's intentions. Even while loosely advocating "civilization," federal officials had continued to press for land cessions, and they assumed that assimilation would eventually bring Native lands under federal or state control. By retaining their tribal identities, the nations clung more firmly to their claims to the lands they had left. Creeks and Cherokees, in fact, imposed the death penalty on any tribe member who tried to sell land to whites. The Cherokees meanwhile demonstrated their intention to use "civilization" to their advantage when tribal leaders in 1817 set up an American-style government, with a bicameral legislature, a court system, and a "National Council" of chiefs to serve as an executive branch.

Among white Americans, objections to Natives' presence only increased. Frontiersmen never paid much attention to the government's "civilization" policy and viewed the inhabitants as dangerous obstacles to their settlement. State governments in the South meanwhile insisted on their right to extend their authority over Native territories within state boundaries. At the same time, federal officials started promoting the removal, or "colonization," of Natives from American society. Thomas Jefferson first suggested moving Natives after completing the Louisiana Purchase; lands that Natives possessed east of the Mississippi River, he reasoned, could be exchanged for an equal amount of acreage in the west, where Natives could continue to move toward civilization and citizenship unmolested by American expansion. Jefferson's encouragement persuaded around one thousand Cherokees to move to Arkansas, and by the 1820s even sympathetic officials advocated removal as Natives' only hope for survival. Ignoring Natives' changes, removal proponents continued to describe them as a primitive people dependent on hunting, and they pointed to the alcoholism, impoverishment, and degradation present in some tribes as the unavoidable effects of a less-sophisticated people's contact with "civilized" Americans. Promoters also more often justified removal in racial terms: Natives were not simply "untutored" people, they claimed, but a different breed of humans than white Americans, naturally unsuited for life in the modern world.

Georgia's demand for Cherokee lands brought national attention to Natives' fate. When Georgia ceded the western lands to the federal government in 1802, federal officials promised to extinguish all Native claims to land within the state. For years, authorities made few efforts to carry out the promise, but the state stepped up its demands after Andrew Jackson forced the Cherokees and Creeks to give up millions of acres in the 1814 Treaty of Fort Jackson. Claiming that Natives were merely "tenants" with only temporary rights to lands within a state, Georgians threatened to extend the state's authority over Cherokee lands regardless of Natives' treaties with the federal government. In response, Cherokee leaders held a convention in June 1827 to write a constitution that declared their people a sovereign and independent nation; as such, Cherokees claimed to belong to the international community of nations and held sole jurisdiction over the area within their borders. President John Quincy Adams rejected the Cherokees' assertions, but he stood behind the Cherokees' right to occupy their lands free from Georgia's harassment. After Jackson defeated Adams in the 1828 presidential election, though, the Georgia legislature passed a law extending the state's authority over Cherokee lands as of June 1, 1830. After that date, any remaining Cherokees would be subject to Georgia law as a "free person of color," with no right to own property in the state.

Georgia acted because it knew the new president wholeheartedly supported removal. Unlike his predecessors, President Jackson considered Natives to be conquered peoples, subject to the will of the US government. After his victory at New Orleans, Jackson emerged as the Union's most active advocate of moving Natives west. Though he had ample opportunity to witness Natives' move toward "civilization," he persisted in describing them as primitive hunters whose contact with white society would inevitably lead to their extinction. Removal, he proclaimed, presented a humane policy necessary for Natives' well-being, and once in the presidency he made it his administration's first priority. Rebuffing Cherokee petitions for protection, President Jackson instead upheld Georgia's claim that treaties only granted Natives "permission" to live in the state. Then, in his first annual message to Congress, the new president proposed the establishment of an area west of the Mississippi where the nations might be taken to live "subject to no other control from the United States than such as may be necessary to preserve peace on the frontier." Congress immediately took up a bill to allocate $500,000 for the president to negotiate treaties and carry out Natives' removal to a region west of Arkansas and Missouri, lands that later would be designated the "Indian Territory." President Jackson stipulated that removal was to be "voluntary," but he made it clear that Natives staying in the east would have to accept the authority of the states in which they resided.

The removal bill sparked significant opposition. Cherokees immediately sent a petition to Congress expressing their desire to remain on the lands of their forefathers, and they expressed concern that the western territories were poorly suited for farming and inhabited by peoples who would consider Cherokees enemies. Social reformers, evangelicals, and abolitionists in the Northeast pointed to Natives' progress in adopting American practices as evidence of "civilization's" success, and they denounced removal as an inhumane betrayal of Natives' rights. Jeremiah Evarts, corresponding secretary for the American Board of Commissioners for Foreign Missions, wrote a series of widely reprinted essays under the pseudonym "William Penn" that described removal as a morally indefensible policy that degraded the Native population. Evarts and Catharine Beecher likewise organized separate campaigns to flood Congress with petitions condemning the proposed bill. New Jersey senator Theodore Frelinghuysen, a committed evangelical, led the resistance to the bill in Congress, and Jackson's political opponents—most of whom had previously expressed little sympathy for Natives—quickly joined in the criticism as a way to weaken the president's re-election prospects. Support for removal remained overwhelming in the South and West, but opposition proved strong enough that several administration backers in the North voted against the bill.

Despite the resistance, Congress narrowly passed the Indian Removal Act in May 1830. President Jackson signed the act into law on the same day it received congressional approval, and he immediately moved to persuade Natives to trade their lands and head west. His administration continued to proclaim removal "voluntary" but at the same time used pressure, threats, and bribery to coerce Natives into accepting treaties. Often agents relied on the long-standing practice of making generous agreements with chiefs of questionable authority, then ordering a military force to "escort" a nation away from its lands. Officials who resisted such heavy-handed methods, including the well-respected Indian Superintendent Thomas McKenney, were dismissed and replaced with less sympathetic appointees. Settlers meanwhile seldom waited for removal treaties before moving onto Native lands, and Alabama and Mississippi followed Georgia in declaring state authority over the Creek and Choctaw nations. Most tribes could present little resistance to these pressures. Over the next decade, federal officials negotiated more than seventy treaties to acquire about one hundred million acres in exchange for lands in the Indian Territory, and by the mid-1840s President Jackson's successors had largely completed moving Natives to the west. As opponents had feared, the human cost was high. Many federal officials had hoped to carry out the policy humanely, but inadequate supplies and inexperience moving large numbers of people produced hardships and a significant number of deaths. An estimated one-third of the Creek population died while the nation was taken west between 1833 and 1835.

Some Natives resisted through violence. In the Northwest, most in the Sauk and Fox tribes followed the counsel of Chief Keokuk and agreed to leave northern Illinois for new homes along the Iowa River. The aging Sauk warrior Black Hawk never reconciled himself to this decision. Believing he would have British support, in April 1832 he led about two thousand followers back to their traditional lands near the mouth of the Rock River. Once Black Hawk realized that Britain would not provide assistance, he tried to surrender his small force, but the Illinois militia sent to oppose him killed his peace emissary and forced him to fight. Black Hawk's men routed the militia, and in the "Black Hawk War" he spent the summer trying to lead his band north to refuge in frontier Wisconsin. An American force finally caught and massacred most of Black Hawk's followers near the mouth of the Bad Axe River on August 2. The Sioux nation—the Sauk's long-term enemies—attacked those who made it across the Mississippi, forcing Black Hawk and about 150 survivors to accept living under Keokuk's authority. Farther South, desperate Creeks raided white settlements and attacked a stagecoach carrying US mail in May 1836 after Georgia's militia tried to oust Creeks who had taken refuge on Cherokee lands. By July, the army had suppressed the "Second Creek War" and immediately deported about twenty-five hundred tribesmen, including eight hundred braves, as the troops prepared for the entire nation's removal.

The Seminoles in Florida presented the strongest resistance. About five thousand Seminoles lived in northern and central portions of the territory. Though Americans considered their lands unsuitable for farming, Southerners demanded Natives' expulsion because the nation frequently harbored escaped slaves. The Seminole nation initially accepted a treaty for removal in May 1832, but the agreement stipulated that Natives would leave only if they were satisfied with the report of a scouting party that would first inspect the western lands. Once the inspectors arrived in the west, however, American officials forced them to sign another treaty requiring the Seminoles' departure from Florida within three years, with little compensation. The nation rejected the new treaty, and on December 28, 1835, a band led by the charismatic warrior Osceola attacked and killed the American agent and four others at Fort King, near present-day Ocala. On the same day, another group of warriors ambushed and killed more than one hundred American soldiers near Tampa Bay. Under Osceola's command, the nation retreated to southern Florida, where warriors launched a series of assaults on American settlements. Gradually, the American army apprehended and deported the majority of Seminoles, but the raids continued for several years even after Osceola's capture—under a supposed flag of truce—in October 1837. The American public meanwhile grew increasingly frustrated with the conflict. Though around five hundred Seminoles still eluded American authority, the army declared the Second Seminole War ended in August 1842—after spending more than $20 million and losing fifteen hundred men for lands that most considered of little value.

The Cherokees tried to defend themselves through the American legal system. The discovery of gold in Cherokee country in 1829 produced a flood of white movement into the nation's land. After passage of the Removal Act, Georgia started to assume control over Cherokee lands, with the legislature dividing the region into counties, appointing local officials, and implementing a lottery system to distribute the lands to white settlers. At the urging of Jackson's political opponents, the Cherokees' National Council hired two of the Union's leading attorneys, John Sergeant and former attorney general William Wirt, to file suit in the Supreme Court for an injunction to stop the state's encroachments. Georgia's government ignored the case, refusing to send representation to the court, while Sergeant and Wirt argued that the state had no power over the Cherokees because they existed as an independent foreign nation within the Union. Chief Justice Marshall expressed sympathy for the Cherokees, but neither he nor his colleagues could accept the Cherokee's claim to exist as a "foreign" nation. In *Cherokee Nation v. Georgia* (1831), the court ruled that the Native tribes were actually "domestic dependent nations," separate from the United States but under the protection of the federal government. Because of this status, Marshall concluded, the Cherokees did not have the necessary standing to sue, and the court had no choice but to dismiss the case.

Figure 7.2 "Ma-Ka-Tai-Me-She-Kia-Kiah, or Black Hawk, a Saukie Brave." An artist's depiction of the Sauk chief whose nation resisted removal. Drawn and printed by John T. Bowen, published by F. W. Greenough (1838). Courtesy Prints & Photographs Division, Library of Congress, LC-USZC4-2677.

Georgia's continued aggression gave Cherokees another opportunity to present their case. American missionaries living among Natives encouraged them to resist removal. To eliminate this influence, the state legislature passed a law prohibiting whites from entering Cherokee lands without a license, and licenses would be issued only to those who took an oath that recognized Georgia's authority over Cherokee lands. Several missionaries were then arrested and pardoned after taking the oath, but Samuel Worcester and Elizur Butler refused the oath and were sentenced to four years of hard labor. Worcester's and Butler's sponsor, the American Board of Commissioners for Foreign Missions, again retained Sergeant and Wirt to file another suit, contending that the legislature had no right to pass the license law because federal treaties recognized the region as under Cherokee authority. This time, the Supreme Court backed the Cherokees' case. In *Worcester v. Georgia* (1832), with only one dissenting vote, the justices declared unconstitutional Georgia's act extending state authority over Cherokee territories. Marshall's majority opinion stated that the Constitution gave to the federal government, not the states, the responsibility of dealing with Native nations. Observing that the missionaries could reside in the Cherokee nation "with its permission and by the authority of the President of the United States," the chief justice implicitly chided Andrew Jackson for failing to protect Natives against state encroachment.

The Cherokees' legal victory proved of little benefit. According to legend, President Jackson dismissed the ruling, with the statement "Marshall has made his decision, now let him enforce it," and his administration continued to deny the Cherokees protection from Georgia law. Several thousand Cherokees bowed to what they concluded to be inevitable and voluntarily went west. The majority tried to cling to their lands, but in December 1835 a small group of tribal leaders signed the Treaty of New Echota, which brought the nation only $5 million while requiring its members to leave within two years of the agreement's ratification. The National Council rejected the treaty and presented a petition signed by almost all of the nation's sixteen thousand members. Nevertheless, the Senate ratified the treaty by one vote. Only a few hundred Cherokees showed up at specified locations on May 23, 1838, the designated date for the official move, but the army rounded up the rest of the nation, often breaking into private homes and using bayonets to force families to leave. While military commanders made preparations for the move, Cherokees were kept in camps, where malnourishment and the outbreak of dysentery and other diseases left them in poor condition. The long trip west took place during an especially bad winter and among Cherokees became known as the "Trail of Tears," as harsh conditions, inadequate supplies, and diseases led to the death of an estimated one-fourth of the nation's people.

A number of Natives managed to avoid removal and remain east of the Mississippi. Several small tribes agreed to live on reservations in the Northwest. Like the Seminoles, groups of Iroquois, Cherokees, and Creeks hid out on undesirable lands in New York, North Carolina, and Alabama. In the South, the lighter skin color of Natives with mixed parentage eventually allowed many to assimilate into white society. For the nations in the west, federal promises that they could govern themselves and live unmolested by further white encroachment soon proved short-lived. As Natives feared, their presence in the new territories provoked hostility from the nations on the Great Plains. Also, by the late 1840s, more and more white settlers were crossing into the Indian Territory. An Indian Appropriations Act in 1851 set up for each nation a reservation under the oversight of federal superintendents. Three years later, the Kansas-Nebraska Act created new federal territories in the northern two-thirds of the region that had been reserved for Natives, reducing the Indian Territory to the area that would later become the state of Oklahoma. Long before that time, Americans in the east had largely forgotten about Natives. Opposition to removal faded as the policy became a reality, and, by mid-century, white Americans agreed that racial differences would prevent Natives from ever becoming part of their society.

African Americans Slave and Free

Despite the challenges the Revolution presented to slavery, white Americans continued to associate blacks with bondage. The vast majority assumed that racial differences prevented whites and blacks from coexisting as equals. In the late eighteenth century, few attributed these differences to inherent distinctions that were fixed in nature. Instead, most believed that history, environment, and experience had created the differences: blacks' toiling in slavery had "stultified" the race, whites reasoned, which limited their intellectual development and rendered them unable to compete with whites in a free society. Eventually, time would overcome these limitations, it was assumed, but the differences were so deeply ingrained that it would take several generations for blacks to reach a level of equality. Until then, African Americans would remain a "degraded" race that, if released into freedom among whites, faced at best gradual extinction and at worst elimination in a vicious and bloody race war. Keeping slavery as a "necessary evil" until the races could be permanently separated, whites concluded, presented a humane alternative to releasing an incompetent people among an advantaged yet hostile white population.

The Revolution stimulated hopes among African Americans that slavery might end, if not for themselves then at least for their children. The "necessary evil" argument, after all, recognized the need to eliminate the institution. Not only did the North abolish slavery, several Southern planters, especially in the Chesapeake region, freed their slaves voluntarily. The rise of cotton, though, dashed these hopes. The careful attention required to produce the fiber created a need for labor that gave slavery an even stronger economic foothold, especially after the prohibition of slave importations in 1808. Slave traders now offered good prices to Chesapeake planters to take to the southwest slaves who in an earlier generation might have been freed. The domestic interstate slave trade became a major business in the Southern economy, as companies like Franklin and Armfield transported perhaps as many as 400,000 slaves from the upper South to the Black Belt's cotton fields. Numerous Northern slaveowners likewise sold their property to the South before state laws requiring them to emancipate their slaves went into effect. Free African Americans faced a constant threat from kidnappers wanting to force them into slavery. As slavery became more concentrated in the lower South from Georgia through Louisiana, blacks became a smaller proportion of the population in the North and in the Chesapeake. As long as slavery remained confined to the South, Northern whites expressed less interest in slavery's elimination, even as planters more aggressively defended the institution.

Planters increasingly grounded their defense on race. As slavery became more entrenched, white Americans more often contended that God and nature had separated the races with deep-seated inherent differences that could never be overcome; whites were given the intellectual and progressive traits necessary to prosper in freedom, while blacks proved naturally suited to physical labor and servitude. Beginning in the 1830s, proslavery writers and spokesmen responding to the abolitionists argued that blacks could flourish only as slaves and pointed to poor conditions in Haiti, Liberia, and the British West Indies as evidence of blacks' inability to succeed in freedom. In the next decade, "ethnologists" like Mobile's Josiah Nott and Mississippi physician Samuel A. Cartwright claimed that blacks had different internal organs and smaller skull sizes than whites—scientific "proof," they claimed, of blacks' inferior intelligence yet better ability to work long hours in difficult conditions. Nott even proposed a theory of *polygenesis*, the belief that blacks had originated as a separate animal species from whites. A few ministers followed with the contention that the biblical account of the creation of man refers to whites, with blacks created either earlier as beasts or at a later time as a different breed of humans. Most whites rejected such extreme views, but the notion of inherent racial differences nevertheless gained widespread acceptance across the Union.

The presumption of permanent black inferiority allowed Southerners to justify slavery in terms of *paternalism*, portraying themselves as loving guardians of childlike wards unable to take care of themselves. At the same time, they tightened their grip on their property. Since the early eighteenth century, Southern legislatures had enacted "Slave Codes" that both defined masters' property rights in slavery and restricted slaves' behavior, and after 1800 both paternalist claims and awareness of slaves' discontent led to the imposition of even more stringent laws. States made the process of manumission more difficult and usually required freed slaves to leave the state. By the 1830s, no state legally permitted slaves to learn to read or write, to leave their homes without permission, to possess firearms, to assemble in a large group without a white person present, or to socialize in the homes of whites or free blacks. Striking a white person, even in self-defense, became a capital offense, and though the law recognized the killing of a slave as murder, few whites were prosecuted for this crime. Male masters had no legal obstructions to the sexual exploitation of their property, but rape of a slave woman by someone other than her owner was considered trespassing. Fear of potential uprisings meanwhile convinced non-slaveholders to uphold the codes. Slave patrols, made up mostly of small farmers, roamed plantation districts at night to apprehend blacks who were away from their plantations, break up gatherings, and enter the quarters looking for legal violations.

As restrictions tightened, slaves recognized that they, along with their offspring, would likely remain in bondage for their entire lives. They recognized, too, that they could do little to change their circumstances. For some, the frustrations proved too much. Some committed suicide. A few even cut off a foot or their fingers to escape their work. A particularly galling incident or unusually unfair treatment might lead individuals to rise up against their masters. Some killed their masters in direct confrontations, others through poisoning, and some by arranging for "accidents" to happen. Strong slaves might fight back against beatings, and owners who wanted to avoid provoking even more resistance—and to avoid an embarrassing reputation as a master who could not control his property—sometimes left unpunished those who resisted whippings. Still, those who fought back or escaped execution remained slaves. They knew that organized resistance likewise offered little hope. Conditions in the South actually discouraged rebellion, since in most regions slaves remained a minority population dispersed across several farms and plantations and under resident owners who kept a close watch on their property. In these circumstances, rebellion would meet only swift and brutal retaliation from more numerous and united whites.

The few uprisings that did occur demonstrated the futility of rebellion. In August 1800, a slave blacksmith in Richmond named Gabriel tried to take advantage of the bitter split between Republicans and Federalists to launch an uprising. With a band of followers, Gabriel planned to seize weapons stored in the state capital and take Governor James Monroe hostage until the state granted them their freedom. Two would-be followers informed authorities of the scheme, however; Monroe ordered the plotters' arrest, and state officials hanged Gabriel and twenty-six co-conspirators. A decade later, Charles Deslondes, a slave brought to Louisiana when his master fled the Haitian rebellion, led about two hundred blacks on a rampage that killed two whites and burned plantations in Saint John's Parish along the Mississippi River. After two days of plunder, a seven-hundred-man militia force decimated Deslondes' army, killing sixty-six slaves in the brief battle. Authorities executed more than forty rebels and displayed their heads on pikes as a warning to other potential malcontents. Another uprising came eleven years later in Charleston. In 1822, Denmark Vesey, a carpenter who had purchased his freedom after winning a lottery, collected more than five hundred weapons for an uprising planned to take place in July. The intentions of his plot remain unclear, but as in Gabriel's Rebellion, some of Vesey's followers revealed the plot to Charleston authorities. In June, officials arrested nearly 140 suspected conspirators. After intense interrogations, Vesey and thirty-four others were hanged, and thirty-seven slaves were sold away from the area.

The last, bloodiest, and—to whites—most frightening rebellion met the same fate. Nat Turner, born in 1800, was a slave whose father successfully escaped bondage. Turner himself learned to read and write at an early age, and he became known as "The Prophet" for his work as a slave minister in Southampton County in southeastern Virginia. Turner acknowledged that his owner treated him well, but in the late 1820s, a series of visions convinced him that God had chosen him to lead his people in a violent uprising against their oppressors. Early on the morning of August 22, Turner and six followers killed their master's family. Over the next two days, his band expanded to about seventy rebels and conducted a series of attacks that killed nearly sixty white men, women, and children. Eighteen white men with rifles finally confronted Turner's army, and the rebels, who lacked firearms, could offer little resistance. Those who survived the battle were soon apprehended, and retaliatory mobs killed or beat perhaps as many as two hundred blacks. Turner himself eluded capture for two months before a hunter stumbled onto the cave where he hid. Ultimately, thirteen slaves, including Turner, and three free blacks were hanged for leading the rebellion, and twelve others were transported out of the state.

Turner's Rebellion terrified white Southerners, especially after Thomas R. Gray, a white attorney, interviewed Turner and presented him as a fanatic zealot in his book *The Confessions of Nat Turner*. For slaves, the event only reminded them of the futility of an uprising. With prospects for peaceful emancipation disappearing, and with violence an unrealistic alternative, the vast majority sought to make the best life they could. Subtle forms of resistance remained widespread. Slaves frequently slowed their work, pretended to misunderstand directions, faked illnesses, or "accidentally" broke their tools. Stealing provided both a form of retaliation and a way for slaves to get what they considered their due. Some secretly resorted to arson, including burning crops just before harvest. Escaping north to freedom was a prospect available only to slaves in the upper South or in port towns with access to ships; even for these African

Figure 7.3 "Horrid Massacre in Virginia." An artist's depiction of Nat Turner's rebellion. Illustration from *Authentic and Impartial Narrative of the Tragical Scene which was Witnessed in Southampton County* (New York, 1831). Courtesy Prints & Photographs Division, Library of Congress, LC-USZ62-33451.

Americans, the prospects for success were slim. Throughout the South, though, many could run away for a few days or weeks to hide out in a wilderness or with other slaves, often receiving only a scolding when they returned. Slaves meanwhile covered up their resistance by acting the part of the childlike, unintelligent simpletons that white racism increasingly assumed of blacks while they cunningly devised ways to avoid the institution's most degrading features.

Traditions and cultural practices brought from Africa helped slaves retain a sense of distinctiveness and worth. The American-born descendants of Africans, who made up the vast majority of the slave population, had no direct memories of Africa, but their ancestors had passed on African folkways to their children and grandchildren. Though modified over time by Anglo-American influences, these traditions helped form a distinct African-American culture that kept slaves from being totally engulfed by the white world. African movements and sounds heavily influenced slave dances and songs, and songs in the fields often used the traditional African "call and response" form, with a worker singing a verse that fellow laborers answered in a chorus. Many passed on proverbs and observed signs and omens from knowledge brought across the Atlantic. Strong belief persisted in the power of their forefathers' potions, spells, concoctions, and remedies. Folk tales and legends that represented African culture were modified to fit New World conditions—especially stories about how small but crafty animals outwitted larger, stupid foes, which for the slaves probably represented how they could manipulate their masters.

Relations with other men and women in bondage also helped slaves cope with their conditions. More than three-fourths of all slaves worked on plantations, with about fifty-five percent working in cotton fields, ten percent on tobacco farms, and another ten percent cultivating sugar, rice, or hemp. Although most slaveowners possessed fewer than ten, the majority of slaves lived on plantations holding more than twenty slaves, with almost half on estates with more than thirty. Living in a group of cabins or "slave quarters" some distance from the planter's home—known among slaves as the "big house"—plantation slaves largely lived away from white oversight when not at work. Here, they could express themselves freely and spend their time as they saw fit. While spending much of their time tending vegetable gardens and supplementing their meager diets through hunting and fishing, their interaction with other slaves in the quarters created a slave "community" that provided a refuge from bondage and that masters left to their control.

Families provided one of the most important ways for slaves to claim their own space. No state recognized slave marriages or the legal existence of slave families, but African Americans nonetheless tried to recreate nuclear family units like those of whites. Most planters encouraged family formation, reasoning mainly that families would create attachments that would make them less likely to rebel or run away. Masters often hosted slave weddings, permitted families to live in their own cabins, and gave slaves primary responsibility for rearing their children. Sometimes owners permitted "abroad marriages"—that is, a union with a slave owned by another master on a different plantation, though more often they encouraged unions among their own slaves or would try to buy a slave that one of their bondsmen wanted to marry. Even when two families had to share a residence, families provided loving and supportive relations as well as a sense of place that belied their status as property. Without their masters' knowledge, many took on surnames different from those of their owners. Parents likewise named their children, resisting names that whites imposed. As children grew older, labor demands usually limited the time parents could spend with their offspring, but parents nevertheless used the family to pass on traditional lore as well as lessons on how to deal with slavery's realities.

Christianity also provided slaves with an important refuge. During the Second Great Awakening, expanding conversions made evangelicalism almost universal among the black population. Masters recognized that Christian principles might counter slaves' desire to resist, and many took an active role in providing religious instruction and opportunities for worship. Several urban congregations served members of both races, though biracial churches always segregated believers into black and white seating areas. More often, planters provided ministers for their slaves and urged them to attend Sunday services held on their plantations. Plantation ministers stressed that slaves who faithfully served their masters would receive their eternal reward in the next world. In a few notable incidents, slaves walked out or protested. Most, though, listened passively but then met privately in semi-clandestine "praise meetings" of their own, forming an "invisible church" that whites knew little about. Gathering in the slave quarters, in nearby woods, or in isolated fields, slaves participated in enthusiastic, animated services characterized by exuberant preaching, high-spirited singing, and lively dancing. Instead of admonitions to be a good slave, black preachers emphasized the story of the Exodus, in which God sent Moses to lead His people out of slavery, and a promised "Day of Jubilee" that would bring freedom and retribution to their white tormentors. Even as slavery gained a firmer foothold in the Union, the promise that God was on the side of the oppressed offered slaves the hope that one day their bondage would end.

Individual slaves, of course, responded differently to their condition. House servants usually felt closer to the white family they served than they did to field workers. Some hands might have accepted their masters' insistence on blacks' inferiority and slavery's benefits. The slave population's rapid expansion—from six hundred thousand in 1790 to more than three million in 1850—showed that owners provided sufficient food, clothing, and shelter to keep slaves healthy enough for the population to continue growing despite the 1808 prohibition of slave importations. The vast majority, though, recognized their bleak existence, and they knew that their refuges from slavery rested on unstable foundations. Slave patrols disrupted praise meetings; the master could break up a family at any time, and many owners sexually exploited their female property. Financial setbacks likewise forced even sympathetic owners to sell family members, and the settlement of estates following the master's death could require the relocation, sale, and permanent separation of slave couples, parents, and children. Although the slave community provided important support, the master remained the most influential person in an individual slave's life, and owners exercised control in an environment that increasingly regarded African Americans as permanent racial inferiors.

Racial assumptions likewise tightened constraints on the Union's free African Americans. Emancipation in the Northeastern states and manumissions in the South raised the number of "free colored" persons from about sixty thousand in 1790 to more than four hundred thousand in 1850. Throughout, though, free blacks remained a small minority, constituting less than two percent of the national population and around ten percent of the Union's African Americans. Relatively few free blacks lived in the cotton states, but the majority lived in the rural South, concentrated mainly in the Virginia and Maryland tidewater counties, in the Virginia and North Carolina piedmont, and in coastal cities like Baltimore, Charleston, Mobile, and New Orleans. The Northern free black population lived mostly in cities, though a few made their homes in isolated rural areas in the Northwest. In the South, free blacks usually worked as farm laborers; in the cities, they took whatever jobs they could find. Many worked as skilled craftsmen in trades that they or their forebears had learned as slaves, and a large number went to sea, making up about one-fifth of the crews on merchant and whaling fleets. Urban free blacks usually lived scattered throughout a city, near the places where they provided services for whites. In cities with a larger free black population, especially in the Northeast, white hostility forced them into the poorest neighborhoods. New York's free blacks, for instance, lived with the city's other undesirables in the notorious Five Points district. Elsewhere, they resided in largely segregated areas like those known as "Nigger Hill" in Boston, "Little Africa" in Cincinnati, and "Hayti" in Pittsburgh, as well as Philadelphia's "South Side."

Whether in the North or South, the vast majority of free African Americans lived in bleak and increasingly oppressive conditions. In the years following the Revolution, free blacks with sufficient wealth often had access to the same opportunities as whites; those who met the property requirement enjoyed the right to vote, and several free blacks gained local recognition for their accomplishments. As democracy expanded to stress the equality of all whites, racial distinctions limited opportunities and firmly relegated African Americans to subordinate status. Within a generation, a few free blacks still worked as carpenters, plasterers, or masons, but competition and declining white patronage limited most to unskilled labor or to service-oriented jobs like barbers, hairstylists, launderers, liverymen, coachmen, and domestic servants. Taverns, inns, and other businesses that once grudgingly served blacks now denied black customers. Officials segregated blacks in hospitals, prisons, and even cemeteries, while churches, theaters, stagecoaches, and steamboats required blacks to sit in separate sections, if they were permitted to enter at all. Railroads created separate cars for blacks that by the 1840s were known as "Jim Crow" seats, so-called after a stock black character ridiculed in popular traveling minstrel shows. Northern public schools meanwhile offered minimal, poor-quality instruction in separate rooms or buildings. Whites most often shunned or abused blacks in personal relations, and harassment led to riots in several Northern cities in the 1830s. Throughout the era, free blacks lived in constant fear of kidnapping and sale into slavery.

Legal changes also made it clear that African Americans stood outside the political community. Like slaves, free blacks had limited access to the courts, as they could neither serve on juries nor testify against whites. The high proportion of African Americans in penitentiaries reflected the legal system's presumption of black guilt. Several states required free blacks to register their presence with local officials; those caught without their "free papers" risked immediate enslavement. Northwestern states passed their own "Black Laws" designed to restrict free persons' behavior and encourage them to leave; some required free blacks to post a $500 or $1,000 bond, and Illinois, Indiana, and Oregon explicitly prohibited free black immigration in their constitutions. Meanwhile, most states denied African Americans the right to vote, often taking away that right at the same time that they expanded the franchise among whites. By the late 1830s, free blacks could vote on the same terms as whites only in Massachusetts, New Hampshire, Vermont, and Maine. New York kept a stiff $250 property requirement on African Americans, while Rhode Island's "Landholder's Constitution" maintained a $134 property requirement after beating back the Dorrites' "People's Constitution," which would have restricted the vote to whites.

Proslavery advocates pointed to the poverty, crime, drunkenness, and vice prevalent in African American neighborhoods as "proof" of blacks' inability to flourish in freedom. Still, a number of free persons gained modest financial security to form a middle-class black elite. African-American ministers became highly respected figures, and several free blacks made a good living providing services for whites as barbers, caterers, cooks, waiters, and coachmen. Black doctors or lawyers, who usually received their training from sympathetic whites, provided their community with medical treatment and legal representation. Storekeepers and small businessmen offered goods that blacks could not obtain from whites, while undertakers provided assistance in the burial of family members. Middle-class blacks often gained an education that set them apart from most free persons and belied racist charges of African-American incompetence. Some colleges offered higher education to a handful. John Russwurm's graduation from Maine's Bowdoin College made him the Union's first black college graduate, and by 1860 twenty-eight African Americans had earned degrees. A few acquired substantial wealth, and a small number in the South became slaveholders themselves. In most cases, black slaveowning involved possession of a spouse, children, or other family member whose freedom faced some obstacle, but in Charleston and New Orleans a few free blacks owned a substantial number for work on their plantations.

Most free black elites identified with their community and provided important civic leadership that helped their fellows cope with their hardships. As among slaves, churches in particular offered comfort. Blacks could be found in all denominations, but most attended either one of the independent Baptist churches, which began separating from white congregations in 1809, or an African Methodist Episcopal (AME) church, a denomination formed when Richard Allen and Absalom Jones led blacks out of Philadelphia's Methodist Church in 1794. Under Allen's leadership as the first bishop, the AME spread rapidly to become the most popular faith among free blacks. Several black Episcopal and Presbyterian churches also emerged, and regardless of sect, these churches served not only for worship but also as meeting halls, recreation and social centers, and havens for fugitive slaves. Leaders formed civic organizations and benevolent societies to offer food and assistance to those in need and to help with funeral costs. Several newspapers voiced African Americans' concerns. John Russwurm and Samuel E. Cornish established the first black newspaper, *Freedom's Journal*, in New York in 1827. Costs kept the publishing lives of most papers short—*Freedom's Journal* survived for only a year—but starting in 1847, the wealthy white abolitionist Gerritt Smith provided financial support for Frederick Douglass' *The North Star*. Published in Rochester, New York, *The North Star* stood as the black community's most influential paper.

As spokesmen for the African American community, urban elites unanimously denounced slavery and racism. Some, including New York ministers Henry Highland Garnet and Alexander Crummell and Pittsburgh doctor and writer Martin Delaney, became convinced that whites would never abandon racial exclusion. By the 1840s, they advocated a form of Black Nationalism that called for blacks to leave the Union for a refuge in Africa. Despite their suspicions, Garnet, Delaney, and Crummell eventually cooperated with the American Colonization Society to help facilitate the transportation of several thousand blacks to a new home in Liberia. The vast majority of black leaders rejected colonization, denouncing the ACS as either a misguided organization or a proslavery plot to remove free blacks and their dangerous influence from the presence of slaves. Within weeks of the ACS's founding, in fact, blacks held meetings in several cities to denounce the society, with more than three thousand gathering in a protest in Philadelphia. As racial constraints hardened, some expressed more interest in colonization, but most black leaders stopped short of Black Nationalism. Recognizing the Union as a land of freedom from which white racism excluded them, they called upon white Americans to live up to the Union's ideals, abandon their commitment to slavery, and stop their hypocritical oppression of blacks.

Disgust with slavery and racism made free African Americans crucial figures in the antislavery movement. William Lloyd Garrison's association with Baltimore's free black community convinced him to abandon colonization for the immediatist and uncompromising stance that characterized the abolitionist movement. Free persons who had experienced slavery offered testimony to the institution's horrors as speakers and writers for the American Anti-Slavery Society, with Frederick Douglass' eloquent account of his life as a slave in Maryland making him perhaps the Union's best known African American. In most cities, men and women formed black auxiliary societies that provided important assistance for the AASS. Free communities also served as important stations on the Underground Railroad, a network of homes and antislavery activists who helped fugitives travel to freedom in Canada, and free black "vigilance committees" thwarted kidnappings intended to force free blacks into slavery and aided runaways seeking freedom. From 1830 through 1835 and again periodically in the 1840s and 1850s, free black leaders held a series of conventions to unite their challenge across the North. Recognizing the need to counter the dissipation prevalent among free blacks, the conventions devoted part of their efforts to promote "self-improvement," hard work, and thrift to counter poverty and demonstrate blacks' ability to thrive in freedom. Mostly, the conventions issued powerful statements denouncing slavery and racism and demanding that whites give blacks the opportunities they deserved.

For the most part, black calls for freedom and equality went unheeded. African-American protests eventually won an important victory when Massachusetts in 1855 approved a law prohibiting racial or religious discrimination in schools. Only three years later, Chief Justice Roger Taney ruled in the case of *Dred Scott v. Sandford* that persons of African descent "are not included, and were not intended to be included, under the word 'citizens' in the Constitution." Instead, Taney concluded, they constituted "a subordinate and inferior class of beings, who had been subjugated by the dominant race, and, whether emancipated or not, yet remained subject to their authority." Northerners widely condemned the *Dred Scott* decision, and lawyers as well as political opponents criticized Taney's legal reasoning. Most critics, though, focused on the chief justice's attempt in the decision to deny congressional authority to prohibit slavery in US territories. Although white Americans argued over slavery's expansion, relatively few disputed the law's denial of citizenship to the Union's black population.

Domesticity and "True Womanhood"

Unlike with slaves, few Americans emerged from the Revolution with a desire to challenge the legal subordination of women. Every state continued to enforce the principle of coverture, leaving wives completely under their husbands' authority. Traditional assumptions limited their expected contributions to acting as "Republican Mothers" who encouraged their children to grow up with morality, responsibility, and virtue. Changes in the early nineteenth century, though, stimulated a reconsideration of women's status. Economic growth and manufacturing expansion tended to separate the workplace from the home, both in reality and in ideals. Instead of working in farm fields surrounding the house or in artisan workshops at a craftsman's residence, men more often "went to work" in shops and factories. Laborers meanwhile increasingly hired out for wages and no longer lived with their employers, leaving wives and children to themselves at home. Gradually, the ideal of the nuclear family of parents and children living together and apart from others replaced the extended kinship household as the fundamental social institution. At the same time, manufacturing made available at low cost many necessities like clothes, soap, and candles, which women once contributed as part of their domestic responsibilities. For some women, the expanding market provided them with more leisure time than they had known before.

As circumstances changed, Americans more often described their society in terms of "separate spheres." A "public" sphere involved affairs outside the home, such as economic production, politics, and community business. The home meanwhile gained recognition as a "private" sphere that offered rest, recreation, and a refuge from the pressures and temptations of an increasingly competitive and corrupt world. The vast majority of men and women alike remained convinced that deep-seated natural differences, differences that went far beyond their physical attributes, distinguished the sexes. Almost everyone believed that men and women varied so much in their outlooks, interests, emotions, and capabilities that God had made them different types of humans. The genders' distinct qualities seemed to suit them perfectly for the newly emerging social spheres. Men's apparent competitiveness, drive to dominate, dispassionate reasoning, and cold calculation made them well-suited for the contested and potentially harsh public sphere. Women's inherent friendliness, submissiveness, emotionalism, and morality meanwhile prepared them for influence and even dominance in the home. Ultimately, Americans concluded that the Union's progress depended on allowing each gender to prevail in its respective sphere. Driven by "the head," men in the public sphere would advance its material success, while women's concern in the private sphere for matters of "the heart" would ensure a well-ordered, peaceful, and virtuous society.

Male and female commentators built on the "separate spheres" notion to expand republican motherhood into a widely accepted ideology that historians have called "domesticity" or "true womanhood." Women's natural characteristics, proponents argued, allowed them to play a crucial social role through their influence in the private sphere. Their natural piety would ensure that the Christian faith had a presence in each family. Domestic skills would help them create a warm, loving environment to which their husbands would want to return. As naturally submissive beings, they would obey their husbands and provide men with examples of self-sacrifice. Finally, women's lack of interest—and even abhorrence—in sex would restrict sexual activity to procreation within marriage, while keeping the family's focus on noble and moral concerns. Women who lived up to these ideals fulfilled their divinely appointed duties, and they ensured the nation's future by instilling proper values in their children. They also made the home a comfortable retreat from the cares of the world, refuges where they could encourage their husbands to live upstanding and virtuous lives despite the public sphere's temptations and frustrations. In this way, even more than as republican mothers, domestic "true" women would serve as the Union's moral guardians, responsible for promoting the virtuous behavior necessary for a successful republic.

"Domesticity" gained almost universal acceptance. "The woman's place is in the home" became a popular saying, and women from all social ranks widely accepted that marriage and motherhood provided the purpose for their lives. Especially among the upper and middle classes in the urban Northeast—where hired servants performed most household duties and families limited the number of children—women consciously tried to live out the precepts of "true womanhood." Even in rural and frontier areas, where farmers still worked the land they lived on, the expectation that wives should keep a good home, and that mothers bore responsibility for their children's guidance, increasingly governed women's existence. Wealthy Southerners meanwhile modified domesticity to fit the traits of the "Southern Lady" or "plantation mistress." Southerners described planters' wives and daughters as ideal women: dainty, passive, graceful, and compassionate creatures who represented all things good and pure in a slave society. As the plantation mistress, she upheld the family's virtue through managing the manor house and overseeing the feeding, clothing, and physical and spiritual care of the white family and its slaves.

The responsibilities of domesticity encouraged greater acceptance of providing women with an education. Outside of New England, colonial Americans had considered women's literacy unnecessary, since their fathers and husbands dealt with business outside of the family. After the Revolution, Americans recognized education as a crucial skill that helped women fulfill their domestic duties. Parents first sent their daughters with their sons to district and field schools, and state-sponsored public schools always accepted girls in the primary grades. By 1850, most white women could read and write, and the proportion of literate women equaled that of men. Expanding literacy gave privileged women opportunities to pursue a more advanced education. From the late eighteenth century onward, women's "seminaries" like the Young Ladies' Academy in Philadelphia usually stressed the teaching of subjects designed to cultivate a woman's "graces," such as French, music, and dance. After Emma Hart Willard established Troy Female Seminary in New York in 1821, many offered curricula similar to what was taught in men's academies, emphasizing mathematics, history, and geography. Women's academies omitted the classical languages, and colleges still accepted only men, but after 1837, Mary Lyon's Mount Holyoke Female Seminary in Massachusetts demonstrated women's ability to complete a college-level program. Oberlin College in Ohio meanwhile enhanced its reputation for radicalism as the Union's first co-educational institution, although women were not permitted to speak in class or to participate in graduation ceremonies.

Increased women's literacy gave rise to a boom in the publication of etiquette books, magazines, short stories, and novels written specifically for female readers—literary works that reinforced the presumptions of domesticity by providing models of "true womanhood" for women to imitate. Sentimental "domestic novels" like those of Catherine Maria Sedgwick, the era's most popular female writer, presented idealized female characters while romanticizing family life. Catharine Beecher, the daughter of Lyman Beecher and the sister of Harriet Beecher Stowe, emerged as one of the Union's leading proponents of domesticity. Beecher established a Female Seminary in Hartford in 1823 and strongly encouraged women's education and their opportunities as teachers. Though she never married—her fiancé died before their wedding could take place—she produced several guides on women's proper behavior in the home and in public. Sarah Josepha Hale meanwhile gained recognition as domesticity's principal spokesperson. After her husband's death in 1822, Hale supported herself by writing novels and children's books. Her success as editor of Boston's *Ladies' Magazine* convinced Philadelphia publisher Louis Godey to hire her as editor of *Godey's Ladies' Book* in 1837. Over the next forty years, until Hale's retirement at age ninety, *Godey's* stood as the most popular women's magazine, with readership peaking at 150,000.

Figure 7.4 "Sarah Josepha Hale." Hale edited the nation's principal ladies' magazine for nearly fifty years and was one of the leading proponents of women's domestic roles. Painting by W. H. Chambers (1850). Courtesy Prints & Photographs Division, Library of Congress, LC-USZ62-35926A.

While admonishing women to live up to domesticity's proper behavior, Hale also encouraged them to assume a more public role in vocations consistent with women's natural characteristics, such as social workers, teachers, and Sunday school leaders. Ladies with leisure time often participated in activities outside of the home that were considered appropriate for women. The belief in women's natural piety, for instance, both encouraged and reinforced a widespread number of female conversions during the Second Great Awakening. More women than men converted during the revivals, and in most churches women comprised at least one-half to as much as two-thirds of the members. Although Charles G. Finney encouraged women to speak in churches, and a few female preachers gained a following, tradition excluded women from ministerial or leadership positions in most congregations. Behind the scenes, however, women provided important administrative assistance and helped organize Sunday schools and female missionary societies to send missionaries to foreign lands. "Maternal Associations" in several churches provided information to promote "Christian Motherhood" among the faithful, while "Children's Aid Societies" sought to assist working-class children by teaching their mothers proper domestic skills like needlework, cooking, and housecleaning.

Women also played active roles in reform organizations. Many assumed leadership positions in associations dealing with issues affecting wives and children. Although the American Temperance Society disallowed female members until 1854, the crusade against alcohol especially gained support, in part because advocates considered alcohol abuse a major contributor to broken families and domestic violence. By 1840, over thirty thousand women belonged to the Daughters of Temperance, the female auxiliary to the American Temperance Society. Other women directed their attention to opposing prostitution. Society traditionally attributed prostitution to the "evil seductress" who seduced unsuspecting men, but domesticity's principles shifted the blame to manipulative men who forced innocent victims into a life of sin. In 1848, several local anti-prostitution associations united to form the American Female Guardian Society, a national organization to encourage state legislatures to outlaw the practice while opening shelters and providing education for women wanting to escape a dissolute life. Stories of masters' brutal treatment, disruption of slave families, and sexual abuse of female slaves drew thousands of Northern women into the abolition movement. Their work gaining signatures for petitions, lobbying legislators, and raising funds helped sustain the American Anti-Slavery Society through its early years. A few women activists gained notoriety for their public testimonials condemning slavery's evils—most notably South Carolina planter's daughters Sarah and Angelina Grimké, who moved to Philadelphia to oppose slavery. In a six-month tour through 1837, the Grimkés addressed an estimated forty thousand listeners.

Even among the most privileged, though, few could aspire to domesticity's high standards. Elite women in the cities sometimes had the leisure time needed to carry out "true womanhood's" idealized maternal and moral roles, but experiencing normal human emotions like selfishness or sexual desire caused many to express feelings of inadequacy. The realities of life kept most others far removed from domesticity's expectations. Unmarried women from the working class often had to take jobs outside the home in textile factories, in sewing or needle trades, or as domestic servants. Many employers relied on the "separate spheres" doctrine to justify paying women lower wages, since they were not expected to support families and their labor would presumably prove of poorer quality and less efficient than would men's work. For the majority of women, farm chores and the daily upkeep of the home preoccupied their time. Because rural families still needed as many laborers as possible, the lives of most farmers' wives continued to center upon the regular cycle of pregnancies and births in environments where rates of death in childbirth and infant mortality remained high. Even the "plantation mistress" was expected to bear several children while carrying out the demanding tasks of managing a plantation household and hosting balls and parties. Often, too, planters' wives daily faced evidence of their husbands' infidelity in the form of light-skinned children of female slaves.

Women with a solid education and better opportunities likewise found their experience constrained by the "separate spheres" doctrine. Middle-class single women could work outside the home, but only if they pursued callings that coincided with presumptions about women's "natural" characteristics. More than six hundred newspapers and magazines employed women as writers and editors, mainly so they could promote domesticity's ideals. Notwithstanding industrialization, many women still ran shops as dressmakers or milliners—hatmakers—skilled trades that provided a good income. Others opened bakeries and catering shops or ran boarding houses. Women's presumed maternal instincts made teaching seem an appropriate position, though they could teach boys only in the primary grades. Schools often preferred female teachers, not least because women would work for only one-third to one-half of the salaries of their male counterparts. The medical field, however, seemed an inappropriate one for delicate creatures like women. Outside of some rural communities, midwives all but disappeared as male doctors increasingly oversaw the birthing process. Most Americans assumed, too, that the law's complications were too demanding for women—who were believed to be irrational and emotion-driven—to become lawyers. All women were expected to give up their work once they married so they could concentrate on their duties to their husbands and children. Commentators like Catharine Beecher, in fact, described the work of a housewife as a profession in itself. Regardless of social status, married women remained under the doctrine of coverture, under their husbands' authority and with no legal existence of their own.

A few successful women directly challenged the "separate spheres" presumptions. In the 1830s, the writer Margaret Fuller won repute as the best-read person in New England, and she gained national attention in the 1840s reviewing books for Horace Greeley's *New York Tribune*. Her 1845 book *Woman in the Nineteenth Century* argued that women had the same intellectual capabilities as men, and she demanded educational and occupational opportunities so women could achieve their full potential. Another writer, Amelia Bloomer, established her own newspaper, *The Lily*, in Seneca Falls, New York, in 1849. Initially *The Lily* focused on promoting temperance, but Bloomer soon used the paper to advocate women's rights, including less cumbersome and restrictive dress. During the 1850s, radical women often wore "Bloomers"—a suit of loose-fitting trousers gathered at the ankles and covered by a short dress and a vest—to symbolize their rejection of convention. An interest in women's health meanwhile convinced Kentucky teacher Elizabeth Blackwell to apply to medical school. Expecting it would demonstrate women's inability to study medicine, twenty-nine schools rejected her, but Geneva College in New York offered her a seat in its entering class in 1847. Blackwell's abilities impressed the faculty and her fellow students, and she finished first in the 1849 graduating class. After further study in Europe, she opened a clinic for poor women and children in New York City, and her encouragement led to the foundation of several women's medical colleges in the 1850s and 1860s.

Calls for an organized movement for women's rights mainly emerged from abolitionism. Some women, like Abigail Kelley, joined the abolitionists because they believed antislavery to be one cause in the fight for human freedom, and from the start they pressured the American Anti-Slavery Society to stand for women's rights. Most female abolitionists came to antislavery because they believed their moral duty as republican mothers compelled them to act against a national sin. Their work against slavery—along with public hostility toward female antislavery speakers and moderate abolitionists' efforts to limit their contributions—persuaded many women that they experienced a form of bondage almost as constricting as slavery. The issue of whether to demand women's rights proved a major factor in the American Anti-Slavery

Society's division in 1839. An incident the next year at a World Antislavery Convention in London, England, pushed some activists to make women's rights their priority. The AASS selected eight women, including Lucretia Mott, to join a large number of men to attend the meeting. When they arrived, the American women met a cold reception; after a long debate, the convention voted to deny them admission. Several American delegates threatened to leave, so attendees compromised: The women could listen to the proceedings, but only by sitting in a side room, with a curtain drawn in front of them so the men in attendance could not see them.

Though the Americans accepted the concession, the insult infuriated Mott and Elizabeth Cady Stanton—who had attended with her husband, one of the male delegates. Mott and Stanton returned from London determined to hold a similar convention that would demand greater rights for women. Their marriages to activist husbands and parenting of young children prevented them from acting on their pledge for several years. The two nevertheless revived the plan in a July 1848 meeting at a mutual friend's home near Stanton's residence in Seneca Falls, New York. Within ten days, Mott and Stanton attracted about three hundred men and women from western New York to meet at Seneca Falls' Wesleyan Methodist Church. For two days, the participants publicly denounced the legal, social, and cultural constraints on women. At the end of the conference, sixty-eight women and thirty-two men signed the convention's "Declaration of Rights and Sentiments," which Stanton had drafted the week before. Patterned after the Declaration of Independence, the "Seneca Falls Declaration" affirmed that "all men and women are created equal" and condemned history's "repeated injuries and usurpations on the part of man toward women, having in direct object the establishment of an absolute tyranny over her." After listing specific offenses, the declaration concluded with eighteen resolutions calling for legal changes, educational opportunities, and recognition of women's equality through granting women the right to vote.

Mott and Stanton circulated the convention's proceedings and wrote to several newspapers to publicize its work. Several editors expressed their sympathy, but most papers either ignored or condemned the meeting, denouncing its leaders for unnaturally wanting to rule over men. For the next two decades, advocates for women's rights remained few in number and associated with the radical fringes of society. Still, their calls for women's equality aided an important legal change that helped crack the foundation of coverture. In 1839, the Mississippi legislature had approved a law giving married women the right to own property. Planters in the state favored the law so they could put their estates in their wives' names to prevent creditors from seizing their plantations in case of debt or a bad cotton harvest. New York and Pennsylvania passed their own Married Women's Property Acts in 1848, and women's lobbying efforts and petitions helped secure passage of similar laws in several other states through the 1850s. Stanton's efforts particularly helped New York to pass a more expansive law in 1860 to give women the right to buy and sell property on their own, to sign contracts, to sue in court, to keep any wages they earned, and in case of divorce to gain joint custody of their children. Other states soon approved similar laws, but few Americans would go further. Activists had to wait for a future generation to secure for women the right to vote.

Long before then, Americans enjoyed a reputation as the most democratic people in the world. Foreign observers like Alexis de Tocqueville recognized that "the people" ruled American society and culture as well as political affairs. Americans defined "the people" to include adult white men, regardless of property or status, but, in the process of expanding democracy, they set limits that effected nonwhites and women for years to come. They did so, too, at a time when they faced crucial issues affecting the Union as it moved from a confederation to a nation.

Suggested Readings

Allgor, Catherine. *Parlor Politics: In Which the Ladies of Washington Help to Build a City and a Government* (Charlottesville, 2000).

Blassingame, John W. *The Slave Community: Plantation Life in the Antebellum South* (New York, 1972).

Boydston, Jeanne. *Home and Work: Housework, Wages, and the Ideology of Labor in the Early Republic* (New York, 1990).

Brooke, John L. *Columbia Rising: Civil Life on the Upper Hudson from the Revolution to the Age of Jackson* (Chapel Hill, 2010).

Bynum, Victoria E. *Unruly Women: The Politics of Social and Sexual Control in the Old South* (Chapel Hill, 1992).

Cave, Alfred A. *Prophets of the Great Spirit: Native American Revitalization Movements in Eastern North America* (Lincoln, NE, 2006).

Clinton, Catherine. *The Plantation Mistress: Woman's World in the Old South* (New York, 1982).

Franklin, John Hope, and Loren Schweninger. *Runaway Slaves: Rebels on the Plantation* (New York, 1999).

Frederickson, George M. *The Black Image in the White Mind: The Debate on Afro-American Character and Destiny, 1817–1914* (New York, 1971).

Horton, James Oliver, and Lois E. Horton. *In Hope of Liberty: Free Black Culture and Community in the North, 1700–1865* (1997).

Huston, Reeve. *Land and Freedom: Rural Society, Popular Protest, and Party Politics in Antebellum New York* (New York, 2000).

Jeffrey, Julie Roy. *The Great Silent Army of Abolitionism: Ordinary Women in the Antislavery Movement* (Chapel Hill, 1998).

Keyssar, Alexander. *The Right to Vote: The Contested History of Democracy in the United States* (New York, 2000).

Kolchin, Peter. *American Slavery, 1619–1877* (New York, 1993).

Lasser, Carol, and Stacey M. Robertson. *Antebellum Women: Private, Public, Partisan* (Lanham, MD, 2010).

McMillen, Sally G. *Seneca Falls and the Origins of the Women's Rights Movement* (New York, 2008).

Perdue, Theda. *Slavery and the Evolution of Cherokee Society, 1540–1866* (Knoxville, 1979).

Raboteau, Albert J. *Slave Religion: The Invisible Institution in the Antebellum South* (New York, 1978).

Wallace, Anthony. *The Long Bitter Trail: Andrew Jackson and the Indians* (New York, 1993).

Wright, Donald R. *African Americans in the Early Republic, 1789–1831* (Arlington Heights, IL, 1993).

175

VIII

NATIONALISM AND REACTION

At the end of the War of 1812, few could foresee the changes that would sweep the next generation. Most Americans simply celebrated the Union's "victory," convinced that Britain's "defeat" assured American independence. Of course, President James Madison and other Republican leaders knew that the conflict had actually brought the Union to brink of disaster. They hoped to channel national pride into support for measures that would strengthen the Union's defenses and promote its self-sufficiency. They also expected the new policies to result from the cool, dispassionate deliberations of statesmanlike leaders who stood committed to the public welfare. Public backlash to the "disunionist" Hartford Convention left Federalists clinging only to the state governments of Massachusetts, Connecticut, and Delaware. Within a few years, only Massachusetts would remain under opposition control; elsewhere, only a handful of Federalists remained scattered through the Northeast. With their rivals all but gone, Republicans hoped they could now govern the Union as its founders had intended—without the complications of self-interested parties or "factions."

An Era of Good Feelings?

In the midst of the postwar celebrations, the ruins of public buildings in Washington presented Republicans with a disturbing reminder of what might have happened. The British invasion had destroyed all but one public building, and rubble lay within the charred walls of the President's Mansion and the Capitol. President James Madison spent the remainder of his term working in the Octagon House, a private residence a few blocks from the executive mansion that Virginia planter John Tayloe offered for the president's use. Congress meanwhile moved into a hastily constructed Federal-style brick structure that ended up serving as its home for the next ten years. Despite the makeshift circumstances, Republican spirits remained high. The elections held in the fall and winter of 1814 and 1815 returned strong Republican majorities to both chambers of Congress—119 Republicans to 64 Federalists in the House, and 26 Republicans to 12 Federalists in the Senate. Likewise, in contrast to the bickering and factionalism that had plagued the party before the war, the sense of triumph produced among Republicans an apparent commitment to unity and common purpose.

Well aware that harmony might not last, President Madison moved quickly. In his first annual message to the Fourteenth Congress, which convened in December 1815, he recommended a series of measures designed to further national defense and the Union's welfare. His proposals included restoring a "uniform" national currency—which the president acknowledged might involve establishing a new national bank—restructuring the militia laws, completing coastal defenses and ships already under construction, using tariff policy to encourage manufacturing, establishing a network of roads and canals, and founding additional military academies and a national university—institutions that would promote "those national feelings, those liberal sentiments, and those congenial manners which contribute cement to our Union." Congressional leaders warmly welcomed his proposals. Back from the negotiations at Ghent, Kentucky's Henry Clay resumed his position as Speaker of the House and threw his support behind Madison's program. Another "War Hawk," South Carolina's John C. Calhoun, took over management of the president's program in the House and worked tirelessly to ensure its passage.

Clay, Calhoun, and their associates first took up President Madison's call to address the Union's economic conditions. During the war, the House had rejected by one vote a bill to charter a new Bank of the United States, but the Union's unstable finances during the war and the size of the debt at its conclusion convinced most Republicans of the wisdom of a central financial institution. After three months of mild debate, in April majorities in both chambers approved a bill chartering the second Bank of the United States. Like the first Bank of the United States, it would be headquartered in Philadelphia, hold a federal charter for twenty years, be governed by a twenty-five-member board of directors that would elect its president, and have the authority to establish branches throughout the Union. Once again, too, the president would appoint five of the bank's directors, with the other twenty elected by stockholders, and Congress would purchase one-fifth of its stock, though by issuing $35 million in stock the second Bank of the United States would be more than twice the size of the first. As the depository for the federal government, the bank would transfer federal funds without charge and be subject to Treasury Department oversight, and the institution would pay the government a "bonus" of $1.5 million over its first three years of existence.

Two weeks after approving the bank bill, Congress passed the Tariff of 1816, an increase in taxes on imports that was designed to "protect" American manufacturers from foreign competition. Despite the expansion of manufacturing during the war, the Union's workshops and factories could not keep up with Britain's long-established and technologically advanced industries, and the resumption of trade threatened to flood the states with cheaper British goods. The new tariff law would raise the prices of imports and encourage Americans to buy cheaper American-made products; manufacturers could then reinvest their profits to expand their own production, reducing the Union's dependence on foreign goods while building up the industries needed for supplies in case of another war. Opponents charged that farmers would have to pay higher prices for goods, but Calhoun defended the tariff with the contention that the expanding manufacturing sector would guarantee a domestic market for American farm products. Calhoun's argument reassured enough members that the law passed by comfortable margins. In its final form, only goods that Americans could not produce themselves could enter the Union duty-free. Most other imports would be assessed at thirty percent of their value, with the rate falling to twenty percent after three years. The law's "minimum price" principle guaranteed that cotton and woolen cloth would always be assessed at least at twenty-five cents per yard, even though imported cotton actually sold at six cents per yard.

Beyond the bank and the tariff, the Fourteenth Congress approved several other laws designed to strengthen the Union. Lawmakers appropriated $100,000 to extend the National Road, committed $1 million annually for the next ten years to construct eighteen new warships, provided another million dollars to construct forts at the mouths of the Mississippi and Delaware Rivers, and created a general staff for a larger professional army. Throughout the session, leading Republicans expressed little concern for their party's onetime devotion to strict construction of the Constitution. John Randolph of Roanoke led a small core in dissent to the party's seeming adoption of "old Federalism" and warned that a Congress that could build roads could also deprive slaveholders of their property. The majority, though, ignored the "Old Republican" complaints. Even President Madison, who had once pressed President

Washington to reject the first Bank of the United States—signed the second bank's charter with little comment beyond noting that "time and expediency" had resolved his constitutional concerns. The remaining Federalists grumbled and divided over whether to accept their rivals' program, while mainstream Republicans reassured themselves that bank officials, manufacturers, and an active federal government could be trusted as long as the people's representatives kept close watch.

Only the attempt to create a national transportation system appeared to take federal authority too far. In its last significant act, on March 1, 1817, the Fourteenth Congress approved a law popularly known as the "Bonus Bill." Drafted by Clay and sponsored in the House by Calhoun, the act would apply the Bank of the United States' $1.5 million "bonus," along with future dividends received on the bank's stock, to pay for a national network of roads and canals along the lines first proposed in then–Treasury Secretary Albert Gallatin's 1808 Report on Transportation. Resistance from areas that would not directly benefit from the plan almost defeated the bill in the House, but the measure passed by two votes after Calhoun argued that a transportation system would aid the military, increase the country's wealth, and "counter every tendency to disunion." On his last full day in office, however, President Madison shocked Republican leaders by vetoing the act. The retiring president actually favored a national transportation network, and he encouraged approval of a constitutional amendment to authorize its construction. Until the states ratified an amendment, though, he believed that the Constitution did not grant Congress the power to fund internal improvements and that the Bonus Act failed "by any just interpretation" to appear "necessary and proper."

Elections held through late 1816 and early 1817 perhaps suggested wider disapproval of the Fourteenth Congress' activism. Usually about half of the House of Representatives' membership changed hands every two years. This time, only one-third of the sitting members won re-election to the next Congress. Many of those rejected were victims of a popular protest against a Compensation Act passed in March 1816. Low pay had long discouraged service in Congress, so the lawmakers voted to increase their compensation from six dollars a day to an annual salary of $1,500, a figure that still stood lower than the pay of several federal officeholders. Calhoun argued that the increase would "attract and secure quality and integrity to the public service," but critics denounced the law as a "salary grab," especially since the representatives voted the increase for themselves. Only fifteen of the eighty-one members who voted for the act kept their seats; several who had voted against the increase lost because opponents denounced them for accepting the money anyway. Republican leaders assured themselves that the Compensation Act alone provoked voters' displeasure, and in the "lame duck" session that met after the elections, the majority repealed the law for future Congresses—though they kept the raise for themselves. Few considered, though, that the outcry might reflect public unease with the federal government's newfound energy and the scope of its activities.

Republicans expected the next president to stand behind further federal activism. James Monroe, once an Antifederalist and the Old Republicans' candidate in 1808, had regained moderate Republicans' favor with his loyal service as President Madison's secretary of state. His work heading both the State and War Departments during the war convinced him of the need for a strong central government while also making him the frontrunner to succeed Madison, despite the New York legislature's warning that yet another president from Virginia could jeopardize Republican strength in the North. When New York governor Daniel D. Tompkins failed to gain much support outside of his home state, Secretary of War William H. Crawford, a Georgian who had gained the Old Republicans' favor, emerged as Monroe's strongest challenger. Crawford, though, kept his distance from the efforts to nominate him, confident that he could have the office after Monroe retired. Aware that President Madison privately favored

Monroe, a congressional Republican caucus in March nominated Monroe over Crawford by a 65–54 vote, with Tompkins as the vice presidential candidate. The general election proved anticlimactic. Federalists never bothered formally to nominate a candidate. The opposition majorities in the Massachusetts, Connecticut, and Delaware legislatures cast their states' electoral votes for New York senator Rufus King, but Republican strength in the other states gave Monroe and Tompkins an easy victory.

In some ways, President Monroe seemed a relic of a past generation. The last president who had come of age during the Revolution, he often still wore the knee breeches, powdered wig, and three-cornered hat in the style of the late eighteenth century. Though he lacked the intellectual depth of Presidents Jefferson and Madison, experience had made him a skilled politician, and he fully intended to use his abilities to further the Union's independence. While retaining Madison appointees Crawford, Postmaster General Return J. Meigs, and Naval Secretary Benjamin Crowninshield, he chose for his cabinet men who were closely associated with the strong nationalist agenda. Massachusetts' John Quincy Adams—a former Federalist, the second president's son, and the Union's most experienced diplomat—agreed to serve as secretary of state, while Virginia lawyer William Wirt became the attorney general. Clay declined to serve as secretary of war, angry that he had not been offered the more prestigious position as head of the State Department, and he soon emerged as one of the administration's leading critics in Congress. Two others also turned down the office, but Calhoun's acceptance ensured that most of Monroe's cabinet stood solidly behind the Fourteenth Congress's actions.

President Monroe's inaugural address reflected his intention to continue the Madison administration's approach. After praising the Union's "happy state," he stressed the need for strong defenses and the government's "systematic and fostering care" in promoting manufacturing. He intended to call for a federally sponsored transportation network, but after President Madison's surprising veto of the Bonus Bill he toned down his wording to advocate roads and canals "with a constitutional sanction." Once in office, President Monroe undertook several actions to encourage respect for the central government. Eight months after his inauguration, the president moved his family into the still-incomplete President's Mansion—by then popularly called the "White House" because of the bright paint needed to cover burn marks on the outside walls. Monroe also revived much of the formality, pomp, and ceremony that Thomas Jefferson had abandoned. Cabinet members refused to wear a uniform the president had designed for them, but seating at state dinners once again would be determined by seniority or status. Foreign representatives meanwhile could no longer drop in to see the president; meetings would be held only by appointment, and President Monroe insisted official business be conducted through his secretary of state. Meanwhile, he filled the executive mansion with ornate French furniture. Like President Jefferson, President Monroe frequently hosted dinners for members of Congress and government officials, and, like those of Dolly Madison, Elizabeth Kortland Monroe's weekly receptions gained notoriety as lavish affairs.

More significantly, President Monroe tried to bring a clear end to the party division that had split the Union's leaders for the past two decades. Shortly after his inauguration, he embarked on a three-and-a-half month tour of the Middle Atlantic and New England states, officially to inspect coastal defenses but primarily to promote a sense of national unity that might transcend party lines. The warm receptions he received, and his conciliatory gestures to the opposition, led one Federalist newspaper in Boston to proclaim the onset of an "era of good feelings" that might lead to Federalists' appointment to government offices. President Monroe actually had no desire to offer appointments to Federalists; though he paid little attention to party organization, he wanted the Union's leaders to remain faithful to Jeffersonian principles. Nevertheless, he hoped that Republicans could eventually absorb their rivals and return the Union to a government without parties, in which nonpartisan statesmen put the public good above personal interests. His efforts to stand as a president "above party" joined Federalist weakness to bring the spirit of postwar unity to its highest point. Politicians still identified themselves as either Republicans or Federalists, but to many, the "Era of Good Feelings" signaled that party warfare had indeed come to an end.

With a seemingly united nation behind him, President Monroe devoted much of his attention to defending American honor abroad. The War of 1812's conclusion left several issues in foreign relations unresolved while raising new ones that threatened to compromise American independence. The president left face-to-face negotiations to his appointees, but he kept close watch on his administration's diplomacy and made the final decisions himself. He found a kindred spirit in Secretary of State John Quincy Adams. Adams had first dealt with European politicians when he was fourteen and had accompanied his father in the talks to end the War for Independence. Since then he had spent nearly twenty years representing the Union in foreign capitals, and he shared President Monroe's desire to present the United States to the rest of the world as an example of a successful free government. Even more than President Monroe, Secretary Adams perceived that a firm and bold stance could advance American commercial interests. He foresaw the Pacific trade as a potential source of wealth, and he recognized more than did President Monroe that the United States stood as "a great, powerful, enterprising, and rapidly growing nation," destined to dominate the North American continent.

Britain's new outlook on the Union significantly aided President Monroe and Secretary Adams. Saddled with a huge debt after twenty-five years of war, and stung by the embarrassing loss at New Orleans, British leaders concluded that peaceful relations in North America might defray some of the costs necessary to protect Canada. In particular, Foreign Secretary Robert Stewart, Viscount Castlereagh, recognized Southern cotton's growing importance to British manufacturers, and despite the Tariff of 1816, he still considered the United States a major market for British-made goods. Even before President Monroe took office, Castlereagh agreed to resume trade with no discriminatory duties on American shipping, though the West Indies trade still remained closed. Eight weeks after Monroe's inauguration, Richard Rush, acting as secretary of state until Adams could take office, signed an agreement with British minister Charles Bagot that effectively eliminated both nations' military presence on the Great Lakes. The next year, in the Convention of 1818, Britain agreed to compensate Americans for slaves taken during the war, to grant Americans the right to fish off of Canada's Atlantic coast, to renounce British citizens' right to navigate the Mississippi River, and to establish the forty-ninth parallel to the Rocky Mountains as the border separating the United States and Canada. The convention also left the Oregon Territory, the region between the Rockies and the Pacific, "free and open . . . to the citizens and subjects of the two powers" for the next ten years.

Relations with Spain, the other European presence in North America, proved more complicated. The Pearl, Perdido, and Appalachicola Rivers flowed through the American southwest and emptied into the Gulf of Mexico through Spain's Florida territories. President Madison had gained possession of much of West Florida in the War of 1812. Now President Monroe and Secretary Adams wanted to bring the remainder of West Florida and the East Florida peninsula under American control. Spanish officials still refused to acknowledge the Louisiana Purchase and demanded West Florida's immediate return. In reality, the once-powerful nation knew that it stood in a weak position. During the European wars, Napoleon Bonaparte had placed his brother Joseph on the Spanish throne after deposing King Ferdinand VII. Spain's Central and South American colonies rejected the Bonaparte king and began a series of revolutions that ultimately led to their independence. After Ferdinand's restoration in 1813, Spain sent what forces it could to try to suppress the uprisings, and persisting royalist support turned the rebellions into bloody civil wars. Though the survival of Latin American independence remained in question, the region's turmoil belied Spain's claim to stand as a continental power. More practically, the diversion of resources to the south meant Spanish officials barely held on to Florida and could not back up their claims elsewhere in North America.

Latin American independence gained warm support within the Union. The colonial rebels appeared to present another republican blow to Old World tyranny. Henry Clay loudly led a faction in the House demanding immediate diplomatic recognition of the Latin American republics. President Monroe and Secretary Adams understood that the new nations could provide profitable markets for American merchants, but the president initially pledged to remain neutral in the conflict: The fate of the insurgents remained uncertain, and recognition would derail the negotiations that Adams had begun with Spanish minister Don Luis de Onís. Onís wanted the Union to renounce any sympathy for the Latin American cause, and, despite Spanish weakness, his government proposed to cede the Florida Territories to the United States only if the Union accepted a western border at the Mermentau and Calcasieu Rivers—located in the middle of the state of Louisiana—and north of that location at the Mississippi River. The proposal effectively required the United States to give up the Louisiana Purchase. Adams countered with a demand to set the boundary at the Colorado River in central Texas and extending northward from the river's source at the 104th parallel to the Rocky Mountains, which would set the western border about eight hundred miles west of Onís' proposal. Onís refused to budge, and as a skilled diplomat he kept the talks deadlocked for several weeks.

Controversy in Florida threatened to derail negotiations permanently. Creeks who had left Alabama after the 1814 Treaty of Fort Jackson had reinforced the Seminole nation in Florida, and continued conflicts over land and over Natives' providing refuge for escaped slaves led to several violent confrontations with Georgians along the Florida border. In the treaty that Thomas Pinckney negotiated in 1795, Spain had accepted the responsibility of preventing Natives in their territory from harassing Americans. After Native warriors killed forty-six men, women, and children on a hospital boat on the Apalachicola in November 1817, President Monroe concluded that Spain's failure to carry out the 1795 treaty justified a military action that might compel Onís to back down. The president thus directed General Andrew Jackson to lead a force to the frontier to deal with the Seminoles and ordered him to cross the border into Florida if necessary, with "full powers to conduct the war in a manner he may judge best." For some unknown reason, Calhoun never forwarded to Jackson the president's restriction that the general refrain from attacking "any post occupied by Spanish troops."

President Monroe probably expected Jackson to threaten Spain's presence in Florida. Possibly he expected Jackson to seize some of the region, but his vague orders would allow the president to disavow responsibility if the expedition failed. But Jackson went further than anyone in the administration could have imagined. With an army of three thousand American soldiers supplemented by another two thousand friendly Creeks, Jackson oversaw the destruction of several Native villages; he never directly confronted the Seminoles, but his excursion drove the tribes farther south into the Florida peninsula. While in pursuit, Jackson seized the Spanish fortress at Saint Marks on April 6, 1818. The fort's commander chose to evacuate rather than fight against the larger American force, and near Saint Marks Jackson's men arrested Alexander Arbuthnot, a Scottish merchant. Two weeks later, during a raid on some nearby settlements, Americans captured Robert Ambrister, a former British marine. Jackson immediately accused both men of inspiring the Seminole attacks and ordered them court-martialed. The general overruled the courts' recommendation for clemency, and the two were executed on April 29, without an opportunity to appeal their sentence. Incorrectly informed that Seminole warriors had taken refuge at Pensacola, Jackson then occupied West Florida's capital after a brief battle on May 28. Before his departure, the general dispatched the Spanish governor and his troops to Cuba, appointed one of his subordinates as the acting American governor, and ordered a customs officer to begin collecting taxes for the United States.

The European powers quickly condemned Jackson's recklessness. Onís immediately lodged a formal protest and broke off negotiations. In Britain, Lord Castlereagh informed American minister Richard Rush that he could get Parliament to declare war over Arbuthnot's and Ambrister's executions merely "by holding up a finger." In the House, Clay pushed for resolutions condemning Jackson's actions. The movement for a congressional censure failed, but Secretary of War Calhoun led the cabinet in encouraging President Monroe to repudiate the expedition and hold Jackson accountable for his actions. Only Secretary Adams advised President Monroe to back Jackson. Adams surmised that British leaders would not risk damaging relations with the United States over the incident. More significantly, Jackson's actions demonstrated Spain's inability to hold the Floridas. Since the United States could hold out the threat of simply taking the territories, Adams reasoned, Spain would eventually conclude that Onís had to make some sort of concessions to the United States or risk losing the Floridas with no compensation at all.

After several months of deliberations, the president came to agree with Adams' view. He ordered Saint Marks returned and promised to evacuate Pensacola once Spain sent a large enough military force to prevent future Seminole raids. Adams informed Spain that the United States absolved Jackson of any wrongdoing and blamed the affair on Spanish weakness in the territory. President Monroe meanwhile defended the general's conduct to Congress, noting that, though he had exceeded his orders, the general had responded to circumstances on the field. In the end, Adams' predictions of both rival nations' responses proved correct. Castlereagh decided against formally protesting the execution of two British subjects, and once Americans evacuated the forts, the Spanish government instructed Onís to make the best deal he could. When the two completed the Adams-Onís Treaty, or "Transcontinental Treaty," in February 1819, Spain formally ceded East and West Florida in exchange for the Union's agreement to pay up to $5 million to American citizens for claims against Spanish attacks on merchant ships during the Napoleonic Wars. At President Monroe's direction, Adams gave up the weak American claim to Texas, accepting the Sabine River and a line between the Red and Arkansas Rivers as the Union's western boundary. Still, the treaty furthered the American claim to the Pacific Northwest by declaring forty-two degrees latitude the northernmost extent of Spanish claims in North America.

The Adams-Onís Treaty's final approval removed the last obstacle to American recognition of the Latin American republics. Rebel military successes now seemed to secure their independence, so in 1822 President Monroe agreed to receive representatives from Mexico, Chile, Peru, the United Provinces of Rio de la Plata—an area covering present-day Argentina—and "Gran Colombia," which included present-day Panama, Ecuador, and Venezuela. Recognition soon brought another possible challenge. In 1820, Spanish army officers launched a coup that forced King Ferdinand to accept a constitutional government. Two years later, the "Holy Alliance"—an agreement among Russia, Austria, and Prussia to oppose republicanism and back "legitimate" monarchical governments—authorized France to send an army to suppress the uprising and restore the king's unchallenged authority. Rumors quickly followed that the Holy Alliance would send an army to conquer the Latin American republics, an action that threatened to draw the Union into the conflict and possibly challenge its own independence. A similar issue in the Pacific Northwest already imposed on the Union's North American claims. In late 1821, Russia's Tsar Alexander I issued a *ukase*, or imperial edict, defining Russia's territory in North America as extending southward to the fifty-first parallel—well into the Oregon Country that the Union had recently agreed to share with Britain—and warning all nations to keep their ships away from the Russian lands.

As the administration pondered these developments, Britain's new foreign secretary, George Canning, suggested in August 1822 that the United States join with Britain to declare opposition to a European excursion against Spain's former colonies. President Monroe and most of his cabinet members immediately favored Canning's proposal, and Presidents Jefferson and Madison encouraged him to accept the offer. Once again, Adams advised a different course. The secretary of state thought European intervention unlikely, and he recognized that Britain's desire for Latin American trade meant that nation would use its powerful navy to prevent a military expedition regardless of what position the Americans took. In this case, Adams argued, the United States should make a unilateral statement that the Union itself would assume responsibility for the western hemisphere. An independent statement, Adams argued, would enhance American prestige and emphasize the Union's independence from its former mother country. Once again, Adams' assessment of international politics proved correct: the Holy Alliance had little interest in a military expedition, especially when Britain made its opposition clear. Once again, too, President Monroe adopted Adams' views. In his December 1823 message to Congress, the president declared North and South America "henceforth not to be considered as subjects for future colonization by any European power." The United States promised not to interfere in European affairs, but he implied a military threat when he proclaimed any European intervention in the Americas as "dangerous to our peace and safety."

European leaders scoffed at the "Monroe Doctrine." Despite Adams' intentions, Britain came to dominate Latin America's trade and remained a formidable presence in the western hemisphere. Nevertheless, President Monroe's declaration was a milestone in American foreign relations. At a minimum, the bold statement, joined with Adams' vigorous protests, convinced Tsar Alexander I to back down. In 1824, the Russian government agreed to set the southern boundary for Russian America at 54° 40' and opened Russian ports on the Pacific to American ships. More significantly, the Monroe Doctrine marked a shift in Americans' focus. As the European powers turned their attention to expanding their empires elsewhere, the Union's leadership became less preoccupied with European affairs and increasingly acted as the dominant force in the western hemisphere. Within the Union, the Monroe Doctrine stood as the high point of post–War of 1812 national pride. Americans celebrated the Monroe Doctrine as what historians would later call a diplomatic declaration of independence.

The Monroe administration's diplomatic achievements contrasted sharply with its lack of success in domestic affairs. As the president became increasingly preoccupied with international concerns, his annual messages included fewer specific recommendations to Congress. Clay's continuing resentment channeled the representative's energy into strong congressional opposition to any of the administration's specific measures. The lawmakers did eliminate the internal taxes left over from the war, and in 1824 they increased tariff protection on American industry to an average rate of thirty-seven percent of the value of foreign imports. However, they refused to follow up on Monroe's call for a constitutional amendment authorizing Congress to construct a national transportation system. Nationalist Republicans like Clay argued that Congress already had the authority, while Old Republicans continued to oppose any expansion of federal power. For his part, Monroe vetoed an 1822 act that would have allowed charging tolls for use of the National Road, though his veto message acknowledged that the Constitution did allow Congress to appropriate funding for improvements to promote the Union's "general welfare," like military defense and roads for the postal service. President Monroe's concession permitted him to sign a General Survey Bill in 1824, which authorized surveyors to secure estimates on the costs for a system of roads and canals. Likewise, he approved a bill funding an extension of the National Road from Wheeling, Virginia, to Zanesville, Ohio. Otherwise, congressional inactivity led Secretary of State Adams to complain that the lawmakers demonstrated "how a legislature can keep itself employed, when having nothing to do."

Much of Congress's inactivity ironically derived from the weakening of party loyalty. With the Federalists' presence dwindling and President Monroe hoping to transcend party organization, the Republican Party divided into bickering factions. Instead of acting as public-spirited "statesmen," with no party ties or allegiances, members of Congress more often associated with a presidential aspirant and devoted their time to criticizing their favorite's rivals. Two major crises meanwhile distracted the Union's leaders from continuing the vigor displayed immediately after the war, and the crises furthered the backlash against postwar national enthusiasm.

Economic Collapse and Sectional Crisis

A booming economy reinforced the exuberant postwar nationalism. No longer fearing the seizure of their ships, merchants resumed taking American produce abroad. Crop failures in Europe joined with the European powers' clumsy transition to peacetime economies to increase the demand and raise the prices for American cotton, grains, pork, and beef. In 1818, British demand and speculation brought the price of cotton to a high of 34 cents a pound. Merchants shipping American exports invested much of their profits into manufacturing ventures in the Northeast, while states chartered several new banks to provide the money and credit needed to sustain economic growth. In the South and especially the Northwest, farmers used the available cash to fund purchases of the lands recently opened up by Natives' displacement. In the years immediately following the war, the federal government annually sold three or even four times as much public land as it had in the years before the war. Most of the land sold for higher than the minimum price of $2 an acre, with a few choice acres going for $50 each. Federal policies joined the buoyant atmosphere to further the feverish speculation. Buyers only had to put up one-fourth of the total cost at the time of the purchase, with the balance due over the next four years.

The boom came to a crashing halt in late 1818 and early 1819. Despite the Tariff of 1816, the flood of cheap British imports undercut the sale of American-manufactured goods. European agricultural production likewise recovered, lessening the need for American goods, while Parliament's imposition of "corn laws"—tariffs against grain importations—had significantly reduced its importation of American wheat. Overproduction, especially of cotton, likewise contributed to the collapse. Most fundamentally, though, an international shortage of gold and silver intensified the declines in prices and values. The Latin American revolutions had disrupted mining for the precious metals in Mexico and Peru, much of which had ended up in the Union, while the importation of British goods drained gold and silver from the country. Banks had backed their loans and paper money with the promise to redeem them in gold or silver, but shortages of the metals compelled them to refuse to pay as such for the notes they had issued. Paper money became virtually worthless. By the spring of 1819, cotton prices had plummeted nearly sixty percent. Commodity prices likewise dropped, and land values declined to a half or even a quarter of their recent highs.

The "Panic of 1819" inaugurated a period of hard times felt deeply across the Union. Business activity came to an almost complete halt. Factories that did not close down had no choice but to cut back production and lay off workers, leaving perhaps five hundred thousand laborers without the means to support themselves or their families. In Philadelphia, an estimated three out of every four workers lost their jobs. There, as in other major cities, churches and private charities struggled to provide meager meals for the poor. The money shortage forced bankers to demand immediate payment for their loans to merchants, who in turn had to demand payment from their customers. Several leading trading houses nevertheless went out of business; court dockets swelled with lawsuits from creditors seeking payments, while hundreds of debtors were imprisoned for their inability to pay. Even Thomas Jefferson had to scramble to try to cover the debts that he cosigned for his friend Wilson Cary Nicholas, and Jefferson's obligations would force his family to sell his beloved Monticello after his death. 1821 marked the turning point of the crisis, but recovery would take a decade. In the short term, the collapse in prices and property values threatened Northwestern and Southern farmers and planters with foreclosure on the lands they had bought on credit.

International forces brought on the Panic of 1819, but the complexities of money and credit led Americans to blame the crisis on an institution closer to home. The second Bank of the United States, which opened its doors for business in January 1817, did bear some responsibility for the crisis, as its policies contributed to making conditions worse. Proponents originally intended for the bank to check issuances of paper money by state banks, since the B.U.S. could collect an unstable state bank's notes and threaten to demand their immediate redemption in gold or silver. Instead, the bank's directors and president, William Jones, authorized the bank and its seventeen branches to offer generous issuances of its own money; perceptive investors then regularly acquired and redeemed the bank's notes for gold and silver, seriously draining its reserves. By July 1818, the bank held only $2.4 million in gold and silver in its vaults to cover the more than $22 million in liabilities it had issued. Jones then reversed his course, but not quickly enough to satisfy the horrified directors. Langdon Cheves replaced Jones as president in January 1819 and dramatically cut the bank's expenses while calling in its loans and demanding redemption for state bank notes. Cheves' actions restored the bank's solvency; by 1823 it had tripled its reserves while reducing its obligations to $10 million. Cheves' ruthlessness, though, made the bank appear the source of the money shortage and deflationary spiral. As Philadelphia's William Gouge observed, "The Bank was saved and the people were ruined."

Hostility toward the central bank broadened into resentment toward all banks. State banks especially provoked hostility because they demanded payment from debtors while refusing to pay gold or silver on their notes. A few proposed eliminating all banks so the currency would consist only of gold and silver coins; others contended that the states should help the banks remain solvent until the crisis ended. More common were calls for the banks to act responsibly and to relieve individuals from the worst consequences of their debts. With the right to vote expanding, popular frustration soon transformed into demands that the states take action. In several states, ambitious politicians gained control of legislatures by championing reform programs that they contended represented the will of "the people" against the "aristocratic" banks. By 1821, more than half the states had passed some sort of relief for debtors, usually in the form of "stay laws," which postponed payment due dates; and "minimum appraisal laws," which tried to ensure that property seized for sale at auction would bring in enough to cover one's debts. Pennsylvania and Vermont ordered their banks to resume gold and silver payments, while five states created government-owned institutions to compete with the chartered private banks. Most states also raised the requirements for private investors to get bank charters, expecting the more stringent conditions to limit the number of banks while ensuring their stability.

While the states took action, few looked to Congress for assistance. Despite the postwar activism, Americans still expected the federal government to focus on foreign affairs and on relations among the states. Internal conditions remained the responsibility of local governments, even if a problem originated from circumstances beyond a state's control. For their part, congressional representatives expressed little inclination to address the crisis. Congress did approve a law in 1820 that ended credit sales of public lands while lowering the minimum price from $2 to $1.25 per acre. Another act allowed public land purchasers to return their unimproved acres in exchange for canceling their outstanding debts. Manufacturers' pleas for more protection contributed to an increase in tariff rates in 1824. The House also discussed establishing a national paper currency without gold or silver backing, as well as a prohibition against exporting precious metals. Nothing came of these ideas, though, and in January 1820 the Senate rejected a resolution to close the branches of the B.U.S. Other than grousing about the bank's *"partialities* and *favoritism,"* no significant movement emerged to extend federal power to implement a national public relief program.

While the economy collapsed, an even more portentous crisis emerged. In February 1819, the House took up an act to allow voters in the Missouri Territory to prepare a constitution and apply for admission as the Union's twenty-third state. Since slaves made up about ten thousand of the Territory's seventy-six thousand inhabitants, Missouri appeared on track to come in as a slave state. New York representative James Tallmadge, however, proposed an amendment to prohibit the future importation of slaves into Missouri and impose a gradual emancipation program that would free all slaves born in the state when they reached the age of twenty-five. Tallmadge's proposal would transform Missouri into a free state within a generation. It also divided the House along sectional lines and provoked the most contentious arguments seen in Congress in years. A few free state representatives opposed the amendment, but the Northern majority nevertheless carried the bill, with Tallmadge's restriction attached, by a respectable though close majority. The Senate, though, struck out the amendment and instead approved the law to allow Missouri's admission as a slave state. The two chambers refused to back down on their versions of the act, so the Fifteenth Congress adjourned in March with the lawmakers deadlocked over Missouri statehood.

The Missouri Crisis brought into the open sectional resentments that had smoldered for thirty years. Northern representatives reminded Southerners that human bondage contradicted the American Revolution's ideals; the founding generation had conceded the institution's existence because of the large number of slaves left over from the South's colonial legacy, but slavery's expansion into Missouri would take it into the "unsettled" portion of the Louisiana Purchase region—beyond its "natural boundaries" at the Ohio and Mississippi Rivers. Stopping slavery's expansion westward, Northerners claimed, would move the institution one step closer to its elimination. Few Southerners in the debates defended slavery in principle; some, in fact, argued that slavery's expansion would "diffuse" the institution and quicken its eventual abolition. Nevertheless, Southerners insisted that the founders recognized slavery's fate to be the states' responsibility. Prohibiting slavery in the territories would violate slaveowners' rights to their property, and placing an antislavery condition on Missouri's admission would set a dangerous precedent that could later be used to attack slavery in all Southern states. Politics actually sparked the controversy, Republicans charged: the most outspoken restrictionist in the Senate proved to be New York's Rufus King, the only remaining Federalist with any claim to national prominence, and Southerners contended that Federalists dredged up the issue to unite Northerners behind King or another candidate who could challenge President Monroe's re-election.

No Federalist plot existed, but the status of slavery in Missouri could indeed have an impact on the Union's future. By 1819, the Union contained eleven free states and eleven slave states. Northerners continued to complain about the Constitution's three-fifths clause, which counted three-fifths of the slave population in determining Southern states' representation in Congress. The added representation, they argued, gave the South's white citizens an unfair advantage in the federal government. Southerners, though, noted that faster population growth in the North had produced a clear free-state majority in the House of Representatives. When the Fifteenth Congress first took up the Missouri bill, 105 free state representatives outnumbered the 80 members from the slave states. All expected the margin to grow wider in the future, so Southerners relied on the balance of free and slave states in the Senate to protect their interests. Missouri's admission with slavery protected, along with the future addition of a few more states carved out of the Louisiana Purchase, would strengthen the South's protection against any move to abolish slavery. A congressional restriction on slavery's expansion, though, would bring in the western territories as free states, tipping the Senate's balance in favor of the North and establishing the South as a permanent minority, subject to Northerners' economic interests or antislavery whims.

While congressmen awaited their next session, Northern opponents of slavery threw their support behind Tallmadge's proposals. Public meetings demanded slavery's restriction in Missouri. Emotions reached the point that, once the Sixteenth Congress assembled in December 1819, members from both sections openly spoke of the possibility of disunion and civil war. Despite the passions, Union loyalty and effective political management provided an opportunity for compromise. The previous June, the Massachusetts legislature had finally agreed to a long-standing petition to allow its northeastern counties to form the separate state of Maine. The Senate quickly linked Maine's admission with the Missouri issue to keep the Senate balance between free and slave states. Senators also added a proposal from Illinois' Jesse B. Thomas to divide the Louisiana Purchase at 36° 30', Missouri's southern boundary. In the future, slavery would be permitted in territories south of the line but prohibited north of it. Initially the House rejected the Senate's package, but Speaker Henry Clay deftly appointed compromise supporters to key House positions while dividing the issue so the members could vote on each question separately. Once fourteen Northern representatives agreed to accept Missouri's admission as a slave state, Southerners withdrew their objections to prohibiting slavery in the territory. The cabinet unanimously assured President Monroe that Congress had the constitutional authority to stop slavery's expansion, so he signed the Missouri Compromise into law on March 6, 1820.

Some Southerners expressed concern about conceding to Congress the power to prohibit slavery in territories, but most welcomed the compromise because it upheld a state's authority over slavery within its boundaries. Although the agreement banned slavery in most of the Louisiana Purchase, the agreement actually appeared to divide the remaining available lands equally, since the northern and westernmost portions of the region—popularly known as the "Great American Desert"—seemed either too mountainous or too dry for settlement in the near future.

The compromise proved unpopular in the North, however. Simmering discontent threatened to unravel the agreement. Missouri's constitution prohibited the migration of free blacks and mulattoes into the state. Since New York and Massachusetts recognized free African Americans as citizens, Northern representatives charged that Missouri's provision violated the federal Constitution's "privileges and immunities" clause, which prevented a state from discriminating against the citizens of other states. While representatives rehashed most of the arguments from the previous year's controversy, Clay proposed that Congress accept Missouri's constitution on the condition that its legislature declared that it would never pass a law that contradicted the privileges and immunities clause. Securing the necessary votes again required careful management of the House, but in another close vote Congress finally accepted Clay's solution. In August 1821, President Monroe proclaimed Missouri admitted to the Union.

Missouri's legislature never accepted Clay's condition, but Republican leaders proclaimed the crisis at an end and pledged to support the Missouri Compromise. Arguments about slavery's future quickly receded behind other issues. Nevertheless, the tensions stirred up in the controversy persisted. Northerners continued to resent the supposed advantage the three-fifths clause gave to the South, and Southern demands to extend slavery westward convinced many in the free states that slavery was not a dying institution but actually gaining strength. Southerners meanwhile recognized that they stood only one step away from becoming a permanent minority in the Union, and many sought additional guarantees to prevent a hostile or misguided free state majority from abolishing slavery without Southerners' consent. Otherwise, they would have to either accept the consequences of a biracial population without a system of racial control or reconsider the value of the Union.

Neither the sectional tensions stirred up by the Missouri Crisis nor the economic frustrations raised in the Panic of 1819 threatened President Monroe's re-election in 1820. Federalist prospects had fallen so low that the opposition never bothered to nominate a candidate. Several Republican aspirants—including three members of the cabinet—declined to press their claims, well aware that a challenge to President Monroe had little chance of success and would only divide the party. As a result, President Monroe ran unopposed, with the public giving little attention to the election. Even Federalists accepted a second term for President Monroe, as the Virginian carried all but one vote in the electoral college. The lone dissenter, from New Hampshire, voted for John Quincy Adams because he thought Adams better suited for the presidency, though a legend soon arose that he wanted to maintain for George Washington the honor of a unanimous election.

The outcome of the 1820 election showed that voters did not consider the federal government the proper forum for addressing the economy's collapse. Nor did Americans appear willing to force an immediate decision on slavery's future. Instead, the competition to determine the next president became politicians' most pressing concern. The contest commenced almost as soon as the incumbent's second term began.

The "War of the Giants"

Unlike his predecessors, James Monroe refused to indicate, even privately, the person whom he thought should succeed him as president. Treasury Secretary William H. Crawford considered himself the favorite, since he could have challenged President Monroe in 1816. From retirement, both Thomas Jefferson and James Madison favored Crawford. Even though he now made his home in Georgia, his Virginia birth and planter status made him the logical continuation of the "Virginia Dynasty." Monroe, though, had little personal respect for Crawford, and during Monroe's administration, Secretary of State John Quincy Adams, Secretary of War John C. Calhoun, and Speaker of the House Henry Clay had all established valid claims to the office. With so many capable aspirants, President Monroe chose to remain neutral in the competition that a Richmond newspaper labeled the "War of the Giants."

Convention, tradition, and principle prevented candidates from openly campaigning for the presidency: George Washington had established the precedent that a trustworthy candidate would not seek the office, and republican ideals suggested that an aspirant who openly expressed a desire for the Union's most important position revealed dangerous ambitions. While publicly remaining quiet, Crawford, Adams, Calhoun, and Clay kept in touch with supporters who openly worked to secure their election. Crawford's associates first took the initiative, promoting the Treasury secretary as the obvious choice. Resentment at President Monroe's refusal to endorse their candidate made them the most vocal critics of the incumbent, but to weaken Adams' and Calhoun's claims they positioned their man against Congress' post–War of 1812 activism. Describing themselves as "Radicals," in opposition to the "Prodigals" who had abandoned "pure" republicanism, Crawford's backers demanded cuts in the supposedly lavish spending that funded the expansion of federal power, and they promised that Crawford would restore the strict construction, states' rights, and simple government ideals that they argued characterized Jefferson's presidency.

The Radicals' reactionary appeal brought Crawford the following of Virginia's Old Republicans. State loyalty assured him of Georgia's support, and his personal connections gained him followers in North Carolina and Delaware. Elsewhere, Crawford excited little enthusiasm, but as the presumptive candidate he also gained the backing of New York's new senator, Martin Van Buren. Van Buren led New York's faction of "Bucktails"—so called because of the deer tails worn on their hats—that challenged George Clinton's and his nephew DeWitt Clinton's long-standing dominance of the state. Van Buren's battles with the Clintonians convinced him of the importance in a republic of a unified, well-organized, and well-managed political party. Once in Washington, Van Buren recognized that President Monroe's attempt to govern without a disciplined party organization had produced not statesmanlike leadership but fragmentation and drift from the Republicans' original principles. Division threatened to give Federalists an opportunity to slip back into power, the senator concluded, so he came to Washington determined to revive the New York–Virginia alliance of "plain republicans of the North and planters of the South" on which the party had been built. Through reviving and celebrating the importance of party, Van Buren believed, Republicans could return to their core principles and restore the general government to its democratic, strict construction, and limited government roots.

Crawford's rivals openly championed the nationalist version of Republicanism. Calhoun's promoters worked to join his South Carolina base with bank and tariff advocates in the Middle Atlantic states to present their man as the national alternative to Crawford. The other candidates linked their national accomplishments to their regional identities to build on resentments over Virginia's long dominance of the presidency. Adams enjoyed a solid following in his native New England, and his recent diplomatic triumphs gained him widespread respect in the South and the West. Clay meanwhile used his position in the House to promote joining tariff protection, federally funded internal improvements, and responsible use of public lands into a comprehensive program that would unite the developing sections' economies. Clay knew that the "American System"—the label attached to his proposals—would not gain him enough support to win the election outright, but uniting his western base with manufacturing and commercial interests in Pennsylvania and New York could bring him the votes necessary to prevent a rival from gaining a majority in the electoral college. In that case, responsibility for selecting the president would fall to the House of Representatives, where Speaker Clay could likely sway the outcome in his favor.

Calhoun, Adams, and Clay also rejected the insistence on party loyalty that Van Buren worked to revive. The Crawford men insisted that the congressional caucus remained the Republican method of nominating a candidate, but his opponents' supporters attacked what to a growing number of Americans appeared an outdated institution. Republicans may have needed the caucus in the 1790s, when they had to unite against Federalists, but the Federalists' demise now made the meeting unnecessary. President Monroe had won re-election without a caucus nomination, and Crawford's rivals had little interest in reviving an institution that might further the Treasury secretary's prospects. Critics charged that the caucus represented an "aristocratic" effort of political insiders to "dictate" their presidential choice to the people. Contending that institutions closer to the people had as much right to put forward candidates, the Missouri and Kentucky legislatures nominated Clay in November 1822. Unofficial meetings of legislators in Massachusetts and Maine formally nominated Adams in January 1823. The following October, South Carolina's legislature nominated Calhoun, but the secretary of war expected his most important boost to come from a Pennsylvania state convention that would be held in Harrisburg in March of the following year.

While the main contenders' proponents skirmished, a wild card entered the race in July 1822 when Tennessee legislators met informally to nominate Andrew Jackson. The men behind the nomination had little belief that Jackson might actually win. The general had long associated with the cohort of planters and land speculators who controlled Tennessee politics, and though he had stayed out of state affairs for years, he maintained a close friendship with John Overton, the head of the faction. In the backlash to the Panic of 1819, reformers seized control of the state government, gaining a majority in the legislature and electing William Carroll to the governorship on a platform to discipline the state banks that Overton and his allies directed.

189

By promoting Jackson for the presidency, Overton's men hoped to use the hero's popularity to recapture the state government. They also expected Jackson's nomination to advance their own presidential candidates' prospects. Most Tennessee leaders preferred either Adams or Clay, while a small rival faction promoted Crawford; nominating Jackson would prevent Crawford's forces from gaining any momentum in the state, and once it became clear that Jackson could not win the national contest, Overton's faction could direct the state into either Clay's or Adams' column.

Overton's associates soon realized that they had tapped into a force too powerful for them to manage. Jackson's candidacy quickly gained a following outside of Tennessee. Over the next year, movements for Jackson emerged in states across the South and West and into the Middle Atlantic. Then, in March 1824, the Harrisburg Convention on which Calhoun rested his hopes nominated Jackson instead. Meanwhile, Jackson showed signs that he actually wanted to be president. His election would provide popular vindication of his actions in the Florida invasion and thwart the ambitions of Crawford and Clay, both of whom Jackson blamed for the movement to disgrace him in the House of Representatives. More ominously, Jackson also began voicing to them his own hostility toward banks and paper money. Without Jackson's knowledge, the Overton clique secretly tried to subvert the movement it had started by quietly backing a Crawford supporter's re-election to the Senate in October 1823. Re-electing a senator who was openly opposed to Jackson would demonstrate a lack of support for the general in Tennessee and effectively end his candidacy. Jackson thwarted their plans, though, when he allowed his supporters to put his own name before the legislature for the seat, and he made an unexpected visit to the state capital to demonstrate his willingness to serve. The legislatures then elected Jackson to the Senate, keeping his presidential prospects alive.

The other candidates at first saw little danger in Jackson's candidacy, since his career seemed to show him completely unsuited for the presidency. Other than brief, undistinguished stints in the House and the Senate during the 1790s, the general had virtually no experience in elected office, while his popularity as a commander stoked republican fears that a "military despot" might use his army to make himself a dictator. Unlike George Washington, the Union's first military hero, Jackson appeared less guided by virtue and principle than he was driven by passion and hatred. Thomas Jefferson abhorred the idea of Jackson's election, recalling that in Jackson's first Senate service the Tennessean often could not speak because his anger made him "choke with rage." More recently, his order for Alexander Arbuthnot's and Robert Ambrister's executions and his brief but turbulent term in 1821 as governor of the Florida Territory—where his arrest of the former Spanish governor nearly provoked a war—clearly demonstrated his disregard for the law and his capacity for rash, shortsighted decisions that would make him dangerous as chief executive. These characteristics, as well as Jackson's lack of political connections outside his home state, assured the other candidates' supporters that they did not need to take the general's nomination seriously.

Washington politicians, however, failed to pick up on the growing strength of the democratic impulse. By the early 1820s, several states had already lowered or eliminated their property requirement for the right to vote, extending the franchise to the vast majority of white men. States also gave to voters the power to choose the state's electors; in the 1824 contest, popular elections would select the electors in eighteen of the twenty-four states. Local politicians' appeals to "the people" to express their will likewise produced consistently high voter turnout. So far, popular participation had bypassed federal politics, but Jackson's candidacy caught the voters' imagination. As he was a Tennessean, Southerners and Westerners both could claim him, and his standing as the "Hero of New Orleans" made him the only candidate with a national following. For humble citizens, support for the general became a way to express their frustrations and unspecified concerns provoked by federal expansion, economic collapse, and sectional tensions. Since Jackson's personal opinions mostly remained unknown, voters could impose their own views on the candidate, and endorsing him as a Washington "outsider" allowed them to convey their dissatisfaction and demand for change. In many areas, politicians found themselves unable to contain the swell of grassroots support for Jackson, while opportunists came out for the hero with the hope of riding his coattails into power.

The Harrisburg Convention's surprise nomination of Jackson ended Calhoun's candidacy. The South Carolinian grudgingly accepted an endorsement for the vice presidency from the Adams and Jackson men. Adams, Crawford, and Clay now realized that Jackson might actually win. As the general's prospects soared, the presumptive front-runner's campaign unraveled. In September 1823, Crawford experienced a serious illness—possibly a stroke—that at times blinded and paralyzed him. He recovered enough to resume his Treasury Department duties in early 1824, and the severity of his illness was largely kept from the public. Still, in spite of his supporters' assurances, politicians questioned whether he had the strength to serve as president. Attacks on the congressional caucus as undemocratic proved equally damaging to Crawford's chances. When representatives called for a caucus, 181 of the 261 members of Congress signed a public address refusing to participate. Only sixty-six congressmen attended on February 14, 1824. Those present duly nominated Crawford, with Albert Gallatin as their vice presidential choice, but the demonstrated lack of support within Congress for the "Virginia Dynasty" candidate left the presidential race wide open.

For the most part, the candidates' promoters approached the 1824 contest like previous presidential elections. In states where voters chose electors, a few stump speakers tried to reassure the public about a candidate's merits, but the campaigns concentrated mainly on winning the allegiance of prominent local figures, whose influence they expected would bring votes to their cause. The Jackson men moved to broaden popular participation, holding rallies and parades to demonstrate their candidate's strength. The general meanwhile proved a masterful politician. Taking his seat in the Senate in December 1823, Jackson acted the part of a mild-mannered Southern gentleman, countering depictions of him as an uncivilized brute. Through published replies to letters from voters, he provided vague but satisfying answers to questions about his views, effectively presenting himself as a modest citizen who preferred retirement but if elected would submit to the people's will. Fellow Tennessee senator John H. Eaton likewise produced a widely published series of letters under the pseudonym "Wyoming" depicting the general as the heir of the Revolution and standing against a government that had lost touch with the American people.

The public's role in the contest still remained limited. The traditional focus on local rather than national affairs, the lingering influence of deference, limited organizations behind the candidates, and the fact that the outcome appeared uncertain in only a few states contributed to a voter turnout of only about twenty-five percent. Those who did vote showed the strength of Jackson's following: He won the plurality of the popular vote, winning forty-two percent of the votes cast and carrying eight of the eighteen states that held popular votes. He proved the favorite in most of the Southern and Western states as well as in the Mid-Atlantic, winning Pennsylvania and New Jersey while losing Maryland to Adams by only 109 votes. Adams' solid support in New England joined a respectable showing in other sections to bring him in second with thirty-two percent of the vote, with Crawford and Clay trailing with about thirteen percent each. Crawford's loyal following in his home states gained him Virginia, Georgia, and Delaware, while Clay carried only his home state of Kentucky plus Ohio and Missouri.

The result, though, failed to give Jackson the 131 electoral college votes he needed to win the presidency. The low population of many of the states he carried, and divisions in several states, brought him a total of 99 electoral votes. Adams came in second with 84, while Crawford with 41 and Clay with 37 took the remaining votes. Eighty-four of Jackson's votes came from states where voters chose the electors, while 36 of Adams' electors were appointed by state legislatures. Nevertheless, since no candidate won a majority, the Constitution directed the House of Representatives to select a president from the three candidates who had received the most electoral votes. Because he finished fourth, the representatives could not choose Henry Clay, but all recognized that the Speaker of the House could play a crucial role in the outcome.

Clay never announced publicly which candidate he would support. For weeks, he relished the attention poured on him as the one who could select the next president. Actually, the Speaker's choice was an easy one for him. Though he disliked Adams personally, the Secretary of State alone shared his nationalistic outlook and his conviction that an active central government should lead the Union forward. Crawford's Radical and Old Republican support rendered the Treasury secretary unacceptable, even if his health fully recovered. Despite Jackson's popularity, Clay considered him unqualified, a military commander whose elevation might bring a tyrant into power. Moreover, Jackson's rise threatened Clay's presidential prospects by undermining the Speaker's image as the hero of the West, whereas defeat would likely send the general into retirement on his Tennessee plantation. By mid-December, Clay was hinting to friends in Kentucky that he intended to support Adams. Once back in Washington, the two met in early January 1825 to discuss the possible direction of an Adams administration. According to Adams' diary, the meeting concluded with Clay "stating that his preference would be for me."

Though not decisive, the Speaker's support did help the New Englander win the presidency. After counting the electoral votes, the House took up the issue on February 9. The Constitution directed each state would cast one vote, and the winner would need to win a majority of the twenty-four states. On the first ballot, the three states that Clay had carried in the general election cast their votes for Adams—even though Kentucky's legislature had instructed the state's representatives to vote for Jackson. Adams needed more than just Clay's three states, though. Three states that Jackson had carried also voted for Adams: Louisiana through the influence of Clay; Illinois because its lone representative was Adams' friend and likewise refused to support a slaveholder like Jackson; and Maryland because Massachusetts representative Daniel Webster assured Maryland Federalists that Adams would offer appointments to Federalists. New York proved the decisive state. With its thirty-four representatives evenly divided between Adams and Crawford, an old Federalist "Manor Lord," Stephen Van Rensselaer, intended to vote for Crawford, but he waffled after intense lobbying from Adams' supporters. Still uncertain as the representatives began voting, he bowed in prayer to ask for direction, and when he opened his eyes he saw a paper ballot on the floor with Adams' name on it. Accepting the ballot as the answer to his prayer, he put it in the ballot box to give his state's vote to Adams.

The "War of the Giants" thus ended with Adams receiving the necessary thirteen states on the House's first ballot. Though disappointed, Jackson accepted the result stoically. The night after the House election, he expressed his regards to Adams at a reception that President Monroe held for the president-elect. Then, as he prepared to return to Tennessee, he learned that Adams had offered, and Clay had accepted, the office of secretary of state—the most prestigious position in the cabinet and one that would make him the leading candidate to succeed Adams. To Jackson, the significance of Clay's appointment seemed obvious: The "Judas of the West" had conspired to steal the presidential election from the American people. No evidence actually exists of an agreement between Adams and Clay; though the two likely had an understanding of some sort, Clay's political record and diplomatic experience made him a reasonable choice for the post. Nevertheless, politicians and the public soon echoed the charge that a "corrupt bargain" had determined the election's outcome. Jackson returned home to his plantation as he planned, but now he resolved to return in four years to claim the office that he believed the people had actually bestowed on him.

Lost in the focus on the contest in the House, and in the furor over the "Corrupt Bargain," was an important signal in the 1824 election. In giving a combined majority to Jackson and Crawford, the electorate had rejected the government activism and national vision promised in Adams' and Clay's candidacies. Still reeling from the effects of the Panic of 1819 and the controversy over slavery's expansion, a large number of voters wanted the general government to step back to its traditional, more limited role, properly balanced with the authority of the states. Unfortunately for Adams, neither he nor Clay picked up on this message.

Democracy Triumphant

John Quincy Adams well knew that a majority opposed his election. In his inaugural address, he referred to the Union as a "representative democracy," which seemed to show that he recognized the shifting political tide. Adams, though, wanted to use his administration to further national development. Brushing aside Republicans' long-standing strict construction constraints, President Adams believed that the central government had the responsibility of promoting the Union's economic growth and improving the condition of its individual citizens. His first annual message, presented to Congress in December 1825, thus outlined an ambitious agenda that would take post–War of 1812 nationalism to a new level. After directing the lawmakers' attention to the reports produced by the General Survey Act, Adams recommended an expansion of the navy, the establishment of a naval academy, the foundation of a national university, the institution of a national standard of weights and measures, the reorganization of the federal judiciary, the creation of a new cabinet department to relieve the State Department of its domestic responsibilities, support for domestic and international expeditions to promote "geographical and astronomical science," and the erection of an astronomical observatory.

Under any circumstances, President Adams' bold program would have provoked a skeptical response. But President Adams misread the smoldering resentments against the "Corrupt Bargain" and the depth of distrust toward federal activism. The sweeping conclusion to his message handed his political enemies the ammunition they would need to label him a Federalist and a tyrant. As the message reached its close, he admonished his countrymen to remember "that liberty is power," and "that the nation blessed with the largest portion of liberty must in proportion to its numbers be the most powerful nation upon earth." Then, he challenged members of Congress to act—notwithstanding the reservations of American citizens. "[W]ere we to slumber in indolence or fold up our arms and proclaim to the world that we are palsied by the will of our constituents," he asked, "would it not be to cast away the bounties of Providence and doom ourselves to perpetual inferiority?" Alluding to the recent completion of the Erie Canal and the foundation of the University of Virginia, he dismissed long-standing states'-rights concerns for the expansion of federal power. The central government, he claimed, could carry out "works important to the whole and to which neither the authority nor the resources of any one State can be adequate."

President Adams' dismissal of public opinion and states' rights bolstered the impression that a president chosen by politicians now wanted to force his will on the people. Ironically, President Adams had no intention of forcing his will on anyone. In fact, he actually renounced using means that could have helped direct his proposals through Congress. He wanted to continue President Monroe's effort to govern by consensus, without the "baneful weed of party strife." He hoped his own administration could bring together independent men of "talents and virtue" who would cooperate to promote the Union's well-being. He appointed a Federalist,

Rufus King, to the prestigious post of minister to Great Britain because he thought King the best person for the job, and he refused to use his power to appoint or remove officials or offer any other executive gifts that might win the support of members of Congress. This approach only weakened the administration's political influence. King's appointment seemed to confirm the administration's Federalist disregard for public opinion. Potential congressional supporters meanwhile had no incentive to put up with the popular criticism that would follow from endorsing President Adams' proposals. Appointees within the administration likewise quickly realized that since Adams would not dismiss them but the next president might, it was in their interest to openly oppose Adams' re-election in order to ingratiate themselves to whoever beat him in the case that he lost—which already seemed likely early in his term.

As a result, President Adams' initiatives mostly went nowhere. Congressmen did appreciate his generous interpretation of the Constitution regarding federal power to fund and construct improvement projects. During his term, President Adams would sign more internal improvement acts into law than all preceding presidents combined. The lawmakers ignored the General Survey Act's plans for a comprehensive national network, though, so the vast majority of these projects reflected local interests with questionable national value. Beyond encouraging roads and canals, President Adams' vision gained little ground. A House bill to fund a naval expedition to the South Pacific, similar to British captain James Cook's voyages of discovery, failed in the Senate. Another law, to create a naval academy, narrowly passed the Senate but was rejected by the House. Neither chamber took up his proposals to standardize weights and measures, establish a university, or construct an observatory. Instead, "lighthouses of the skies," the phrase President Adams used to describe observatories, became a popular term of derision for the president's overblown agenda.

Even in foreign affairs, where as secretary of state Adams had achieved much, the new president mostly met frustration. The administration successfully worked out trade agreements with Denmark and Prussia, but negotiations to open the British West Indies to American imports went nowhere, hampered both by President Adams' insistence that Britain allow American ships to trade in the region with no restrictions and by Foreign Secretary George Canning's resentment against American tariff policy and the Monroe Doctrine. The deadlock finally compelled President Adams in March 1827 to close American ports to ships coming from British colonies. Meanwhile the president suffered a major political setback when he proposed to send Kentucky's Richard C. Anderson and Pennsylvania's John Sergeant to a conference of the Latin American republics in Panama in June 1826. President Adams and Secretary Clay hoped that American participation could foster closer ties to the new republics and gain trade advantages for American merchants. Congressional opponents lambasted Adams' nominations as a departure from President Washington's admonition to avoid "entangling alliances" with foreign nations, while Southern representatives charged that cooperation with the mixed-race republics that had recently abolished slavery would weaken slavery in the United States. Opposition delayed congressional approval of the nominees until April 1826, a date so late that the Union remained unrepresented at the conference. Sergeant refused to travel through the Caribbean during its sickly season and arrived after the conference had ended; Anderson took the risk, caught a tropical fever, and died in Colombia.

While obstructing Adams' administration, the opposition worked to coalesce around Jackson as his replacement. The Tennessee legislature nominated the general in October 1825, before the first Congress under President Adams even met. Jackson's associates—including John Overton, now firmly in the hero's camp—formed a committee that met frequently at Jackson's Nashville plantation to oversee his campaign, while in Washington, Jackson's recent rivals came together to promote his cause. Vice President Calhoun made the first overtures toward the general. Recognizing that Clay's "bargain" likely blocked his own advancement to the presidency, the South Carolinian wrote to Jackson in June 1826 to offer his services in the upcoming election. Van Buren likewise saw Jackson as the best hope of reviving the Republican alliance of "plain republicans of the North and planters of the South." Meeting in Virginia on Christmas day, 1826, the New York senator and the vice president agreed to unite their efforts behind Jackson. Calhoun would keep the vice presidency under Jackson, while Van Buren would bring Crawford's supporters into the Jackson coalition. Van Buren likewise worked regularly with Jackson confidants John Eaton and Missouri senator Thomas H. Benton to coordinate the opposition in Washington with the work of the Nashville committee. By the next spring, the New Yorker clearly stood, in Adams' words, as "the great electioneering manager for General Jackson."

The midterm congressional elections demonstrated the opposition's growing strength. For the first time, opposition candidates based their campaigns on their favorite in the presidential election, and when the Twentieth Congress convened, Jackson men held clear majorities in both the House and the Senate. Only one issue threatened to disrupt the momentum behind Jackson. In the North, proposals to raise tariff rates gained increasing favor as a way of improving the economy. Notwithstanding the increase in 1824, New England's young textile industries continued to demand higher rates to shield them from cheap British imports. Pennsylvanians demanded protection for the state's iron industry, while several other producers, including small farmers, wanted tariff increases on imports competing with their produce. In the South, though, cotton planters blamed the tariff for the fiber's continuing low prices: Southerners charged that, to retaliate against the tariff, British manufacturers restricted their cotton purchases, while the higher cost of protected American goods made Southerners "serfs" of the North. As the tariff's popularity grew in the North, Van Buren sensed that President Adams' well-known support for high tariffs would hurt Jackson in the crucial state of Pennsylvania and possibly in New York as well. In early 1827, the opposition managed to defeat an administration-sponsored bill to raise tariff rates, with Vice President Calhoun casting the tie-breaking vote in the Senate. The popularity of a pro-tariff convention held in Harrisburg the following summer, though, convinced Van Buren that the Jackson men needed to respond.

Van Buren recognized that New England would support President Adams, while the South would back Jackson, regardless of any tariff revisions, so he worked to make tariff revision an issue in the crucial states. One of his political lieutenants, New York congressman Silas Wright, authored a bill that would raise rates on Pennsylvania iron, Kentucky and Missouri hemp—a fiber grown for manufacturing rope and bags—and raw wool sheared from sheep raised by farmers throughout western New York and the Northwest. Wright's tariff would also raise costs for New England shipbuilders but reduce the tax on the imported wool cloth that planters bought to dress their slaves. Southern Jacksonians dutifully helped the bill get through the House, probably expecting New Englanders to join with Southerners to defeat the bill in the Senate. This strategy would allow the opposition to blame the administration for the bill's defeat and defend Jackson as a tariff proponent in the Middle Atlantic states but uphold his image as a free trader in the South. The Senate, though, restored enough protection for wool manufacturers to bring the New England votes it needed to pass; despite Southern protests, President Adams signed the Tariff of 1828 into law. As Van Buren expected, the act neutralized the tariff issue in the Middle Atlantic and West. Betrayed Southerners denounced the law as the "Tariff of Abominations," but with President Adams so objectionable, they trusted that Jackson's status as a cotton planter, along with the South Carolinian Calhoun's expected influence, would steer the next administration in an anti-tariff direction.

With the tariff issue somewhat resolved, Jackson's backers campaigned to win even more popular votes than they had in 1824. Every state except Delaware and South Carolina adopted the general ticket system, meaning the voters would choose the vast majority of presidential electors. The Jackson coalition thus adopted the name "Democratic Republican" and formed an extensive organization designed to make sure Jackson voters turned out at the polls. Jackson himself remained out of public view, and a central committee in Washington officially managed the national campaign. Through his Nashville associates, though, Jackson oversaw the campaign, coordinating with the central committee through Van Buren, Calhoun, and Eaton. In Washington, Calhoun's friend Duff Green established the *United States Telegraph* to act as the campaign's "organ," while members of Congress used the "franking" privilege, which allowed them to send mail to their constituents at no charge, to provide local committees with campaign literature for distribution in their home districts. State committees nominated tickets of electors who would conduct speaking tours for Jackson, while "Hickory Clubs" established newspapers and held rallies, barbecues, and parades to drum up enthusiasm. Much of the money for the campaign came from the Middle Atlantic's wealth, with Van Buren acting as campaign treasurer. "Five-dollar-a-plate" banquets likewise provided important funds while reinforcing the campaign's grassroots appeal.

The Democratic-Republicans' message in 1828 built on the case made for Jackson four years earlier. Jackson's supporters presented the general as the hero who stood with the people against entrenched interests in Washington. The "Corrupt Bargain" had allowed an illegitimate regime to seize control of the central government; just as Jackson had routed the republic's enemies at New Orleans, now he would oust "aristocrats and tyrants" from the capital and restore the government to the people. The campaign avoided committing the candidate to specific opinions on issues, emphasizing simply that the general championed "reform" and intended to restore the presumed principles and simplicity of the Jeffersonian era. At the same time, Democratic-Republicans mounted a smear campaign to demonize the incumbent. Jacksonians described President Adams as a pampered elitist and Secretary Clay as a gambler, reprobate, and rank opportunist. They likewise denounced the presence in the White House of an elaborate chess set and a billiards table as evidence of the administration's extravagance and moral degeneracy—even though President Adams had actually purchased them with his own money. Jacksonian ministers pointed to President Adams' Unitarian beliefs as proof of his "heresy," while editors in urban centers claimed that the incumbent denounced Catholics as ignorant bigots. New Hampshire editor Isaac Hill meanwhile twisted a story from Adams' service as minister to Russia. An American family had asked Adams to introduce their fourteen-year-old daughter to the tsar because she wanted to meet him, but Hill turned the story into a salacious account of a degraded diplomat offering an American girl to satisfy a European despot's lusts.

While Jackson's forces gained momentum, President Adams remained committed to his ideals and refused to use his office to advance his re-election. Notwithstanding Clay's insistence, he even refused to fire Postmaster General John McLean despite McLean's appointment of local postmasters who used their positions to advocate Adams' defeat. With his own political future at stake, Clay took the lead in organizing a popular campaign. The incumbent already enjoyed the support of the Union's most prestigious newspaper, Joseph Gales' and William Seaton's Washington *National Intelligencer,* as well as the backing of well-established papers in most states, but Clay nevertheless shifted several government printing contracts to local papers that could provide Adams' cause with even more support. Daniel Webster used his connections with eastern merchants and industrialists to raise funds, and Clay corresponded with local leaders to provide campaign literature. He likewise pushed state conventions that could formally nominate Adams, with Treasury Secretary Richard Rush as the vice presidential candidate to replace Calhoun, and appointed Adams' electors who were willing to campaign against Jackson's electors. District and county committees arranged rallies and events to drum up excitement for the incumbent similar to the enthusiasm stirred by the Jacksonians.

The Adams campaign presented voters with a clear alternative. Adopting the name "National Republicans," his backers aggressively espoused a strong, active national government and championed "The American System" as a slogan, to represent the federal actions they believed offered the key to the Union's prosperity. They likewise launched a campaign to vilify Jackson, matching the character attacks that Democratic-Republicans hurled against President Adams. Along with charges of Jackson's inexperience and his rash course in the Florida campaign, they recounted stories of Jackson's numerous brawls and duels to portray him as an uncontrollable ruffian and a cold-blooded murderer. Philadelphia editor John Binns' "coffin handbill"—a broadsheet headed by silhouettes of six coffins—related how Jackson had once ordered a firing squad to execute six militiamen, including a sixteen-year-old, for desertion, when actually their terms of service had expired. Cincinnati editor Charles Hammond meanwhile claimed to provide evidence showing that Jackson had lured his wife Rachel from her first husband and lived with her for two years before marrying. National Republicans even denounced Jackson's mother as a "common prostitute, brought to this country by British soldiers" and who "afterwards married a mulatto man, with whom she had several children, of which number General Jackson is one!!"

President Adams' prospects received an unexpected boost after the outburst following the disappearance of William Morgan, a Virginia stonemason who had recently relocated to western New York. Morgan claimed to belong to the "Ancient Order of Free and Accepted Masons," a fraternal organization that had emerged in eighteenth-century Britain to promote Enlightenment ideals, rational religion, and benevolence. Freemasonry's secret rituals, elaborate hierarchies, and sense of fellowship made it popular among prominent early Americans. In the early nineteenth century, many aspiring young men joined the Masons as a way to make social connections that could further their business prospects. Nonmembers, though, increasingly distrusted the secret organization's apparent prevalence among local officeholders. Government officials' favoritism for brother Masons seemed to reveal an exclusivist, elitist influence in public affairs, and the order's mystic rituals and rejection of orthodox traditions convinced many that it threatened Christianity as well as democracy. Morgan hoped to use these suspicions to exact his revenge after his drinking and crude behavior led Masons in Batavia, New York, to doubt his claims to membership and deny him admission to their lodge. Morgan knew enough about Freemasonry that his threat to publish a book revealing the Masons' secrets incited mobs to ransack his home and to burn the press that intended to print his exposé. After Morgan's arrest on a minor charge in September 1826, the jailer released him at night into the custody of two men, who forced him into a carriage that carried him off to a fate that remains unknown.

Official responses to Morgan's disappearance kicked off a widespread protest against Freemasonry's supposed power. Masons in strategic positions seemed to delay or block formal investigations into the crime. Members refused to discuss or testify against implicated brothers. Suspected individuals either fled before arrest, were released on technicalities by judges who were Freemasons, or were acquitted by packed juries. Masonic lodges denied any involvement with Morgan's disappearance, but most declined to condemn his presumed murder, with many Freemasons stating publicly that he received his just reward. Hordes of Masons resigned their membership in protest; popular meetings denounced Masonry as a dangerous aristocratic faction that had to be rooted out of the government. Led by Rochester editor Thurlow Weed and aided by Auburn lawyer William H. Seward, the protests gradually organized as an "Antimasonic Party" and elected fifteen Antimasons to the New York legislature. The movement soon spread into Pennsylvania and through New England into the Northeast. In New York, its popularity compelled Van Buren to give up his Senate seat in 1828 to run for governor, as he was the only Democratic-Republican popular enough to defeat an Antimasonic candidate. Though National Republicans hesitated to join forces with the new party, the Antimasons

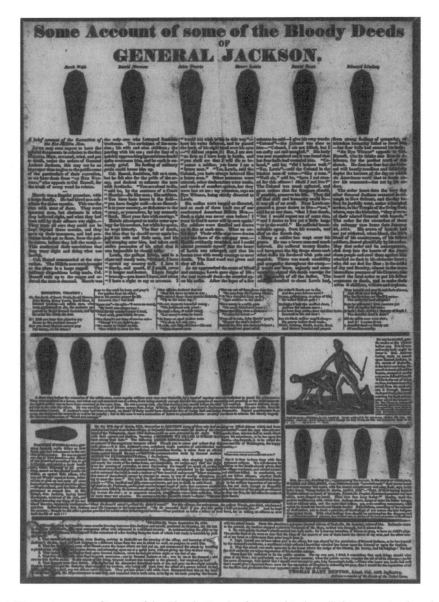

Figure 8.1 "Some Account of Some of the Bloody Deeds of General Jackson." This campaign broadside published during the 1828 electoral campaign popularly became known as the "Coffin Handbill." Woodcut by John Binns (1828). Courtesy Prints & Photographs Division, Library of Congress, LC–USZ62–43901.

endorsed Adams for the presidency, for the incumbent had once openly denounced Freemasonry, while Jackson stood as a high-ranking Mason, proud of his long association with the order.

Neither Antimasonic support nor National Republican attacks could diminish the groundswell of support for Jackson. The assault on Jackson's marriage presented his opponents' strongest charge, but Democratic-Republicans countered its effect by claiming that the hero had rescued Rachel from an abusive husband: The couple had married in Natchez in Spanish territory when they thought Rachel's first husband had divorced her, and they immediately remarried when they learned that Lewis Robards had not completed divorce proceedings before their first marriage. Other National Republican charges failed to derail Jackson's support, while Clay's obsession with denying the "Corrupt Bargain" prevented the campaign from effectively exploiting Jackson's ambiguity on the tariff issue. Still, with the two parties competing in almost every state, the contest brought out more than half the eligible voters and established the conviction that the people, rather than electors, now chose the president and vice president. The result was a major victory for Jackson and Calhoun, who won more than fifty-six percent of the popular vote—a record majority that would not be surpassed for seventy-six years. President Adams remained the favorite in New England, although Democratic-Republicans managed to win thirty percent of the region's vote. The incumbent also carried New Jersey and Delaware, and Antimasonic support helped him split the vote in New York, as he did in Maryland. Jackson, though, swept the West and the South and handily won Pennsylvania, giving him a strong 178–83 majority in the electoral college.

The 1828 election marked a new phase in the Union's politics. The democratic impulse long stirring within the states now directed its attention to the federal level. From this point on, popular campaigns would try to win the presidency. Democratic-Republican success demonstrated the crucial role that party organization could play in crafting candidate images and getting out the vote. Once again, too, voters rejected a strong federal government. Though they avoided committing their man to specifics, calls for "reform" indicated that Jackson would somehow step away from the centralized national Union that American leaders had advocated since 1815. Few knew where Jackson actually stood on most issues. His decisions as president would establish the grounds of conflict for the next generation.

Suggested Readings

Baxter, Maurice G. *Henry Clay and the American System* (Lexington, KY, 1995).

Cole, Donald B. *Vindicating Andrew Jackson: The Election of 1828 and the Rise of the Two-Party System* (Lawrence, KS, 2009).

Cunningham, Noble E. *The Presidency of James Monroe* (Lawrence, KS, 1996).

Dangerfield, George. *The Awakening of American Nationalism, 1815–1828* (New York, 1964).

Goodman, Paul. *Towards a Christian Republic: Antimasonry and the Great Transition in New England* (New York, 1988).

Hammond, Bray. *Banks and Politics in America from the Revolution to the Civil War* (Princeton, 1957).

Hargreaves, Mary W.M. *The Presidency of John Quincy Adams* (Lawrence, KS, 1985).

Heidler, David S., and Jeanne T. Heidler. *Old Hickory's War: Andrew Jackson and the Quest for Empire* (Mechanicsburg, PA, 1996).

Forbes, Robert Pierce. *The Missouri Controversy and Its Aftermath: Slavery and the Meaning of America* (Chapel Hill, 2007).

Lewis, James E. Jr. *The American Union and the Problem of Neighborhood: The United States and the Collapse of the Spanish Empire, 1783–1829* (Chapel Hill, 1998).

May, Ernest R. *The Making of the Monroe Doctrine* (Cambridge, MA, 1975).

Parsons, Lynn Hudson. *The Birth of Modern Politics: Andrew Jackson, John Quincy Adams, and the Election of 1828* (New York, 2009).

Peterson, Merrill D. *The Great Triumvirate: Webster, Clay, and Calhoun* (New York, 1987).

Russell, Greg. *John Quincy Adams and the Public Virtues of Diplomacy* (Columbia, MO, 1995).

Skeen, C. Edward. *1816: America Rising* (Lexington, KY, 2003).

IX

ANDREW JACKSON'S UNION

Usually few people besides government officials attended presidential inaugurations, but Andrew Jackson's election brought thousands to Washington to witness the installation of the hero's administration. Most of the estimated twenty thousand people who showed up at the East Portico of the still-incomplete Capitol building could not hear his brief inaugural address, but they cheered when the new president took the oath and bowed to the spectators to acknowledge the people's sovereignty. After the ceremony, the crowd followed President Jackson to a reception at the White House, with hopes of giving him their best wishes personally. There the scene became chaotic. Tightly packed into several rooms, the visitors damaged thousands of dollars' worth of china, glasses, and furniture. Jackson himself had to escape through a back door to avoid injury, and servants finally lured out the crowd by setting up bowls of punch on the lawn. Even with order restored, President Jackson's opponents feared that the commotion marked the onset of what Supreme Court Justice Joseph Story called "the reign of King Mob."

The boisterous celebration contrasted with the new president's own mood. His beloved wife Rachel had died of a heart attack shortly after the election—killed, he was convinced, by the slanders of his opponents. He himself suffered from chronic poor health that kept him a gaunt 140 pounds stretched across his six-foot-one frame. Approaching his sixty-second birthday, he was the oldest person to date to assume the presidency, and his body still carried two bullets—one lodged dangerously close to his heart—as the legacy of a duel and a brawl both fought several years before. Washington insiders assumed that he would last only one term. More experienced and cunning politicians expected to easily control him. But supporters and foes alike underestimated the new president. His soldiers had given him the nickname "Old Hickory" to celebrate his toughness. Now, the strength of his will, his innate political skill, and his sensitivity to the public's democratic expectations would permanently alter the Union's direction.

Old Hickory Takes Command

The campaign that carried Jackson to the presidency stressed the need for reform. Political observers understood that he intended to somehow scale back the federal government activism that had been expanding since 1815 and return the Union to Jeffersonian principles. Beyond these generalities, exactly what "reform" involved remained unclear. The broad coalition that had elected him added to the confusion. The "Jackson Party" stood less as a coherent political organization than as a loose association of Southern planters, Northeastern and Western small farmers, and "mechanics"—artisans, journeymen, and workers in the Union's cities and industries. The new president also remained an outsider in Washington politics. Newspapers reported that "Jackson men" held clear advantages in both chambers of Congress, but many such men identified with the president to take advantage of his popularity and expressed only token loyalty to the new administration. Several held deeper connections to more established aspirants, especially Vice President John C. Calhoun and the recently elected governor of New York, Martin Van Buren, each of whom intended to position himself as the obvious choice to succeed President Jackson.

Observers expected President Jackson's cabinet appointments to indicate whether Calhoun or Van Buren had gained the president's favor. Instead, they demonstrated his independence. Van Buren himself accepted President Jackson's offer to serve as secretary of state—the one office with as much prestige as Calhoun enjoyed in the vice presidency—but the new president avoided appointing any of Van Buren's "Old Republican" allies. Instead, he acknowledged his Southern support by naming Georgia's John M. Berrien as attorney general and North Carolina's John Branch as secretary of the navy. The Treasury Department went to Samuel D. Ingham from the crucial state of Pennsylvania, and President Jackson's desire to have at least one close friend among his official advisers led to the appointment of fellow Tennessean John Eaton as secretary of war. To some, the appointments seemed to favor Calhoun. Only Eaton was associated with Van Buren, while Ingham and the lone holdover from Adams' administration, Postmaster General John McLean, were thought to support the vice president. Also, Duff Green, the editor of the *United States Telegraph*, a newspaper widely thought to speak for the administration, loyally supported the South Carolinian. McLean's appointment to the Supreme Court soon after Jackson took office, though, allowed the new president to replace him with another unaligned figure, Kentucky's William T. Barry, preserving the image that the cabinet allied with neither aspirant.

The public generally expressed disappointment with President Jackson's choice of appointees. Other than Van Buren, the appointees seemed second-rate figures. Opposition newspapers labeled the group the "Millennium of Minnows" and charged that Van Buren's association with such an undistinguished group would diminish his reputation. The president brushed aside the complaints and instructed his cabinet members to address his first "reform": removing "corrupt" officials from federal positions. Since President Jefferson had replaced Federalists with loyal Republicans a quarter-century earlier, presidents seldom dismissed appointed officials unless they clearly proved crooked or inept, so most officeholders had held their positions for years. President Jackson, though, thought long-standing officeholders constituted a privileged aristocracy, unresponsive to the public will. Within weeks of his inauguration, the administration began firing officials and filling their positions with recess appointments, who would hold their offices pending confirmation at the Senate's next session. In its first eighteen months, Jackson's administration would replace more than nine hundred federal officials—about nine percent of all federal appointments. Removals slowed after the initial wave, and during Jackson's presidency ninety percent of all officeholders actually kept their jobs. Still, the large number of replacements after years of inactivity produced the widespread impression that the new president intended to completely remake the executive branch.

Opponents accused President Jackson of removing qualified public servants to replace them with incompetent hacks as rewards for their subservience to the general. New York senator William L. Marcy added fuel to this charge when he defended the removals with the smug declaration "To the victor belong the spoils of the enemy." While critics denounced the "Spoils System," President Jackson defended the removals as "rotation in office," a reform necessary to keep officials responsive to the people they served. When the Twenty-First Congress assembled in December 1829, he explained that the tasks of any federal position should remain "so plain and simple" that any intelligent man could perform them; "no one man has any more intrinsic right to official station than another," he argued, and keeping terms of service short would remind officeholders that their appointments represented a public trust, not a right.

The administration meanwhile conducted investigations revealing that dismissed officials had embezzled $457,000. Still, several of the dismissed officials had performed ably and responsibly, and as the administration proceeded, it focused less often on corruption than on opening up spots to reward political supporters. Future presidents likewise would distribute offices on the basis of political loyalty rather than qualification. For the next fifty years, the "Spoils System" served as the principal means of rewarding political activists.

A social scandal threatened to derail Jackson's presidency and soon overtook attention to the removals. During his brief term in the Senate in the early 1820s, Jackson had lodged with fellow senator John Eaton at William O'Neale's Franklin House, one of Washington's best-known boarding houses. There they socialized frequently with Margaret Timberlake, O'Neale's vivacious and beautiful but brash young daughter. Margaret's ease at discussing politics and gossip with Franklin House's male guests led Washington's social elite to dismiss "Peggy" Timberlake as a crass social upstart. Elizabeth Kortland Monroe had banished her from the White House as rumors spread that she carried on an affair with Eaton while her husband, a naval purser, was away at sea. In the summer of 1828, word reached the capital that John Timberlake had died near Spain. Washington society erroneously concluded that he had committed suicide because of his wife's infidelity. Whether John Eaton and Margaret Timberlake had an inappropriate relationship remains uncertain, but by the time of John Timberlake's death Eaton clearly loved Margaret and believed their marriage would restore her reputation. He convinced her to ignore a widow's customary yearlong mourning period, and they married on January 1, 1829—six weeks before President Jackson invited Eaton to join his cabinet.

Instead of rejuvenating Margaret's reputation, the marriage only confirmed her unworthiness to Washington society. Neglecting a respectable grieving for her first husband seemed to prove she had had an extramarital affair with Eaton. Regardless of her new husband's position, Washington's ladies refused to accept her, and their obstinacy soon infected the government. Federal officials' wives snubbed her at President Jackson's inauguration. Only a small number paid her the expected courtesy visits at the Eaton's home. When President Jackson held his first formal dinner, the other cabinet members' wives' displeasure with her attendance ruined the occasion. Berrien, Ingham, and Branch refused to host the customary dinners expected of cabinet officers; Branch's and Ingham's wives declined invitations to Van Buren's dinner, as did Berrien, who was a widower. Emily Donelson, who was the president's niece and the administration's hostess, reluctantly agreed to receive her in the White House, but she resisted calling on Mrs. Eaton at her home. Cabinet meetings became unbearably uncomfortable as John Eaton tried to work with the colleagues who ostracized his wife. Tensions finally reached the point that the president stopped holding meetings and instead met with each officer individually.

The president's response only made the "Eaton Affair" worse. President Jackson became the Eatons' chief defender and insisted that his administration extend to Margaret the respect her husband's position deserved. For more than two years, he devoted hours to securing evidence to disprove rumors of her promiscuity. Much of his determination stemmed from his loyalty to Eaton. President Jackson, in fact, had encouraged the couple to marry immediately rather than wait for the customary mourning period. More importantly, he convinced himself that politics lay at the heart of the scandal. Although he genuinely liked Margaret, he projected on her the image of his recently departed Rachel—another innocent victim of political slander and gossip. Brushing aside the marriage's violation of tradition, President Jackson concluded that Henry Clay had instigated the charges against the Eatons to embarrass the administration. Defending Mrs. Eaton thus provided a way for President Jackson to demonstrate his political strength while upholding both Margaret's and Rachel's honor.

To halt the opposition's scheme, President Jackson met with his cabinet except Eaton on September 10, 1829, along with his private secretary Andrew Donelson and two ministers who had encouraged Jackson to repudiate the Eatons. Demanding that they accept Mrs. Eaton socially, he shut down all attempts to question his evidence with the proclamation, "She is as chaste as a virgin!" The president's declaration failed to end the standoff, however. Instead, the rift in the administration gave Secretary of State Van Buren the opportunity to increase his standing with the president. Though President Jackson long respected Van Buren, the two had never developed a close relationship, but as a longtime widower, the New Yorker faced no personal obstacle to throwing his full support behind the Eatons. President Jackson deeply appreciated Van Buren's respectful treatment of Margaret as well as his attentiveness to his frustrations and physical condition. Never much of an outdoorsman, Van Buren took up riding so that he could accompany the president on his daily morning outings. In their discussions, the secretary's good political sense impressed the president, who likewise recognized the similarity of their political principles. By the end of the year, President Jackson had come to regard Van Buren as one of the Union's most competent and trustworthy leaders, so much so that, when the president became seriously ill in December, he indicated that, in the event of his death, he thought Van Buren should succeed him.

Of course, had Jackson died in 1829, Vice President John C. Calhoun would have succeeded him, but as Van Buren's stature rose, the vice president increasingly fell out of the president's favor. As with Van Buren, the Eaton Affair partly determined Calhoun's fate. Though he paid little attention to social affairs, Calhoun's wife Floride stood well-respected among Washington's ladies. Before returning to South Carolina after the inauguration, Floride Calhoun received a visit from the Eatons, but she never paid the expected return visit. Most of Margaret Eaton's detractors in the administration associated with the vice president. Even without the Eaton Affair, political developments drove a wedge between President Jackson and Vice President Calhoun. Cotton prices remained low after the Panic of 1819 through the 1820s, and throughout the South, slaveholding planters blamed federal tariff policy for their difficulties. Protection for American industries through taxes raised the price of imported goods, they reasoned, so in retaliation Great Britain—the leading importer to the United States—had cut back their purchases of the South's principal crop. After Denmark Vesey's failed slave rebellion in 1822, too, South Carolina planters feared that the federal government might reach farther and try to abolish slavery. South Carolina planters thus took the lead in demanding the elimination of protective tariffs. As a consequence, Calhoun—once the Union's leading nationalist—found he had to move toward sectional extremism to retain support in his home state.

Rather than reduce the tariff, Congress raised rates when it passed what Southerners denounced as the "Tariff of Abominations" in 1828. Radical South Carolinians called for the state's secession—that is, its withdrawal from the Union. Most Southern leaders hoped that the election of Jackson, himself a cotton planter, and Calhoun could resolve the problem. Still, a committee in the South Carolina legislature asked Calhoun to prepare a statement challenging the tariff. His essay, published anonymously in the fall of 1828 as the *South Carolina Exposition and Protest*, denounced the tariff as "unconstitutional, unequal, and oppressive" and proposed "state interposition," or "nullification," as a means of resistance. Calhoun contended that the Union represented a compact among the states; building on the challenge first presented in 1798 in the Kentucky and Virginia Resolutions, he argued that state governments could "interpose," or effectively veto, a federal law that violated the rights of its citizens. Despite their membership in the federal Union, Calhoun argued, the states retained their original sovereignty. If the federal government approved a law that encroached upon a state's authority, a state convention could declare the law null and void within its boundaries. Federal officials thus could not enforce the law until it received the endorsement of three-fourths of the states—the proportion necessary to ratify a constitutional amendment. Once enough states upheld the law's constitutional status, the nullifying state would have to either accept the law or withdraw from the Union.

Calhoun presented his theory to counter the secessionist threats coming from his state. He thought state interposition offered a constitutional remedy to the tariff, and he hoped that simply promoting the theory might present a sufficient threat to encourage Congress to revise the law. President Jackson, though, concluded that the vice president himself advocated secession. Though the South Carolina legislature published the *Exposition and Protest* anonymously, several Washington politicians—most likely including the president—knew of Calhoun's authorship. Then, in January 1830, Calhoun's ally, South Carolina senator Robert Y. Hayne, openly defended state sovereignty, nullification, and secession in a Senate debate with Daniel Webster. The president sympathized with his fellow planters' economic plight, but he held no doubts about the constitutionality of the tariff; in fact, he favored keeping rates temporarily higher in order to secure the revenues needed to pay the national debt. More importantly, notwithstanding his respect for the states' powers, he believed the Union existed as a permanent agreement among the people of the United States. For him, the states had no right to secede, and any effort to withdraw from the Union constituted treason. Coupled with his supporters' rejection of Margaret Eaton, the nullification theory persuaded the president that Calhoun, rather than Clay, had instigated the Eaton Affair to undermine his administration.

Despite the Eaton Affair's distractions, President Jackson began taking action on several issues. Working with Secretary of State Van Buren, he instructed Louis McLane, the minister to Great Britain, to open talks that would culminate in the reopening of trade with Britain's West Indian colonies in October 1830. Van Buren's diplomatic efforts produced treaties settling claims and opening trade with several European, Asian, and South American nations, which contributed to a 70-percent increase in American exports and a 250-percent increase in imports during Jackson's presidency. President Jackson instructed his cabinet members to cut unnecessary expenditures and direct federal revenues toward paying the national debt. Most significantly, when the Twenty-First Congress convened in December 1829, he proposed removing Natives to lands west of the Mississippi River. Several of the president's Northern supporters resisted, but enough joined with solid Southern support to pass the Indian Removal Act in late May 1830.

President Jackson's position on internal improvements shocked many of his supporters. The day after Congress approved the Indian Removal Act, he vetoed an act to build a road from Maysville to Lexington in Kentucky. Four days later, he vetoed a second road project, and he killed two additional acts—to construct a canal near Louisville, and to appropriate funds to construct several lighthouses—through "pocket vetoes"—that is, he prevented them from becoming law by refusing to sign them after Congress had adjourned. Some projects, however, met President Jackson's approval. He signed bills to extend the National Road and to conduct surveys for future roads. During his presidency, in fact, he would authorize federal construction of more roads and canals than any preceding president. Still, his vetoes demonstrated that he opposed a national transportation "system" and would hold more firmly to President Monroe's standard that the federal government could spend money only for improvements that clearly satisfied national goals. His message accompanying the veto of the Maysville Turnpike—written by Van Buren with assistance from young Tennessee congressman James K. Polk—explained that the road was a local project that did not sufficiently satisfy a national need to justify federal assistance. The Maysville Veto also furthered the president's political aims. While blocking a project in the home state of the "American System's" champion, Henry Clay, it reassured Southern planters—who might be tempted to accept South Carolina's claims for nullification—that he would keep the federal government's activities within the Constitution's limits.

By the time President Jackson issued the Maysville Road veto, his differences with his vice president had become public. Throughout the congressional session, the president made no public statement about nullification, and Duff Green's *United States Telegraph* conveyed the impression that the president agreed with Calhoun's and Hayne's extreme position on states' rights. Still, insiders recognized Calhoun's declining influence in the administration, especially after Jackson loyalists helped defeat a South Carolina representative's proposal to reduce tariff rates. Needing to regain the initiative, Calhoun tried to force the president's hand. Missouri senator Thomas H. Benton arranged a dinner to honor Thomas Jefferson's birthday on April 13, 1830. Benton agreed to let Hayne deliver the keynote address and also serve as chair of the arrangements committee. Through Hayne, Calhoun scheduled to follow Hayne's speech with a series of twenty-four toasts that would both proclaim states' rights and implicitly attack the tariff. After the *Telegraph* published the program and revealed the prominent role of Calhoun's friends, President Jackson concluded that the event would be "a *nullification affair altogether*," and he resolved to rebuke Calhoun's disunionist allies. Following the aggressive planned toasts, the president had the opportunity to present the first "volunteer" toast. Raising his glass and staring directly at Calhoun, he declared, "Our Union—it must be preserved!"

President Jackson's statement dramatically revealed Calhoun's alienation from the president to the public. Van Buren moved quickly to ensure that the breach remained irreparable. Later in April, Georgia senator John Forsyth secured a letter from former Treasury secretary William H. Crawford revealing that, as secretary of war, Calhoun had encouraged President Monroe to punish Jackson for his unauthorized invasion of Florida in 1818. When Van Buren then arranged to share the evidence with the president, President Jackson wrote to Calhoun to demand an explanation. The vice president's indignant and exhaustive fifty-two-page reply presented an unsatisfying mixture of self-justification and indictments against Crawford. President Jackson's own response accused Calhoun of betrayal and declared their communication ended. Insisting on having the last word, Calhoun wrote three more letters, accusing his political foes of slander and hinting that Van Buren was the source of the "false accusations." The president spent the next eight months marshaling evidence to back his claim that President Monroe had privately authorized Florida's seizure—which the aging Monroe vehemently denied—but Calhoun's decision to publish his correspondence with President Jackson in February 1831 demonstrated to all observers that the vice president had lost all credibility in the administration.

Van Buren then provided the means for President Jackson to escape the lingering complications of the Eaton Affair. The rift in his cabinet continued to frustrate the president. Secretaries Ingham and Branch and Attorney General Berrien still rejected the Eatons socially, and the three moved closer politically to Calhoun as the vice president grew estranged from the president. Several times, President Jackson threatened to dismiss the troublesome secretaries, but he knew that their firing would give the impression that he was under Margaret Eaton's influence. Eaton's resignation, on the other hand, would signal that his wife's detractors had forced the president's hand. Soon after the Twenty-First Congress adjourned in March 1831, Van Buren himself offered to resign, claiming that Calhoun's insinuations might make him a distraction to the administration. The president resisted at first, but he quickly came to see the wisdom of Van Buren's move. Linked with Eaton's resignation, Van Buren's departure would allow President Jackson to claim the need to reorganize his entire cabinet, forcing out Calhoun's allies without appearing pressured either by the Eaton controversy or by political strains. Thus, in mid-April he accepted Van Buren's and Eaton's resignations and immediately requested that Berrien, Branch, and Ingham also resign. By June, all but Postmaster General Barry had left office. The president then appointed Eaton as governor of the Florida Territory, removing from the capital the couple at the center of the scandal that had dominated his presidency's first two years.

Unlike the first cabinet's "Millennium of Minnows," President Jackson's new appointees enjoyed widespread prestige and respect for their abilities. Each officer placed his primary loyalty to the president, demonstrating how the hero had stamped his character on the executive branch. Cabinet reorganization also showed how his administration began to transform the loose coalition of sectional interests that had elected him into an organized political party. His response to the major issues yet to face him would further clarify what his party stood for.

Nullification and the "Bank War"

President Jackson had long distrusted banks—especially the Bank of the United States. He believed that only gold and silver coin qualified as the Union's "constitutional currency." Paper money, he thought, mainly provided a means for the unscrupulous to defraud honest, hard-working citizens. Even when banks promised to back their money with gold or silver, too many closed their doors or simply suspended payments in hard times, leaving their notes worthless. Like others, President Jackson blamed the Panic of 1819 on the Bank of the United States' reckless behavior. Moreover, he remained convinced that the Constitution did not authorize Congress to charter a national bank and that its ability to establish branches without a state's consent violated states' rights. The bank was a private institution, but its stockholders enjoyed unfair privileges not available to the average citizen. Its thinly veiled association with his political enemies, including Henry Clay and Daniel Webster, persuaded him that it used its financial resources to advance their political ends. Most importantly, President Jackson feared that, as a large and wealthy corporation that operated across the Union, it could become more powerful than the federal government itself.

When President Jackson took office, few Americans held the same resentment toward the Bank of the United States. The widespread hostility that the Panic of 1819 had stirred largely subsided as the economy recovered. Following Chief Justice John Marshall's ruling in *McCullough v. Maryland* (1819), most Americans accepted the bank's constitutionality. Under the direction of its third president, Nicholas Biddle, the bank had come to play a major role in promoting national economic stability as a backer of paper money across the Union. From his office on Chestnut Street in Philadelphia, Biddle monitored state banks' currency issuances and practices. When a bank appeared to issue more paper than its gold and silver reserves could support, Biddle would order the nearest Bank of the United States branch to exchange money for the state bank's notes; then, the Bank of the United States could demand that the state bank redeem its notes with gold or silver. If the state bank could pay, the public could confidently trade its notes; if not, the federal bank could drive it out of business without causing widespread economic disruption. These services won support for "Biddle's Bank" even from most state bankers. Congress had chartered the bank in 1816 for twenty years, so to continue its work uninterrupted it would need a new charter approved no later than 1836. Since its existence no longer appeared controversial, no one expected President Jackson to stand in its way.

President Jackson thus disturbed his cabinet advisers when his first message to Congress included a statement that the bank's constitutionality remained "questioned by a large portion of our fellow-citizens" while it had "failed in the great end of establishing a uniform and sound currency." The House Ways and Means committee responded to Jackson's charge with "respectful but decided dissent," but the president reiterated his concerns in December 1830 when he suggested replacing the bank with a government-owned institution with no private stockholders. Congress again ignored his warnings, and in February 1831 the Senate defeated Thomas Hart Benton's resolutions opposing the bank's recharter. Jackson's administration meanwhile sent out mixed signals about the bank. Bank supporters still dominated the cabinet after its reorganization in the spring of 1831. In particular, all knew Treasury Secretary Louis McLane as a champion of the institution, and in December President Jackson allowed him to endorse re-chartering the bank in a Treasury Department report to Congress. Though the president's reservations remained an obstacle, most Americans expected him to work with lawmakers to modify the bank's charter to meet his objections.

The need to deal with the Bank of the United States likely contributed to President Jackson's decision to accept another term as president. In January 1831, the *Washington Globe*, which had recently replaced the *United States Telegraph* as the administration's organ, reported that the president would agree to continue in office if re-elected. Although Democrats widely supported another Jackson administration, several challenged President Jackson's desire to replace Calhoun as vice president with Van Buren. The "Sly Fox of Kinderhook" still carried a reputation as a political schemer, and Southerners resented the New Yorker's initial promotion of the "Tariff of Abominations" while questioning whether a Northerner could adequately defend their slave property. To unite President Jackson's followers, in June 1831 Amos Kendall—a Treasury Department auditor who emerged as one of the president's most trusted advisers—urged Democrats in New Hampshire's legislature to call for a national convention to nominate a vice presidential candidate. The *Globe*'s editor, Francis Preston Blair—who, like Kendall, became one of the president's closest confidants—quickly endorsed the proposal and suggested that the convention meet in Baltimore in May 1832. The *Globe* then encouraged Democrats to accept the convention as the surest way of keeping the choice of a president and vice president in the hands of the people.

For most of 1831, the leading aspirant for the nomination appeared to be Blair's and Kendall's preference, Kentucky congressman Richard M. Johnson. An unexpected development, though, united Democrats behind Van Buren: The former secretary of state left to assume his new duties as US minister to Great Britain in August 1831, before the Senate had the opportunity to confirm his nomination. When Congress came into session in December, the administration's opponents mustered enough votes to reject the appointment. To provide his rival with a measure of revenge, Calhoun's allies arranged the vote in January 1832 to result in a 23–23 tie so the vice president himself could cast the deciding vote. Van Buren's detractors expected his defeat to destroy his career. Instead, the public saw him as the victim of selfish, jealous, and petty politicians. Promoting him for the vice presidency now became a means of vindicating "the will of the people" against President Jackson's enemies, so when Democrats gathered in Baltimore, Van Buren's nomination was a foregone conclusion. The delegates decided that the states would vote as units—that is, each state would cast all of its votes for one candidate—and they instituted a rule requiring a nominee to receive at least two-thirds of the votes. These decisions would prove crucial at future Democratic conventions, but in 1832 they posed no threat to Van Buren, who received 208 votes to 26 for Johnson and 49 for federal judge Philip P. Barbour, the favorite of Virginia's "Old Republicans."

By the time the Democratic Convention met, President Jackson's opponents had already held their own nominating conventions. Thurlow Weed and William Seward hoped to unite the Antimasons with National Republicans behind Henry Clay, but when Clay refused to renounce his association with Freemasonry, Antimasons held the first national party convention in Baltimore in September 1831 and nominated former attorney general William Wirt. Eleven weeks later, National Republicans held their own convention, also meeting in Baltimore, to nominate Clay. The incumbent's popularity made it unlikely that either candidate could win, even if the opposition could unite, so Clay persuaded Biddle to take a bold step: Rather than wait four more years to ask Congress to re-charter the Bank of the United States, he pushed Biddle to apply for the charter's renewal immediately. Enough Jackson men still favored the bank that their votes could help a re-charter bill pass Congress, Clay reasoned, and public support for the bank might then compel President Jackson to sign the act to avoid a backlash that might jeopardize his re-election. More likely, the president would veto a re-charter bill, but the effective destruction of the institution might prove so unpopular that it could provide Clay with the issue he needed to give him a chance of winning the presidency.

Biddle hesitated at first, fearful that the move might incite the president's hostility, but Clay's reasoning assured him that the move could only work to the bank's advantage. With the opposition's blessing, Pennsylvania Democrat George M. Dallas presented a resolution to the House in January 1832 calling for the charter's renewal. Though several Jacksonians tried to delay a vote until after the election, on July 3 Congress approved a bill extending the bank's charter until 1851. The re-charter passed both chambers by close but respectable margins, and as Clay expected, President Jackson vetoed the bill on July 10. Clay failed to anticipate, though, how President Jackson would turn the bank issue to his advantage. When the president returned the bill to Congress, he accompanied it with a carefully crafted 8,100-word veto message, drafted principally by Kendall, Attorney General Roger B. Taney, and Navy Secretary Levi Woodbury. Previous veto messages had only provided brief explanations of a president's constitutional objections to a bill. In contrast, the Bank Veto message bypassed Washington politicians, presenting the president's case against the bank directly to the public and framing the bank issue as part of his defense of the people against the aristocratic political and social interests that tried to deny the people's right to rule.

Much of the veto message did deal with rejecting the case for the bank's constitutionality. Despite the Supreme Court's decision in *McCullough v. Maryland*, President Jackson claimed that the president also had the right to decide an act's constitutionality. Though proponents proclaimed a federal bank "necessary and proper" for the executive branch, President Jackson—the executive—reminded lawmakers that he had never been consulted about its usefulness. Mainly, though, he charged that the bank was "subversive of the rights of the States, and dangerous to the liberties of the people." The charter gave the bank a monopoly on banking privileges under the federal government's authority while granting a "gratuity of millions to the stockholders." Only "a few hundred of our own citizens, chiefly of the richest class," owned its stock, and foreigners—mostly Britons—owned a significant amount; should the Union find itself in another war, President Jackson asked, "what would be our condition?" Biddle publicly admitted that state banks existed only because of the central bank's "forbearance," and a congressional investigation's early findings revealed evidence of "gross abuse and violation of its charter." Rather than a vital fiscal agent, the message concluded, the bank represented an unjust special privilege granted to "the rich and powerful." "When the laws undertake . . . to make the rich richer and the potent more powerful," the president thundered, "the humble members of society . . . have a right to complain of the injustice of their Government."

The veto message infuriated President Jackson's enemies. Antimasons joined National Republicans to denounce it as proof of the president's "tyranny." Biddle concluded that its ridiculous charges and poor constitutional reasoning showed the president's incompetence, so he ordered thirty thousand copies printed for distribution before he recognized its effect. Several Democratic leaders privately expressed discomfort with the assault on the bank, but most rallied behind the president. After the Senate failed to override the veto, the bank became a central issue in the fall elections. President Jackson's personal popularity raised few doubts about his re-election, but the results revealed a public deeply divided over the bank's future. The incumbent's proportion of the popular vote declined slightly from his victory four years earlier—from fifty-six to fifty-four percent. Still, he carried sixteen states, to earn him 219 votes in the electoral college. Clay won thirty-seven percent of the popular vote, giving him six states, for forty-nine electoral votes. Wirt carried Vermont's seven electoral votes while gaining eight percent of the votes cast, and South Carolina's legislature threw the state's eleven electoral votes to Virginia's advocate for states' rights, Governor John Floyd. President Jackson's Democratic allies, though, suffered setbacks in congressional and state contests. In the House of Representatives, the Democrats' majority fell from fifty-nine to forty-six seats, while the opposition gained an eight-seat advantage in the Senate.

Immediately following the election, President Jackson faced a greater threat than the Bank of the United States. Trade had boomed throughout his first term, but because cotton prices remained low, radicals won control of South Carolina's legislature in 1830. President Jackson indicated a willingness to accept a reduction in tariff rates, so Treasury Secretary McLane drafted a new tariff bill that John Quincy Adams—now returned to Washington as a representative from Massachusetts—revised and championed in the House. Adams' version of the bill easily passed Congress, lowering the average tax on imports from forty-five to thirty-three percent while still protecting iron and cotton textiles. As a concession to Southerners, Adams' bill also cut to five percent the duty on the cheap woolens used to clothe slaves. Most Southern planters accepted the Tariff of 1832 as a fair compromise, but Nullifiers rejected it because it still upheld the principle of protection. In October 1832, Nullifiers won the two-thirds majority in South Carolina's legislature needed to put Calhoun's nullification theory into effect. Meeting in late November, a state convention overwhelmingly approved an ordinance declaring the Tariffs of 1828 and 1832 null and void in the state. Should the Union attempt to collect the tariff after February 1, 1833, South Carolinians would "thenceforth hold themselves absolved from . . . their political connection with the people of the other States" and "forthwith proceed to organize a separate Government."

Nullification infuriated President Jackson. He believed Calhoun's frustrated ambition lay at the root of the challenge. Behind the former vice president, Nullifiers intended to destroy the Union and form a new confederation that they could rule. As soon as he read the convention's ordinance, he began to draft a formal response. After revisions by Secretary of State Edward Livingston, on December 10 President Jackson issued a Proclamation on Nullification, which declared the theory "incompatible with the existence of the Union" and "contradicted expressly by the letter of the Constitution." The judiciary and the people alone could determine a congressional act's constitutionality, he contended. If the Constitution allowed nullification, "this Union would have been dissolved in its infancy." The Constitution plainly authorized Congress to assess taxes, including tariffs, and as chief executive the president had a duty to enforce the law. He rejected the claim that the Union represented a compact of the states, concluding with a strong defense of the Union as a nation. As colonies, "we had no separate character," and in the Constitution the American people created a "more perfect" Union by forming "a government, not a league." Secession—Nullifiers' true object—would only destroy "the unity of a nation." "Be not deceived by names," Jackson warned: "disunion, by armed force, is treason."

For a time, violent confrontation between the central government and South Carolina appeared likely. South Carolina's convention called for volunteers for a twenty-five-thousand-man army to defend the state against federal action. President Jackson had already reinforced the garrisons at Fort Moultrie and at Castle Pinckney in Charleston Harbor, and he ordered General Winfield Scott to prepare for an invasion of the state. Eight thousand Unionists within South Carolina volunteered for a militia to fight their state's leaders. President Jackson asked Congress to approve a "Force Bill" that would authorize a military response if South Carolinians attacked federal installations in the state. Meanwhile, public meetings throughout the Northern and Western states—often led by the president's National Republican foes—rallied to pledge their support for action to suppress nullification. Behind his bombastic rhetoric, though, President Jackson worked to avoid conflict. He stipulated that he would use force only in response to Nullifiers' aggression, and even before the crisis he ordered two revenue ships to patrol the coast so they could intercept merchant ships and collect the tariff before they reached Charleston's harbor. Four days before he issued his proclamation, his annual message to Congress avoided mentioning nullification while indicating that he would accept a further reduction of tariff rates. New York representative Gulian C. Verplanck then introduced a bill into the House that would cut tariffs in half, a proposal that all understood had President Jackson's support.

South Carolina leaders also wanted to avoid civil war. When Governor James Hamilton, one of the state's most adamant radicals, resigned to take charge of the state's army, the legislature selected Senator Robert Hayne as his successor. Hayne supported Calhoun's more moderate understanding of nullification, so he ordered the militia to train at home rather than in Charleston, where their presence might provoke an incident that could lead to conflict. To replace Hayne in the Senate, the legislature selected Calhoun himself, who resigned the vice presidency on December 28 to take his seat. Despite President Jackson's accusations, Washington insiders knew that Calhoun regretted his state's action and would use his new position to try to resolve the standoff. Most significantly, South Carolina found itself isolated. Radicals expected other Southern states to back their challenge to the tariff and advance nullification as a potential protection for slavery. Other than in Georgia and Virginia, however, the stand gained little support. Several Southerners broke with the president over his strong nationalist declaration to form independent "State Rights" organizations, and the legislatures of North Carolina, Alabama, Mississippi, and—surprisingly—New York refrained from endorsing the Nullification Proclamation. But no state publicly endorsed South Carolina's course of action, and eight Southern state legislatures joined nine Northern states to pass resolutions condemning the principle of nullification.

With few options available, Nullifiers held a public meeting in Charleston on January 21, 1833, and decided to delay nullification of the tariff until some undetermined time after the February 1 deadline. In Congress, Calhoun fought against the Verplanck bill and instead endorsed a compromise proposed by Henry Clay. President Jackson found it distasteful to accept a proposal that gave his nemesis the credit for solving the crisis, but he indicated that he would accept Clay's bill so long as Congress approved the Force Bill—partly to ensure that South Carolina carried out any agreement, but mainly as a symbol of the Union's permanence and of the federal government's authority. Nine Southern senators abstained rather than endorse the Force Bill, and Southern representatives provided most of the votes against the measure in the House, but Congress easily approved both the Force Act and Clay's tariff on March 1, 1833. In its final form, the Compromise Tariff of 1833 established a scale to reduce rates each year until 1842, when they would stand at twenty percent for all imports, with no protection for manufacturers. Nine days after President Jackson signed the acts, South Carolina's convention reconvened and repealed its nullification of the tariff laws. Before adjourning, Nullifiers carried out one final act of defiance: They approved a new ordinance that nullified the Force Act.

Radicalism remained a force in South Carolina, but nullification's defeat allowed President Jackson to turn his attention back to the Bank of the United States. Interpreting his election as a mandate to destroy the bank, he decided to attack the institution at its most vulnerable point: He would order the withdrawal of all of the federal government's deposits. Federal funds made up almost half of the bank's total capital; withdrawing them would take away the bank's major asset, seriously weaken its position in the economy, and deprive it of the political influence it needed to secure a new charter. To carry out this assault, President Jackson would have to overcome several obstacles. Secretary of the Treasury Louis McLane would actually have to withdraw the funds, and McLane still wanted to work out a compromise to keep the bank.

Also, the bank's charter required that the government's money remain in the bank unless Congress concluded that the institution was financially unstable, and in early 1833 the House voted 109–46 to affirm that the funds were safe in the bank. If President Jackson could secure their withdrawal, the funds might be placed in state banks, but most state bank executives feared Biddle's retaliation if they accepted federal money. Politically, support for some sort of central financial institution remained widespread, even among Democrats. Within the administration, only Kendall, Blair, and Attorney General Roger Taney enthusiastically favored removal. McLane and Secretary of State Livingston threatened to resign if President Jackson ordered the withdrawal. Others, including Vice President Van Buren, warned that the public would see removal as unnecessarily provocative.

President Jackson never wavered from his decision, however. In May 1833, he appointed Livingston as the American minister to France so he could elevate McLane to the State Department. To replace McLane in the Treasury Department, he appointed William J. Duane, a Pennsylvania lawyer and longtime opponent of the Bank of the United States. That summer, Kendall toured the Northeast and found seven state banks willing to accept federal funds. Then, in August, the president outlined to the cabinet his plan to withdraw the deposits on October 1. To the president's shock, Duane refused to carry out the withdrawal. The new Treasury Secretary opposed re-chartering "Biddle's Bank," but he concluded that removing the deposits without congressional approval would be illegal. Moreover, as an opponent of paper currency, he protested to President Jackson that depositing the money in state banks would only expand their paper money issuances and "plunge the fiscal concerns of the country" into "chaos." Frustrated, President Jackson fired Duane on September 23—the first time a president dismissed a cabinet officer without securing his resignation—and replaced him with Taney, who had no reluctance about challenging Biddle. Taney sidestepped challenges to the withdrawal's legality by slowly taking funds from the bank when needed to pay the government's expenses; then, when he received the revenue from tariff collections and public land sales, he deposited the money into the seven "pet banks" that Kendall had identified. By the end of 1833, the withdrawals had reduced the government's balance in the Bank of the United States from more than $10 million to $4 million. Within another year it would stand at zero.

Biddle responded to the loss of the federal deposits with vengeance. As soon as Taney began to withdraw funds, the bank started calling in its loans and demanding payments on notes from state banks. The sudden contraction of currency and credit sent the economy into a recession. The crisis never reached the levels following the Panic of 1819, but land values and the prices of farm goods fell, while business failures and rising unemployment revived memories of the Panic of 1819's hardships. Biddle claimed that he had to adopt these policies because the federal deposits' withdrawal deprived the bank of the capital it needed to survive. Actually, the bank called in more money than the withdrawals had taken out, and Biddle privately acknowledged that he wanted to create the financial panic to compel the public and the state banks to demand congressional action to stop President Jackson's assault. Through early 1834, Biddle's strategy appeared to be working. Public meetings and newspapers throughout the Union called upon President Jackson to restore the deposits and end the crisis.

The economy's setback gave the president's political opponents a potent weapon. They charged that his vetoes, his apparent disregard for the Constitution and the laws, and his reckless firing of Duane had transformed his presidency into a dictatorship. The Senate took the lead in condemning his "executive usurpation" during its "Panic Session" in early 1834. Amid several blistering speeches, the senators in February declared Taney's reasons for removing the deposits to be "unsatisfactory and insufficient." In late March, they approved by a 26–20 vote Clay's set of resolutions censuring President Jackson for assuming "authority and power not conferred by the Constitution and laws, but in derogation of both." Attacks on the president's "executive tyranny" gradually expanded into an assault on the Democrats' growing emphasis on party unity. Critics claimed that political hacks and incompetent "spoilsmen" carried out President Jackson's orders so they could gain power and enjoy political privileges. These accusations provided the issue upon which Antimasons and National Republicans could unite. In local elections in the spring of 1834, opposition candidates in New York began to refer to themselves as "Whigs," the label for the opponents of King George III during the Revolution.

Figure 9.1 "King Andrew the First." A caricature of President Jackson that emerged during the "Bank War" and provided common ground for the opposition to unite as Whigs. Lithograph, New York (1833). Courtesy Prints & Photographs Division, Library of Congress, LC-DIG-ppmsca-15771.

Clay picked up the term to identify President Jackson's enemies in a speech to the Senate in April, and by the fall the Democrats' adversaries throughout the Union had begun calling themselves "Whigs" to stress their resistance to "King Andrew I."

Despite public demands that he restore the deposits, President Jackson refused to back down. Throughout the deadlock, he kept the focus on Biddle's influence and irresponsibility. When business leaders and politicians asked him to return the deposits to the bank, he told them, as he responded to a delegation from New York, "Go to Nicholas Biddle. We have no money here, gentlemen. Biddle has the money." In time, as President Jackson expected, public attention shifted from his withdrawal of the deposits to Biddle's contraction of the currency and credit. Biddle, after all, had more influence on the nation's money supply, and his policies' effects seemed to confirm the president's warning about the dangers of the central bank's power. In April, Democrats in the House gained enough support to pass resolutions upholding the removal and opposing the bank's recharter. Biddle meanwhile damaged his cause when he arrogantly refused to cooperate with a congressional investigation into the bank's conduct. When state elections held in the late summer and fall produced Democratic victories, even Biddle realized his failure. With no hope now of renewal of the bank's charter, Biddle in September restored the bank's loans and currency issuances, and he made arrangements to receive a charter from the Pennsylvania legislature so it could continue to operate as a state bank, with neither the size nor influence it had once enjoyed.

Biddle's surrender signified the end of the "Bank War." President Jackson had destroyed the bank as a national institution and defined the Democratic Party as the organization that protected the people against the wealthy and powerful. In the process, he had driven a deeper wedge in the electorate than any since the division between Federalists and Republicans forty years earlier. But he also left his party with the challenges of managing the nation's finances and guiding the Union's economy without the aid of the Bank of the United States.

From Old Hickory to Sly Fox

Much would happen during the last two years remaining in President Jackson's term. In January 1835, his administration celebrated paying off the federal debt for the first and only time in the Union's history. Later that month, he experienced the first presidential assassination attempt when a mentally deranged house painter tried to shoot him on the Capitol's east portico. After John Marshall died in July, the president appointed Roger Taney as chief justice as a reward for his service in the Bank War. A dispute with France almost led to war. In July 1831, France had agreed to pay $4.6 million for its spoliations—damages to American merchant ships—during the Napoleonic Wars. When the French Chamber of Deputies delayed approving the payment, in December 1834 President Jackson threatened to retaliate. The House approved a bill giving him permission to seize French merchant ships, and though the bill died in the Senate, the French government recalled its minister as the two nations broke diplomatic relations. The Chamber of Deputies finally approved the spoliations payment, but only on the condition that President Jackson explain the meaning of his threat. The president refused to apologize, but his assurance that he intended no "menace or insult" or "charge of ill faith" sufficiently appeased French leaders. The Deputies backed down, and the Treasury received the spoliation payments in May 1836.

President Jackson's most important concern at this point was to secure Martin Van Buren's election as his successor. To forestall the emergence of rivals, he urged Democratic leaders to hold the party's national convention early. Delegates thus gathered in Baltimore in May 1835 and dutifully nominated Van Buren unanimously, with Kentucky congressman Richard M. Johnson selected as the vice presidential candidate. Divisions among the opposition appeared to put Van Buren in a strong position. Antimasons had cooperated with Whigs during the Bank War, but they still held on to their separate identity. Rivalries among presidential aspirants meanwhile convinced Whig leaders that a national convention would only drive its factions farther apart. Whigs hoped that nominations of local favorites might put forth a candidate who could gain a national following. When none of the nominees gained national attention, three regional candidates ended up standing against Van Buren. Massachusetts Whigs nominated Daniel Webster in January 1835, but the senator failed to gain much support outside of his home state. Pennsylvania's Antimasons nominated William Henry Harrison in December 1835. The sixty-two-year-old hero at the Battle of Tippecanoe a quarter-century earlier emerged as the most popular challenger in the Western and Mid-Atlantic states, but he failed to gain a following in the South. In that region, dissident Jacksonians joined State Rights men to throw their support behind Tennessee senator Hugh Lawson White, a onetime Jackson ally who resented his lack of influence with the administration.

Van Buren, though, lacked President Jackson's heroic stature, making it difficult for Democrats to muster enthusiasm for their candidate. At first, Whig leaders hoped that promoting regional favorites might bring out enough voters to help the opposition gain control of Congress. Gradually, they realized that their nominees could carry enough states to deny Van Buren an electoral college majority, which could give the House of Representatives the chance to elect one of the Whig candidates. Despite his age and relative obscurity since 1811, Harrison enjoyed the reputation of a military hero and Indian fighter; also, President Jackson had dismissed him as American minister to Colombia, making him now appear a victim of the new party machinations that the Democratic nominee represented. Van Buren particularly appeared vulnerable in the South. White's supporters cleverly presented the senator as a loyal Jacksonian who now rejected the president's attempts to "dictate" his successor to the voters. Van Buren's initial promotion of the "Tariff of Abominations" showed that he had little respect for Southern interests, they claimed, and the candidate's New York background—along with the fact that vice presidential candidate Johnson openly lived with his mulatto mistress—showed that Southerners could not trust the Democratic ticket to defend their human property rights or protect them from slave rebellion.

Political concerns weighed heavily on President Jackson as he tried to deal with the Union's finances. Without the Bank of the United States, the economy lay on an unstable foundation. Biddle's decision to relax credit at the end of the Bank War coincided with increasing supplies of gold and silver, brought by British investments in state internal improvement projects, Mexican purchases of American goods, and Chinese merchants' shifting preference for British credit rather than silver when selling their products. With more gold and silver available, the number of state banks nearly doubled. Political pressures compelled President Jackson to increase the number of deposit banks to thirty-three by mid-1836, and without the restraints imposed by "Biddle's Bank," state banks increased the amount of paper money available from $172 million in 1834 to $276 million in 1836. More money meant an increase in prices and property values, but it also stimulated widespread inflation as well as a mania for speculation in western public lands. Before 1834, annual government revenue from land sales had never exceeded $5 million, but land sales brought in $15 million in 1835 and another $25 million in 1836. The government began to accumulate an embarrassingly high surplus that in 1836 soared from $17 million to $42 million.

The expansion of the "credit system" he despised disturbed President Jackson. Despite the boom, he was determined to move the Union closer to an exclusively "hard money" currency. Influenced by the book *A Short History of Paper Money and Banking* by William M. Gouge, a Philadelphia printer whom he appointed a clerk in the Treasury Department, President Jackson thought that gold and silver coins could provide enough money for most people's everyday use. Paper money should be available only in large denominations for more substantial deals. Keeping federal funds in a smaller number of state banks, he concluded, might allow the government to promote more coins and reverse the rampant expansion of paper money. Careful regulation of the government-selected banks that held the federal deposits could then restrict the amount of paper they issued, which would increase the use of gold and silver, uphold the value of the deposit banks' notes, and compel other state banks to reduce their paper issuances as well. To implement this plan, Treasury Secretary Taney issued an order in April 1834 that forbade deposit banks from issuing or accepting notes worth less than five dollars. Taney likewise encouraged Congress to change the valuation of gold and silver from 15:1 to 16:1—that is, valuing sixteen ounces of silver as equal to one ounce of gold—to encourage the minting of more gold coins.

In June 1834, Congress approved a Coinage Act, changing the ratio of silver to gold to 16:1 and increasing the minting of "Jackson eagle" gold coins. Even after elections strengthened the Democratic presence in Congress, though, the president's program gained little ground. His own party put up much of the resistance. "Radical" hard-money Democrats became known as "Locofocos" after working-class Democrats in New York City lit candles with newly developed friction matches—called *locofocos*—in protest at a party meeting in October 1835. "Conservative" Democrats, who enjoyed close ties to state banks, had supported the Bank War to free the state banks from Nicholas Biddle's restraints, and now they wanted to make sure their banks got their fair share of the available funds. When Taney's successor at the Treasury Department, Levi Woodbury, again encouraged Congress to enact regulations on the deposit banks, conservative Democrats instead joined with Whigs in June 1836 to pass Henry Clay's Deposit and Distribution Act, which required the government to place federal funds in at least one bank in every state and territory—increasing the number of deposit banks to eighty-one. The act also instructed the Treasury secretary to distribute the federal surplus to the states in three installments beginning on January 1, 1837, with each state's share determined by the size of its representation in Congress.

President Jackson seriously considered vetoing the Deposit Act. The opportunity to strike down another one of Clay's policies tempted him, but more importantly he expected distribution and expanding the number of deposit banks to produce more paper money, inflation, and reckless speculation. Reluctantly, he concluded that he had to sign the act. The bill had passed with strong enough majorities in the House and the Senate that Congress would likely override a veto. Also, with conservative Democrats accusing the administration of privileging certain "pet" banks, a veto would likely damage Van Buren's prospects in the election. To counter the Deposit Act's effects, President Jackson directed Secretary Woodbury in July 1836 to issue an order requiring the Treasury Department to accept only gold or silver coins as payment for public lands. Jackson defended the "Specie Circular" as necessary to counter the rampant speculation and to promote a "uniform currency." Whigs denounced the order as more evidence of the president's executive tyranny. Conservative Democrats worried about the effects of what they considered an ill-advised decision at best. Nevertheless, the president refused to rescind the order, even though it only modestly slowed land sales because speculators simply withdrew gold and silver from banks to complete their purchases.

More than financial matters threatened to complicate the campaign for Van Buren. Although abolitionists only gained a small number of followers, their efforts to take the antislavery cause directly to slaveholders threatened to bring sectional tensions into the election. The American Anti-Slavery Society postal campaign mailed nearly one million antislavery tracts directly to planters and politicians in Southern states in early 1835. Southern state legislatures had banished antislavery literature in their states, but the federal postal service had a legal responsibility to deliver mail to its intended recipients. Abolitionists hoped the pamphlets might persuade slaveholders to adopt immediate emancipation. Instead, the mailings provoked widespread, often hysterical fears that the pamphlets would fall into slaves' hands and incite bloody rebellions. When the first tracts arrived in South Carolina, Charleston postmaster Alfred Huger placed them in separate bags in a corner at the post office. He then wrote to Amos Kendall, who had taken office as postmaster general the previous May, for direction on what to do with the pamphlets. Before he could send his missive, a group broke into the post office, seized the bags, and burned the pamphlets—along with effigies of abolitionist leaders—before a crowd of about three thousand onlookers at the city's parade grounds on July 30. Elsewhere in the South, postmasters refused to deliver the pamphlets and waited for instructions from the administration.

The abolitionists' postal campaign presented President Jackson with a dilemma. Most Northerners rejected abolitionists' pleas, but after the nullification controversy and the Charleston riot, they had little patience with Southern defiance of the law. The president agreed with other Southerners that circulating the pamphlets might incite slave rebellion, and he recognized that forcing the tracts' delivery might damage Van Buren's reputation in the South. The administration thus moved to suppress the mailings' impact. Postmaster General Amos Kendall instructed Southern postmasters to withhold antislavery literature unless an addressee specifically requested its delivery. Likewise, he informed Northern postmasters that they could refuse to accept abolitionist pamphlets addressed to the South. President Jackson meanwhile encouraged Southern newspapers to publish the names of anyone who requested abolitionist tracts—a move that ensured that no one requested the pamphlets. When Congress convened in December, he recommended passage of a law allowing the postmaster general to censor the mails to stop "incendiary publications." The lawmakers rejected his suggestion and instead reaffirmed federal responsibility to deliver all of the mails, but Southern postmasters continued to withhold antislavery publications. Starting with Kendall, postmasters general for years conveniently overlooked Southerners' dismissal of federal law.

Antislavery advocates then shifted their offensive to petitions to Congress. The first amendment guaranteed for citizens the right to petition the government for "redress of grievances." A member of Congress would submit a petition to either the House or the Senate; the clerk of the House or the secretary of the Senate would read the petition to the body and enter the request in its official records before sending it to a committee. In late 1835, abolitionists began flooding Congress with thousands of petitions asking for slavery's elimination in the District of Columbia. Many petitions included long preambles denouncing slavery as a sin and slaveholders as tyrants. Insulted Southerners insisted that Congress refuse to accept antislavery petitions, but Northern representatives defended the right to petition as a form of free speech, even if they had no desire to carry out abolitionists' request. Administration supporters moved to reassure Southerners on Van Buren's fidelity to slavery. The Senate quietly accepted Pennsylvanian James Buchanan's suggestion to accept the petitions but then immediately "table" them—that is, postpone considering them until a later time—with an understanding that the Senate would never actually take them up. Most petitions went to the House, and after an extensive debate, Northern Democrats provided the necessary votes on May 26, 1836, to approve what became known as the "Gag Rule," a rule implementing the Senate's practice of accepting all petitions but immediately tabling antislavery requests without reading the petition.

Still another potential sectional obstacle emerged when Texas sought to join the Union. After Mexico gained independence from Spain in 1821, the new republic's leaders invited American Southerners to help develop its sparsely populated state of Texas. Mexico's 1824 constitution already allowed its states a great degree of self-control, and to attract more settlers, officials exempted Americans from paying customs duties and ignored the requirement that they convert to Catholicism. Mexican officials soon regretted these policies. By 1835,

Figure 9.2 "Abolition Frowned Down." In this satirical cartoon, two slaves watch as South Carolina representative Waddy Thompson repels John Quincy Adams' challenge to the "Gag Rule" with the statement, "Sir, the South loses rest whenever she suffers this subject to be discussed here: it must be indignantly frowned down." Adams concludes, "I cannot stand Thomson's [*sic*] frown." Two slaves comment in a parody of slave dialect: "Hi! Sambo! de dern Babolishn [Abolition] is down flat!" "Ah, Sal, Massa de Boy! he know how to scare 'em." Lithograph by Henry Dacre and Henry R. Robinson (1839). Courtesy Prints & Photographs Division, Library of Congress, LC-USZ62-9916.

the number of Americans in Texas had grown to thirty thousand—twice the number of Hispanic *tejano* residents—along with about five thousand slaves. The flood of Americans caused Mexican officials to doubt the region's loyalty. Following a coup in 1830, President Anastasio Bustamante prohibited further American immigration, abolished slavery, and ordered Texans to obey Mexican laws. Three years later, General Antonio López de Santa Anna established himself as a dictator, and in October 1835 he personally led six thousand troops into Texas to enforce his government's authority. Texans declared their independence on March 2, 1836. Despite the slaughter of nearly two hundred Americans at the Alamo near San Antonio, and of another three hundred at the town of Goliad, General Sam Houston's army routed a portion of the Mexican army and captured Santa Anna at San Jacinto on April 21. As a condition for his release, the humiliated dictator had to sign the Treaty of Velasco recognizing Texas as an independent republic.

Once free from Mexican authority, Texans began laying plans to apply for admission to the United States. President Jackson had long wanted to acquire Texas. Like Thomas Jefferson, he considered the region part of the Louisiana Purchase, and he thought John Quincy Adams had needlessly bargained the region away in the 1819 treaty with Spain. Soon after he became president, Jackson sent Colonel Anthony Butler to try to buy Texas from Mexico. Now, though, President Jackson hesitated to endorse annexation. He had proclaimed the United States neutral during the Texas Revolution, but Butler's bungling and obnoxious diplomacy and President Jackson's decision to send an army into northern Texas—officially to protect Louisiana from Native raids—convinced Mexican authorities that President Jackson had instigated the rebellion. Mexico's congress repudiated the Velasco Treaty, meaning that annexation would probably result in war. Southerners called for the state's immediate annexation, but abolitionists' recent activities had heightened sectional tensions to the point that the admission of a large new slave state under suspicious circumstances would make slavery an issue in the presidential election. Concerned about Van Buren's liabilities in the South, President Jackson determined it best to delay Texas' annexation. Throughout the campaign, he made no public statement to encourage the state's admission.

Keeping Texas out of the political arena helped the administration dampen sectional tensions in the election. White's campaign continued to insist that Southerners could trust no Northerner to stand against the abolitionists, but nationally the opposition mainly condemned President Jackson's attempt to "dictate" Van Buren's election. Whigs likewise ridiculed the Democrats' emphasis on party loyalty, deriding administration men as office-hungry "spoilsmen" who now worshipped "at the mere shrine of party idolatry." Democrats meanwhile released a statement in July that mentioned Van Buren only once and stressed instead President Jackson's accomplishments and the party's commitment to the rule of the people. Campaign activities brought out enough votes for Van Buren to win the election, but the results proved closer than Democrats expected. Opposing candidates attracted 200,000 more votes than Clay had won in 1832; Webster won only his home state, but Harrison carried seven Northern states, while White carried Tennessee and Georgia and won forty-nine percent of the South's popular votes. South Carolina's legislature again gave the state's electoral votes to a protest candidate—this time North Carolina senator Willie P. Mangum—and the refusal of Virginia's Democratic electors to vote for Johnson denied him an electoral college majority, forcing the Senate to elect him to the office the following January. Still, Van Buren won fifty-one percent of the votes and carried fifteen states—including seven of the eleven slave states—for a clear victory.

With Van Buren's election secured, and with Democratic majorities in both chambers of the upcoming Congress, President Jackson prepared to retire, confident the Union would remain in secure hands. As his term wound to a close, Democrats in the Senate gave him personal vindication when they voted in January 1837 to "expunge" the censure passed during the Bank War: The secretary of the Senate drew a black box around the censure resolution in the official journal, with a note that the Senate now rejected it. Financial conditions still worried the president, as currency expansion and inflation persisted. Conservative Democrats joined with Whigs to pass a bill to rescind the Specie Circular, but in his last official act, President Jackson killed the act with a pocket veto. Otherwise, he had no choice but to leave the growing financial conundrum to his chosen successor.

"Martin Van Ruin"

President Martin Van Buren pledged that his administration would continue his illustrious predecessor's policies. The new president anticipated facing some serious issues, but his inaugural address declared his expectation that he would serve "a great, happy, and flourishing people." Shortly after he entered office, though, the economic boom that had persisted through most of Jackson's presidency finally imploded. In February 1837, cotton prices suddenly dropped. In mid-March, two weeks after Van Buren's inauguration, word reached Washington that Hermann, Briggs, and Company, one of New Orleans' largest cotton brokerage firms, had gone bankrupt. The company owed a substantial sum to a major New York banking firm, which in turn was forced out of business. Several other cotton brokers and merchant companies likewise had to close, including abolitionist Arthur Tappan's mercantile house, and fears of further collapses incited runs on the city's banks—note holders rushed to exchange their paper money for gold or silver before a bank ran out of the precious metals. On May 9 alone, nervous New Yorkers withdrew $652,000. The next day, the city's bankers agreed to suspend paying gold and silver until further notice. By the end of the month, all but six of the Union's nearly eight hundred state banks had also suspended gold and silver payments, marking the onset of the "Panic of 1837."

The Panic of 1837 set off a deeper economic downturn than the recession that Nicholas Biddle had induced three years before. This time, the lack of reliable paper money produced widespread hoarding of gold and silver. Commodity prices and land values plummeted, and industries dismissed thousands of workers. The Union's fiscal conditions had done much to bring on the collapse. Without the Bank of the United States' restrictions, several state banks had issued more notes than their gold and silver reserves could reasonably support. Jackson's "Specie Circular" had reduced the holdings of eastern banks as speculators withdrew gold and silver to pay for public lands in the west, and the Distribution Act weakened New York banks' reserves because the federal government moved its surplus from east to west for delivery to the states. Decisions made across the Atlantic actually set off the Panic of 1837. Experiencing its own reduction in gold and silver reserves, the Bank of England in late 1836 raised the interest rates it charged on firms that imported American cotton, which drove down the prices for the Union's principal export. The bank also called in its loans on companies involved in the American trade, forcing British firms to demand payments from American traders and driving many American firms out of business. A setback would have occurred regardless of President Jackson's policies or the amount of money that state banks issued. Still, the Union's financial circumstances had created an unstable environment that made the financial panic far worse than it might have been.

Politicians nevertheless wasted no time blaming the Panic of 1837 on their opponents. Democrats charged that the banks had acted irresponsibly: They had recklessly expanded their paper money issuances and now arrogantly refused to honor their obligation and redeem their notes. Recent memories of the Bank War gave the Whigs the stronger case: In destroying the Bank of the United States, President Jackson had eliminated the institution that provided the Union with a sound and stable currency. His "experiment" with the deposit banks then encouraged the state banks' overextensions, which he undermined with the Specie Circular and its consequent drain on the banks' specie reserves. Most Whigs avoided promoting specific remedies, and the focus on blaming Democrats for the economy's ills helped them unite as a coherent party. Building on the appeal first developed during the Bank War, Whigs portrayed themselves as the party of responsible leaders who had stood against President Jackson's abuse of executive authority and the greedy Democratic "spoilsmen." Across the Union, Whigs promised to return the government to "the people" and enact whatever measures necessary to restore prosperity. Even Southerners who had supported Hugh Lawson White in 1836 as President Jackson's true heir now openly proclaimed themselves "Whigs," and they pledged to support "statesmen" who could deliver the Union from the selfish politicians who had wrecked the economy.

President Van Buren's formal response to the Panic of 1837 drew a clearer distinction between the parties. He first had to address some problems presented to the administration by the banks' suspensions of gold and silver payments. The Deposit Act prohibited the federal government from keeping its funds in banks that had suspended gold and silver payments. Officials thus had nowhere to deposit government receipts from tariff collections and public land sales. Many merchants meanwhile lacked the funds to pay the tariff when they arrived in American ports, and with revenues reduced, payment of government expenses dramatically reduced the government's reserves after three distributions of its once-huge surplus. Five days after New York's banks suspended payments in gold and silver, President Van Buren issued a call for Congress to convene early in a special session. When the session opened on September 4, he recommended postponing the final installment of the distribution's surplus, allowing merchants to defer tariff payments, and a temporary issue of $10 million in Treasury notes—paper money backed by the federal reserves—so the government could pay its expenses. He made it clear that he opposed establishing a new national bank because it would "disregard the popular will." However, he also refused to recommend a plan to relieve the public distress, since "such measures are not within the constitutional provinces of the General Government." Instead, his messages focused on creating an Independent Treasury, a system that, as Democratic supporters claimed, would "divorce" the federal government from the Union's banks.

The Independent Treasury became the central issue of Van Buren's presidency. If enacted, the plan would no longer require the federal government to deposit its money in banks; instead, it would hold gold and silver in vaults in several cities across the Union. Hard-money "Locofoco" Democrats called for the elimination of all banks, but they supported the idea of an Independent Treasury because the system would deprive the banks of capital and limit their paper money issuances. Despite its association with radicals, though, President Van Buren presented the Independent Treasury as a moderate proposal. One of the president's closest lieutenants, Silas Wright, put forth the president's plan in the Senate. Wright's bill would have allowed the Treasury to accept the notes of gold-and-silver-paying banks. The Treasury secretary would then frequently present the notes to the banks for redemption, supplying the check on the state banks' paper money issuances that "Biddle's Bank" had once provided. Through this approach, the Independent Treasury could provide a constitutional means for holding the Union's funds while promoting a stable currency: It would permit the continued existence of the state banks to satisfy his party's conservatives, but in deference to Locofocos it would separate the government's daily operations from private banking while effectively limiting the banks' paper money issuances. Politically, the Independent Treasury would allow Democrats to unite behind a clear alternative to a powerful, dangerous institution like a national bank, which President Van Buren expected Whigs to adopt as their defining issue.

Congress easily approved the president's call to postpone distribution and tariff payments and to issue Treasury notes. In the Senate, President Van Buren's onetime rival, John C. Calhoun, came out in favor of the Independent Treasury, signaling his return to the Democratic Party. But Calhoun based his support on his preference for a hard-money currency, so he proposed an amendment to Wright's bill that would limit the Treasury to receiving and paying out only gold and silver. Calhoun's "Specie Clause" would eliminate the Treasury's regulatory function over state banks, and it made Van Buren's proposal appear more radical than the president had intended. Locofocos backed the Specie Clause, but conservative Democrats balked at what now appeared to be a scheme to promote an exclusively hard-money economy. The Senate approved Wright's bill with Calhoun's amendment attached, but conservative Democrats joined with Whigs to defeat it in the House. Whigs meanwhile downplayed desires for a new national bank. Instead, they concentrated on defending state banks against the administration's supposed war against paper money. Rather than presenting voters a choice between a Bank of the United States and an Independent Treasury, as President Van Buren had hoped, "hard money" versus the "credit system" became the main issue dividing Democrats and Whigs.

Several Conservatives eventually abandoned the Democrats. Congress again failed to approve the Independent Treasury in its regular session, and President Van Buren's party suffered significant losses in state elections held in late 1837 through 1838. By mid-1838, though, Democratic fortunes looked more promising as the economy started to improve. The Bank of England had relaxed its credit on American trade earlier that year. Demand for cotton and other American commodities picked up; states spent much of their shares of the federal surplus on internal improvement projects, and with gold and silver available, English investors purchased most of the bonds that states issued to cover the projects' remaining costs. With their reserves recovering, New York banks resumed gold and silver payments in May. Later that month, Congress finally overturned the Specie Circular, with President Van Buren quietly giving his approval. In August, Biddle's Bank of the United States of Pennsylvania joined most other banks in renewing gold and silver payments, and the crisis appeared over. By September, prices and property values were again rising, and Democrats won back six state legislatures in elections held in late 1838 and 1839.

The respite proved short-lived. Facing another drain on its gold and silver, the Bank of England in May 1839 raised interest rates to new highs. The increase coincided with a booming cotton harvest the previous fall and a decline in demand from British manufacturers, producing another sharp drop in cotton prices. Biddle's bank had speculated heavily in the fiber and had also underwritten several bond issues for western states, and the drain on its gold and silver reserves forced it again to suspend payments in October. The bank's troubles produced another general suspension across the Union, marking the beginning of the Panic of 1839. This time, the collapse set off a currency contraction even more serious than two years before, and the economy entered a depression that lasted for several years. As money disappeared, prices and property values again plummeted while unemployment in the cities shot up. Public land sales all but stopped. Internal improvement construction in the states also came to a halt, with eight states, along with the Florida Territory, defaulting on their bond payments. Biddle's bank itself went out of business in 1841. State banks did not resume gold and silver payments until 1842, and the economy showed few signs of recovery until mid-1843.

Figure 9.3 "Specie Claws." A Whig cartoon depicting an unemployed worker and his family suffering the consequences of Democratic financial policies. Lithograph by Henry Dacre and Henry R. Robinson (1838 or 1839). Courtesy Prints & Photographs Division, Library of Congress, LC-USZ62-36585.

Well-wishers encouraged President Van Buren to provoke a war, arguing that a conflict would unite the public behind him and distract voters from their economic troubles. Two incidents presented him with opportunities to inflame public passions against the Union's oldest foe. In western New York, several Americans volunteered to assist a Canadian rebellion against British authority. A joint American-Canadian force captured Navy Island in the Niagara River in December 1837, and seven British ships brought a force of fifty men across the river to seize and burn the *Caroline*, a private steamship that delivered supplies to the island. Fourteen months later, Governor John Fairfield of Maine sent two hundred men to expel British loggers from the Aroostook Valley, which lay in a twelve-thousand-square-mile area that Maine and Britain's New Brunswick colony both claimed because the 1783 Treaty of Paris left the border separating the regions unclear. The governor of New Brunswick, in turn, threatened to retaliate against Fairfield's action with force.

President Van Buren refused to exploit either conflict. Instead, he presented a strong response that kept the incidents from escalating into war. Regarding the *Caroline* Affair, he lodged a formal protest with Britain but also issued a proclamation upholding American neutrality in the Canadian rebellion. Likewise, he asked Congress for more authority to enforce the Union's neutrality laws, which forbade American citizens from participating in foreign rebellions, and he sent General Winfield Scott to Buffalo to oversee the controversy, with orders to maintain peace with honor. In the "Aroostook War," President Van Buren pledged to defend Maine but refused publicly to approve Fairfield's occupation of the disputed territory. Privately, the president chastised the governor for failing to notify New Brunswick officials before ordering his excursion. British authorities recognized President Van Buren's peaceful intentions. After British officials suppressed the Canadian uprising in late 1838, Queen Victoria's government backed down from its protests against the Americans' actions. Scott's skillful negotiations meanwhile persuaded the Americans to abandon Navy Island. President Van Buren then sent Scott to Maine, where he convinced the governors of Maine and New Brunswick to accept joint responsibility for the contested territory until the British and American governments could resolve the border dispute.

President Van Buren also worked to contain the potential revival sectional disputes. Abolitionists continued to flood Congress with petitions, and John Quincy Adams used a series of parliamentary maneuvers to try to give the petitions a hearing in the House. Adams' moves provoked several raucous arguments, but Van Buren's Northern Democratic allies remained firm and approved the "Gag Rule" in every session. Adams' irritations raised concerns that a more substantive issue might provoke a confrontation over slavery. Thus, when in August 1837 Texas representative Memucan Hunt formally requested the "Lone Star Republic" be annexed by the United States, President Van Buren rejected the proposal, arguing that the Constitution did not clearly authorize the annexation of a sovereign state. His decision disappointed Southerners, but he balanced his sectional support with his decision to intervene on slaveholders' behalf in the *Amistad* case. The Coast Guard had seized the merchant vessel *Amistad* in August 1835 after forty-nine Africans took control of it and tried to sail it to Africa. In January 1840, a federal district judge ruled that the thirty-six surviving Africans had been illegally enslaved and should be freed, but President Van Buren urged the district attorney who prosecuted the case to appeal to the Supreme Court. The justices' final decision to uphold the district court's ruling came out in March 1841—too late to affect the presidential election—but the president's position helped reassure slaveowners of his commitment to defend their human property rights.

Van Buren's reliance on Southern support and the Whigs' apparent indifference to slavery contributed to moderate abolitionists' decision to create the Liberty Party and nominate former Alabama planter James G. Birney as a presidential candidate dedicated to ending slavery. Nevertheless, the economic collapse overshadowed slavery and all other concerns in the contest. Whigs sensed they would be victorious as long as they handled their campaign carefully. An opposition congressional caucus met in May 1838 and issued the call for a Whig national convention to meet in December 1839. By the time the delegates gathered in Harrisburg, Pennsylvania, Henry Clay remained the Whigs' front-runner and as a slaveowner stood as Southern Whigs' favorite. Still, several party leaders feared that Clay's association with "Biddle's Bank" would drive away potential votes. William Harrison, the strongest Whig candidate four years earlier, had kept his prospects alive, while Thurlow Weed and William Seward promoted Winfield Scott as a younger version of Harrison—a popular military hero with little political baggage. At the convention, Weed and Seward threw their support behind Harrison after Harrison backers convinced Southerners that they could not trust Scott to defend slavery. Four Southern states weakened Clay's strength when they held true to their "antiparty" convictions and refused to send delegations, and the convention nominated Harrison on the third ballot. After five Clay supporters turned down the vice presidential nomination, the delegates settled on former Virginia senator John Tyler, a personal friend of Clay who reportedly wept when the convention rejected the Kentuckian.

Though disappointed, Clay dutifully endorsed Harrison's nomination. Under the Whig banner, the Democrats' opponents entered the presidential contest more unified nationally than ever before. Whigs adopted the organization and tactics of their opponents and relied heavily on popular activities to bring out the vote. Democrats unwittingly provided a central theme for the Whig campaign. The *Baltimore Republican* dismissed Harrison as an old and undistinguished figure who would be content with "a barrel of hard cider" and "a pension of two thousand a year," and to "sit the remainder of his days in his log cabin . . . and study moral philosophy." Whigs seized on the charge to portray Harrison as a "man of the people," a humble citizen born in a log cabin in contrast with the condescending and elitist politicians who led Democrats. The candidate actually had been born in the Virginia plantation home of his father, a signer of the Declaration of Independence. Still, Whigs throughout the Union used log cabins as campaign headquarters and portrayed Harrison as a humble man who preferred a private life but would return to public service if his country needed him. Torchlight parades, with marchers singing catchy songs like "Tippecanoe and Tyler, Too!" and "Little Van Is a Used-Up Man," attracted potential voters to campaign activities. Distributing broadsides, ribbons, and hard cider and "Old Cabin Whiskey" in bottles shaped like log cabins—produced by Philadelphia distiller E.G. Booz—kept up the enthusiasm, while crowds pushed huge leather balls covered with anti-Democratic slogans to remind Whigs to "keep the ball rolling" until they won the election.

Much of the "Log Cabin" campaign concentrated on mocking President Van Buren as a pampered elitist. Ironically, the president actually had been born in a log cabin, but a festive and high-toned atmosphere at Van Buren's White House opened the incumbent to accusations that he was actually a "democrat by profession and an aristocrat in principle." The opposition claimed that while the country suffered, the Democratic Party's unprincipled officeholders lived in ease off the public treasury. Whigs presented the president himself as the worst offender, wasting thousands on refurnishing the White House while dining on French meals served on gold plates and dressing in foppish outfits to admire himself before gold-framed mirrors. Amid the hoopla, Whigs portrayed Harrison as a clear alternative to "monarchy" and economic hardship. Like President Jackson, "Martin Van Ruin" abused executive power while doing nothing to help the suffering people, they charged, and Harrison's election would return the government to "the people" and restore the Union's prosperity. The candidate himself broke precedent and made twenty-three public appearances, where he promised to serve only one term and to veto only clearly unconstitutional laws. While admitting that he favored paper money, Harrison denied charges that he was a "Bank Man," though he promised to approve a law chartering a new Bank of the United States if the people's representatives in Congress approved it.

Democrats loyally lined up behind President Van Buren. A national convention dutifully nominated the incumbent for another term in May 1840. Southern discontent with Richard Johnson's black mistress and unconventional family prevented his re-nomination, though in most states Democrats promoted Johnson as if he were the official vice presidential nominee. To counter the Whigs' ambiguity on specific issues, the convention approved a party platform—a statement of principles and policies that the party promised to carry out—that opposed federal activism in the economy or on antislavery proposals while endorsing the government's separation from banks. President Van Buren staked his hopes on the Independent Treasury, which Congress finally passed in July 1840 after Democratic victories during the economy's brief recovery provided the necessary votes. Even though the Treasury included Calhoun's "Specie Clause," the president proclaimed the law a "second Declaration of Independence" and expected the Treasury's "divorce" from the banks to turn the economy around. Campaign activities then stressed the administration's continuity with Jackson's presidency and, while trying to match their opponents' popular enthusiasm, Democrats criticized the hysteria of the "log cabin campaign" for distracting the people from the real issues at hand. Deriding the sixty-seven-year-old Harrison as "Old Granny," Democrats ridiculed the Whig nominee's supposed military accomplishments and labeled him "General Mum" for his party's silence on specific issues. Likewise, they trumpeted their own party's standing as the people's defender against wealthy and powerful "aristocrats" whose main goal remained the restoration of the Bank of the United States.

The economic slide, though, blunted the Democrats' appeal. Whigs assured voters that Harrison's election alone would initiate recovery, but President Van Buren's backers had no answer for the depression. The Democratic platform contained no reference to the hard times, while economic conditions continued to decline despite the Independent Treasury's passage. Campaign activities brought out 364,000 more votes than President Van Buren had won in 1836, and eighty percent of eligible voters cast ballots—a higher turnout than in any previous presidential contest. Yet Whigs attracted thousands of new voters to the polls in recent state elections, and the Log Cabin campaign succeeded in getting them to turn out for the presidential contest. The Liberty Party's hastily organized campaign proved no factor in the outcome, as the party gained only seven thousand votes out of a total of almost two and a half million. Harrison won fifty-three percent of the popular vote and carried nineteen various states, for 234 electoral votes. Van Buren carried seven states—including South Carolina—for sixty electoral votes. Whigs also enjoyed success at the state level, recapturing the legislatures lost during the brief recovery in 1838 and 1839. When the next Congress convened, for the first time Whigs would hold a majority in both chambers, winning a 142–99 advantage in the House and twenty-nine of the fifty-two seats in the Senate.

The election appeared to bring the Age of Jackson to an end. Reflecting on the effectiveness of the "Log Cabin" campaign, Democratic leaders agreed with the *Democratic Review*'s lament that "We have taught them how to conquer us." Still, President Jackson's followers remained confident that the "sober second thought of the people" would soon restore them to power. Whigs meanwhile eagerly awaited their opportunity to undo the damage the Jacksonians had done.

Suggested Readings

Belohlavek, John M. *Let the Eagle Soar: The Foreign Policy of Andrew Jackson* (Lincoln, NE, 1985).
Cole, Donald B. *The Presidency of Andrew Jackson* (Lawrence, KS, 1993).

Ellis, Richard J. *The Union at Risk: Jacksonian Democracy, States' Rights and the Nullification Crisis* (New York, 1987).

Feller, Daniel. *The Jacksonian Promise: America, 1815–1840* (Baltimore, 1995).

Grimsted, David. *American Mobbing, 1828–1861: Toward Civil War* (New York, 1998).

Howe, Daniel Walker. *What Hath God Wrought: The Transformation of America, 1815–1846* (New York, 2007).

Jones, Howard. *Mutiny on the* Amistad: *The Saga of a Slave Revolt and its Impact on American Abolition, Law, and Diplomacy* (New York, 1987).

Marszalek, John F. *The Petticoat Affair: Manners, Mutiny, and Sex in Andrew Jackson's White House* (New York, 1997).

Miller, William Lee. *Arguing about Slavery: John Quincy Adams and the Great Battle in the United States Congress* (New York, 1998).

Pessen, Edward. *Jacksonian America: Society, Personality, and Politics* (Urbana, IL, 1985).

Remini, Robert V. *Andrew Jackson and the Bank War* (New York, 1967).

Schlesinger, Arthur M. Jr. *The Age of Jackson* (Boston, 1945).

Sellers, Charles. *The Market Revolution: Jacksonian America, 1815–1846* (New York, 1992).

Stevens, Kenneth R. *Border Diplomacy: The Caroline and McLeod Affairs in Anglo-American Canadian Relations, 1837–1842* (Tuscaloosa, AL, 1989).

Temin, Peter. *The Jacksonian Economy* (New York, 1969).

Van Deusen, Glyndon G. *The Jacksonian Era, 1828–1848* (New York, 1959).

Watson, Harry L. *Liberty and Power: The Politics of Jacksonian America* (New York, 1990).

Wilentz, Sean. *The Rise of American Democracy: From Jefferson to Lincoln* (New York, 2005).

Wilson, Major L. *The Presidency of Martin Van Buren* (Lawrence, KS, 1984).

X

THE UNION AT A CROSSROADS

The 1840 election not only brought Andrew Jackson's opponents into power, but it also established the two-party competition that would dominate the Union's politics for the next fifteen years. In what historians refer to as the Second Party System, Democrats contended against Whigs in a series of close elections fought along the same lines and following the same pattern on which they had battled in 1840. New issues would emerge, but the parties absorbed them into their established conflict. Throughout, they presented distinctly different visions for the Union's future, and circumstances eventually allowed the Democratic vision to prevail. In the process, Whig and Democratic leaders institutionalized a mass two-party system as a permanent feature of American politics, even as they tried to sidestep the Union's most divisive issue.

The "Money Power" vs. the "Spoilsmen"

The Whig and Democratic battles presented the Union's first competition between two organized parties with mass followings in a national, democratic electorate. To be sure, Democratic-Republicans challenged and overthrew the Federalists in a series of hard-fought elections in several states during the 1790s, and Democratic-Republicans especially had organized to coordinate their campaigns and to get voters to show up at the polls. In the Second Party System, though, parties developed to fit the more democratic political culture that had emerged in the second quarter of the nineteenth century. Federalist and Republican leaders, for instance, mainly came from the social elite, and as in the colonial era they considered public service a duty associated with their status. Whig and Democratic officeholders also usually came from society's wealthiest ranks, but party leaders more often rose to wealth from middling or poor status. Many operatives, in fact, acted as "professional" politicians, devoting their lives to their party—partly from principle, but also to further their own fortunes through gaining office or taking advantage of opportunities. Democrats and Whigs likewise organized more extensively than the earlier parties. Politicians regularly scheduled conventions to unite the party behind a candidate and to coordinate its message for a campaign. Activists established committees at the local and state levels as well as the national level to schedule party activities and to make sure voters showed up at the polls.

The Federalists and Republicans of the 1790s had also held on to the traditional view of parties as dangerous "factions"—that is, groups of politicians joined together to promote their selfish interests against the public welfare. They reluctantly accepted party allegiance as a temporary expedience because they believed their opponents threatened to take control of the federal government, subvert the citizens' liberties, and make the Union subservient to a foreign power. Once the Federalists no longer seemed a serious threat, most Republicans, like President James Monroe, saw little need for further party organization. The Whigs of the 1840s tended to hold on longer to the previous generation's "antiparty" sentiments, but like Democrats they eventually accepted political parties as permanent institutions that benefited the Union. Since freedom's enemies persistently threatened the republic, the danger that their rivals might slip into power helped keep the "true" party—whether Democratic or Whig—united and committed to republican principles. Party loyalty, in fact, became a way for citizens to demonstrate their virtue: Even when a person disagreed with his party, a patriot put aside his own selfish opinion for the sake of party unity and the good of the Union.

On one level, Democrats and Whigs continued to fight the ideological war that developed during Andrew Jackson's administrations. Relying heavily on republican rhetoric, spokesmen for both parties claimed to represent "the people" against the foes who wanted to take away their freedom. For Democrats, the "rich and powerful" remained the enemy—not those who had gained their fortunes honestly through hard work, but the financial and propertied elite who according to Democrats manipulated institutions like banks to steal from common citizens the fruits of their labor. Like the old Federalists, this "Money Power" rejected the premise that the people could govern themselves; instead, they thought their wealth gave them the right to rule as a European-style aristocracy. Whigs meanwhile pointed to the Democratic Party itself as the biggest threat to the people's liberty. In the Whig view, ambitious and scheming political hacks had attached themselves to President Jackson mainly so they could get into power, either by riding the general's popularity to win elections or by relying on the "spoils system" to secure appointments to government offices. In either case, the "spoilsmen" flattered and deceived voters to keep their positions while plundering the public treasury and ruling the republic according to their own whims rather than the people's will.

Notwithstanding the oratorical excesses and conspiratorial overtones, the parties' rhetoric reflected a serious disagreement about the nature and role of government in a republic. Whigs condemned President Jackson's activism because they insisted that Congress, not the president, should act as the federal government's leading branch. The House of Representatives embodied the collective will of the people, and the Senate provided a popularly based method of refining the people's will. As the people's representatives, Congress should decide national policy and make the laws. Whigs also expected public officials to act as "statesmen": independent, conscientious, and intelligent public servants who based their decisions on the public welfare rather than on local or petty interests. The president's role, in contrast, was to act as the Union's "chief executive," whose main responsibility was to enforce the laws passed by the national legislature. Whigs recognized that the Constitution authorized the president to veto acts of Congress, but they contended that the executive should limit his use of this power to occasions on which lawmakers exceeded the powers that the Constitution had granted to them. In no case, though, should the president use the veto to shape policy, for then the executive would be exerting his own will over that of the people. To issue as many vetoes as had President Jackson—he vetoed twelve acts of Congress during his eight years in office, while his predecessors had vetoed only ten in the previous thirty years—represented the acts of a tyrant.

Democrats, in contrast, insisted on the need for a strong chief executive, to ensure that the government remained committed to serving the public. In the Democratic view, the president stood as the only official in Washington chosen in a national election; House members represented the constituents in their districts, while Senators upheld the interests of their states, but the president represented the collective will of all the people of the United States. As the people's direct representative, the president had the responsibility to ensure that the lawmakers served the Union. In a legislative body like Congress, senators and representatives faced the constant temptation to bargain away the public interest as they intrigued with each other to pass laws for their own benefit. The lawmaking process likewise inevitably invited corruption, for the "Money Power" could use its wealth and influence to buy off members to secure legislation granting special privileges and favors to the rich and powerful. The founders, Democrats concluded, wisely gave the president the veto power, not just to protect the Constitution, but to prevent the government from acting only in the interests of an influential few. Even after President Jackson's retirement, Democrats viewed the president as more than the lawmakers' servant. As the hero himself explained, he was "independent" of Congress and stood as the representatives' "coequal" as a servant of the people.

Beyond their divergence over the executive's role, Whigs and Democrats presented dramatically different understandings about the type of society and economy the federal government should promote. Whigs particularly encouraged the changes that the expanding economy and the early stages of industrialization brought to the Union. Rejecting the notion that industrialization would produce class conflict, Whigs contended that the Union's various sections and interests should cooperate to transform the United States into an economic power. Development would end the Union's dependence on foreign trade and eventually secure American economic independence. Expanding national wealth would likewise improve the condition of all Americans, raising the standard of living and encouraging citizens to live the best possible lives. Because a person's efforts should determine his condition, Whigs believed, the opportunity for farmers, planters, and laborers to work their way up to financial security and social respectability would inspire them to gain an education and to live the morally responsible lives necessary for a successful republic. Evangelicals among Whigs believed that economic development could bring on the millennium by creating a virtual heaven on earth to which Christ could return. Secular Whigs likewise remained optimistic that furthering industry and trade could create a good life for all Americans by freeing them from isolation, ignorance, and poverty.

Confident in the promises that development offered, Whigs contended that government could play an important role in bringing about economic transformation. Federal officials could use their resources to promote the economy's growth, while Congress would oversee the changes to make sure they benefited all Americans. Henry Clay's "American System" presented the most visible expression of how the government could act as a positive and unifying force. As Clay proposed, protective tariffs would promote industrial development; the Bank of the United States could establish a national currency, ease trade across the Union, and offer the capital needed for investment; and federally funded internal improvements would provide the facilities to enhance national communication and internal trade. Through these policies, the government could harmonize the Union's various sections so that their strengths could complement each other as the nation moved toward self-sufficiency. Southern planters would ship their cotton and other raw materials to factories and workshops in the Northeast rather than to Britain, while Western farmers would profit from the "home market" for their goods that protective tariffs would expand, providing food both for factory workers and for the slaves on Southern plantations.

Whigs encouraged government activism at the state level as well. State bank charters received legislative support more often from Whigs than from Democrats. After the Panics of 1837 and 1839, Whigs defended from legislative action banks that had suspended gold and silver payments. Local transportation needs profoundly influenced legislators' votes on internal improvements, so Democrats often supported projects that benefited their constituents. Overall, though, Whigs proved more likely to support transportation systems within their states. The assumption that state governments should promote the health, welfare, and morals of the people meanwhile encouraged Whigs to promote legislation for what many called "parental" care for the people, including the establishment of such institutions as public schools, asylums for the disabled, and penitentiaries. Notwithstanding their support for state activism, Whigs tended to express stronger confidence in federal authority. More often than their opponents,

Whigs openly concluded that the central government stood as the Union's final authority. Although they agreed that the states had primary responsibility for local concerns, Whigs usually supported federal authority in conflicts between state and central authority.

Democrats presented a sharply different understanding of society and government. Most importantly, they held on to the belief that a citizen's freedom rested on his personal economic independence. Identifying "the people" as the Union's farmers, planters, and artisans, Democrats insisted that the producing classes should create the wealth they needed to support themselves. In a democracy, small farmers and craftsmen should make up the bulk of the population, and voters should insist that politicians carry out the majority's will. Most Democrats agreed with President Jackson's defense of the Union's permanence, but they placed greater faith in local and state governments because they stood closer to the people. At all levels, though, Democrats expected politicians to follow the people's direction, rather than having citizens subserviently defer to their public servants. Voters and state legislators, in fact, had a duty to present direct instructions to representatives or senators whose personal views might contradict the majority's will. Still, Democrats expected government to keep its activities limited. Especially at the federal level, they considered protecting citizens' property and equal rights and enforcing the law against criminals to be the government's chief responsibility. Otherwise, authorities should remain out of citizens' lives to let them live freely and pursue happiness in the way they saw fit.

Democrats thus looked skeptically at the economic developments that excited their opponents. Commercial and manufacturing expansion would not improve all Americans' lives, Democrats maintained. Instead, economic transformation would unleash forces that would undermine democratic government. Industrialization would create a large class of permanent wage earners under the control of a small group of factory owners whose wealth gave them the pretensions of an aristocracy. Expanding trade meanwhile would make farmers less self-sufficient and more dependent on distant, unpredictable markets and on a bewildering financial system based on credit, banks, and paper money. Individuals had every right to pursue their fortunes through commerce and industry if they desired, and men who became wealthy through hard work and honest effort deserved the public's respect. But the poor man who remained a subsistence farmer and supplemented his family's diet through hunting and fishing had the same rights and deserved the same respect as the rich, and government had a duty to protect these citizens from the "Money Power's" schemes. Under no circumstances should the government act to promote economic development, for in doing so it only granted special favors to the rich and powerful and threatened the democratic freedoms that government had a responsibility to preserve.

Based on this outlook, Democrats contended that the government should use its power with the approach that later generations would refer to as *laissez-faire*: Public officials should enforce the law, stay out of economic affairs, and act only when the people faced a threat to their liberty. If left to themselves, Democrats assumed, the people's natural inclinations would keep agriculture at the economy's center, and farmers would remain the republic's predominant citizens. The presidential veto presented an important tool to check the "Money Power's" schemes, and Democratic policies would ensure that the laws treated all citizens as equals. At the state level, radical and conservative Democrats divided over whether to encourage or discourage local banks, although they agreed that local governments could construct roads and canals when a state constitution authorized them. At the federal level, though, Democrats united to oppose chartering a new Bank of the United States while championing the Independent Treasury's "divorce" of federal funds from the banking system. Most Democrats likewise rejected high tariffs, arguing that protecting American manufacturers reflected government favoritism and forced humble citizens to pay higher prices. Likewise, federal construction of a massive internal improvement network benefited only those who lived along transportation routes—and the companies that secured the contracts to complete the projects.

Party rhetoric provided points around which Whigs and Democrats could unite. Some politicians cynically parroted the party line to further their careers, while others held these views sincerely. Most likely, party principles represented the majority of their supporters' beliefs. Still, both parties acted as broad coalitions of voters who had to cooperate with each other in order to win elections. As a consequence, they included factions with interests that contradicted some of the party's stated ideals. Democrats in the crucial state of Pennsylvania, for instance, knew that outright opposition to protective tariffs would seriously damage their prospects with the state's numerous manufacturers and workers. In the underdeveloped states north and west of the Ohio River, the party favored federal assistance to help construct transportation routes. The State Rights Southerners who broke with President Jackson during the Nullification Crisis joined the Whigs to condemn Old Hickory's "executive tyranny," even though they had little sympathy for the government activism central to Whigs with National Republican roots. Many voters chose their party allegiance because of long-standing local disputes that had little to do with the national confrontation, or because they identified a party as a friend or enemy to their own ethnic group. Irish Catholic immigrants overwhelmingly voted Democratic, primarily because they associated the Whigs' evangelical moralism and paternalism with the English oppressors they had escaped. Most German migrants also voted Democratic, but Protestant immigrants from Britain generally assimilated more easily into American culture and more often found a home in the Whig Party.

Figure 10.1 "Political Cock Fighters." Cartoon showing the two-party competition both as entertainment and as a serious business. Cocks representing Henry Clay and James Polk fight to the death while Daniel Webster, Martin Van Buren, John C. Calhoun, Andrew Jackson, and others watch. Lithograph by James S. Baillie (1844). Courtesy Prints & Photographs Division, Library of Congress, LC-USZ62-1972.

Still, the parties' economic appeals provided the primary attraction for most voters. Throughout the Union, Whigs gained most of their support from cities, towns, and economically developed areas; from regions with relatively easy access to trade; and from rural counties that would most immediately benefit from an internal improvement—all areas whose inhabitants had something to gain from the Whigs' economic policies. Democrats' votes more often came from areas more isolated from transportation routes and trade—where voters usually held less wealth and proved more skeptical of the supposed benefits of development—and from urban workers who recognized that they were becoming permanent wage laborers. Economic appeals also brought the parties national followings that transcended sectional loyalties. Whigs and Democrats competed against each other in every state but one, with Whigs gaining their strongest followings in New England and in the upper South—including Andrew Jackson's home state of Tennessee—and Democrats relying on solid support from the lower South and the Northwest. The parties divided closely in most states, including the four with the most congressional representatives and electoral votes: New York, Pennsylvania, Ohio, and Virginia. Only South Carolina remained outside the national party competition. There, John Calhoun's prominence, the legacy of the Nullification Crisis, and the state constitution's limitations on popular participation kept most voters out of either organization.

The parties' national followings produced a narrow division among voters across the Union. In the 1840, 1844, and 1848 presidential elections, Whigs won forty-nine percent of all votes cast, while Democrats carried slightly more than forty-six percent. Modern statistical studies indicate that more than ninety percent of the era's voters long continued to support the party they chose in 1840. Turnout in these years averaged seventy-seven percent of all eligible voters, with only a small proportion of citizens remaining unaffiliated with a party. Democrats and Whigs both had an opportunity in every election to win control of the federal government and of the majority of states. In this environment, political strategists concluded that stirring up the party faithful's enthusiasm and ensuring that voters turned out at the polls presented them with the best chance of winning. Rather than try to win the support of the few independents, activists relied on debates, barbecues, parades, and songs to excite party loyalists. Whigs particularly encouraged women to participate in campaign activities, with the hope that they would pressure their menfolk to vote for Whig candidates. Local issues sometimes crept into state or district contests, but the powerful symbolic appeals concerning the Union's future meant the Whig and Democratic conflict focused mainly on national confrontation. Politicians interpreted state contests as referenda on national questions, and in an era before modern political polling, they monitored the results of state elections to gauge their party's prospects in the congressional and presidential elections.

Because the parties needed national followings, Whig and Democratic leaders carefully tried to avoid taking firm positions on the Union's most potentially divisive issue. Party rhetoric actually revealed a slight difference in their approaches to slavery. The Democrats' emphasis on the equality of all white men reflected a belief in white supremacy based on the presumed inferiority of African Americans. Southern Democrats more often defended slavery as a positive good, while most Northern Democrats either appeared indifferent to the institution or stressed that their constitutional principles prevented federal action against it. In the North, too, Democrats often held harsher racial views than Whigs, which led them to favor measures designed to keep blacks out of white society. Whigs accepted the belief in racial differences, but their emphasis on individual effort and responsibility opened many to the idea that some African Americans could elevate themselves through education and hard work. In a few Northern states, Whigs favored giving property-owning blacks the right to vote. In the South, Whigs more often than Democrats expressed regret over slavery and sympathized with colonization as a way eventually to rid their region of the institution. Both parties, though, insisted on

Southerners' right to determine slavery's future for themselves. Southern Whigs and Democrats both pledged to defend the institution while charging their opponents' Northern wings with conspiring with radical abolitionists. Nationally, party leaders recognized that the safest course remained to sidestep the issue and emphasize the states' responsibility to determine slavery's fate.

Despite politicians' intentions, slavery-related issues still sometimes entered the political arena. Northern Democrats regularly provided the votes to renew the House of Representatives' "gag" on antislavery petitions until pressure from constituents forced enough to accept the rule's repeal in December 1844. When 135 slaves rebelled and seized control of the American brig *Creole* and sailed to freedom in the (British-controlled) Bahamas, Southern representatives demanded their return. Ohio congressman Joshua Giddings instead proposed a set of resolutions in support of the slaves' uprising. The House censured Giddings; he resigned in protest, but then he overwhelmingly won the special election to fill the seat he had vacated. The threat remained, too, that aspirants outside of or loosely connected to the major parties might use the slavery issue to further their own goals. While the Liberty Party lay plans for a better-organized presidential campaign in 1844, abolitionists continued to lobby congressmen to act against slavery where they could. A handful of antislavery politicians won seats in Congress and in state legislatures, while several Southern politicians harped on states' rights and limited government as the best means of protecting their human property. Most Southern rights advocates remained in the Democratic Party, though President Jackson's condemnation of nullification drove some to the Whigs. Yet President Jackson's former vice president returned to the Democrats, and John C. Calhoun hoped to unite Southerners behind a firm defense of Southern rights as the best way to defend slavery and win for himself the party's presidential nomination.

In the aftermath of the Whigs' victory in 1840, slavery seemed a minor issue for most party politicians. Still, it remained a disturbing undercurrent behind the warfare over whether the "Money Power" or the "Spoilsmen" would control the Union's future. Arguments over slavery would re-emerge in the 1840s as the battle between the political parties took several unexpected turns.

The Whigs' Implosion

Whigs eagerly awaited their chance to take the reins of government even before the 1840 election's results were in. Right principles and honest men would again lead the Union, they believed, and once in office they would direct the Union away from the disastrous course that Andrew Jackson and his "spoilsmen" had set. William H. Harrison would be the president, but Kentucky senator Henry Clay still appeared the party's actual leader to most Americans—including Clay himself. Confident that swift government action alone could end the economic depression, Clay and his Whig colleagues taunted Democrats in the Twenty-Sixth Congress' last session with promises to repeal the Independent Treasury, limit executive authority, and enact the far-reaching agenda long outlined in the "American System." They expected these measures to revive prosperity, solidify the party's support, and establish the Whigs as the national majority for the next generation.

A personal clash among the party's leading figures hinted at difficulties. Clay turned down an expected appointment as Harrison's secretary of state even before the president-elect could extend the offer. Clay wanted to remain in the Senate to oversee passage of the Whigs' legislative program, which would assure him of his party's nomination to succeed Harrison in 1844. The next choice to head the State Department, Massachusetts senator Daniel Webster, also harbored presidential ambitions. Harrison's other cabinet choices were known to be Clay's political friends, but Webster's influence kept Harrison from offering an appointment to Delaware's John M. Clayton, a strong proponent of a national bank whom Clay especially wanted on the cabinet. Even without Webster's cajoling, Harrison quickly grew annoyed with Clay's arrogance, his dictatorial manner, and the popular presumption that he himself was merely Clay's puppet. An early meeting between the two reportedly degenerated into a shouting match. Possibly due to pride, Harrison initially rejected Clay's demand that he call Congress into session immediately so Whigs could get on with their program, rather than wait for the constitutionally mandated convening in December. Clay's patronizing letter instructing the president-elect on the need for the session—which included a draft of a proclamation to announce the decision—provoked a forceful reply from Harrison that Clay angrily interpreted as an edict banishing him from the White House.

Few Whigs expected the rift to impede the party's progress. In his inaugural address on March 4, 1841, President Harrison reiterated his pledges to serve only one term, to respect the will of Congress, and to use the veto sparingly. With these public commitments, the new president appeared unlikely to let personal irritations derail the Whig agenda. Likewise, President Harrison reluctantly agreed to call the special session of Congress that Clay had demanded. After Treasury Secretary Thomas Ewing reported that the government debt would increase another $11 million unless Congress found new sources of revenue, President Harrison summoned the lawmakers to convene on May 31. The extra session's chief purpose would be to address the Union's financial constraints, but the president's recommendation to consider other "sundry important and weighty measures" provided all the authority congressional Whigs would need to start working on their program.

President Harrison would not live to see the special session open. At age sixty-eight, he was the oldest man yet to assume the presidency, so he made a conscious effort to demonstrate his vitality. Arriving in Washington in mid-February, he spent the weeks before his inauguration in almost constant dinners, receptions, public appearances, and meetings with important politicians, including a pleasant courtesy call on outgoing president Martin Van Buren. Despite cold temperatures and freezing rain, he refused to wear an overcoat to his inauguration, and he took off his hat to deliver his nearly three-hour-long address—the longest inaugural message of any president. Once in office, he faced a barrage of meetings with office-seekers, but he still insisted on taking daily walks in the city and making regular forays to markets to buy the White House's provisions. The flood of activities wore him down. At some point he caught a cold that quickly degenerated into pneumonia. His doctors' treatments, including harsh laxatives and blistering, likely weakened him further, and he died in the early morning of April 4, only one month after taking office.

A president had never before died in office. Along with most Democrats and leading legal authorities, most Whigs assumed that the vice president would not take over as president. Instead, he would merely perform the office's necessary duties as a caretaker until the next election. In their official letter notifying Vice President John Tyler of the president's death, the cabinet members addressed him as the vice president and agreed among themselves to refer to him as "Vice President, acting as President." Publicly, Whigs mourned the president's death, but privately many thought his passing would further their cause. The absence of a fully empowered chief executive would leave Henry Clay as the Whigs' uncontested leader, and even if Tyler asserted himself in office, he appeared likely to approve congressional Whigs' actions. Though he came from the party's Southern Rights wing, his rejection of President Jackson's "executive tyranny" indicated that he accepted the party's belief in leaving policy initiatives to Congress. Moreover, he had favored Clay for the presidency in 1840, and the party's Harrisburg convention had nominated him for vice president largely to appease Clay's disappointed supporters.

Like President Harrison, though, Tyler had no desire to be anyone's puppet. In fact, he rejected the notion that he should act as a caretaker. When he received the cabinet's official notice of the president's death, Tyler immediately returned to Washington from his Virginia plantation. Shortly after his arrival on April 6, he met with the cabinet and asked all the members to stay in office, but he also informed them that he considered himself not an "acting president," but the head of the administration, with all the responsibilities and duties of the presidency. Later that day, a circuit court judge administered to him the oath of office, and he instructed his staff to return unopened any correspondence addressing him as "vice president." On April 9 he issued an "Address upon Assuming the Office of President of the United States," which effectively served as an inaugural address. Unlike President Harrison, President Tyler offered no promises to defer to the will of Congress or to leave the office at the end of the term. With these actions, President Tyler established the precedent for future vice presidents to follow, assuring that they would assume the full powers of the presidency when a predecessor vacated the office.

President Tyler also expected to use the office to further his own political objectives. In contrast to President Harrison, at fifty-one he was the youngest man yet to become president, and he hoped to win the office in his own right in the next election. He would need congressional Whig support to accomplish this goal, so he wanted to develop a good working relationship with Clay and his allies. But he also had serious reservations about parts of Clay's program. President Tyler liked and respected Clay personally and had worked closely with him in the Senate to promote the compromises that ended the Missouri and Nullification Crises. As a strict construction "Old Republican," though, he never endorsed Clay's "American System," and he rejected the claim that Congress had constitutional authority to charter a national bank or impose protective tariffs. Shortly after taking office, President Tyler asked Clay to delay discussion of the bank until after the special session, citing widespread public division about the issue. As for the tariff, President Tyler realized that the government needed additional revenue. The scheduled expiration of the Compromise tariff law on July 1, 1842, would require Congress to increase tariff rates above the current level of twenty percent. As a consequence, he opposed Clay's proposal to distribute to the states the income from public land sales to pay for internal improvement projects; distribution would deplete the federal reserves, and in President Tyler's opinion, it served merely to justify raising the tariff to unacceptably high protective rates.

Despite President Tyler's constitutional reservations, Clay and his congressional allies pressed on. Convinced that they had a mandate to act immediately to end the economic crisis, they interpreted the president's willingness to cooperate as evidence that they could convince him to change his mind. If he did prove obstinate, they expected public demands and congressional Whig unity could pressure him to back down from his personal objections and approve all of their measures. Clay thus announced early in the special session his party's intention to introduce several bills to relieve the Union's distress. President Tyler assisted the party on most of the proposals. By the time the session adjourned on September 14, he had signed laws to repeal the Independent Treasury, establish a national bankruptcy law, and authorize the Treasury secretary to take out a $12 million loan to cover the government's short-term expenses. A new land law granted to squatters the right of pre-emption, meaning that those who had settled on public land before it was surveyed now had the first option to buy up to 160 acres. The land law also authorized distribution of the land revenues to the states, though to win President Tyler's approval it ended distribution if tariff rates went above twenty percent.

But a national bank stood at the center of the Whig program, and on this issue President Tyler remained firm. For Clay and his allies, the United States needed a central bank, with branches located throughout the Union, that could regulate state banks' currency and discount promissory notes—that is, the bank could purchase privately held debts at prices lower than the face value on written promises from individuals who promised to pay the debt. Discounting in particular would provide the capital that Whigs believed necessary to revive the economy. President Tyler not only doubted Congress' authority to charter a national bank, but also he believed that a state had the right to keep a central bank's branches out of its boundaries, especially when the branches competed with state-chartered banks through practices like discounting. Nevertheless, by a straight party vote the Whig majority passed a bill establishing a bank that would be capitalized at $30 million, be headquartered in Washington, and have the authority to establish branches in states regardless of the state government's consent. To appease President Tyler, the act included a provision that would allow a state legislature to temporarily delay a branch's establishment. The president recognized no compromise in the law's concession. Annoyed with Clay's arrogance and condescension, President Tyler vetoed the bank bill on August 16. His message explaining his decision stressed that the Constitution did not authorize Congress to create a bank that could establish branches of deposit and discount without a state's approval.

Publicly, congressional Whigs denounced the veto as a Jackson-like abuse of executive authority. Privately, they had anticipated President Tyler's decision, and Clay's fellow Kentuckian, Attorney General John Crittenden, suggested an alternative: since President Tyler opposed branches because they competed with state banks, Whigs could alter Clay's bill to prohibit branches from making loans or discounting promissory notes. This change would satisfy President Tyler's principal objection to the bank, Crittenden reasoned, but the bank could still help the economy as long as its branches could discount bills of exchange—that is, commercial notes that merchants received from customers promising to pay for goods being shipped to them. Eventually, too, the bank's operations would show the need to expand the branches' responsibilities, and in the future a more cooperative Whig president could sign laws expanding their activities. Crittenden discussed his proposal with President Tyler, and Whig leaders assumed that the plan had the president's approval and modified the bank bill, renaming the institution the "Fiscal Corporation" and calling its branches "agencies"—terms they thought the president would find more acceptable. Once again the bill passed with overwhelming Whig support. But Crittenden had misinterpreted President Tyler's interest as approval. The Whigs' personal attacks after his bank veto aggravated the president, as did their rejection of his request to delay the bank issue until the next congressional session. Convinced that Whigs were trying to force him to accept an unconstitutional bank, President Tyler vetoed the Fiscal Corporation act on September 9.

President Tyler still hoped to salvage a working relationship with Whig leaders, so his second veto message complimented Congress for its other accomplishments and expressed hope of resolving their differences on a bank at the next session. Clay and his allies, though, refused to acknowledge the president's conciliatory gesture. Two days after the second veto, all but one cabinet member resigned. Only Daniel Webster remained in office; the secretary of state claimed that he needed to continue his delicate negotiations for a treaty with Great Britain, but he also hoped to help President Tyler wrest control of the party away from Clay. Then, on September 13, about sixty Whig congressmen held a party caucus, denounced President Tyler's "maladministration" and "usurpation," and formally expelled the president from the Whig party. Across the Union, party spokesmen and newspapers endorsed the Washington Whigs' actions and labeled President Tyler "His Accidency" for his abusing the office of the presidency.

President Tyler refused to leave the party easily. Working with Webster and relying on the advice of associates whom his critics labeled the "Virginia Cabal," he appealed to moderate Whigs to try to establish himself rather than Clay as the party's leader. He removed several Clay supporters from federal positions, and he replaced the departing cabinet members with

Whigs who, like himself, had once been Democrats. When Congress reconvened in December 1841, he proposed to resolve the bank issue with his own plan to create the "Exchequer": a government-run institution in Washington with "agencies" in several states that would hold government funds and issue paper money without competing with state banks for discounts or deposits. With the government still needing revenue and the compromise tariff set to expire, he acknowledged that tariff rates would have to go up, and he indicated to lawmakers that he could accept a tariff that provided "incidental protection" for American industry, though he still opposed distributing public land sale revenues if the tariff went above twenty percent.

President Tyler's program gained little support. Democrats as well as Whigs ignored his Exchequer plan. Twice Congress passed bills linking tariff increases with distribution, both of which the president promptly vetoed. After the second veto, John Quincy Adams chaired a House committee that condemned the president's conduct as impeachable. Whigs lacked the votes to press for impeachment, so they reluctantly divided distribution and the tariff into separate acts. President Tyler pocket vetoed the distribution bill, but the administration's desperate need for money convinced him to sign the tariff act in 1842, which aggressively restored protective rates while expanding the number of goods subject to the tariff. As congressional Whigs feared, President Tyler's continued efforts to claim party leadership contributed to the party's devastating losses in the elections held in the summer and fall of 1842. In the largest turnover since the furor over the Compensation Act in 1816, the Whigs' 142–99 majority in the House of Representatives fell to a 73–149 minority, with the Whig majority in the Senate reduced from six seats to three. Part of the backlash stemmed from the unpopularity of the Bankruptcy Act that Whigs had promoted in 1842. The Bankruptcy Act's generous terms allowed irresponsible borrowers to escape their debts too easily, and many of the Whigs who had promoted the act helped repeal it in March 1843. As long as President Tyler could make any claim to Whig leadership, voters considered the party hopelessly divided and unable to govern.

For most Whigs, uniting behind Clay seemed the only solution to the party's setbacks. Widespread endorsement for him as a presidential candidate would leave no doubt about who led the party. Standing behind a national bank and the "American System" would present Whigs as the clear alternative to Democrats and further the claim that President Tyler actually was a Democrat at heart. Party newspapers had already promoted Clay for the presidency in late 1841, and Clay himself resigned from the Senate in February 1842, officially for health reasons—he may have suffered a mild heart attack—but also to concentrate on a presidential run. Later that year, Whig conventions in several states nominated the Kentuckian and repudiated Whigs who remained loyal to President Tyler. Throughout, they blamed the president for blocking the measures necessary to restore prosperity. Success in New England and upper South state elections in late 1842 confirmed the strategy's effectiveness. By mid-1843, no significant opposition to Clay remained in the party. Even Webster had to acknowledge Clay's preeminence. He resigned as secretary of state in May 1843 because he recognized that remaining in office associated him too closely with "His Accidency" and damaged his future prospects as a Whig.

President Tyler now found himself without the backing of a party. Still, he hoped to use his office to boost himself as a candidate in 1844. As Whigs moved solidly behind Clay, President Tyler began making overtures to their rivals. In the summer of 1842 he removed several Whigs from federal offices and offered the positions to Democrats. Democrats, though, had little interest in promoting President Tyler. Although they praised his bank vetoes, they still regarded him as having betrayed President Jackson. The few Democrats who accepted his patronage usually used their offices to promote their own presidential candidates. With both organizations rejecting him, President Tyler moved to form his own party. Federal appointments to Whig and Democratic moderates, he thought, would allow him to form a coalition that could offer voters a middle path between Clay's extreme federal activism and the Democrats' hard-money "Locofocoism." It might also provide the organization he needed to regain an influence in Congress—and to nominate him for his own term.

Foreign relations offered a foundation to build a case for President Tyler's election. The Constitution allowed the president to act in foreign affairs with fewer congressional restraints than he faced on domestic matters. With little influence in the legislature, some diplomatic triumphs could bring him the support needed for his third party. Webster had already provided his administration with a significant accomplishment in August 1842 when he completed a treaty with British representative Lord Ashburton. The Webster-Ashburton Treaty settled the boundary between Maine and Canada—resolving the issues that had brought on the "Aroostook War"—and established terms for the two nations to send naval patrols to the African coast to suppress the Atlantic slave trade. President Tyler hoped for more substantial accomplishments. Notwithstanding his states'-rights "Old Republican" principles, the president believed that the United States stood destined to become the dominant nation in North America and that the Union would eventually rise to the status of an international power. Territorial expansion would eventually bring the western lands along the Pacific coast to the Union, providing new lands for generations of farmers and easing sectional tensions by providing new homes for pioneers from both free and slave states. The west coast would also give American merchants easier access to potentially lucrative Asian markets. Also, President Tyler assumed—as would later generations of imperialists—that activity in the Pacific would help Americans fulfill their responsibility to promote freedom and progress to the world's less fortunate peoples.

President Tyler thus explored several possible avenues to promote the Union's international interests. While Webster worked on his treaty with Britain, the president instructed him to explore a possible settlement for the Oregon Territory in the Pacific Northwest, which the two nations had occupied jointly since 1818. At the same time, he encouraged Webster to sound out Ashburton about asking the British government to persuade Mexico to sell California to the United States. The British minister rejected the California scheme and eventually agreed with Webster to postpone a resolution for Oregon. When President Tyler learned that Britain had defeated Chinese forces in the First Opium War, he dispatched former Massachusetts congressman Caleb Cushing to Asia to gain for Americans similar trading rights to what the British had won. Cushing's efforts produced the 1844 Treaty of Wangxia, which opened five ports to American merchants and granted the Union "Most Favored Nation" status, giving Americans the best trade terms that China would award to any foreign nation. The lobbying of missionaries and concern that Britain or France might try to seize Hawaii, an important stop for American ships, drove President Tyler to issue a statement in December 1842 that became known as the "Tyler Doctrine," which upheld Hawaiian independence and opposed any other nation's attempt to take the islands as a colony. Similarly, President Tyler instructed Henry Wheaton, the American minister to Prussia, to open negotiations for a treaty with the *Zollverein*, the customs union among several German states. Wheaton's efforts produced an agreement that would have lowered tariffs and increased trade with central Europe, though the president's political troubles caused the Senate to reject it.

In his most consequential decision, President Tyler revived efforts to secure Texas' annexation by the United States. Instead of winning him the presidency, the issue provided what Democrats needed for their revival.

The Texas Bombshell

President Tyler long favored adding Texas to the Union. Since President Jackson declined the former Mexican state's request for annexation in 1836, Texas had remained the weak "Lone

Star Republic" along the Union's southwestern border. After President Van Buren likewise rebuffed Texas' appeals, its government renounced its desire to join the Union, but enough sentiment for annexation remained on both sides of the border to encourage President Tyler to revive the subject. The battles with the Whigs and the negotiations for the treaty with Great Britain prevented him from pushing annexation early in his administration, and Daniel Webster discouraged the idea while he was the secretary of state. After Webster resigned, however, President Tyler persuaded Abel P. Upshur to leave his post as secretary of the navy and replace Webster as head of the State Department. Like the president, Upshur strongly favored Texas annexation, and acquiring the state now became an administration priority.

As President Tyler well knew, several obstacles stood in the way of acquiring Texas. The acquisition of a huge slaveowning region would provoke opposition in Northern states. With the 1844 presidential election on the horizon, the backlash would strengthen the appeal of the antislavery Liberty Party while discouraging Northern politicians from taking up the Texas cause. Northern Whigs and Democrats would likely join together to block the ratification of an annexation treaty, which would require approval by a two-thirds majority in the Senate. The Mexican government meanwhile refused to recognize Texas' independence and protested its claim that its land extended to the Rio Grande and westward to the river's source in the Rocky Mountains—more than a hundred miles west of the Nueces River, the boundary that all nations had acknowledged while Texas was a Mexican state. Mexicans would consider annexation an offense to their national sovereignty and an assault on their territorial integrity. Though currently Mexico was too weak to reconquer Texas, the insults could provoke a declaration of war. The previous rebuffs to their requests, too, made Texans leery of American intentions. Even if their leaders could be persuaded to begin treaty negotiations, many Texans doubted whether an American president could get the Senate votes needed for ratification, and they feared invasion should the Mexican government learn about the move to join the Union.

At the same time, several circumstances encouraged annexation's prospects. The Texas government had amassed a substantial debt while fighting for its independence. Most of the debt's bondholders were wealthy Americans who might use their influence to promote annexation, with the hope that the United States government would take over its payment. The president could count on Southerners to support annexation, and not simply because of slavery; with the economy still in a depression, eastern Texas' rich farmlands offered struggling small farmers the chance for a fresh start in a new location under the American government's protection. President Tyler also thought he could present Texas as a national rather than a sectional issue. Confident that Americans agreed with him about the Union's destiny, his administration could argue that acquiring Texas would help spread freedom and democracy across the continent, with Oregon and California soon to follow. Annexation could also be presented as necessary for national security. Duff Green, whom the president had sent to England in the fall of 1843, sent back sensationalized reports of a supposed British plan to offer military protection and force Mexico to recognize Texas independence in exchange for the Lone Star Republic's abolition of slavery. If true, this scheme would halt American expansion and make Texas a refuge for fugitive American slaves, a refuge that would encourage more runaways and rebellions, destabilize the institution of slavery in the South, and irritate sectional relations to a point that might dissolve the Union.

Actually, a British official in Texas had suggested the abolition scheme without his government's approval, and Britain's foreign minister denied any intention to interfere in Texas' affairs. Nevertheless, Secretary of State Upshur kept the British threat at the center of his operations for annexation. Beginning in September 1843, he anonymously published several articles in the administration's newspaper, the *Madisonian*, warning of the "Designs of the British Government." At the same time, he began secret, informal talks with Texas' representative in Washington, Isaac Van Zandt, for an annexation treaty. With no sign of gaining Mexican recognition, Texas president Sam Houston gave his approval to negotiations in January 1844 and sent James P. Henderson to assist Van Zandt and sign a treaty. The secretary of state meanwhile conversed with several Northern Democratic senators to lay the foundation for ratification, warning of the British threat to national security while luring support with promises to secure American interests in Oregon. By the time that Upshur and Van Zandt completed a draft for a treaty, Upshur's lobbying had gained the support needed for its ratification. The proposed agreement would annex Texas as a state, recognize Texans as American citizens, and have the United States assume Texas' debt in exchange for Texas' public lands. By the end of February, all that remained was for Henderson to arrive in Washington to sign the treaty.

While Upshur moved toward accomplishing President Tyler's primary goal, the president's hope of gaining the Democratic Party's nomination started to seem more realistic. Martin Van Buren had emerged as the Democratic front-runner. "Hard-money" Democrats and party insiders promoted his re-election in 1844 as a vindication of Jacksonian principles. The bland and colorless "Sly Fox" never enjoyed a widespread popular following, though, and to many Democrats his defeat in 1840 justified a search for a stronger candidate. Conservative "soft money" Democrats in Northeastern and Western states considered several alternatives before settling on Michigan's Lewis Cass, the recent American minister to France, as their candidate. Van Buren's onetime nemesis, John C. Calhoun, hoped to unite working-class radical support in the urban Northeast with his Southern followers to secure the nomination for himself. After state conventions in New England and New York nominated Van Buren in late 1843, Calhoun concluded that he lacked the Northern support needed for the nomination, and he withdrew his name from consideration. With Van Buren the leading contender, Cass promoted mainly as a protest candidate, and Calhoun out of the way, President Tyler hoped that the announcement of an annexation treaty would rejuvenate his standing with Democrats and convince the party's convention to nominate him instead.

An unexpected tragedy suddenly derailed President Tyler's plans. Prior to becoming secretary of state, Abel Upshur had served for almost two years as secretary of the navy, where he strongly pushed for the expansion and modernization of the Union's naval forces. Congress balked at his proposals to establish a naval academy and to build a fleet half the size of Britain's, but lawmakers did approve funds to build a new warship, U.S.S. *Princeton*. Constructed in Philadelphia and launched in September 1843, the *Princeton* was the Navy's most advanced ship, the first propelled by a steam-powered screw. It carried twenty-four pivoting guns and two large cannons nicknamed the "Oregon" and the "Peacemaker"—the latter with a fifteen-foot barrel, making it the largest gun to date constructed of wrought iron. On February 28, 1844—the day after Upshur and Van Zandt completed the draft for a treaty—the *Princeton*'s commander, Captain Robert F. Stockton, hosted the president, his cabinet, and more than three hundred guests at a party on board as it cruised down the Potomac River. During the excursion, the crew twice fired the "Peacemaker" to demonstrate its power. Navy Secretary Thomas W. Gilmer then requested a final shot, and, against his better judgment, the captain complied. This time, the cannon exploded. The blast wounded Stockton and several bystanders, but it killed Gilmer and seven others—including Secretary of State Upshur.

President Tyler was below deck during the last firing and escaped injury. Most likely, he recognized immediately that the explosion not only deprived him of two reliable advisers but also seriously jeopardized his Texas project. Gilmer had strongly supported annexation, while Upshur had effectively negotiated a treaty while laying the groundwork for its acceptance in the Senate. President Tyler's Southern advisers now urged him to appoint their true favorite, John C. Calhoun, as Upshur's replacement. The president never greatly admired Calhoun, whom he considered overly ambitious and arrogant—privately, he mockingly referred to the

Figure 10.2 "Awful Explosion of the 'Peace-Maker' on board the U.S. Steam Frigate, Princeton, on Wednesday, 28th Feby. 1844." Lithograph by Nathaniel Currier (1844). Courtesy Prints & Photographs Division, Library of Congress, LC-USZ62-2526.

egotistical South Carolinian as "The Great I Am." Undoubtedly, too, he suspected that Calhoun would use the office to advance his own presidential prospects. Also, while Calhoun avidly supported annexation, he approached it as a Southern issue, rather than as the national cause as President Tyler framed it. Nevertheless, no other prospect with Calhoun's prominence and experience appeared willing to take the post. Calhoun also had the necessary reputation to win easy confirmation in the Senate, and the appointment would appease the administration's Southern friends—one of whom, Virginia's Henry Wise, had already notified Calhoun that President Tyler intended to offer him the position. Rather than create a potentially embarrassing situation, the president offered the appointment to Calhoun, probably hoping that he would turn it down. If he did take the job, the president hoped that Upshur had already established a foundation for annexation too strong for Calhoun to shake.

But Calhoun accepted, and as President Tyler feared, his new secretary of state proved unpredictable and uncontrollable. Calhoun immediately began meetings with Van Zandt and James Henderson, who had arrived in Washington a few days before Calhoun assumed his office on April 1. On April 12, the three concluded a treaty on the same terms of the draft that Upshur had completed, except that the agreement now included an explicit promise of American military protection for Texas. Before submitting their work to the Senate, however, Calhoun wrote a letter to Richard Pakenham, the British minister in Washington, expressing "deeper concern" over Britain's international commitment to abolition. He went on to defend annexation as necessary to protect slavery from Britain's abolition designs; likewise, he justified slavery as beneficial for the African race and concluded by proclaiming the institution "essential to the peace, safety, and prosperity of those States of the Union in which it exists." Then, he included his Pakenham Letter in the documentation that accompanied the treaty when he sent it to the Senate. As Calhoun possibly expected, a Northern senator leaked the treaty to the press, along with the "Texas bombshell," as Senator Thomas Hart Benton labeled the Pakenham Letter.

The New York *Evening Post* published both documents on April 27, placing annexation at the center of public attention and thrusting the issue into the upcoming presidential election.

News about the treaty came as no surprise to Whig and Democratic leaders. They doubted that annexation could revive President Tyler's fading electoral hopes, but they also recognized the potential popularity of geographic expansion—just as they realized its potential conse-quences. The possible pitfalls convinced the front-runners to downplay the subject. Washing-ton insiders had kept Henry Clay and Martin Van Buren well informed about the negotiations even before the Senate received the treaty. Both concluded that annexation would likely strain sectional relations, possibly to the point of disunion. After Upshur's death, the Senate now appeared likely to defeat the treaty, so keeping their parties from endorsing annexation could isolate Texas as a minor issue associated with political outcasts like President Tyler and Secretary Calhoun. Thus, on the same day that the *Evening Post* published the treaty, Washington's leading Whig and Democratic papers printed separate letters from Clay and Van Buren announcing their opposition to annexation. Both based their decision on the fact that the move would lead to war with Mexico. Clay's letter in the *National Intelligencer*, written from Raleigh, North Carolina, dismissed charges of a British plot to abolish slavery in Texas and stressed his belief that annexation would irritate sectional arguments about slavery. Van Buren's letter to Missis-sippi congressman William H. Hammet appeared in the *Globe* and acknowledged Britain to be a threat to the Union, but the candidate claimed to see no concrete evidence showing British interference in Texas' affairs.

Whigs dutifully followed Clay's lead. Several Southern Whigs favored acquiring Texas, but they accepted geographic expansion as a secondary concern to promoting economic devel-opment. Four days after the publication of the Raleigh Letter, the Whig national convention met in Baltimore and nominated Clay unanimously. To balance the slaveowning Kentuck-ian with a Northerner—and to counter Clay's personal reputation as a rakish gambler and womanizer—the delegates selected former New Jersey senator Theodore Frelinghuysen as the vice presidential candidate. Popularly known as the "Christian Statesman," Frelinghuysen had gained renown as a leader of several moral reform causes. Still, the delegates signaled clearly that Whigs would focus their campaign on the issues at the center of their appeal since 1841. The convention's brief platform omitted any reference to Texas annexation while affirming the party's commitment to "a well-regulated currency"—which Whigs understood could be established only by a new Bank of the United States. The platform likewise endorsed pro-tective tariffs, distributing public land sale revenues, limiting presidents to a single term, and amending the Constitution to reform "executive usurpations."

While Whigs rallied behind Clay, Van Buren's Hammet Letter stunned his fellow Democrats. Though they had little regard for President Tyler, most Democrats enthusiastically favored extending the Union's boundaries. Southern partisans particularly desired access to Texas' lands, while many of their Northern compatriots accepted annexation as a first step toward warding off the British menace and fulfilling the nation's "Manifest Destiny," the term coined in 1845 by New York editor John L. O'Sullivan to describe the Union's "right" to dominate North America. Prominent Democrats had already endorsed President Tyler's treaty and expected Van Buren to follow suit. Instead, Van Buren's opposition guaranteed that the already-tarnished candidate would have difficulty whipping up excitement for him within his own party. Several state conventions, though, had met before the Hammet Letter's publication, and the meetings had chosen a majority of delegates committed to vote for Van Buren at the national conven-tion, which would meet in Baltimore in late May. President Tyler's handful of supporters scheduled their own convention to meet in Baltimore at the same time as the Democratic meeting. If Democrats went ahead with Van Buren's nomination, Southern delegates might abandon the party, join the other convention, and unite behind President Tyler and Texas. This move, party leaders feared, would ensure Clay's election and leave the national Democratic Party severely divided, perhaps for years.

The convention, though, took an unexpected turn. A majority of delegates came committed to Van Buren, but enough broke with the candidate to support the rule adopted at previous national conventions to require the nominee to receive at least two-thirds of the delegates' votes. Once adopted, the rule produced a deadlocked convention. Van Buren gained the most support in the early ballots, but his total fell short of the two-thirds requirement. Lewis Cass emerged as the New Yorker's strongest challenger and passed Van Buren as the front-runner on the sixth ballot, but Van Buren supporters refused to concede. Small contingents remained loyal to Kentucky's Richard Johnson and Pennsylvania's James Buchanan. Behind the scenes, a handful of delegates pushed a compromise candidate recommended by the party's elder states-man, Andrew Jackson. James K. Polk, a former Speaker of the House, had hoped to emerge from the convention as Van Buren's vice presidential candidate. Polk had publicly endorsed the Texas treaty, which satisfied the delegates behind Van Buren's rivals, while Van Buren support-ers appreciated his continued loyalty to the New Yorker after the publication of the Hammet Letter. Southern Democrats likewise found the slaveholding Tennessean preferable to Cass, a western man whose views on slavery they still questioned. After a night of tense and compli-cated negotiations, the convention accepted the Tennessean as a satisfying compromise. On the ninth ballot, the delegates unanimously nominated Polk for president, with former Philadel-phia mayor George M. Dallas as his vice presidential candidate.

Whigs mocked the Democratic candidate as a political nobody, asking derisively, "Who is James K. Polk?" Anyone who followed political affairs, however, knew Polk well, and his surprising nomination suddenly revitalized his party. At age forty-eight, the Tennessean now stood as the youngest presidential nominee to date—a sharp contrast to the party's bland older contenders. His unexpected emergence as the convention's choice generated a sense of excitement. Embracing geographic expansion as the campaign's central theme likewise excited Democrats. Reviving largely forgotten claims, the convention approved a platform declaring "the reoccupation of Oregon and the re-annexation of Texas at the earliest practicable period" to be "great American measures"—thus once again nationalizing the expansion issue by offer-ing new lands for Northern as well as Southern pioneers. The candidate himself wisely stated that if elected he intended to serve only one term, allowing other aspirants to unite behind Polk with hopes to succeed him in four years. Though Polk had stood by President Jackson during the Nullification Crisis, his status as a slaveowner satisfied most in the party's Southern rights wing. The Tyler convention obediently nominated the incumbent, but Secretary of State Calhoun supported Polk with the hope of keeping his office and dominating a Polk adminis-tration. When South Carolina extremists threatened to call for secession if the Senate rejected annexation, Calhoun used his influence to stop the move and persuaded most of the radicals to promote Polk.

As expected, the Senate rejected President Tyler's annexation treaty on June 8. Van Buren Democrats joined the Senate's Whigs to produce thirty-five votes against the agreement to only sixteen votes for it. The solid margin persuaded Whigs that they had successfully removed the expansion issue from the campaign. Confident of the seeming inevitability of Clay's elec-tion, Whigs revived the rallies, songs, parades, and other popular activities from the "Log Cabin" campaign four years earlier to generate enthusiasm for their candidate. Party spokesmen harped on the need for federal enactment of the American System to restore prosperity while con-trasting Clay—the "Harry of the West"—with the supposedly second-rate Polk, who had twice recently lost re-election to the governor's office in Tennessee. Important developments, though, worked against the Whig campaign. An increase in government revenue and in the Union's gold supply—ironically brought on by the Whigs' Tariff of 1842—had produced an upturn in trade and in commodity and land prices. These signs of economic recovery reduced the urgency of the need for the Whigs' program, since government action no longer seemed essential to restoring prosperity. More disturbing, expansion proved to be a more popular and powerful issue than Whigs anticipated. Rather than neutralizing the drive for expansion, the Senate vote instead made the election a referendum on annexation. Clay's Raleigh Letter put his supporters on the defensive, and in the South, Democrats used the candidate's opposition to annexation to charge that he sympathized with Northern abolitionists.

Clay's concern for the Texas issue prompted him to act. On July 1, he wrote a letter to the Tuscaloosa *Monitor*, an Alabama newspaper, that repudiated any sympathy with abolitionism while reiterating his concern that annexation might endanger the Union. Three weeks later, on July 27, he wrote a second letter, to the Tuscumbia *North Alabamian*, stating that, if the obstacles could be removed, he would "be glad to see" Texas annexed, "without dishonor, without war, with the common consent of the Union, and upon just and fair terms." These letters produced a strong backlash among Northern Whigs and antislavery voters, many of whom concluded that the candidate now supported annexation. Clay thus felt compelled to write a third letter in late September—this one appearing in the *National Intelligencer*—affirming that he still opposed annexation on the grounds that he first stated in his "Raleigh Letter." Technically, Clay's position on annexation had remained consistent, but his attempted explanations created the appearance that he wavered on the election's most pressing issue. His apparent reversals drove away moderate antislavery voters in the North while bringing him no significant additional support in the South.

The reinvigorated Democrats meanwhile matched the Whigs' popular campaigning. Democratic spokesmen focused on the supposed British scheming in Texas as well as the benefits of expansion—to Texas for the South and to Oregon for the Northwest. While his party portrayed Clay as a morally depraved gambler, drunkard, and philanderer, Polk followed tradition and remained out of public view. Behind the scenes, though, he acted to address potentially damaging concerns. Most significantly, Polk prevented his well-established record as an enemy of tariffs from weakening his appeal in Pennsylvania, a crucial manufacturing state where most Democrats endorsed tariff protection. Nine days after his nomination, he responded to a question from Philadelphia's John K. Kane with a letter stating that he opposed tariffs "for protection *merely*" but always favored "moderate" duties for revenue that provided "reasonable incidental protection for our home industry." The ambiguously worded Kane Letter allowed Pennsylvania Democrats to promote Polk as a supporter of the highly protective "Democratic Tariff of 1842"—while the candidate privately assured Southerners that his administration would try to reduce tariff rates. Similarly, Polk persuaded the dying Andrew Jackson to send an indirect message assuring President Tyler that a Polk administration would receive Tyler's supporters back into the Democratic fold. President Tyler had long given up hopes of remaining in office, but Jackson's appeals satisfied him enough that he formally withdrew as a candidate on August 20 and encouraged his followers to vote for Polk.

Both parties remained confident, and the totals produced the closest outcome of any presidential election yet. All considered the result a monumental upset. Polk ended up winning 49.5 percent of the popular votes and carried fifteen states—two by margins of less than two percent, and two others with less than half of the votes cast. Clay gained 48.1 percent of the votes, but he won only eleven states, giving Polk a 170–105 victory in the electoral college. The prominence of the Texas issue and Clay's fumbled attempt to finesse his position possibly determined the outcome. In Southern states, Whigs captured about the same number of votes they had won in 1840, but the Democratic tally increased by twenty-six percent as Polk carried four lower South states that Van Buren had lost four years earlier. The Whig totals in Northern states likewise remained virtually the same as in the

1840 election, but Liberty Party candidate James G. Birney won three percent of the popular vote—including sixteen thousand votes in New York, which Polk carried by a margin of only 5,106. A shift of only one-third of Birney's New York votes would have given Clay the state's thirty-six electoral votes and elected him to the presidency. Whigs largely blamed their loss on the immigrant vote, though. In New York and Philadelphia, local Whig organizations had agreed to support local anti-immigrant "nativist" candidates in exchange for their votes for Clay. The strategy backfired: The deal produced an unusually high turnout among the cities' Irish Democratic voters, who contributed significantly to Polk's winning the Union's two largest states.

Clay's defeat shocked and dismayed Whigs. Compounding their troubles, state and local elections also went against the party and gave Democrats solid majorities in both chambers of the next Congress. While Whigs grieved and Democrats celebrated, John Tyler used his last few months as president to accomplish what had become his administration's highest priority. After the Senate had rejected his annexation treaty in June, President Tyler suggested to the House of Representatives that Congress admit Texas immediately as a state. That action would require a joint resolution approved by simple majorities in both chambers of Congress and bypass the need for the Senate's two-thirds approval of a treaty. With the presidential campaign in high gear and President Tyler officially a candidate, the House adjourned without acting on the proposal. When the lawmakers assembled in December for the final session of the Twenty-Eighth Congress, President Tyler again urged them to admit Texas through a joint resolution. Polk's victory presented a popular mandate for annexation, the incumbent claimed, and further delay would only jeopardize acquiring the region.

President Tyler's urgings produced a bitter and acrimonious debate that dominated the lame-duck session. Some of the arguments focused on the weak constitutional grounds for annexing Texas with a joint resolution: The Constitution clearly directed the president to deal with foreign states like Texas, and opponents insisted that annexing an independent republic required a Senate-approved treaty. Mostly, the proposal reopened disputes about the terms by which Texas should be admitted. Their recent electoral victory encouraged most Democrats to support a joint resolution, and Polk aided the move with hints that he would use his patronage to reward members who voted for Texas' admission. Finally, in late February 1845, the House approved a resolution to offer Texas admission without assuming its debt but allowing the state to keep its public lands. The border separating Texas and Mexico would be determined later, but up to four new states could be carved out of Texas' territory. The Senate amended the House resolution to give the president the option either to offer admission to Texas on the resolution's terms or to open talks for a new annexation treaty; the House concurred, and President Tyler signed the resolution on March 1, three days before the end of his term. Many lawmakers accepted the Senate amendment because they thought the decision on whether to pursue a new treaty would be left to Polk. However, on the day before he left office, President Tyler sent a message to Texas offering the state admission to the Union.

The Polk Administration

Popularly known as "Young Hickory," President James K. Polk strongly adhered to President Jackson's belief that the president stood as the people's direct representative in Washington. Despite his close election and the fragile condition of the Democratic Party, he intended to execute the office independently through bold and direct leadership. Against Jackson's wishes, he refused to discuss possible appointments with two former fixtures in Old Hickory's "Kitchen Cabinet," Amos Kendall and William B. Lewis. When offering cabinet positions, he indicated to each prospect that he expected his official advisers to publicly renounce their presidential aspirations so they could focus on their duties. No one in the cabinet came from the party's Calhoun or Van Buren wing. Once in office, the new president purged the executive branch of Whig appointees and of Democrats who he suspected might obstruct his goals. Soon after his inauguration, he oversaw the establishment of a new administration newspaper, the Washington *Union*, to supplant the long-standing Democratic organ, the Washington *Globe*, and its editor, Jackson's compatriot Francis Preston Blair.

The new president's assertiveness irritated Democratic insiders. The party's old guard viewed him as a placeholder who was merely supposed to occupy the presidency until more qualified Democrats could work out their differences. Instead, President Polk quickly established himself as the leader of his party and of the Union. He had definite objectives in mind: He intended for his administration to return the federal government to the Democratic principles overturned during the brief Harrison-Tyler aberration, and he wanted to acquire the western lands—mainly California—necessary to establish the Union as the dominant presence in North America. A cold, introverted, and secretive individual, President Polk revealed the full extent of his plans to few if any of his cohorts, and he recognized that he lacked the personal appeal that had contributed so much to Andrew Jackson's success. But President Polk knew how to play the political game, and experience taught him that decisive and determined leadership, along with effective use of the presidency's resources, could overcome his bland personality to achieve his aims.

President Polk acted as if his narrow election margin had given him an overwhelming popular mandate. He wasted no time taking on the central issues of his campaign. The Oregon dispute, he concluded, could best be resolved through compromise. In his inaugural address, he asserted that the United States had "clear and unquestionable title" to the territory, but he knew that American claims never extended to its northern boundary at 54° 40' latitude, a region that included present-day British Columbia. In past discussions, American representatives had proposed to divide the territory at the forty-ninth parallel, the border separating the United States and Canada east of the Rockies. This proposal would give more than half of Oregon to Britain but preserve for the Union the rich farmlands of the Willamette Valley, where about five thousand Americans had settled by 1845. British interest in the Pacific Northwest centered on acquiring furs for trade, so Her Majesty's government always countered the American proposal with a demand to extend British possessions to the Columbia River, which would ensure the river's use for the Hudson's Bay Company, the largest trading company in the territory. During Tyler's administration, Edward Everett, the American minister in London, appeared to have found a resolution. Everett suggested extending the boundary along the forty-ninth parallel but conceding to Britain all of Vancouver Island, which would give British ships access through the Juan de Fuca strait at the island's south end. Lord Aberdeen, the British foreign minister, indicated that his government would accept a deal based on Everett's proposal. Only the Tyler administration's preoccupation with Texas prevented the two nations from moving closer to an agreement.

President Polk replaced Everett with Democratic loyalist Louis McLane, but the new president considered the Whig diplomat's proposal a reasonable solution. Politically, he could blame his predecessor for moving toward a compromise that compelled the new administration to back away from the demand for all of Oregon. Still, he believed he had to take a strong public stance. An approach that was too conciliatory might imply weakness, encourage Britain to demand more, and damage his support among Democrats in northwestern states, where the claim to all of Oregon enjoyed great popularity. Thus, when Secretary of State James Buchanan formally offered to begin discussions with Britain in July 1845, at President Polk's direction he conceded less than Everett had suggested. Instead of yielding Vancouver to Britain, Buchanan proposed to divide the island, with the United States granting British merchants free use of

American ports on the Pacific. At the same time, Buchanan indicated in a note to McLane that, while the president might concede Vancouver, he would never accept granting British ships the right to navigate the Columbia River. Both documents framed the offer as a gracious concession of American rights, rather than as a fair settlement to resolve a dispute over a region to which both nations had legitimate claims.

Instead of moving the two sides closer to an agreement, President Polk's posturing produced an international crisis. The bold claims in his inaugural address offended British leaders. Prime Minister Robert Peel responded in a speech in Parliament with the reminder that Britain also had "clear and unquestionable" rights in Oregon. The self-righteous tone of Buchanan's message likewise appeared to present an ultimatum rather than a starting point for negotiations. Richard Pakenham, the British representative in Washington, rejected Buchanan's initiative without referring it to his government. Foreign Minister Aberdeen soon disavowed Pakenham's action, but the apparent insult infuriated President Polk. He instructed Buchanan to withdraw the offer to negotiate, and when Congress convened in December he recommended the lawmakers approve a resolution notifying Britain that the United States intended to terminate the joint-occupation agreement after one year, when Americans would assume control of the entire Oregon Territory. Northern Democrats lauded Polk's stance. Behind the slogan "Fifty-Four Forty or Fight!" they called for war if Britain refused to concede all of Oregon. Prime Minister Peel's government began mobilizing its forces in Canada, and war between Britain and the Union increasingly appeared likely.

Despite the backlash with Britain, President Polk pursued a similarly aggressive approach with Mexico, even though prospects for a peaceful settlement with that nation also appeared encouraging. Mexico had long threatened war if the United States annexed Texas. Two days after Polk's inauguration, the Mexican minister left Washington and formally broke diplomatic relations. However, Mexican president José Joaquín de Herrera realized that his politically fragile and heavily indebted country lacked the resources for extensive military operations. Instead, he tried to prepare his nation to accept the loss of Texas while seeking to salvage what he could to benefit his nation. In May 1845 he offered to recognize Texas' independence on the condition that the state reject American statehood. Then, in October, he allowed Foreign Minister Manuel Peña y Peña to tell an American agent that his government would receive an American envoy if President Polk would send a representative to "settle the present dispute" separating the nations. If he could not stop annexation, President Herrera hoped he might receive some sort of compensation for Texas. In particular, he wanted to persuade the American government to renounce Texas' extravagant claims and limit the state to its long-recognized boundary at the Nueces River.

President Herrera's efforts met strong resistance at every front. The Texas Congress rejected his recognition offer. Instead, a state convention unanimously accepted annexation and in July began the process that would culminate in its formal admission to the Union in December. President Polk meanwhile signaled that he no longer considered annexation a subject for negotiation. Convinced of Mexicans' racial and economic inferiority, he expected a demonstration of American force to intimidate the Mexican people to accept the loss of Texas while coercing their government to sell the country's northern lands. Even before Texans accepted statehood, he sent General Zachary Taylor and four thousand American soldiers to Corpus Christi, in the disputed area on the southern banks of the Nueces. At the same time, he strengthened the American naval force in the Gulf of Mexico, and he instructed Commodore John D. Sloat, the commander of a naval squadron in the Pacific, to prepare to seize San Francisco in case the United States and Mexico went to war. Meanwhile, the president directed Captain John C. Frémont to lead a small band of men on an "exploratory" mission to the Rockies, with orders to move into California if necessary.

Backed by the threat of force, President Polk responded to President Herrera's offer to begin talks with an assertion of American demands. Though Peña y Peña had indicated that Mexico would receive a "commissioner" to discuss restoring diplomatic relations, President Polk instead appointed former Louisiana congressman John Slidell to go to Mexico as a "minister plenipotentiary," a title that in international law assumed that a diplomatic relationship already existed. If the Mexican government received Slidell as a minister, then formal relations between the Union and Mexico implicitly would be restored, with Mexico accepting Texas annexation as an established fact. The president's instructions to Slidell thus assumed that Mexico recognized Texas as an American state and authorized him to offer $3.25 million to pay for American citizens' claims against the Mexican government if Mexico would accept the Rio Grande as Texas' border. The minister's main task, though, was to propose $25 million to buy California while offering another $5 million to buy the province of New Mexico, which also included most of present-day Arizona.

While awaiting Mexico's response, President Polk pursued his domestic goals with the same tenacity that characterized his dealings with foreign rivals. More than any of his predecessors than perhaps John Quincy Adams, President Polk used his first message to Congress to lay out a legislative agenda, one that would once again place the Union on a Democratic course. After reporting on foreign affairs, the message criticized the Whig Tariff of 1842 because its high rates offered "protection merely." President Polk argued that lower rates assessed on an *ad valorem* basis—that is, on the market value of goods rather than on a minimum price set by the government—would increase government revenue by increasing the volume of imports. Likewise, the message contended that putting federal money in private banks had brought "ruins to thousands" and called for the restoration of the Independent Treasury—or, as President Polk preferred to call it, a "constitutional treasury"—as the only safe depository for public funds. Though he made no mention of his desire to acquire more western lands, the president recommended setting public land prices on the basis of their value, rather than a set minimum price. Graduated land prices, he contended, would discourage speculation and give the "hardy and brave men of the frontier" the chance to buy their own homesteads.

More than any of his predecessors, President Polk proved willing to bargain, pressure, and strong-arm members of Congress to win their votes. His influence helped get his major proposals enacted. The Democratic majorities in both chambers in June 1846 easily approved a bill re-establishing the Independent Treasury. Lowering the tariff proved more of a challenge. In February 1846, Treasury Secretary Robert Walker submitted a bill to the House listing what he concluded were the highest rates that could be assessed on specific foreign-made products without discouraging their importation. Once amended, the bill set most rates at thirty percent of a good's value, and the House passed Walker's tariff even though eighteen Democrats—including eleven from Pennsylvania—broke with the administration and voted against it. The strength of the resistance compelled Vice President George Dallas—also a Pennsylvanian—to announce that he would vote for Walker's tariff if the Senate vote ended in a tie, but the votes of two new senators from Texas and of a Tennessee Whig provided the support needed to pass the bill by a one-vote margin in late July. Differences over details kept the two chambers from agreeing on a bill to revise land prices. In August, northwestern Democrats joined with Whigs to allocate $1.4 million to improve conditions on rivers and harbors, but President Polk vetoed the bill—as he would veto two similar internal improvement bills in 1847—to remind his party of the Constitution's restraints on Congress.

Foreign affairs, though, remained at the forefront of the administration's concerns. Fortunately for President Polk, Robert Peel's government had little interest in a war for Oregon, especially as the growing presence of American settlers seemed to destine the territory's southern portion as a Union possession. Congressional moderates also encouraged a settlement. The president's call to terminate the joint-occupation agreement sparked an extended debate that dominated Congress through the first five months of 1846. Northwestern Democrats demanded the Union occupy the whole territory, but the termination notice that the House approved in February avoided blustering demands and called for an "amicable settlement" of American and British interests. President Polk meanwhile directed Louis McLane to inform Foreign Minister Aberdeen that the United States would probably accept a settlement if Britain first made a proposal. Once the Senate agreed to the House's termination resolution in mid-April, Peel's government accepted its mild terms as sufficient acknowledgement of British rights. In May, Aberdeen formally proposed to divide Oregon at the forty-ninth parallel, with Britain occupying all of Vancouver and recognizing the Hudson's Bay Company's navigation rights on the Columbia. President Polk submitted Aberdeen's terms to the Senate. After the senators gave their consent, he quickly worked out an agreement—ending the Oregon controversy and allowing President Polk to claim that the Senate, rather than the president, bore responsibility for the concessions.

By the time the Senate ratified the Oregon treaty in June, the Union had been at war with Mexico for a month. The administration's firm stance seemed to leave Mexico with no option but submission or war. John Slidell's arrival in Mexico City in early December 1845 only undermined President Herrera's already fragile government. The Mexican press and public expressed outrage at President Polk's audacity, while political rivals labeled President Herrera's willingness to sacrifice Texas as treason. In January, General Mariano Paredes replaced President Herrera in a coup. Publicly, President Paredes took a more militant anti-American stance, but privately he also wanted a settlement. Like President Herrera, though, he insisted that Slidell ask President Polk to change the diplomat's credentials to designate him as a commissioner rather than as a minister, a demand that Slidell indignantly refused. To increase the pressure on President Paredes, President Polk ordered General Taylor to move his army from Corpus Christi to the Rio Grande, where the general set up fortifications across the river from the town of Matamoros. Nevertheless, President Paredes formally rejected Slidell's mission on March 12. Upon his return to Washington, the diplomat briefed the president about his experience on May 8. Two days later, President Polk met with his cabinet and prepared a message to Congress recommending a declaration of war.

President Polk had instructed Slidell to delay his return from Mexico, probably to give the administration time to move closer to a settlement over Oregon. Possibly, too, the president hoped that something might happen to provide stronger grounds for war than Mexico's refusal to receive an American diplomat. If so, the delay paid off. Four hours after the cabinet concluded its May 10 meeting, President Polk received news from General Taylor of an encounter with a Mexican army. Near Matamoros on April 25, Captain Seth B. Thornton's sixty-three-man reconnaissance force ran into a two-thousand-man Mexican brigade that had crossed the Rio Grande. The brief clash that followed killed eleven Americans and wounded six others, with the rest of Thornton's men taken prisoner. Once he received this report, President Polk immediately revised his message. Proclaiming that "American blood has been shed on American soil," he now contended that a Mexican invasion produced a state of war between the two nations. To avoid a lengthy debate over the cause of the hostilities, Democratic leaders in Congress proposed a bill that simply acknowledged the conflict while providing $10 million and fifty thousand volunteers for a military response. Several Democrats abstained, and a handful of Whigs opposed the bill, but the lawmakers easily passed the act. Most Democrats either welcomed the war or accepted it because of party loyalty. Whigs suspected that President Polk had provoked the conflict, but they feared political repercussions if they voted against the war or opposed providing supplies for soldiers on the battlefield.

President Polk expected a quick and easy war. Well aware of Mexico's financial difficulties, he assumed that seizing the lands he wanted would compel the Mexican government to sell them to the Union at whatever price he offered. At first, the conflict played along the lines he expected. In early May, Taylor's army defeated a larger Mexican force in battles at Palo Alto and Resaca de la Palma on the northern side of the Rio Grande. After occupying Matamoros, Taylor won another victory in September to capture the city of Monterrey. By that time, a hastily assembled "Army of the West" under General Stephen Kearny had moved out from Fort Leavenworth west of Missouri and in August easily occupied Santa Fe, New Mexico's capital and trade center. Captain John Frémont's band had entered California several months earlier and conspired with American settlers to proclaim California's independence in July as the "Bear Flag Republic"—mocking the Hispanic *californios'* reference to Americans as *los osos*, or "bears," because of their shabby and wild appearance. Commodore Sloat's fleet likewise captured a port also named Monterey on the Pacific coast on July 7, and three days later Sloat's forces occupied San Francisco. Upon receiving news of the war, Frémont's "Bear Flag Republic" declared its loyalty to the Union. Frémont and Robert F. Stockton, now promoted to commodore and replacing the ailing Sloat, bickered over who had primary authority, but with Kearny's assistance the two cooperated enough to suppress the resistance of the *californio* population and establish firm American control of California by January 1847.

Despite the reversals, the Mexican government refused to give up. The prospect of a larger and longer conflict soon contributed to growing antiwar sentiment. The claim of an invasion, and Taylor's early victories, at first stimulated widespread support, but as the initial popular enthusiasm waned, Whigs openly challenged the questionable circumstances surrounding the war's onset. The opposition denounced "Mr. Polk's War" as a selfish attempt to seize Mexican lands, and Northern and Western Democrats increasingly noted the contrast between the administration's eagerness to compromise away most of Oregon while provoking a war for more southwestern lands. Sectional resentments burst out on the floor of Congress in August. When President Polk asked for $2 million for "extraordinary expenses," which he intended to offer as a down payment for the occupied Mexican lands, Pennsylvania congressman David Wilmot—a Van Buren Democrat—proposed to amend the bill so that it would prohibit slavery in any territories acquired in the war. The Wilmot Proviso sparked an intense, bitter debate, and the sectional division defeated the appropriation. President Polk secured enough Northern Democrats the following spring to get an appropriation for $3 million without the Wilmot Proviso attached. Before then, the elections held over late 1846 and into 1847 dealt the administration a stern rebuke. Democrats held on to the Senate, but Whigs gained thirty-seven seats in the House, to transform a sixty-three-seat Democratic majority to a four-seat Whig advantage.

The president's involvement in an unsavory conspiracy compounded his political difficulties. In February 1846, he met privately with Alexander J. Atocha, an agent representing Antonio Lopez de Santa Anna, the former Mexican dictator now exiled in Cuba. Atocha assured President Polk that Santa Anna would sell his country's northern territories to the United States if the Americans would assist his return to Mexico. At first President Polk rebuffed the plot, but with the two nations at war, in July he sent his own representative to Havana to work out the details of an agreement. Later that month, the American fleet in the Gulf of Mexico permitted a British merchant ship carrying the general to pass through its blockade of the Mexican coast. Santa Anna arrived in Mexico City in mid-August. Within a month he had re-established himself as his country's de facto dictator. Instead of suing for peace, however, the general reorganized the Mexican military and in February 1847 launched an offensive against Taylor's army at Angostura Pass near Buena Vista, 160 miles from Monterrey. Though Santa Anna's army outnumbered Taylor's three to one, superior American artillery helped repel the Mexican assault in what proved to be the American commander's greatest victory. Long before then, though, Whig representatives had revealed President Polk's deal with Santa Anna to the press, and the president grudgingly acknowledged the intrigue in December 1846.

Nevertheless, President Polk pressed on. Reluctantly, he appointed a Whig, General Winfield Scott, to lead a naval landing at Veracruz on the Gulf Coast, followed by a march two hundred miles northwest through mountains and jungles to Mexico City. President Polk and General Scott quarreled almost constantly, but the general executed his mission brilliantly, aided by superior technology and the poor training of General Santa Anna's conscripted troops. Landing on the Mexican coast in March 1847, his twelve-thousand-man force captured Veracruz and in April defeated Santa Anna's army at Cerro Gordo on the road to the Mexican capital. The expiration of his volunteers' one-year terms of service delayed Scott's advance for ten weeks while he waited for reinforcements, but in August, his army of fourteen thousand overwhelmed the Mexican defenses at Contreras and Churubusco on the outskirts of Mexico City. At this point, Scott believed the war might end without further hostilities. President Polk had sent Nicholas Trist to accompany Scott's army with the authority to negotiate a treaty, so at Santa Anna's request the general agreed to an armistice to allow Trist to begin peace talks with Mexican officers. After several unproductive meetings, Scott realized that Santa Anna had used the cease-fire to gain time to rebuild the city's defenses. President Polk ordered Trist back to Washington, while the American commander terminated the armistice. In September, Scott attacked Santa Anna's fortifications. After two bloody battles at Molino del Rey and Chapultepec, the Mexican army withdrew, and Scott's army occupied the Mexican capital.

PLUCKED:

THE MEXICAN EAGLE BEFORE THE WAR! THE MEXICAN EAGLE AFTER THE WAR!

Figure 10.3 "Plucked, or The Mexican Eagle before the War! The Mexican Eagle after the War!" Illustration in *Yankee Doodle* (1847). Courtesy Prints & Photographs Division, Library of Congress, LC-USZ62-130816.

With the loss of Mexico City, rivals overthrew Santa Anna and formed a temporary government at Querétaro, 120 miles west of the capital. The new government continued to resist for several weeks before officials agreed to discuss a settlement. With peace seemingly at hand, Trist decided to disobey President Polk's order to leave. He resumed talks with Mexican officials in January 1848, and on February 2 he completed a treaty in the Mexico City suburb of Guadalupe Hidalgo. In the treaty, Mexico agreed to cede California and New Mexico to the United States and recognize the Rio Grande as Mexico's boundary with Texas. In exchange, the United States paid Mexico $15 million and assumed the $3.25 million in American citizens' claims against the Mexican government. Trist's disobedience infuriated President Polk, who dismissed him from his State Department post. The treaty's terms likewise disappointed the president. With Mexico City occupied, some congressmen now called for the Union to annex all of Mexico, leading President Polk to think he could probably acquire more land than Trist's treaty provided. Nevertheless, the deep divisions in Congress and the war's continuing unpopularity persuaded the president to accept the agreement. Whigs opposed taking any territory, and some Democrats wanted still more, but the desire to end the conflict produced the Senate support necessary to ratify the Treaty of Guadalupe Hidalgo on March 10 by a 38–14 vote.

President Polk honored his promise to serve only one term. When he retired from office in March 1849, he left behind a Union remarkably different from the one that George Washington had reluctantly come out of retirement to serve sixty years earlier. The thirteen states along the Atlantic coast with just under four million people now extended—in large part thanks to President Polk—to the Pacific Ocean, containing thirty states and a population of twenty-three million. Farming remained the principal means of support for most, but cotton now stood as the Union's major crop. A growing manufacturing sector had reduced dependence on British goods and gave the Union the potential to rival its onetime mother country as an industrial nation. Religious revivals had brought thousands to evangelical denominations and made their lay-oriented beliefs and practices an important cultural force. Many believers joined their secular-minded countrymen to promote a variety of reforms designed to improve their world. Most significantly, American leaders no longer described their states in classical republican terms, with citizenship limited to property owners who were expected to defer to their betters. Instead, Americans understood their Union to be a democracy. White male citizens now expected both the state and national governments to follow the direction of the "people," and two mass political parties worked to unite politicians, mobilize voters, and put their principles into law.

As he left Washington, President Polk might have reflected on how a change in one or a few events of the previous decade would have sent the Union on a different path—if President Harrison had survived his bout with pneumonia; if President Tyler had proven willing to accept a central bank; if President Tyler had decided against pursuing Texas; if Abel Upshur had chosen to forego witnessing the last firing of the "Peacemaker"; or if Henry Clay had addressed the annexation issue with more political skill. A shift in any of these outcomes might have allowed Whigs to implement their economic program and delayed the pursuit of a continental empire. At a minimum, Polk would never have become president. Even if the Union had acquired Texas, a war for California probably would not have followed. Instead, the course of events brought "Young Hickory" to the White House, and his administration determined that the government would follow President Jackson's domestic principles while aggressively pushing to expand American interests abroad—even as the Union experienced the type of industrial transformation that Whigs had foreseen.

But Polk's administration paid a high price to accomplish its goals. The Mexican-American War cost nearly $100 million and almost thirteen thousand American lives, significantly more than had been lost in any previous war. Even within the president's party, many recognized the conflict as a selfish attempt to steal a neighboring republic's lands, and Polk's heavy-handed style of governing and rigid adherence to his ideology left his party deeply divided. Frustration with the war and Democratic infighting brought a Whig—Zachary Taylor—to the White House as President Polk's successor. More ominously, the war brought sectional conflict to the center of politics. The bitter arguments sparked by David Wilmot's proposal to prohibit slavery in territories would persist for the next fifteen years. As many in President Polk's generation feared, those arguments would be resolved only through a civil war that would determine the fate of the American nation.

Suggested Readings

Altschuler, Glenn C., and Stuart M. Blumin. *Rude Republic: Americans and Their Politics in the Nineteenth Century* (Princeton, 2000).

Carwardine, Richard J. *Evangelicals and Politics in Antebellum America* (New Haven, 1993).

Clary, David A. *Eagles and Empire: The United States, Mexico, and the Struggle for a Continent* (New York, 2009).

Crapol, Edward P. *John Tyler: The Accidental President* (Chapel Hill, 2006).

Greenberg, Amy S. *Manifest Manhood and the Antebellum American Empire* (Cambridge, UK, 2005).

Haynes, Sam W. *Unfinished Revolution: The Early American Republic in a British World* (Charlottesville, 2010).

Henderson, Timothy J. *A Glorious Defeat: Mexico and Its War with the United States* (New York, 2007).

Holt, Michael F. *The Rise and Fall of the American Whig Party: Jacksonian Politics and the Onset of the Civil War* (New York, 1999).

Howe, Daniel Walker. *The Political Culture of the American Whigs* (Chicago, 1979).

Johnson, Reinhard O. *The Liberty Party, 1840–1848: Antislavery Third-Party Politics in the United States* (Baton Rouge, 2009).

Johnson, Timothy D. *A Gallant Little Army: The Mexico City Campaign* (Lawrence, KS, 2007).

Kohl, Lawrence Frederick. *The Politics of Individualism: Parties and the American Character in the Jacksonian Era* (New York, 1989).

Peterson, Norma Lois. *The Presidencies of William Henry Harrison and John Tyler* (Lawrence, KS, 1989).

Pletcher, David M. *The Diplomacy of Annexation: Texas, Oregon, and the Mexican War* (Columbia, MO, 1973).

Silbey, Joel H. *Storm over Texas: The Annexation Controversy and the Road to Civil War* (New York, 2005).

Varon, Elizabeth R. *We Mean to Be Counted: White Women and Politics in Antebellum Virginia* (Chapel Hill, 1998).

Winders, Richard Bruce. *Mr. Polk's Army: The American Military Experience in the Mexican War* (College Station, TX, 1997).

INDEX

Aberdeen, Lord 245–6, 248
abolition, abolitionists 143–8, 158, 162, 168, 215–18, 222, 232, 240, 243; and women 172–4
Adams, Abigail 8
Adams, John 8, 15, 23, 28, 39, 40–1, 97, 99, 108, 121; as president 41–3, 45–9, 55, 57, 58
Adams, John Quincy 87, 89, 91, 99, 209, 247; congressman 146–7, 217, 209, 222, 236; in election of 1824 188–93; in election of 1828 195–9; president 99, 157–8, 193–4; secretary of state 179–83
Adams-Onís Treaty 182
Adams, Samuel 23
African Americans 10, 52, 120, 144–5, 148, 150, 152, 162, 164–5, 231; free ix, 121–2, 143, 166–9, 187
African Methodist Episcopal Church 168
Alabama 94, 99, 100, 102, 117, 156, 158, 161, 181, 210
Alamo 217
Albany, New York 5, 86, 93, 104, 105, 154
Alcott, William Andrus 138–9
Alexandria Gazette 111
Algerine War *see* Second Barbary War
Algiers 62–3, 97, 154
Alien and Sedition Acts 43, 45, 48
Alien Enemies Act 43, 55
Alien Friends Act 43, 55
Allen, Richard 168
Ambrister, Robert 181–2, 190
American and Foreign Anti-Slavery Society 147
American Anti-Slavery Society 144–7, 168, 172–4, 215
American Bible Society 132
American Board of Commissioners for Foreign Missions 156, 158, 161
American Colonization Society 122–3, 143, 168
American Female Guardian Society 172
American Home Missionary Society 132
American Medical Association 138
American Phrenological Journal 139
American Physiological Society 138
American Sunday School Union 132
American System 189, 197, 204, 228, 232, 234, 236, 242

American Temperance Society 133, 172
American Tract Society 132
Amistad 148, 222
Anderson, Richard C. 194
Andover Seminary 138
Anglican Church 125–7, 131; see also *Episcopal Church*
Annapolis Convention 17, 18
Antifederalists 22–3, 26, 39, 51, 52, 178
Antimasonic Party 197–9, 207–8, 212, 214
Anti-Rent War 154–5
Appeal to the Coloured Citizens of the World 145
Arbuthnot, Alexander 181–2, 190
Arkansas 100, 117, 157, 158
Arminianism 130–1
Armstrong, John 80, 87–8, 90–1
Army 12, 33, 36, 56, 70, 79–80, 83, 161, 177; in Mexican-American War 246, 249–50; 1798 Provisional 43, 45–7; in War of 1812 84–9, 91, 93
Aroostook War 227, 237
Articles of Confederation 11–16, 17, 18, 20, 21, 25, 30, 45
Asbury, Francis 127–8
Ashburton, Lord 237
assimilation policy 156–7
asylum movement 135–7, 228
Atocha, Alexander J. 249
Auburn, New York 197; Auburn System 135

Bagot, Charles 180
Baltimore 3, 90–2, 101, 106, 110, 112, 128, 134, 143, 166, 168, 207, 213, 241
Baltimore and Ohio Railroad 105
Baltimore Republican 223
Bank of Augusta v. Earle 112
Bank of the United States 220, 224, 228–9, 233–6, 241; first 31–2, 37, 41, 45, 56, 66, 81, 85, 110; of Pennsylvania 213, 221; second 110, 176–8, 185–6, 206–13, 214, 219, 223
Bankruptcy 111, 234, 236
Bank Veto message 208
Bank War 206–15, 219
Baptist Association of Danbury, Connecticut 125
Baptists 127–8, 130, 131, 133, 145, 148, 168